# THE MAN WHO OUTGREW HIS PRISON CELL

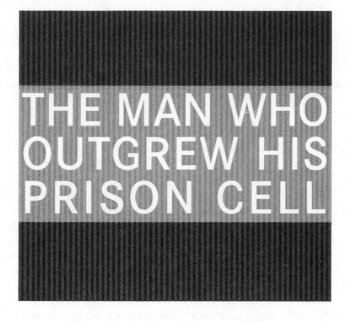

# THE MAN WHO OUTGREW HIS PRISON CELL

## Confessions of a Bank Robber

# Joe Loya

*An Imprint of* HarperCollins*Publishers*

HarperCollins books may be purchased for educational, business, or sales
promotional use. For information, please write: Special Markets Department,
HarperCollins Publishers Inc., 10 East 53rd Street, New York, NY 10022.

FIRST EDITION

*Designed by Daniel Lagin*

Printed on acid-free paper

Library of Congress Cataloging-in-Publication Data

Loya, Joe
    The man who outgrew his prison cell : confessions of a bank robber /
Joe Loya.—1st ed.
        p. cm.
    ISBN 0-06-050892-2
        1. Loya, Joe.    2. Brigands and robbers—California—Biography.
3. Bank robberies—California.    I. Title.

HV6653.L69A3 2004
364.15'52'092—dc22
[B]                                                      2004042826

04   05   06   07   08   DIX/RRD   10   9   8   7   6   5   4   3   2   1

*Dedicated to my wife, Diane—*
*for the certainty of your belief in me, and for your laughter.*

## Acknowledgments

Although it is I who physically wrote this memoir, it wouldn't be accurate to say I wrote it by myself: I couldn't have completed the work without the profound bolstering of those I need to acknowledge below:

Lisa Perez and Danny Shaw, who visited me in prison—if you had not walked in, I would not have walked out; Paul Loya and Joe Loya Sr., for the beauty of our nearness; my secret sharer, Richard Rodriguez, whose letters reached into that lonely prison cell and comforted me; my editor at the Pacific News Service, Sandy Close, whose true faith in me and frequent support made this book a reality; to my stepmother Brenda Liebowitz, for exposing me to great literature at a young age, and who never allowed me to be at war with the English language; Ofelia Cuevas, for her singular, sisterly gift of love; my close friends who I have been able to rely on in the midst of trouble, and who step up for me consistently with generosity and deep affection: Kerry Tremain, Marilyn Berlin Snell, Lisa Margonelli, Barbara Ramsey, Jeff Silberman, Ben Ehrenreich, Robbie Baitz, Mark Salzman, Jessica Yu, and Danny Gallegos; Father Mark Serna, whose laughter made my time in prison lighter toward the end; Leo Karlyn, whose financial support and hilltop hikes with me (in my early days out of prison) kept me focused and optimistic;

Jimmy Armistead and Elizabeth Bernstein, for their fine reads of my manuscript; my agent, Sam Stoloff, and my editor, Rene Alegria, for helping me to bring forth a manuscript that didn't always want to come; Andrea Montejo, for doing tons of little work that amounted to much achieved; The Sundance Institute, Ovid Foundation, and the Ojai Play- wright's Conference, for their generous contributions during the writing of this book; And lastly, I want to give special praise to my friend Jaime Kibbens, who with his actions—his multiple talents and regular good humor—taught me to remember the Shakespeare quote that "the near- ness of death exalts life."

# Contents

# Introduction

*By Richard Rodriguez*

Ten years ago, I received a bundle of folded binder-paper from a man named Joe Loya, who asked if we might correspond.

Joe Loya was serving time for vainglorious bank robbery. Apparently a thug with a golden ear—he quoted Larkin and Eliot. He professed his love for nineteenth-century Russians, particularly Dostoevsky (who, he reminded me, had murdered).

For two years, we exchanged letters. Mine to him were always typewritten; his to me were in a controlled, painfully minute hand. We were self-consciously secret sharers—we were like Conrad's secret sharers—our letters were nothing if not allusive.

Over time, he rehearsed, always with a fine sense of narrative structure, cellblock altercations, as well as many of the stories of his criminal life that you will read here.

The nagging question I posed, in many letters, in various ways, concerned two men named Joe Loya: How was it possible the man I was addressing each week and reading—the Joe Loya of fine sensibility—was also the criminal who had been so dangerous to himself, and, eventually, to others?

His mother died in East L.A. when he was a boy. His father—a Heathcliff—was so crazed by grief he turned murderous against his own sons. The father (as much a puzzle as the son) was an evangelical Protestant minister and a scholar of Hebrew and Greek.

In an early letter, Joe Loya admitted his interest in Dr. Jekyll and Mr. Hyde, and the Victorian notion that the monster and the gentleman reside at the same address. (Had I forgotten that nineteenth-century insight?) Joe Loya remembered how his father's congregation seemed to have no idea of their pastor's dark behavior at home.

There is no Augustinian moment of conversion in this book. Nevertheless, enough of the "born again" Protestant survived in Joe Loya that he would insist to me (as he will tell you) that his dark days are behind him.

Whenever I would ask him if Joe Loya, in his darkest aspect, could ever have been in correspondence with me, or, if he and I were in prison, might the two of us have been friends, his answer was unqualified: No.

Some weeks there were more than twenty pages stuffed into the envelope. We descended further and further into the past.

I wrote of my travels (once to a school a few miles from his prison). But I resisted Joe Loya's several invitations to see him in prison. I did not want a personal relationship (in many ways I am the colder of the two of us). Instead, I asked a friend, a Benedictine monk in Rhode Island, to visit him.

The letters were implicating enough. What need did I have to face Joe Loya in a fluorescent lit visiting room?

*How was the drive?*

*Fine. Some rain.*

No. No. The letters were everything. For me, it was like having a correspondent from another century. And all the great themes our postmodern age will not name were in his letters: good, evil, sin, grace, fall, redemption—beginning with the almost-biblical rendition of the son turning a knife against his father.

As the term of his imprisonment grew thinner, I told Joe Loya I would be honored to help him with his readjustment to the outside, but I did not need to see him. I did not want to. I felt the meaning of our relationship waning with the end of his imprisonment.

(I was right. Once free of the luxury of austerity, Joe Loya would never again send me letters of the sort he had written to me from prison.)

And yet he was insistent that we actually meet, in the first weeks of his parole. We met at his brother's apartment in Los Angeles. Nouns and adverbs became voice, face, arms; I was greeted with a very Russian bear hug. And then, for almost four hours, he told me prison stories.

It was as though he were rehearsing a public, spoken version of the material he had introduced to me in his letters.

Since he has been free, he has reconciled with his family. He has married. He has gathered around him a large circle of friends. And why not? The drama of the two Joe Loyas is seductive, for he tells us of darkness in a voice that does not frighten.

Among his friends, he counts a large number of writers. Also actors. Joe has himself become a theatrical. A year ago, in San Francisco, I watched him on stage, performing an autobiographical piece, describing the adventures of Joe Loya, criminal and convict. There was more than a hint of the Ancient Mariner in the strangeness of the evening. At one point, during the re-creation of a prison fight, it became difficult to tell where an actor's control ended and the criminal's mind triumphed.

In these pages, Joe Loya is implacably dogged by Joe Loya. The criminal has not been disposed of. Or, more: The exorcism represented by this memoir requires summoning Mr. Hyde. Indeed, the criminal Joe Loya gives the writer Joe Loya his material and thus draws him to his lips.

But instead of the crude notes the criminal pushed toward a bank teller—scrawled words of threat and demand—Joe Loya now passes the reader pages of refined prose.

I have found Joe Loya, while channel-surfing motel TVs. There he is on Court TV, cheerfully explaining to the host the clockworks of some crime or behavior. Or on CBS explaining to the hosts of *48 Hours* how, when he was on his way to rob a bank in San Diego, his overwhelming impulse was to pull over and take a nap.

I grab the attention of high school students with the lesson of Joe Loya ("a bank robber I know . . ."): Words can save you. Knowing how to sound and speak is essential when getting a job. Or when the cop pulls you over. . . .

Joe Loya parodies my point with his tale of hitching a ride with two California highway patrolmen, after he had just robbed a bank. The police were looking for bad grammar and never guessed that they had their man in the back seat.

*St. John Chrysostom, of the golden tongue, patron of rhetoric, protect Joe Loya!*

Joe's tongue saved him, continues to save him. Reading saved him. The cherished texts of his youth saved him—his father's King James Bible; the nineteenth-century novels beloved of his stepmother; the nervous but lucky habit he acquired of reading everything he could find saved him.

The French word for "word" is what we call our society's conditional license to the convict, making him, briefly or not, an "ex".

We grant Joe Loya parole.

I have no doubt the criminal believes he yet breathes through the pen of the author—falsifying, justifying: *What dupes they all are!*

But, in the end, words pin the robber down onto the page, rendering him, forever, a sentence.

# ORIGINAL SIN

# i

want to cry. And I need to vomit. I've eaten Chinese food three days in a row, once for lunch and dinner on the same day, so I know what's likely to come out of me if I do. I'm supposed to go onstage in thirty minutes but I'm basically paralyzed, lying on the floor of the men's room, backstage. I have to keep my eyes shut or I'll puke. That's how serious things have become. My head is between the toilet and a wall that has no doubt received its fair share of piss splatter over the years.

I have Ménière's disease. Excess salt in my diet is the prime suspect, what kicks off these debilitating episodes. Apparently a membrane in my ear swells up with fluid and begins pressing against something else in my inner ear, and that's what sends my equilibrium all to hell. Thirty minutes ago I suddenly felt a small vacuum-suction sensation in my right ear, followed by a sharp, high-pitched ringing. Then I became slightly buzzed, as if I'd guzzled a pint of Guinness. I usually like that dizzy feeling, but I hadn't drunk any alcohol, so I became worried. I asked someone to escort me to the men's room.

That's how we got here. I opened my eyes a minute ago (briefly, since the seasick feeling is relentless) and saw where the blue-plastic molding met the floor, and I thought, "Great. A room with a mouse's view."

My wife, Diane, arrived a few minutes ago and knelt down to comfort me. Now she's sort of petting me on this dark bathroom floor.

My eyes are closed, but it still feels like I'm on the Mad Hatter's Tea Cups ride at Disneyland. I can hear the buzz of the crowd gathering in the lobby. I've already performed fourteen shows here at the Thick House in San Francisco, and this is supposed to be my second to last performance, although it's looking more and more every minute like I'll have to cancel tonight's show.

The producer is hoping that things will miraculously improve.

My stage manager, director, producer: They've all come to see me stuck to the floor. I fear they may perceive me as a diva. Delicate and spoiled. I mean, I'm not bleeding or otherwise obviously injured. Nothing broken. I'm simply lying here talking about "dizziness," but for all they know I could be faking it. Like women fake headaches to get out of sex. I may as well say I'm having an attack of the vapors for all this Ménière's thing makes sense to anyone.

I'm feeling like a failure as I lie here on this cold floor, a man who will disappoint those people who believe in him the most. I mean, let's face it, another twenty minutes and the show is cancelled, and I will have let down an entire audience. And I have friends out there: The three friends, who came up to see me rather than attend a funeral in Los Angeles; my busy editor at the Pacific News Service; my wife's aunt and uncle, who drove an hour from their home even though the aunt is suffering from debilitating arthritis; several friends who saw my show once and have now brought their brothers and friends; and ten ex-felons who now work in the theater as a way to exorcise their demons. (I had planned on talking to them after the show.)

But first and foremost I'm disappointing myself, betraying my own sense of my strength. It pains me to be so close to the stage, yet helpless as a baby to stand up. I'm embarrassed when people come to the bathroom door and see me laid out. I'm embarrassed because my massive helplessness is on full and elaborate display. At five foot ten, two hundred ten pounds, I'm a burly fellow, broad shouldered and barrel chested from a time back when I did six hundred push-ups a day in prison. That once-solid muscle has turned almost gelatinous, so that I now have two evenly defined male breasts. Almost hugging the toilet throne, I'm mumbling about the exotic pain.

It's one thing to know that you are helpless, another to be willing to talk about it, and something quite different to have your helplessness become public spectacle. Believe me when I tell you, it's no fun when folks come in here and see my fat ass laid out like some sort of beached manatee.

In my one-man show, *The Man Who Outgrew His Prison Cell,* a prisoner named Heavy D is characterized as so obese (673 pounds) that he sometimes falls off his bed and gets stuck between the post at the foot of his bed and the toilet. Heavy D can't lift himself up, and the pressure of weight on his lungs makes it difficult for him to breathe. Seeing me lying there on the men's room floor, my director, Karen Amano, says, "Maybe this is Heavy D's revenge. You know, theaters are full of ghosts." I chuckle and get dizzier and tell her to go away. But now she has me thinking. I've been haunted by the dead before. Perhaps the ghost of Heavy D— the original man who outgrew his prison cell is saying to me from the Great Beyond, "You see, punk? See how fun it is to fall and not be able to get up? Now it's your turn to learn the lesson: the same thing that'll make you laugh will also make you cry."

# Maravilla

*God possesses the heavens, but He covets the earth.*
                                                    —W.B. Yeats

S he's seated on her throne in the school gymnasium, a bouquet
    of roses in her arms and a pageant banner draped across her
    dress. The principal, a Troy Donahue look-alike, is adjusting a
dainty silver crown on her head. It's 1959, and fourteen-year-old Basilia
Jesus Martinez, whom everyone calls Bessie, looks sweet and pretty
in her white-chiffon hoopskirt, the crinoline made of tulle—a dressier
outfit than the one she'll wear in two years when she rushes to marry my
father. Voted the "Tower Queen" of D. W. Griffith Junior High School
in East Los Angeles, she is, according to her friends, the Mexican-
American version of the popular Mouseketeer Annette Funicello. But
the photographer has caught her at an unexpected moment, when
she looks more uncomfortable than pleased. Her look communicates
misunderstanding—the sudden flash was a bad augur—as if even she,
with her cheery optimism and sentimental faith in the world, senses
the farce: she, with her dark, full, Indian face, as a symbol of contest
beauty in Sandra Dee's bobby-sock America.

My father, Joey, her escort, stands next to her, weighing a little less
than a hundred pounds. He's wearing a dressy black jacket, a white shirt,
and a tie with clip. His arms are in front of him, his left hand clasped over
the hand of his polio-withered right arm. Despite his small stature, he

has a dangerous reputation. There are rumors that he once beat a boy with a baseball bat. He is a member of the neighborhood gang *El Lote Mara* ("The Lot"), considered by some to be the oldest gang in Los Angeles. In the photo his head is erect, as if he is staring over the heads of a crowd we cannot see. He's intentionally not smiling, either to act tough or to hide the gap between his two big front teeth, or both. The pursed lips and the head that is slightly cocked back are the juvenile pose of the pachuco—a pose that I, too, would eventually assume.

This yearbook photograph is the earliest evidence of my parents' courtship.

Scribbled on the inside flap of my father's Tower yearbook that year is my eighth-grade mother's sworn affection for him:

*Honey, I don't have very much to say but that it was very nice sharing a lot of things with you. (You know what.) Don't ever forget every thing we had in school because I won't. Hope to see you in all my periods at Garfield. Don't forget I will always love you. Yours always, Bessie p.s. Love always and always and always.*

▪▪▪▪▪▪▪▪▪

A religious movement burned through the Maravilla housing projects in the mid-1950s, halcyon days for the hallowed East Los Angeles elect, when the young evangelist Billy Graham's altar call from midfield ignited the jam-packed football stadium at the nearby community college. (My father's mother, Nellie, was one of thousands who rose in the bleachers in response to the call to surrender her soul to Christ.)

A few miles away, in downtown L.A., Pastor J. Vernon McGee of the Church of the Open Door (or C.O.D.) encouraged Ruth Burke to use the Maravilla housing projects as her mission site—two missionary boards had denied her a post in Japan—since she had already started a chummy evangelical Bible study group there known as the Good News Bible Club.

Ruth Burke was born in Palestine, Texas. She had come to Los Angeles to attend Biola College, whose campus in those days was the Church of the Open Door. Heeding her pastor's advice, she moved into a store-front across the street from the projects.

With a sweater worn across the back of her shoulders like a cape, Ruth walked around the neighborhood knocking on doors, distributing pamphlets, and asking parents if their children could come to her Good News Bible Club.

In the Good News Bible Club, Ruth preached a personal and Protestant relationship with the Bible. Each child was awarded a Bible for attending the club. A child first learned the order of all sixty-six books in the Bible through an easy-to-remember, Sesame Street sort of sing-along song. Then they'd play "Bible drill": Ruth would shout out a verse, such as John 3:16, and the older kids would race to locate it. The winner would then read it aloud. The younger kids, who couldn't read, merely pretended to know what they were doing as they flipped through the Bible's pages. They were being trained, nonetheless: they would know the Bible themselves and not need to rely upon the interpretation of Catholic priests.

Very few Protestant churches in East Los Angeles at the time preached in English, so the candies Ruth offered weren't the only incentive to attend the club. Mexican immigrant parents sent their children to her club to learn English.

Soon the neighborhood mothers invited Ruth to their homes, telling her she was too skinny and plying her with tamales and Mexican sweet bread. At the end of her day, Ruth could be seen walking home carrying homemade tortillas wrapped in a scarf, a gift from one of the grateful women of Maravilla. Ruth Burke, the Irish Protestant who converted Mexican Catholic families, became a sort of honorary barrio mascot.

▉▉▉▉▉▉▉▉▉▉

My mother was a sophomore in high school when she got pregnant with me. Her father, my grandpa Nieves, was a gentle man and he wouldn't be upset, she thought. But her father didn't live at home anymore, so it was her mother, Frances, she really worried about. My mother and my father swore not to tell anyone their secret. But my mother soon confided in my aunt Maggie, her older sister closest in age.

Unfortunately, as protective as Maggie generally was, she reacted badly to the news. Maggie didn't like my dad, whom she considered a little punk, an insecure boyfriend, and an altogether unsafe bet as a boyfriend. Maggie had seen Bessie cry, deeply remorseful after Joey berated her for something as innocuous as talking to another boy after school.

Like my father, Maggie had had polio as a child, in her leg, which forced her to walk with a pronounced limp. Short like my father, she was also his equal in temperament, with a reputation for refusing to back down from any fight.

In prison I met a Mexican Mafia associate who as a young gangster had once made the mistake of getting romantically involved with my aunt Maggie's only daughter, my cousin Terry. In my cell he pulled up his pant leg and showed me where my aunt Maggie, after chasing him down the street, had bit him in the ankle just as he was pulling his foot into a car.

Maggie felt compelled to tell her older sister, Nena, about my mother's pregnancy.

*Pinche fregada! You know Mami will kick your ass if she finds out that Bessie's knocked up and you didn't tell her. Bessie's gotta tell Mami tonight or I'll tell her myself.*

Ten years older than Maggie and much tougher, Nena understood more acutely that for propriety's sake it was better to get married before the belly got too big. If telling their mother was a bitter pill to swallow, then so be it. Nena figured that there were plans to be made. Her little sister Bessie had already wasted too much time worrying and hiding. She needed to take her lumps and move on. So Nena confronted my mother with a threat: *You tell or I tell. I don't care, but one way or the other, Mami's gonna know about that baby by tonight.*

My mother ran to tell my father that because of her sister's threats she had no choice but to confess that night. My father agreed and swore to tell his parents too. They hugged, kissed, and assured each other that no matter what happened, they loved each other more than life itself. (*Love always and always and always.*)

And, as might have been expected, that night, my grandmother,

Frances, got mad, slapped my mother, yanked her around the house by her hair, and whipped her with a coat hanger.

## Joe Loya Begat Joe Loya Who Begat Joe Loya

My father's father, Joe, was a brooding Korean War veteran stationed at Fort MacArthur in San Pedro. The police had several times carted him off to jail for beating his kids, for getting drunk, for punching his wife, Nellie. (My grandmother's favorite taunt to his fist: *Go ahead. Hit me again. You hit like a girl.*)

Joe wasn't much better behaved when sober, when he would boast of his superior knowledge of the "real world" (where my father would one day have to go out and earn a living to support a family). *Then and only then will you be any kind of a man.* A martial man, my grandfather ran his home like a drill instructor, barking orders and treating his wife and children as if they were enlisted pieces of human garbage.

For several years my father had been thinking of nothing but how to get out from under his father's brutal, overbearing rule. My mother's pregnancy, for all the grief it had caused him, and for all the grief it might cause him in the near future, promised to be a way out of being treated like a boy by his father. He would himself be a father and therefore the man of his family. A man among men. That would earn him some standing in his father's eyes. Surely his father would stop beating him if he got married and got a job.

So, while my poor, scared mother was being chased around the house by her mother a few blocks away, my scrawny sixteen-year-old father sat down for dinner—intentionally across the table and out of punching distance from his dad—and very nonchalantly told my grandpa Joe that his girlfriend was pregnant. Unexpectedly, sergeant first class Joe Loya, Sr., in a rare show of restraint, merely harrumphed, turned his head to the kitchen, and shouted to my grandma, *Nellie, do you want to know what your oldest son went and did? This suato went and got Bessie pregnant.*

Since my parents had been on-again-off-again boyfriend and girlfriend since age fourteen, both sets of their parents powwowed and determined that the two lovebirds should marry. And both sets of their parents agreed that, of course, my mom and dad would have to drop out of school after their sophomore year at Garfield.

On March 24, 1961, my parents were married down the road at the tiny Lorelei Chapel on Beverly Boulevard in Montebello. My mother wasn't the only pregnant female in the family wedding photograph. My thirty-six-year old paternal Grandma, Nellie, was eight months pregnant with Lucy, her seventh and last child. (Grandma Nellie appears dizzy in the wedding photo, as if she is going to faint, vomit, or give birth right there in front of the camera.)

My mother's oldest brother, David, helped my parents out. A quiet, polite man in his late thirties, David was an ex–Golden Gloves boxing champ known for his graceful moves in the ring and had served seven years in prison for murdering a man. He offered to try to find my father a job, and found them a place to live. A little cottage behind the home he rented had become vacant, so he talked to the landlord and got my parents in there after the wedding ceremony. My grandparents split the rent, fifteen bucks apiece.

For a few weeks my dad worked as a construction laborer, but then he caught whooping cough and had to go on welfare. Ten days before I was born, he got a job sweeping floors at a machine shop on Ford Boulevard, not far off Brooklyn Avenue—the future Cesar Chavez Boulevard—where on Sundays he bought Mexican chocolate and sweet bread at the *panadería* and where my mother purchased cooked lamb's head at the *carnicería*. She'd bring the *cabeza* home and place the warm paper bag on the center of the kitchen table, tear open the bag, peel back the Saran Wrap, then finally unwrap the foil to reveal the meaty, steaming sheep's skull. My parents used hot corn tortillas like gloves to tear off chunks of the facial meat.

My father took a second job dumping indigent and unidentified corpses into the furnace at an L.A. County crematorium, and was able to save enough money to move us into a one-bedroom apartment in the Maravilla housing projects shortly after I was born, on August 11, 1961.

Two weeks later my parents took me to the Church of the Open

Door, to be near God in the basement nursery. In their pew upstairs my parents prayed and thanked their God for a healthy son, while I lay in my crib, drank holy formula, and shitted my diapers.

Ruth Burke had converted my father to the Protestant faith at age ten, and four years later he converted my mother. So my mother referred to Ruth as her "spiritual mother-in-law." Ruth had invited them to attend the Church of the Open Door, and they were always happy to please her. It was nice for my parents, along with other Christian families, to leave the neighborhood once a week after Sunday school to picnic at Griffith Park and have long discussions about Biblical prophecy or the veracity of the gift of tongues in the modern age.

The Church of the Open Door was a large, middle-class church. Very few brown, much less black, Angelenos attended services there. The church wasn't actively inhospitable to us, more like cool, with manners foreign to young Mexicans of East L.A. Understandably, most of the new Protestants in Maravilla felt more comfortable at local Spanish-speaking churches, like the Mexican Evangelical Memorial Church, where Sal Delgado was pastor. But my parents weren't intimidated by C.O.D. They chose to attend regularly and make the church their home.

A year and a half after I was born, my parents' new religious lifestyle left them at a crossroads. Salvation had aroused in my father's heart the memory of himself as a pious little boy who used to lie on the lawn of his grandparents' home in El Paso, contemplate the heavens, and think about becoming a priest. I suspect that his premarital sexual activity with my mother was guilt that he thought great piety might erase. Eager to distance himself further from what he considered early sins of sexual lust, he flung himself into the minutiae of Scripture. Believing he was a "new man," theologically repaired, he aspired to become a Baptist preacher.

Up until then, my father and mother hung out with their childhood friends from high school, worldly people, Catholics—considered by my parents' new Protestant friends to be non-Christians—who, on the weekends, were more likely to be drinking liquor and dancing to rock-and-roll music than attending church services. People, in other words, whose behavior was openly hostile to my father's code for holy living.

Finally, my father decided that he and my mother would give up those friends of their youth, cut off contact with anyone who couldn't understand what they were becoming as born-again Christians. He took literally St. Paul's exhortation to Christians to be in the world but not of it.

So, in the trash went his Johnny Mathis and Paul Anka albums. Soon the music of Beethoven and Handel, Mario Lanza crooning Neapolitan love songs, and folksy gospel music hovered over the boxy RCA turntable in our apartment, contrasted with the Big Bopper or norteño mariachi music played loudly elsewhere in the projects.

■■■■■■■■■■

I was raised closer to Galilee than Guadalajara.

In those days, our home was a place of Bible studies. Weeknights, the Guerrero, Delgado, and Andrade families from church would gather around our kitchen table and pore over the Scriptures and discuss tricky theological riddles: Why did Jesus tell the good thief hanging on the cross next to him that he would see him in Paradise later that day even though Jesus didn't actually ascend to heaven until a few weeks later? Or, if God's righteousness cannot tolerate sin in His presence, and all humans are born sinners, how can God allow into heaven babies who are born without volition to repent and accept the shed blood of Jesus? With all these discussions going on, I knew what the words *hermeneutic* and *exegesis* meant before I knew how to greet my great-grandmother in Spanish.

At age nineteen, my father started teaching himself Hebrew and Greek, two of the three original languages of the Christian Bible. He bought Bible commentaries to study for enjoyment. Odd, I know, for a brown boy in the housing projects to spend his free time engrossed in the theological realms of Calvin's Lake Geneva or popular nineteenth-century British Bible expositors. But because of his daily Old Testament readings, in my father's imagination, ancient empires like Mesopotamia and Assyria were contemporary places.

Sometimes our apartment was the scene of marathon prayer meetings, where the men tried to outdo each other's religious stamina by seeing who could pray the longest. My dad swore off those prayer meetings after he fell asleep several times during one of Ruben Garcia's three-hour prayers.

These men—truck drivers, desk makers, unemployed laborers—concentrated on the lineages of the twelve tribes of Israel:

> *Two years after the flood, when Shem was 100 years old, he became the father of Arphaxad. And after he became the father of Arphaxad, Shem lived 500 years and had other sons and daughters. When Arphaxad had lived 35 years, he became the father of Shelah. And after he became the father of Shelah, Arphaxad lived 403 years and had other sons and daughters.*

My father admired the orthodox rabbis because he believed, as they did, that life's answers were revealed through God's holy inspired Word. The Jewish and Christian ideas of what constituted God's Word were partially antagonistic to each other, but my father concentrated on the obscured similarities in their beliefs, mostly because he fervently believed that the Jews were always God's "chosen people."

The fundamentalist Baptist doctrine my father and his friends subscribed to taught that every word in the Bible was inerrant—absolutely true and without error. They could cite chapter and verse for every abomination listed in the Scriptures. They talked of the Latin Vulgate, Septuagint manuscripts, and the Masoretic Text as if they'd actually read them. They knew about the Levites, Philistines, and concubines, about Sabbath traditions, about Jewish prophets and kings. In fact, these men of Mexican descent—some Mexican nationals—could more easily recite the names of the first five kings of Israel or the names of the thirty-nine books of the Old Testament, than name the last five presidents of Mexico.

They spoke of identity, of being "new men." But Judaism and the Old Testament, rather than their own Mexican heritage, were the premises from which they drew their conclusions. It was as if I was being raised in some cult of Judaism. We memorized and claimed as true the origin myths of the Jews (Methuselah lived to be how old?), but never once while I was growing up did I hear a single adult talk of the Mayans, Toltecs, or Aztecs.

▇▇▇▇▇▇▇▇▇

My mother noted in my baby book:

> *Baby's name is Joe Loya.*
> He looks like his father.
> First haircut given by his daddy. May 29, 1962.
> First word: *Papa.*
> Mother's notes: *Doctor said he had a lot of sense for his age, she said he will be smart and to send him to college.*
> Our baby's type: *He has muscle arms it runs in his father's side.*
> Baby's Temperament: *He has a temper. I guess he takes after his father's temper.*

One Saturday, when I was almost two, our family attended a picnic with our Christian "brothers and sisters" from our old house of worship, the Mexican Evangelical Memorial Church. At one point my dad sauntered away to play football with the guys. He thought he'd left me securely with my mother, who sat on a blanket chatting with friends. *She* thought I was going with *him*. I waddled after my father. They noticed that I'd wandered off just in time to see me step into a sandpit and into the path of an older boy on a swing. The swing's collision with my chubby, wobbly body broke my collarbone. When they lifted me they noticed blood on the torn seat of my shorts. I had sat on pieces of broken glass.

The doctor put my arm in a tiny sling and gave my parents a bottle of St. Joseph's baby aspirin—chalky, pink pills that looked and tasted like candy. The glass shards were removed from my butt as well, permanently scarring the crease.

That same night, shortly after eight thirty, my mother noticed that I was struggling to breathe. The first thing my dad did was go for the baby aspirin. But the bottle was on the floor. Cap off. Empty. The bottle had been on a shelf above a counter. Apparently, I had climbed on a chair and then a table, grabbed the bottle, and gnawed off the cap. My father raced me to Rowan Clinic, where my baby brother, Paul Peter—named after the two most famous apostles—had been born sixteen months after me.

A doctor at the small clinic examined me briefly, then told my father that he should take me to the larger County General Hospital where, in his opinion, I'd receive abler treatment.

My father: *Today I know better. But back then I was only an eighteen-year-old kid from the* barrio. *I didn't second-guess a doctor. Today, if a doctor told me he couldn't admit my dying son into the hospital, I'd at least make him use a paramedic to transport you somewhere else. I don't know why he just let your mother and me drive you in our old beat-up DeSoto all the way to County.*

Someone from the Rowan Clinic telephoned the county hospital, so by the time my father and mother arrived with me, there were staff waiting outside for us. One doctor, a young white male, quickly looked me over. He glared at my parents before he rushed us into the emergency room.

My father: *When he spoke to your mother and me, we could tell that he was upset with us. He was probably thinking, "All you Mexicans love to have children but you don't even know how to take care of them."*

I cried and squirmed in my father's grip while the doctor shoved a tube down my throat to pump my stomach. Then I was put into the Intensive Care Unit. The aspirin had already spread throughout my system, so pumping my stomach didn't help much. The doctor recommended that my family pray for me, saying that the first forty-eight hours would be critical.

At 4:30 A.M., my parents, who'd kept the crisis private up to that point, went home and began telephoning family and friends.

My grandma Nellie rushed over. So did Ruth, and Ruben and Lily Garcia.

My father again: *I think it was Virgie Andrade who came to the house and said she'd called people from the Angelus Temple—you know, Aimee Semple McPherson's church in Echo Park. She told us that they had a twenty-four-hour prayer chain going for you. Can you believe that? Total strangers were praying for your tiny life hanging in the balance. Of course, I put mine and the Temple's theological differences aside. I didn't care who sent the prayers, just so long as they got to God.*

I spent four days in critical condition, eight days in the hospital. A genuine brush with death. My parents were mortified. So, when my father went alone to Ruth's house on the second day, he decided to plead and bargain with God for my soul.

*You have to understand. You were the son I always wanted. I loved you more than I'd ever loved anyone. I told God that it would just tear me up inside if He took you to be with Him. But I also told God that if my son was going to grow up and turn away from Him, and live an unrighteous life, then I wanted Him to take you, right then and there. It was all about your soul for me. I knew that if He took you I'd suffer for the rest of my life here on earth. But at least knowing that I'd be able to spend eternity with you in God's kingdom could comfort me.*

The threat to my life had been serious. The prayer vigil, hospital bed, bloody gauze on my ass, tube shoved down my throat and needle poked into my vein were real enough. But the rest is family lore.

Family and friends believed that I was wrested from the Reaper's grasp by the power of the Christ who compels death. God had miraculously answered my father's prayer. My future was a done deal. I was going to glorify God's name with my life, and that was that.

My father always told the story of his bargaining with God as if he were Abraham himself, down from the mount, recounting to his tribe just how close he came to sacrificing his only son out of obedience to God's sacred command. Like Isaac, I sat and listened to his proud telling of the tale. Sometimes I can't help but wonder if my father would have felt even more pious if God had answered his prayer and accepted his sacrifice.

▐▌▐▌▐▌▐▌▐▌

On November 3, 1964, my mother noted in my baby book that I had accepted Jesus as my Savior in a Good News Bible Club meeting. *Faith Gerlach led him to the Lord.* I was three years old. I couldn't tie my own shoes and barely comprehended buttons, but apparently Jesus was a snap.

A baby book entry the following year notes that *Joey feels a call to the missionary field. To tell the parents and preach in India the gospel. He is 4 years old.*

I sense that I was something of a showman, not quite like those freaky six-year-olds on soapboxes in documentaries about crazed Christian Bible-Belt fundamentalists—tiny boys shouting at the crowd, denouncing wicked lewdness, ranting about the corruption of the flesh and an evil world full of fornication, thumping the Bible, and quoting verses to claim the power of the Holy Spirit to cast out demons. No, my showmanship wasn't quite hell fire like that. But on my parents cue I'd sing songs I'd learned in church to family friends in our kitchen.

*Jesus loves me, this I know,*
*For the Bible tells me so.*
*Little ones to him belong,*
*They are weak, but he is strong.*

Several times I was heard comforting my brother, Paul, when he cried at night, afraid of the dark: *Paul, don't cry. Jesus said let not your heart be troubled, neither let it be afraid.*

The bulk of my best memories come from those early years. Dad would come home from work, and Paul and I would race to the front door to wrestle with him. And he'd become our horse, down on all fours, with two little boys holding on to the back of his shirt, feet dangling over the side of his torso, kicking his sides and telling him to move faster. Whenever I see the old photos that capture those playful scenes, my memory conjures a whiff of fat crayons and the fresh scent of a new coloring book opened for the first time.

I'm smiling in all the early photos, either pandering to the camera—my shoulders hunched as if I were trying to contain myself from bursting with glee at the seams of my flesh—or shoving out my tiny bird's chest, with my face lifted to the lens. In every shot, my body looked like it was in some sort of convulsion of excitement.

On Easter Sunday evening when I was five years old, my parents and I watched the film *The Greatest Story Ever Told* on television. It was the story of Jesus of Nazareth, with a very young Max Von Sydow in the role of Christ, the Paschal lamb. Near the end, Jesus finally goes limp and hangs dead on the cross.

I wept.

My mother and father were shocked. They lifted me onto the couch and tried to comfort me with adult logic. They told me to wait, not to be sad, that the movie wasn't over. I still wept. A few scenes later, when Jesus appeared alive again on the screen, I slid off the couch. Amazed, I pointed at the TV and looked back at my parents, as if they'd been the ones crying and I was proving to them that Jesus had indeed risen. I laughed, jumping, spinning, singing. *Jesus isn't dead! Jesus isn't dead!*

In their room that night, my mother and father knelt at the foot of their bed. Crying, they thanked God for giving them a sensitive child, a boy who, with God's blessing, would become a righteous man.

▌▌▌▌▌▌▌▌▌▌

When English is your first language, but Spanish is spoken all around you—swirling in the steam above a stack of freshly made flour tortillas or in the whiff of *chorizo con huevos* sizzling in Grandma's cast-iron skillet—you process words differently, notice their ironies, find the hidden likenesses, their comical distinctions, like the Russian Nabokov did with his English-as-a-Second-Language (ESL) prose.

I referred to my sweet drunkard grandpa Nieves as Grandpa "Ice Cream," the literal English translation for the Spanish word *nieves*. And Maravilla became a Spanish word synonymous with tenements, the barrio, teenage pregnancy, high school dropouts, welfare, *cholo* gangbangers (in other words, all the clichéd Latino pathologies)—a place poor people aspire to leave for a better life elsewhere.

For a brief time in prison, I was proud of the rumor that the Mexican Mafia was formed by thirteen male inmates in California State Prison who were all from Maravilla. But for most of my life, "Maravilla" meant extreme embarrassment. Only after I was out of prison for four years did I discover that the more accurate English translation for *Maravilla* is the word *marvel*.

# ii

After one year of solitary confinement on the West Coast, I was transferred to Pennsylvania, where I was placed in another special housing unit (SHU) at the Lewisburg Penitentiary. This was standard procedure after a transfer: The prison administration had to verify that an incoming prisoner had no known enemies at the prison before they could release him into the general population.

During my brief wait for prison clearance in the SHU, I was able to get out of my handcuffs and stab a prisoner named Griffith.

My loathing for Griffith was ancient. He'd been my friend Paddy's lackey at Lompoc Penitentiary. He was a bookie. A lying, sneaking, weasly motherfuckin' shady scoundrel who had the same build and stroll as Shaggy from the Scooby-Doo cartoon. Same funky little goatee, too. Griffith was a constant source of grief for Paddy, getting into debt with the wrong guys or spouting off at the wrong time, even daring to skim profits off Paddy's books. As Paddy's bagman, he came in contact with all Paddy's money.

There was one month at Lompoc Penitentiary when my best friend, Creeper, and I seriously contemplated stabbing Griffith because we felt he had cheated us out of our proper share of dope. But we gave him a pass after Paddy asked us not to harm his boy. Paddy said that he would take care of things himself. He straightened things out by giving us free dope from his next shipment.

We liked Paddy because he was a man of his word. And he was the only man I knew who was a literal knock-out artist. He had hands like a pit bull's head: thick and sinewy and angry. On the way to the chow hall Paddy would punch the wall to keep his knuckles tough. If during a disagreement Paddy became upset, he would simply throw one punch to the offender's jaw and turn out the guy's lights.

I'll never forget the time Paddy and I stood outside his cell, on the third tier, leaning against the rails and looking down at Griffith, who was below passing out betting tickets.

"See that kid? He's such a fuckin' thorn in my side."

"Yeah, Creeper and I can't figure out what the payoff is, why you keep him around."

"I know. Don't think I don't regret taking him under my wing. Sometimes I have a good mind to put him out of my misery."

This contempt, plus what he had done to Creeper and me, made me despise Griffith. So, at the Lewisburg SHU, after he got drunk one night in the cell across from mine, he called me out and all pumped up on liquid courage, told me he knew I never liked him so why didn't I do something about it? I said, okay, if he was that tough, then I would meet him on our way to recreation. The next morning I said to a guard that I wanted to go to recreation with the first group, after I saw that Griffith was going with them. They have to search us before we go into the recreation cages, so, for a brief moment, we would all be unhandcuffed together. I knew that that's when he intended to stab me.

All prisoners are searched before leaving their cells, but when we step out of our cells and are standing on the tier, the food traps on the doors are still open from breakfast. When I stepped out of my cell that morning I walked over to a friend's cell with my hands handcuffed behind my back. He reached out of his cell and undid my cuffs with a paper clip. Then he handed me a knife. I started walking toward Griffith with my hands behind my back as if they were still cuffed. As soon as I got near him I kicked him in the balls, and then I stabbed him once on the arm. I was immediately held down by the guards. They handcuffed me and took me to a holding cell in the basement. I lay down and relaxed as they cleaned out a cell for me in the super-max, high-power basement tier of cells.

# Omen

## 1966, Maravilla Housing Projects, East Los Angeles

My mother often went to visit her mother-in-law in the mornings. Grandma Nellie would be propped up in bed on pillows like a lazy duchess, watching her favorite Spanish-language soap operas on Telemundo. My mother would slip under the blankets with her. To my aunts Margie and Rosemary, four and six years younger than my father, my mother was still the beauty queen of Griffith Junior High, and they deferred to her as if she were their own glamorous older sister.

▐▐▐▐▐▐▐▐▐▐

Every writer from East L.A. has his Whittier Boulevard memory. This is mine:

It was 1966 and I was four years old, almost five. Paul was two, shaking a rattle in his stroller as my mother—dressed Hepburnish in pedal-pushers and sunglasses with a summer scarf covering her bouffant hairdo—pushed him. My grandma Nellie held my hand as we strolled alongside them. We were out to go shopping on Whittier Boulevard, a street made infamous years later by bad Hollywood movies about Mexicans in the barrio, illegal cruising, and gang-banging.

Sometimes we'd take the Kern bus to get onto Whittier Boulevard, where the men's clothing store Richard's stood. We'd stop at Grayson's Clothing Store for women, where inside my mother and grandma would peek at but not purchase—never purchase—expensive gloves and handbags. (They usually bought their clothes at lower-end stores.) Back on the sidewalk we'd pass Curley's clothing store for men, across the street from the Army-Navy store, where my father bought his Sir Guy shirts and baggy khaki pants, a bastardized zoot-suit look and the popular uniform of the local cholos. On our way to Johnson's market, my mother and grandmother would pay their weekly bills at Stone's, a furniture store owned by a popular Jewish man who spoke Spanish to his customers and offered them furniture on credit. Mr. Stone's promotional schtick was advertising on Spanish TV as "El Chaparito" Stone. You'd think that this gimmick would have given Shorty Stone one up on his competitor, Wenger's Furniture Store down the street. But Mr. Wenger also spoke Spanish and offered credit to his customers.

I remember that I used to feel special on Whittier Boulevard, where women, friends of the family and other Maravilla folks—in knock-off pillbox hats, boxy-shouldered suits or angora sweaters, and pointy-toe pumps—congregated in front of the Golden Gate Theater, gossiping and commenting on how smartly my mother had dressed Paul and me.

There were five movie theaters in the one-mile stretch of Whittier Boulevard. The Center Theater and Boulevard Theater for starters. My father saw *The Man Who Shot Liberty Valance* with his friend Abraham Ayala at the Egyptian Theater. During that 1966 summer, double features like *Born Free* and *The Lion in Winter* or *The Sound of Music* and *The Russians Are Coming, The Russians Are Coming* ran at the Golden Gate Theater. The United Artists Theater down the street wasn't to be outdone. The previous year, Richard Burton starred there in *The Spy Who Came in from the Cold*. In 1966, Elizabeth Taylor and Richard Burton tore up the screen in two Oscar-winning performances, as George and Martha in the Academy Award winner for Best Picture, *Who's Afraid of Virginia Woolf?* That's when the entire world was fascinated by the passionate offscreen romance between Burton and Taylor.

After the shopping, bill paying, and sidewalk schmoozing, we'd end up in front of Thrifty's drugstore, at one of those photo booths that, for a dime, would spit out four black-and-white photos the size of large postage stamps. Afterward, we'd walk to the soda counter located at the back of the store. My mother would always order the strawberry sundae, and she'd let me pick the cherry off the top. I'd stick my finger into the whipped cream and suck on it.

Bessie and Joey were fourteen years old when they had their first date in one of the booths at the back of Thrifty's drugstore. Bessie pointed at Joey's open palm held firmly in her hand.

*You see this? That means you are going to live a long life.*

*How can you tell?*

*Because a lady read my palm and told me that this line is the lifeline. She told me that I'm not going to live a long life.*

Ten years later, when Joey drove Bessie to Harbor General Hospital for her first dialysis treatment, he recalled that conversation about mortality. He wondered if Bessie recalled the palm reader's prophecy.

## 1966, Manzanar Street, Pico Rivera

My aunt Nena's two eldest sons went to fight in Vietnam. When Aunt Nena went to live with her latest boyfriend we moved into her home on Manzanar Street in Pico Rivera, ten miles east of Maravilla.

There are two things from those years that I will always identify with my aunt Nena: avocados and leopard-skin print. Avocados because a large avocado tree in the backyard meant that we ate them regularly. As guacamole or sliced as a side dish with breakfast, lunch, and dinner or salted and smeared onto a warm tortilla to make an avocado burrito.

Leopard-skin print because that was my aunt Nena's fashion motif: leopard-collared coats, leopard scarves, leopard lining in her slippers, leopard drapes and sofa, leopard blouses, and leopard tights. Wispy leopard sashes covered lamps or were laid across the coffee table under bowls of hard candy and glass figurines of Don Quixote on horseback and Sancho on his burro, bought at the Mexican-American border after a day's visit into Tijuana.

My aunt Nena was the kind of woman who would playfully slap or punch her boys or boyfriends when they made her feel uncomfortable, such as when her son kissed her and embarrassed her in front of other family members (Slap! *Ay, Frankieee, quit playing around, you're messing up my hair*) or when her boyfriend made a sour face, pretending that her cooking was bad (Punch! *Yeah, Okay* pinche pendejo, *see who cooks for you from now on*).

My mother and Aunt Nena had different fathers. Nena's real name was Maria Felix. This was also the name, fittingly, of Mexico's leading onscreen femme fatale (described in her obituary as Mexico's Marilyn Monroe), who appeared in more than forty films. Maria Felix made her film debut in 1942 in *El Penon de las Animas* ("The Crag of the Soul") alongside Jorge Negrete, the Mexican Clark Gable, with whom she later became romantically involved. She'd been romantically linked also with the famous muralist painter Diego Rivera. I grew up imagining my aunt Nena as a femme fatale, with a hard-ridged heart—stony, impossible to crack—and with crags in her soul. Aunt Nena was tough, diffident, and pouty. She was caught squinting a lot in her photos. I don't recall her ever happy or smiling—only slyly, like a caricature of a villain in cartoons. She's the reason I first read the villainous Cruella DeVil as a vampish Latina in Disney's *101 Dalmatians*.

▮▮▮▮▮▮▮▮▮

My dad assembled my Schwinn bike—complete with training wheels—on our first Christmas morning on Manzanar Street. He propped me up on the bike then walked beside me, one hand holding the front bars, the other on the back of the black seat, guiding me down the sidewalk.

Soon after the training wheels came off, I went riding to the other end of the block, in the middle of the street—a complete no-no. Some boys jumped out from behind a large bush and charged me, yelling and swinging sticks. I panicked, sped up, and turned the handlebars sharply . . . straight into a curb. It was a cartoonish scene, with the bike stopping dead while I flew over the handlebars and hit my head on the pavement. A gash opened up above my right eyebrow.

The boys scattered, and a neighbor ran out of her house when she heard me crying and yelling for my mommy. She held my hand and walked me home. My dad answered the door. He lifted me up into his arms so that as we passed through the living room I could see myself in the mirror above the fireplace. I'd always been too short to look into that mirror, and I didn't recognize myself at first because the blood obscured my features.

I knew that I was the boy in the mirror because the boy was crying and being carried by my father, like me. But without those obvious clues, the boy in the mirror seemed like a stranger whose tragedy I was observing independently. The detachment I felt from my own traumatic experience baffled me. I expected to own myself more forcefully, to know and feel my experience more acutely. It was as if the large mirror were a film screen and I were watching a blurred movie about my life.

■■■■■■■■■■

As a high school dropout with no real skills my father didn't earn a lot of money. But by the time I was old enough to enroll in kindergarten, he had worked hard to pay for tuition at St. John's Lutheran Elementary School. My father understood that St. John's was commendably conservative. He knew, for instance (and was proud to know this), that the school was affiliated with the "Lutheran Church—Missouri Synod," an institution so conservative that a new moderate Lutheran Church was later created in protest of the tight doctrinal parameters the synod orthodoxy had set at a convention in 1973.

My father's favorite radio program was (the widely heard) *The Lutheran Hour,* started by Walter Maier. Maier was an inspiration to my father, who yearned to be both a preacher and language scholar. (Walter Maier earned his Ph.D. in Semitics at Harvard in 1929, and published, my father believed, the definitive commentary on the Book of Nahum in the Old Testament. And Billy Graham bestowed the highest testimonial on Dr. Walter A. Maier when he called him *the greatest combination of preacher and scholar that America has produced.*)

My father suspected, almost expected, that I would one day do graduate work, so the fact that the Lutheran school would teach German to first graders appealed to his sense of posterity and scholastic pedigree. Having become familiar with language studies and the hierarchy of languages in his theological world, he concluded that nothing could beat German for graduate-school prep.

## 1967, Deland Street, Pico Rivera

When I was in second grade, our family moved to an apartment on Deland Street, not far from Manzanar Street. That's when I was transferred from St. John's Lutheran to Brethren Elementary School in Whittier, where teachers expected their fourth-grade charges to memorize entire chapters from the Bible, in my case, Luke 2 and John 14.

Throughout elementary school my father allowed Paul and me to order any books we wanted from a catalogue handed out to us in class. We'd check off what we wanted—Dr. Seuss, *Curious George*—turn the slip in to our teacher, and then wait two weeks for our boxes of books, mine usually stuffed with ten thin books, twice as many as the next student. Same with my brother and his class.

My father's splurging took the sting away from the fact that the student body at Brethren Elementary School was almost entirely white and middle class. To my mind, middle class might as well have been Boston Brahmin for all its exoticism. The only way I felt equal was academically. I was the best student in my classes.

My father also always gave me an outrageous amount of cash whenever I went on field trips. When my class went to Disneyland, he placed a twenty-dollar bill in my hand and kissed me proudly. When I got to school I was surprised to learn that the other kids had been given only five or ten dollars by their parents. I could tell that the teachers thought that my father had given me an inappropriate amount of money. But I was proud. The money would show my friends that I wasn't some poor Mexican. You know, *them:* uncouth and without class—like my aunts, whose boisterous laughs were unladylike or who farted while getting out of cars and then crossed themselves—the ones who couldn't appreciate the great Protestant instruction I was receiving from the Brethren.

Desperate to distance myself from the *barrio* class, I surrendered myself to the delusion of equal wealth, if only for a day. The money my father lavished on me for books and field trips seemed to elevate me somehow, make my classmates take me more seriously. And with good reason: With all that cash I got to treat them to extra ice cream or cotton candy when their chump change ran out. Still, I knew my standing with them was somewhat artificial and only temporary. Like Cinderella at the ball, I knew that by the end of the day I'd lose my fiscal sheen and be reduced again to my lower, house-cleaner status.

*Put your money away, Joe. Put it in your pocket.*

Miss Halbern scolded me when I flashed the twenty-dollar bill, but her chastisement only assured me that the money did in fact make me more noticed, picked out of the crowd. It also taught me an important lesson: Money altered people's perception of me, and how I handled my money became their concern. There was a public ethic about money. And the most important lesson of all: if you had money, pretend like it didn't matter.

■■■■■■■■■

My parents were obsessed with sharing the good news that God so loved the world that he sent His only begotten son Jesus to die for our sins. They evangelized with equal zeal, and saw every new introduction as an opportunity to proselytize.

One time my mother was reaching for a box of Rice-A-Roni on a shelf at the local Von's supermarket when a thin, scraggly woman yanked my mother's purse out of our shopping basket. My mother cried out and chased the woman. The store manager joined in the chase.

When I finally caught up with them, the store manager was yanking the cutpurse's arm up behind her back, the way Joe Friday held a burglary suspect hard against the hood of a car. The purse snatcher's face was twisted with anger.

My mother was deep in discussion with the store manager. I couldn't understand what they were saying but it was clear that my mother was trying to convince the manager of something. I thought it a bit odd when the manager suddenly shoved the cutpurse's wrists out of his grasp with a sneer. Stranger still: once he let her loose, the woman did not run. The manager walked back to the store.

A Christian who was devoted to Jesus as she was devoted to my father, my mother believed the Gospel was all that the world needed to straighten itself out. So she shared this good news with the probably jonesing purse-snatcher (like Jesus with the publicans, sinners, and tax collectors), telling her how God loved her, and how He had indeed sent Jesus down to earth to die for her sins. A prayer was said. Tears flowed there in the parking lot.

▉▉▉▉▉▉▉▉▉

My parents trained me to desire "good," to consider the moral consequences of my thoughts and behavior. By age seven, modeling myself on my father's rectitude and my mother's evangelical style, I took up the cause of converting my Catholic neighborhood friends on Deland Street to my brand of Protestant Christianity.

I'd gather them in a circle of bicycles in front of our apartment and then I'd Bible-thump with righteous indignation like a tiny Jimmy Swaggart. I preached about the sly serpent in Eden. I scared them with Bible stories about angry prophets, fallen angels, and the Lake of Eternal Fire in Hell. I converted them to my fears of fire and brimstone, my apocalyptic vision of the future, my mediocre version of salvation.

With a flannel board propped on an easel—the same board my mother used to teach Bible stories to children who attended the Good News Bible Club meetings she held in our home—I would tell them the story of Samson and Delilah.

With their steady diet of Saturday-morning television my audience could relate to the world I was describing. When I said Goliath was a giant, they believed me because they faithfully followed the *Adventures of Gigantor,* our favorite cartoon. When I said Samson fought and slew an entire army with only the jawbone of an ass as a weapon, they didn't doubt it because on television we had watched Superman still the earth's rotation for a moment to save it from annihilation. And of course, we all recognized Delilah's kryptonite-like weakening effect on mighty Samson. We understood girls to be crafty. If superheroes could be lured and trapped, like Batman was by his feline nemesis, Catwoman, then simple boys like us were defenseless.

When I finished preaching, my mother would make us lemonade or iced tea. Then we'd set off in a short caravan to play army camp under the old green bus parked permanently behind the corner church. Or we'd get our tires pumped up with air at the bicycle repair shop across from the church.

One summer day an unfamiliar boy rode his bike full speed onto our street, one hand on the handlebars, the other strangely pressed down on his head. He was no older than I, yet he clearly possessed a freedom beyond our seven years. I was wildly impressed as I watched him navigate his bicycle down the center of the street.

When the boy saw me standing in front of my apartment building, he smiled and pedaled toward me as if we'd arranged to meet there. Like mine, his smile was front-toothless, but his skin color was pale, his cheeks pink. Although he was a white boy, he looked even more bleached-out than my white classmates.

He plopped his bicycle onto the sidewalk next to mine and boldly introduced himself. His name was Bobby. I looked at his disheveled light brown hair and sensed something amiss in it.

I was impressed to learn that Bobby had ridden his bicycle from his home three blocks away in search of new friends. Three blocks, unescorted, on a bike! He may as well have declared himself to be from Africa, Jupiter, or the upper class. Each place was equally distant in my imagination, and with its own exotic associations.

After our introduction, Bobby and I rode bikes together—with him following me up and down the block . . . on the sidewalk. I found this humility singularly odd. He was *allowed* to ride in the street, and yet he kept to the sidewalk. If *I'd* been allowed to ride in the street and saw that he was confined to the sidewalk, *I* would have ridden off the curb to just show off, to demonstrate my superiority, my advantage. But he seemed indifferent to that sort of pettiness. Whatever I proposed, he was entirely agreeable to it. And he always rode with one hand on his head.

*How about if we go down to the church at the end of the block and play army camp under the bus?*

*Sure.*

*Let's go get our tires pumped up at the corner bike shop. The owner gives me free air all the time.*

*Sure.*

*Do you want something to drink?*

*Sure.*

*What do you want? Soda or juice?*

*Doesn't matter.*

*I'm gonna get a soda. Is that all right with you?*

*Sure.*

Later in the afternoon Bobby invited me to his house. I asked my mother's permission. She asked him for his phone number. I didn't know mine so I was surprised when he recited his address and phone number.

My mother telephoned his mother, and the sojourn was set for the next day. The plan was for him to return for me the following morning, and then we would ride to his house *(On the sidewalk, okay mijo?).* I was to walk my bike whenever we needed to cross the street.

Bobby and I shook hands like two gentlemen going into business together. Then he hopped on his bicycle and rode off around the corner, his knobby-kneed legs pumping the pedals hard. Looking back, he waved quickly and then returned his hand to its place on that bushy mop of hair growing peculiarly on his bony skull.

The following morning my mother waited outside with me for Bobby. Suddenly he zoomed around the corner, standing while pedaling and concentrating as he furiously pumped his stick-legs. I glanced at my mother, wondering whether she would be alarmed at his riding in the center of the street, but she simply smiled and reminded me to have his mother phone when I arrived. Bobby popped his bike over the curb and stopped next to me, breathing hard.

His hair was as disheveled as it had been the day before. To me, this showed a lack of self-discipline on his part. At that age I felt that it was my Christian responsibility to size up a person's transgressive nature. Trusting that God planned for me to serve Him in the future, to minister to the lost world, I felt privileged to judge the rightfulness or wrongfulness of any person or occasion. So, I knew at our first meeting that I would need to counsel Bobby on the value of a tidy appearance. He, of course, was never aware I was plotting his cosmetic redemption.

*Ready to go?*

*Sure.*

I kissed my mother, mounted my bike like a commander mounting a cavalry horse, and followed Bobby to the end of the block on the sidewalk. I looked back and saw my mother's arm waving high above the low yard fences. Once out of her sight, I did not hesitate to ride my bike into the street. My rule-breaking felt good. Clean and liberating. And even as my bike jumped off the curb, I knew that I had become someone other than the typical goody-two-shoes I was in private. Bobby and I rode faster than my customary sidewalk route had ever allowed.

When we reached his home, we rode our bikes up into Bobby's driveway. I expected to stop near the front door so we could park our bikes and report to the parent in charge. Instead, Bobby's mother waved from the porch as we continued past her up the driveway and into the open garage. I wanted to ask Bobby if his mother's welcome was typical. I was shocked that we hadn't been subjected to some parental list of do's and don'ts.

A large quilt blanket draped from the garage rafters divided the garage into front and back spaces. The front section, where we lay our bikes, was too small to accommodate even the smallest sub-compact car. Bobby dismounted his bike and disappeared behind the blanket. I followed him.

The back portion of the garage was a two-tiered clubhouse equipped with a small wooden staircase leading to a second level. The upper deck was stocked with an old refrigerator, a dusty black-and-white television set, several sleeping bags shoved behind some folding chairs, miniature counters, cabinets filled with bags of cookies and potato chips, and flimsy plastic kitchen dishes for children. Various sports banners and posters of rugged outdoor scenes were taped to the wall. Bobby's clubhouse was expertly prepared for any siege a child could imagine.

While we were walking around the clubhouse, Bobby suddenly took off his wig and tossed it onto a table, casually, as if it were an ink-less pen that has fulfilled its usefulness. He was completely bald.

He went to the refrigerator to get us something to drink. I glanced at him. Variegated patches of pink spots designed his skull like a paisley jacquard print. I looked over at his wig lined with dried loops of scotch tape.

He handed me a drink and then, sensing my incomprehension, casually informed me that he had cancer. His illness, and the therapy he was participating in, had caused his hair to fall out.

I wasn't shocked. I had no idea what that meant, no way to understand the merciless implications of his calm revelation.

As the day wore on we rode our bikes around his neighborhood. We went back to his clubhouse and feasted on bologna sandwiches and potato chips. Somewhere along the way I had forgotten about my intention to convert him.

We rode back to my apartment building, I was disturbed with myself. Bobby's illness, or his humility, his deep mansuetude, had momentarily made me feel something like regret for spoiling everything with my judgmental heart and secret intentions. We shook hands again like grown men and he rode away, waving goodbye. As he turned the corner, my neighborhood squad of religious buddies rode up to me.

*Who was that?*

*Where'd he come from?*

*What's he doing here?*

*Why is he so funny looking?*

*Hey, when are we going to have another Bible story time?*

A few months later on the way to church my father told me that Bobby had gone to be with Jesus. He explained to me how the boy was riding his bike in heaven, how God was now taking care of him. I remember feeling something at the time, but I didn't know what it was or how to explain it to myself. If Bobby was with God, then everything must be all right. This was how I finally was able to put the boy out of my mind.

▮▮▮▮▮▮▮▮▮▮

Frequently my father would take breaks in his day and call me to him to ask, *How much do you love your daddy?* As I was learning about numbers I would call out the highest number I knew. *I love you one hundred, Daddy.*

Or, *I love you one million, Daddy.* Or even *I love you a hundred million million.* But one day when my daddy asked me how much I loved him, I'd just learned about eternity so I said, *Daddy, do you know that numbers never stop?*

*Yes, mijo, I know that.*

*Then, Daddy, I love you as long as counting goes.*

▓▓▓▓▓▓▓▓▓▓

While we were still living on Deland Street, my mother got a job at the Sears department store. Her shift began at 5:00 A.M. On those cold, foggy workday mornings, while Paul and I were still lying in bed, my father would go outside to start the car and turn on the car's heater and defroster. He'd return to the apartment and bundle Paul and me in thick blankets, then carry us outside and lay us in the back seat, pillows and all. Our avocado green Ford Maverick rolled under the early-morning blinking streetlights on the outskirts of downtown Los Angeles on the way to drop my mother off at the Sears corporate building.

Across the street from the building, my mother would kiss my brother and me while we half-dozed, adjusting the blankets to stave off the brisk breeze from the open car door. I recall a blistering Chicago-like winter morning, with steam coming out of our mouths when we moaned—that kind of severe cold. But the temperature was probably somewhere in the typical low fifties range, frigid cold by a Los Angeles native's appraisal.

My father would get out and walk around the car to hug and kiss my mother goodbye. Sometimes I'd move up to the front seat to watch my mother disappear into the mist that blanketed the industrial area around the L.A. River. And I'd be put in mind of those foggy, gloomy London street scenes in the grainy black-and-white Sherlock Holmes films my father invited me to watch with him every Sunday afternoon.

Sears required all employees to submit to physicals when they were hired. My mother's initial blood tests came back abnormal. A Sears administrator told her that she needed to go see her family physician. So she made an appointment with Dr. Anaradian to get more blood work done.

## 1968, Shenandoah Street, Pico Rivera

Dr. Anaradian was the only doctor's name I heard while growing up. His clinic was located a few blocks from the Maravilla projects, so he was something like our tribal doctor, deferred to by everyone I knew. He delivered uncles and aunts into the world, Paul and me too, and of course he was the doctor that my grandparents and great-grandparents visited with all their ailments.

One day Dr. Anaradian telephoned my mother with her blood test results and told her that she needed to go to the hospital immediately. In fact, he urged her to check herself in that same day. She told him that she couldn't go to a hospital just like that. Nobody would know were she was. She needed to finish packing things at home. We were moving that weekend, she said.

*Well, Bessie, then you can go in tomorrow, but please have Joey call me. He's got to take you in for sure tomorrow. This is real serious; you really don't have time to delay.*

My father checked her into the Rowan Clinic the following day, a Saturday, then rushed home to complete our move into a large, yellow house on Shenandoah Street, five blocks from Deland Street. He had to have us completely moved out by Sunday night, and losing my mother's help as well as the time it took him to get her to the clinic, was going to make the move harder.

My mother stayed at the clinic for a few days while the doctors ran more tests. The tests quickly confirmed that disease had so thoroughly polluted her kidneys that even if she were in line for a transplant, which she wasn't, her body would most likely reject it. The doctors tapped her stomach to drain the accumulation of fluid, but some time that week she had a heart attack. The doctors revived her, then stabilized her with medication. They told my father to prepare himself for her death.

We'd just celebrated her twenty-fourth birthday.

Dr. Anaradian had two friends at Harbor General Hospital in Torrance: Dr. Sandler, an internist, and Dr. Johnson, who taught at the hospital. The fact that Dr. Johnson was a Christian who attended Long Beach Brethren Church was not lost on my father, whose faith always sought out these sorts of connections. Drs. Sandler and Johnson moved my mother up on a list of patients whose disease was so advanced that they qualified to be guinea pigs for experimental drug trials. She was admitted to Harbor General.

After her brush with death, the doctors allowed her to go home. She was to return to the hospital several times a week for dialysis treatment. In the following months a pall fell over the home as my mother weakened and my father tried to keep the family together. He'd just started working for Quality Frame and Door, a company in Cerritos owned by Mr. Olsen, an elder at our church. My father drove a truck and delivered doors to all sorts of job sites in southern California, from family homes in Pasadena to the amusement park Magic Mountain, then being built in Valencia, forty miles north of Los Angeles. He often worked late.

▓▓▓▓▓▓▓▓▓▓

My mother's dying years can be bisected into two phases of grief in our home: poised and unpoised.

The first phase was optimistic. Many people rallied around our family. They confidently prayed with us and asked our loving and gracious Father in Heaven to heal my mother. They assured us that God would answer their prayers and bring her home to her husband and boys, who God knew needed her. He was simply testing us, they said, and all we needed to do was trust him and remain faithful. They used Bible speak.

*Don't worry. God loves you. He'll provide. Look at the birds of the air; they do not sow or reap or store away in barns, and yet your heavenly Father feeds them. Are you not much more valuable than they? See how the lilies of the field grow? They do not labor or spin. Yet I tell you that not even Solomon in all his splendor was dressed like one of these. If that is how God clothes the grass of the field, which is here today and tomorrow is thrown into the fire, will he not much more clothe you?*

One anonymous man from church who heard about our family's situation dropped two hundred dollars through our front-door mail slot.

Before my mother got sick, she and my father belonged to a church group of young married couples that called themselves the Joint Heirs. One wife in the group, Andrea Goss, took it upon herself to make the "Loya men" one hot meal a week. (My father spent a lot of time at the hospital after work, which meant that we didn't much eat dinner together.) On Thursdays Andrea and her husband, Larry, would deliver meals to our Shenandoah Street home. Mashed potatoes in Corning-Ware, warm foil-wrapped muffins or corn bread, a ham or chicken dish, my first tuna or turkey casseroles, hot corn on the cob or salad in Tupperware bowls. We enjoyed Andrea's hot meals for an entire year. Sometimes my mother was home for the meals, other times she was at the hospital.

The Joint Heirs also pitched in and bought school clothes for Paul and me. The entire group delivered the new wardrobe to our home one evening. We unwrapped the gifts in the living room and *oohed* and *aahed* the corduroy pants and Keds sneakers and plaid shirts as the adults gathered around us in a large circle. I stood up and thanked them with a little speech. Then I offered to lead them in prayer. They bowed their heads, and all the men and women cried, impressed with the serenity of my tiny but triumphant godly spirit.

In the mornings my father fed and dressed Paul and me. Then he went to work for ten hours as a truck driver. When my mother was at the hospital, he'd visit her on his way home. After classes, the school van dropped us off at my grandma Nellie's, on Maple Street in Pico Rivera— down the street from a roller rink where, on Friday nights, big women with paunches and washed-up B-movie actors competed on televised *Roller Derby*. My father would pick us up around ten o'clock and take us home.

He never told us that our mother was dying. Obviously I knew she was sick (we sometimes visited her in the hospital), but Paul was too young to know anything other than that our home life had become chaotic and distracted. Still, I had no clue that the doctors were merely waiting for her to die.

The second phase of my mother's illness was the blurring of faith. Our family's falling-apart occurred in 1970, when even my father prayed that God would take my mother "home" to end her suffering. Compassionate death was finally the best that could be expected from God because it was clear that he wasn't going to answer prayers for a miracle.

Paul and I stayed with friends from church, sometimes for as long as a week. Jess and Luz Valencia had two daughters, Sandy and Lillian. Jess was a big, moody man who baked cakes for a living. Luz smelled nice and responded to people with sweet, little squirmy noises as if she'd just been pinched provocatively. Sandy was between my brother and me in age. Lillian three years younger than Paul. I once caught a glimpse of Sandy's budding breast as we leaned over a coloring book. I was shocked because the breast looked long and tubular with a very dark chocolate-taffy–looking knob at the tip. There was nothing round or full about the shape of that thing in her training bra.

We also stayed with Phil and Barbara Grubbs, and their toddlers, and, of course, with the Garcias.

By the end of a full week of sleeping and eating and living with each of these families, I inevitably exasperated the fathers. They'd always end up yanking me around in frustration or sitting me down and hotly scolding me. I vaguely recall being deceptive and the fathers being disappointed with me, having wanted to like me or think of me as a golden boy. I soon came to realize that Paul and I were adorable half-orphans at a distance, but up close we (I in particular) were more than a little taxing. Proximity had dulled our spiritual sheen. I was now just another child who needed to be disciplined and taught the lesson of spare not the rod.

I began to suspect that the grief and fatigue of our mother's long illness, coupled with the adults' realization that God wasn't answering their prayers, had turned family friends against us. We were a reminder of God's fickleness. Perhaps our family was out of favor with God, and by praying for us they'd thrown in their lot with a losing cause. (*Stigmatized* was the word I intuited, although it didn't yet figure in my vocabulary.)

▮▮▮▮▮▮▮▮▮

During my early childhood, it was nothing for my father to yank me around or spank my bottom with his hand or sometimes even pull down my pants and spank me with a belt. But the first instance in which the terror level of his punishment was raised in the home occurred one night when my father was home to help me with my schoolwork. He'd told me to memorize the multiplication table printed on the inside of my Pee-Chee folder. That evening he asked me to stand in front of him and recite all 144 calculations; $1 \times 1 = 1$, $1 \times 2 = 2$, and so on, all the way to $12 \times 12 = 144$. Every miscalculation, he warned me, would equal two whacks with the belt. I missed five out of 144. He did the math and told me I was going to be whipped $5 \times 2$ times.

My mother protested. *Joey, don't hit him. He did good.*

But my father was not to be dissuaded. *He knew that he was supposed to get them right. I told him the consequences. He knows that he was lazy and didn't study them hard enough.*

*He's just a boy. He's not perfect. Don't hit him with the belt for a few mistakes.*

The argument—my mother's pleading, really—went on for a minute. Then my father shouted, *You don't want me to hit him? Then you come over here and hit him.*

My mother cried, standing small and emaciated in the corner of the living room. She pleaded with my father. *Please Joey. He didn't do anything wrong. Please don't spank him.*

*You better come over here and hit him or I'm going to hit him. What'll it be?*

*I don't want to hit him. Don't make me, please don't make me.*

*Bessie, I'm gonna hit him hard.*

*No. No. No. No.*

She continued crying as the belt transferred from his hand to hers. I was embarrassed for her. He barked more threats, even moved to take back the belt. She finally whipped me, feebly. I cried, not out of pain, but more for the anguish she and I felt in that moment of absolute fear. I pulled up my pants when she was done

But my father was not satisfied. *You didn't hit him hard enough. Give me that.*

*No. I hit him hard. I did.*

*Those weren't painful. He didn't even wince.*

I felt stupid for not being a better faker. My father took the belt from her hands and pointed at me.

*You. Pull your pants down again and bend over the couch.*

*No, no, Joey, please. I love you. Don't do this. Don't hit him again.*
*Get out of the way, Bessie.*

I was hit ten more times with the belt and made to cry out in elaborate pain.

■■■■■■■■■■

When I was eight Dr. Anaradian diagnosed me with asthma. Rough breathing often kept me home from school, and I'd get to hang out all day with my mother. We'd watch the old black-and-white movies that were televised every day on *The Early Show*. Tyrone Power was her favorite actor. All the white men looked alike to me, with their suits and hats and greasy, slicked-back hair.

It was those movies that inclined me to fantasy. Zorro, the original superhero with cape and mask, saving the Mexican peasants from corrupt rancheros. Or Elwood P. Dowd, whose best friend was a six-foot-tall rabbit that only he could see. And then there was the movie *Charly*, where a really dumb man became a genius and then went back to being really dumb again for no apparent reason. Then there was my favorite childhood movie, *Zotz!*, about a coin that has awesome powers. The finder of the coin attempts to inform the government about it but is dismissed out of hand as a lunatic. Foreign agents get involved in a huge chase that I, at age eight, found thrilling. About fantastic moments, these afternoon movies were helping me already to imagine a theatrical life for myself. By that I mean they were helping me shape my story theatrically, with a touch of magic and the sensational.

My senses were being primed in all manner of unusual ways—for instance, when my mother would ask me to scratch her back. Due to her illness, a harvest of knotty, boil-like patches grew on her back, the skin around them tough like animal hide. I would close my eyes and with the tips of my fingers memorize the path that would allow me to scratch her gently and safely without touching the infested and repulsive bumps.

During the day a nurse would come to the house and prepare saltless meals for my mother. Going without salt was hard for her. She'd been raised in a family who sprinkled salt not only on all their savory foods but also on their fruit: apples, mangoes, oranges, lemons, watermelon, and pomegranates. When my mother was growing up, the daily family meals were a veritable pickling process. But salt was the bane of her ill-functioning kidneys, so on our dinner table the forbidden mineral was replaced with a blue-bottled salt substitute.

One afternoon, when I was home sick, the nurse prepared two medium-rare steaks for my mother and me. I sat across the table from my mother while the nurse acted as waitress, bringing us condiments, juice, and napkins. Then she brought out our sizzling steaks, and my mother reached for the salt substitute. But when the nurse retreated into the kitchen, my mother quickly yanked her hand back from the salt substitute and reached for her handbag, on the floor, propped against her foot. Engaging the nurse in conversation to keep track of her location, she pulled out tiny salt packets from inside her handbag, no doubt smuggled from the hospital. She briefly panicked when she caught me staring at her, puzzled by her deceit. Then she simply raised her index finger to her pursed lips, eyes full of supplication, and gestured *ssshh.*

She ripped the edges off the salt packets and nervously sprinkled salt onto the meat. Then she wadded the empty wrappers in her fist and shoved them deep into her handbag. The nurse entered the room just as my mother was carving into her steak.

A canopy of dread hung over our lives in those days, and the rules of the house were in flux, family alliances taking a different shape, ideas of right and wrong foggier. All this made it easier for my mother to implicate me in her deception, something which she or I couldn't have imagined two years earlier. The upright leader of the Good News Bible Clubs, responsible for good character development in children, was now a cool corrupter of one.

But I didn't mind. I guessed that she feared that my dad would get mad at her if he found out about the salt stash. I understood the fear of getting caught for disobeying one of his rules and I swore to myself that I would not reveal our secret. I prized the opportunity to, for one, prove myself tight-lipped and trustworthy, and, two, get back at my father for making her hit me for that multiplication-table memorizing lapse. Besides I enjoyed the feeling of conspiracy, the way chicanery felt like immunity.

Naturally, it was only a matter of time before I began to try to recreate that composed feeling of license involved in breaking a rule. One weekday morning the yellow school van pulled up outside our home and honked its horn. Neither Paul nor I went out to board it. Mommy was in the hospital, and my dad was at work, and I'd convinced Paul to ignore the van's horn. I was hoping that when we didn't come out the driver would simply leave. I peeked out of the window when I thought I heard the van pull away. Nope. It was still idling at the curb. The second horn alarmed me. I sat on my bed and silently stared at the window. My brother sat staring at the window, too. I couldn't believe it. I'd plotted a crime and actually followed through on it. This struck me as utterly impressive: challenging those with jurisdiction over me, adults who always seemed to box me in, to treat me like a stupid little boy, unaware that I was onto their tyranny. Walking this line between truth and lies was a dangerous flirtation with moral freedom, and that moment on my bed, my eyes wide open as I waited for that van to pull away, was a thrilling and exquisite one.

What I hadn't banked on was how stupid I'd been to look outside. The driver had seen my big head and had decided to walk up to the door to see if everything was all right. He knew that we were "special condition" kids, that our mother was dying. He knocked and knocked until he figured out that the door was unlocked. My brother and I sat frozen on our beds until a crisp voice scared me so completely—by its clarity and proximity to us—that I yelped and almost fell off the bed.

*You coming or what?*

We turned around. The driver's head was poking into our room through the half-open bedroom door.

Busted! I grabbed my books and pretended not to have just been scared out of my wits. *Oh, uh, huh, yeah. It's just that we didn't hear you honk.*

The lie was as extemporaneous as a pregnant teenage girl claiming that God had knocked her up.

My mother had been extremely ill for several weeks, on the verge of death. When my grandma Nellie last visited her, she was prepared to sit in silence next to a heavily medicated, nearly comatose patient. Instead, when she walked into the room my mother was sitting up in her bed, chipper, happy to feel so healthy and optimistic. If she continued to feel this good, she told my grandma, she'd buy curtains and put them up in the living room on the weekend.

Christmas, just one month earlier, had been a drab time at our home. My mother hadn't had enough energy to clean the house or put up Christmas decorations. In fact, the doctors had initially insisted that she not go home for Christmas at all. But then they relented, and she was allowed a two-day leave. On Christmas morning, my father and mother sent Paul and me into the bedroom while he arranged toys without Christmas wrapping into two piles. When we were called, we ran out of the bedroom and tore the manufacturer's packaging off the toys. My mother sat on the couch, frail but smiling. She wished she could have organized a more elaborate Christmas setup, but was happy when we climbed onto her and our father's laps, and hugged and kissed them.

My grandma Nellie was both surprised and dismayed at seeing her only daughter-in-law in such a fey mood. Superstitious by nature, she believed that unnaturally high spirits always preceded death. She'd seen it before, when a sickly patient on his deathbed snapped out of some deep and static stupor to breathe cleanly again for a brief couple of hours, or days, only to succumb to death soon after. It was as if the Reaper, with a soft spot for his victim, granted the doomed person a momentary reprieve from his choking grasp.

Seeing my mother cheerily animated like that—no longer speaking in stilted tones or murmuring or stammering through a drug-addled stupor, her facial muscles flaccid and slack—my grandmother was shaken. Instead of feeling delighted by this return of my mother's former self, she felt grief stricken, almost taunted by this final glimpse of the lively Bessie she used to know, who was momentarily taking the place of the depleted, lesser version whom, for two years, my grandmother had begrudgingly grown to accept, even at great challenge to her faith in God.

And her faith had been challenged. At one point, she'd even begged God to take her son, my father, in place of Bessie. When that didn't work she tried a different tack.

*I'm an old lady already, God. Bessie is just starting, she's young. Please Lord, take me in her place.*

My mother was full of surprises. A month earlier she'd stunned my grandma.

*Nellie, can I ask you a favor?*

*Sure,* mija, *anything. You know that.*

*If I die, will you promise me that you'll look after the boys?*

My grandmother wanted to say, "Bessie, you're not going to die," but she sensed that what my mother needed was a solid assurance about our future, not the cheap and polite assurance that her Christian friends generally gave to those in real peril. So my grandma avoided a sugar-coated response and simply said, *Of course, Bessie. I promise I'll always look after the boys.* No te precupes.

Three days after her brief interlude of strength, on February 4, 1971, as she lay hooked up to the dialysis machine, my mother's heart lurched. The doctors frantically worked to resuscitate her, but she could not be revived. She was twenty-six years old when she died. I was nine.

Around the time that my mother's body succumbed to cardiac arrest, my brother and I were playing three-man basketball with a neighbor in my grandma Nellie's backyard. I knew something was going on when I walked into grandma's living room and saw Jess and Luz Valencia seated on the couch, dressed in their Sunday best. Sandy and Lillian were wearing white frilly dresses and had pink bows in their hair. My aunt Lucy, the same age as Sandy, was Sandy's pal. I overheard them powwow.

*What's going on, Sandy?* I asked.

*I'm not supposed to tell you why we're here.*

*You can tell me, Sandy,* Lucy suggested.

*Well, I can tell you, Lucy. Only you. But I can't tell them.* She pointed to me and my brother, who stood nearby, clueless. Lucy moved nearer to Sandy.

*Okay. Then tell me.*

*You have to promise not to tell them.*

I thought they were just girls being girls, keeping stupid secrets.

Then my aunt Jessie, my grandma Nellie's older sister, dropped by with her gentle husband, our uncle Campos. For as long as I could remember he'd given me a quarter every time I'd seen him. Then other family members dropped by. Soon it looked like a party, with people jammed wall to wall into that small apartment. But the mood of the place wasn't celebratory.

My father came home finally and nodded to everyone present. The adults moved to hug him. He slipped away from them and took my brother and me by the hand into my grandma's room. My father closed the door behind him. We sat on the bed, the first queen-size bed I ever slept in.

My father told Paul and me that he loved us. Then he said that our mommy wouldn't be coming home anymore, that she was in heaven. He told us that he knew it was going to be hard for us to deal with, that we were really going to miss her badly at times, but he wanted us to be strong little men. I thought he meant that he didn't want us to break down, so I told him that I would never cry. No, he said, he wanted us to cry. It was good to cry. George Washington cried. King David and Jesus cried.

I paused for a moment, confused. I didn't want to cry just because it was allowed. But then the tears came. Slowly at first. My father reached for us and we fell into his arms, nuzzling our faces against his wet cheeks. The three of us wept uncontrollably, our sobs convulsing in unison, like a trinity of souls in one massive body.

After a few minutes we broke apart. He rubbed our faces and wiped our tears and told us again that he loved us. He pulled a pack of Dentyne gum out of his pocket and gave us each a few sticks. We fumbled with the wrappers and popped the stiff, red gum into our mouths.

We stood, and he hugged us again. Then he opened the bedroom door. I stepped out of the room first. Sandy and Lucy were crying in the hallway. As I walked past them and through the house, filled with our friends and relatives, the rooms were silent except for the low, muffled sniffling sounds of soft crying as people moved to hug Paul and me.

For days after my mother's death, adults from our church came to the house to pay their respects and offer their condolences. They'd kiss me, hold my hand, and tell me to rejoice because my mother was no longer suffering. She had now found her peace with Jesus in heaven.

## February 9, 1971

On the morning of my mother's funeral, my brother and I were staying at my Grandpa Joe's apartment, where my aunts Rosemary and Margie were in charge of us while my grandfather worked the night shift at the post office.

Reading his Bible in bed at 6:01 A.M. my father first heard a squeak. Then he felt the bed move, and, because it was on wheels, begin to roll across the wooden floor. Immediately thinking, "Earthquake," he panicked and covered himself with a blanket. Then, realizing that flimsy blankets weren't going to protect him if the ceiling collapsed, he jumped up from his rolling bed to stand in his bedroom doorway.

At that same moment, in my aunt Rosemary's bed, where I was sleeping, I heard the window above my aunt's bed rattle a bit. Then a small candleholder, a picture frame, and a plant in a tiny clay pot fell off the window ledge. A mirror hanging on the wall rattled, then the bed lurched violently, and the mirror crashed to the floor.

*Get the boys!* someone yelled.

My aunt Rosemary came for us. She grabbed our hands and we scrambled across the shifting floor to the dining room, where she positioned us under the dining room table.

*Not there, Rosemary! To the door! Get them to the door!*

My aunt Margie was already yanking Paul and me out from under the table and away from my aunt Rosemary. The three of us finally stood in the kitchen's doorway, looking at my aunt Rosemary trembling between the hall doorjamb.

The Sylmar earthquake—6.6 on the Richter scale—shifted and cracked in two the new (not yet open) 210 Freeway on the east side of the San Fernando Valley. The only other reported major damage was at Sylmar Veteran's Hospital, where an entire wing collapsed.

Later, as my aunts readied us for our mother's funeral, I superstitiously interpreted the quake as a secret message to me. The earth, too, lurched and ached with grief for the loss of my mother. In the reeling world and random hazard of the unsteady earth's convulsions I had found something that resembled my soul's turbulence. I even went so far as to wonder if on that funeral morning an archangel had descended from heaven to wrestle with nefarious beings for the blessed remains of my mother. After all, in my Bible-believing mind there was precedence for this. Scriptures had taught me that an archangel descended from heaven to wrestle with a demon for the bones of Moses. That's how I interpreted the earth's raucous rumbling: as another resurrection.

# iii

fter I stabbed Griffith I was taken downstairs by the guards to be housed in
a more secure supermax fourteen-cell tier. I'm chillin' like a villain in my
holding cell when all of a sudden I hear a high-pitched almost Tweety
Bird–like voice and some giggling. My first thought was, "Damn, they got a woman
in here?" Women weren't allowed to be guards in the maximum-security peniten-
tiaries.

I leapt from my steel bunk and jammed my face up against the crack at the
large cell door's jam. (They had covered the small square bulletproof-glass peep-
hole with tape and cardboard so my only view out of the cell was this crack.) I
could barely see, but I couldn't believe what I was seeing. I mean it was the most
absurd sight. A baby elephant receding down the hallway, trudging slowly. I got
only a quick second glance, but that's what I saw. It was there, then it was gone,
that fast. In the blink of an eye.

I stood at the door, stunned, and wondered, "What the hell are they moving circus animals in here for?" Then I thought that maybe it was the back end of a cow
and they were taking it through the basement to get slaughtered. Maybe that was
the answer to the riddle of the mystery meat on our dinner trays. But the animal's
hide had been dark brown, and I'd never seen a dark brown cow before.

An hour later I was transferred to my permanent cell. My new tier was seriously
locked down, except for one guy called a "runner," who they let out of his cell to

clean the tier and do little errands for us, like pass books back and forth between cells. This runner, Early, came up to my cell door and knocked. "What's up?" He was wearing a headband, like the kind worn by reservation Indians in federal custody. Early claimed to be Native American, but he looked like just another good ol' Dixie white boy to me. He had a pudgy mug that, I imagined, when he aged would make him look like Colonel Sanders himself on the side of a bucket of chicken.

I was unfurling my property roll, which consisted of a mattress, pillow, sheets, and a pillowcase. "Not much. Are you the runner?"

"Yeeh." His accent was deep South.

"All right."

"Howz it smell in there?"

"Like Pine-Sol."

"Yeeh. I had to use a whole bottle of 'monia to get the smell out."

"Is that right?"

"Yeeh, the guy who lived in there was a filthy fucker. They moved him upstairs to the infirmary because he outgrew his cell."

"Cut it out."

"No bullshit." He grinned a little.

I started to get mad, thinking this fuckin' punk thinks I'm gullible. "No one can outgrow these cells. They're six fuckin' feet wide."

Early senses that I'm getting uptight, so he says.

"No, no. Really bro'. He didn't really outgrow the inside of the cell. He just got so fat that it took him a while to get through the door. Seriously man. They escorted him out of here an hour ago."

Then it clicked.

"Fuck. I think I saw the fat fucker. Man. Maaaan! Except he must have been naked. Ugh. Yeah. 'Cause his skin was like a fuckin' elephant's."

"Yeeh. That's heem. That's Heavy D."

# Flux

*A conviction that the world was now a bundle of fragments possessed me without ceasing.*

—W. B. Yeats

A few months after the funeral, my dad took Paul and me to visit grandma Frances at her trailer home in Pico Rivera. My mother's mother was married to Bill Newkirk, a grizzled, retired World War II veteran who lavished her with gifts and called her sweetheart with a Nebraska twang. He also laughed a lot. When he died years later, he left her the trailer and his pension. He was a good man. I knew this because when his name came up in conversation my mother's brothers and sisters would all reverentially refer to him as a good man. Since my aunts and uncles usually couldn't agree about anything, I believed them.

Being a nerdy kid in elementary school, I received academic gifts at Christmas or for my birthday, gifts that piqued my curiosity and reinforced my desire to learn—gifts like a chemistry set. On that day Paul and I visited my grandmother's trailer, I brought with me a white magnetized board, and a baggie full of little stop-sign red plastic alphabet tiles with tiny magnets attached to their back. The alphabet pieces could be arranged into words or sentences on the board.

While the adults talked inside, Paul and I knelt on our grandma's green Astroturf-covered cement patio and arranged the alphabet tiles into words.

Inside, my grandma Frances was making my father what she no doubt considered a generous offer: to assume responsibility for raising Paul and me. For two and a half years, during my mother's illness, my father, sleep deprived and in a state of constant sorrow, had been suppressing his libidinous urges. In fact, since the age of sixteen he'd been forced to take on enormous financial responsibilities, becoming a man at an accelerated pace. Consequently, my grandma imagined that my father would welcome the freedom she was offering him—freedom to pursue the pleasures of the flesh. Why, any man in such a situation would have given up his children.

A man in such a position could easily have justified relinquishing his sons, could easily have argued that letting us be raised by the female members of the family, by the people closest to our dead mother—who would surely give us the maternal warmth we no longer enjoyed—was a sound parental choice.

But my father said no. He'd made a promise to my mother that he wouldn't give us up. He intended to take care of his boys.

My grandmother Frances and my father had never been on good terms. She thought him an uppity boy who considered her a stupid peasant. He disliked her meddling and thought that she considered him unworthy of her special daughter. Dad's choice to reject my grandmother's offer would strain an already difficult relationship.

At one point my grandmother came out to check on us, to let grandpa Newkirk smooth things over inside. We had some random letters magnetized to the board. Grandma stepped out onto the patio and tenderly noted, *Oh, what a nice board, her and all the pretty red letters. She's a nice toy. Oh, there is the J, and the H, the E and the K, and . . .*

I didn't say anything because I instantly grasped that she couldn't read: There wasn't a *J, K,* or *E* on the board. We'd lost those letters. If she had made only one mistake I could've written it off as her misreading a letter, but she'd named three letters that weren't there.

Her charade insulted me. I was hot with resentment toward her. Her lie relegated me to some nether region where children didn't deserve to be told the truth (*This belt whipping is going to hurt me more than it hurts you*), to be exploited for the convenient self-deception of adults.

In that moment I knew that my disgust for her was now, and I regret-

ted that I could judge my dear old grandma so harshly, but her lie triggered in me perplexity and anger, a wild fusion of brokenheartedness
and indignation, converting the shock of estrangement and the shock of
recognition into a single unit of dense rage—volatile stuff that sponta-
neously combusted and cried out for justice. I wanted to yell out to her,
*Don't lie to me!*

But it wasn't only adults who were forcing me to reconsider my belief
that language was a stable thing, not to be misused. Paul's best friend in
first grade was this kid named Julio who lived two houses from our apartment. He and Paul would ride their bikes up and down Deland Street for
hours. One afternoon, back before our mother had died, I heard some
yelling. I poked my head out the back door of our apartment. Paul and
Julio were quarreling vehemently. My brother, typically imperturbable,
yelled something at Julio who then turned and said that he was never
going to speak to my brother again. Paul swore the same hot oath then
carried his small Schwinn bicycle past me into the apartment. I felt bad
that he'd just lost his best friend.

That's why I was so shocked, two hours later, when I heard Julio at the
back door asking my mother if Paul could come outside to play. My
brother leapt up, grabbed his bike, and went outside as if their earlier
terse exchange had never occurred. I couldn't understand how he and
Julio were so readily able to suspend the meaning implied in their earlier
verbal altercation. For me, they were showing a cavalier attitude toward
language. I didn't think of language and meaning that way—as something improvisational, something free.

This devil-may-care attitude toward words was something unfamiliar. This indifference to truth meant that language was more flighty than
my father had taught me to conceive of it when instructing me in the inspired Word of God. For me, words were charged with divine meaning.
They had an objective component. *In the beginning was the Word, and the
Word was with God, and the Word was God.* I was already a convert to the
evangelist's ideal that the power of words was equal to truth.

Up until then I had an exacting preconception that the meaning of
words has only one certain conclusion. Now I was suffering a peculiar

sort of word neurosis. This nervousness led me to worry that words might be used inaccurately around me at any time. Certainty, the type of certainty that I desired, could not be assured.

Eternal oaths were the certainty I had always relied on—the ones born true and that had been true before me—and therefore were not fallible or vulnerable to whimsy or human point of view. If you couldn't trust eternal oaths, how could you trust that God would keep his word and let us into heaven? The idea became more and more unjust in my mind. What if God promised not to let Moses into the Promised Land but then changed his mind and said, *Ah, shucks. Forget what I said earlier, Moses. I was just a little pissed, letting off steam. Of course you can come into the Promised Land.* How fair would that be to the other Israelites who had worked so hard to show their faithfulness? For me it would be the height of injustice if God broke down and couldn't keep his word about destroying and laying bare those who disbelieved his Word. How could I evangelize effectively if I couldn't back up my message with examples of how God's wrath always led to vengeful action?

I believed that we Christians had cornered the market on meaning, on the significance of all those words my father used, like *hermeneutics*, *exegesis*, and *theology*. As a little soldier in God's army I expected to be able to rely on the thrust and intention of God's Word, to use it as another weapon in my spiritual armory to defeat Lucifer's lies and mighty minions.

My grandma Frances was an authority figure, and her lie that day was so startling that I began to lose my trust in the stability of language. Religious custom and social conventions asked me to believe that authority figures were morally superior to me. But now I was concerned that their preeminence was one Great Bluff.

▮▮▮▮▮▮▮▮▮▮

Before my mother died, I suffered an equally shocking change of perception—but this time about school.

I had always felt capable, a star student among my peers. Back then, in Miss Fry's third-grade class, I worked hard to finish my tests before all the other students. Every test was a competition for me. Every project was an opportunity for me to prove myself. At Thanksgiving time, Miss Fry laid a roll of white construction paper across the classroom floor.

Each child was responsible for drawing a part of the Thanksgiving narrative on the section of paper in front of him. Crayons were scattered around our knees. There were brown turkeys with red dangling throats. Green forests. Black kettles over orange flames. Brown log cabins. Orange pumpkins. Pilgrims in black garb, with silver buckles on their shoes. Women wearing black or gray dresses that covered everything from neck to wrists to ankles, white bonnets on their golden-haired heads.

I drew orange brown–faced Indians peering from behind trees on the far, scary side of the Plymouth settlement boundary. Even though I was the chocolate-brown dot in all my early school group photos, I nonetheless drew myself, on that Thanksgiving tableau—me with my Indio face—as a pink-cheeked white boy in black pilgrim clothing. Back then, I felt like I belonged to some brilliant, onward-marching, white Christian future.

But my mother's illness, coupled with the violence in our home and my difficulty breathing due to periodic asthma attacks, began to affect the way I imagined the world, and my place in it. Now I no longer felt I belonged. At recess I'd run around with the other boys playing touch football or chasing them in games of tag. But when I was no longer engaged with them in competition—when the bell rang and we lined up to return inside and I listened to them talk about the cartoon *Johnny Quest* or about their G.I Joes or their favorite Hot Wheels—I felt like a stranger.

I wanted to ask them if they got whipped hard with a belt. I wanted to talk to them about how I hated hospitals and how I felt guilty for not wanting to visit my mother there. I wanted to confess that I felt embarrassed when my mom shuffled down hospital corridors in her fuzzy pink slippers or sat upright in a hospital bed in a room that reeked of pee, wearing nothing but a flimsy hospital gown. I needed to tell someone that I didn't understand why my young mother's appearance was so scary looking. Her bloated belly made her look nine-months pregnant. Her black hair had lost all its body and lay flat and greasy on her head, making her look like Morticia on the *Addams Family* TV show. I wanted to tell them that I had to sit on my mother's left side if I wanted her to hear me because she'd lost hearing in her right ear.

My school friends' parents knew that my mother was very ill, so they generously invited me for sleepovers at their homes. The sleepovers were designed to provide some familial normalcy, to replace my turbulent home life with a stable family environment for an evening, but exactly the opposite occurred. The homes and lives of my friends Randy and Timothy, disconcerting for their cultural foreignness and governed by a white ethic—white, as in the White America motif of optimism and presumption—only made me feel my alienation more acutely.

Redhead Randy Crawford was my best friend at Brethren Elementary School. His older brother Jeff was not only the fastest kid in the school, he was also the first deaf kid I'd ever met. He wore a large flesh-colored hearing aid around his ear.

The first time I heard Jeff speak was one day when Randy's mother was driving us to their home. While Randy and Jeff's younger sister and brother played and screamed in the back of the family station wagon, Jeff argued and joked and answered his mother's questions just like the other kids, except that I could barely understand the garbled grunts and stunted noises coming from his mouth.

I felt an affinity with Jeff. His otherness, his shyness about his difference, his knowing instinctively that when he spoke, people would become confused and feel uncomfortable—all these things drew me to him. I had felt the same way while my mother was dying; handicapped in some way. (After my mother's death, if someone asked me about her I'd have to tell them that I didn't have a mother, that she had died. Then they'd feel embarrassed and apologize profusely. I was the boy who had lost his mother, the boy who was different.) In this way I felt some mystical solidarity with Jeff, for his unlikeness to other kids.

Later I watched as Jeff and his sister ran to hide behind the front door to surprise their father when he entered the house after work. When he arrived, their dad dropped his briefcase and jacket on the rug in the foyer. He tussled Jeff's hair while Jeff squeezed him in a fat hug. Then he lifted his daughter and carried her into the dining room, where Randy's mother met him with a kiss. It was all very *Father Knows Best.*

Later, after dinner, some Milton-Bradley board games were brought out of the hall closet, and Randy and Jeff's parents joined us in games of Operation or Life, showing the same gung-ho glee as their children.

The tight family bond both excited and disturbed me. I was envious of the joy inspired by the presence of Jeff and Randy's father. True, when I was a baby I used to bang my plastic high-chair table with a spoon when my father entered the kitchen after work. But, now, most of the time I dreaded his return home.

Then there was Timothy, whose mother picked us up after school one day. Timothy was excited to show me his favorite after-school activity. When we arrived at his house he dumped his books on his bed and raced to fill up empty plastic spray bottles with steaming hot tap water—so hot, in fact, that we had to hold the bottles by their thick necks. He handed me my own bottle and we walked out his back door. A tall hedge ran along the length of the driveway side of the house. Timothy positioned himself facing the hedge, his bottle holstered in his pocket. How strange, I thought. Then with a quick draw of his squirt bottle he started shooting the hedge, like a gunslinger. I wondered what he was shooting at. Then a swarm of bees filled the air around the hedge.

*Look. If you hit them with the hot water it'll stun them, and they just drop to the ground.*

Sure enough, every bee zapped with the scalding water fell to our feet. I had the sensation of being both slightly disgusted by Timothy's sadism and comforted that he wasn't actually killing the bees. This was sheer technological genius. I'd never have thought to employ hot water to agitate the tranquil bees feeding off flowers near my house. I simply would have flicked them with my finger, if I bothered with them at all.

The writer of the Torah tells us that after the Great Flood, God promised Noah that Man now held primacy over nature. *The fear and dread of you will fall upon all the beasts of the earth and all the birds of the air, upon every creature that moves along the ground, and upon all the fish of the sea; they are given unto your hands.* Remembering Timothy taunting the little winged bees pollinating the lilies in his yard, I finally was able to comprehend that verse. The vanity and presumption ordained to Noah felt like the answer to why so many serial killers ended up being white men: murder being the ultimate audacity and dominion.

▮▮▮▮▮▮▮▮▮

At Brethren, I was a gifted running back on the football field, typically one of the first players chosen when it came time to pick teams. (My family was comprised of athletes, several of them city and state champs in wrestling and track. My uncle David had been a Golden Gloves boxing champ. And growing up, I'd heard stories about how my father had been a superstar running back when he was young. His neighbor Mike Garrett—who went on to become USC's Heisman Trophy winner a few years before O. J. Simpson—schooled my dad in the art of the cross-field cutback.) The other boys nicknamed me Crazy Legs because my legs would twist spasmodically when I saw that some kid was about to tackle me. It was my conceit that I'd never been tackled head-on. I was either shoelace tackled or pushed out of bounds.

Once, during fourth grade, I was returning a kickoff on the playground when all of a sudden I fell flat on my face and had the wind knocked out of me. I rolled over on my back, feeling distressed in an unfamiliar way. It was as if the pain were occurring on a cellular level, with every molecule equally exasperated and gasping for air.

Somebody was pumping my legs. It was the new boy, Glen. Glen was a beefy kid with wild black Brillo pad–like hair. He had the frame of a future dockworker or NFL lineman—thick and already showing signs of muscle definition. And he was supremely confident, especially for being the new kid at school. This cockiness I attributed to his having three older brothers in the upper grades.

After a few minutes, when I had regained my wind, he helped me to my feet. I asked him what had happened. I didn't remember anything. One moment I was returning a kickoff and the next moment the ground was speeding toward my face. Laughing and patting me on the back, Glen confessed that he had body-blocked me. His brothers played Pop Warner football, and they'd taught him how to throw his body at the thighs of a runner in full stride. It was the first time that I'd ever heard of a body block or Pop Warner football. Glen patted me on the back again and walked away. I was afraid of him from then on.

The shock of how fast I went from running with ease to breaking my fall with my face made me wary of carrying the ball for the remainder of that game. Instead I'd lateral the ball or pass it quickly whenever it came to me. Glen was out there somewhere, and I never wanted him to hit me again. There was something bullyish about the whole body-blocking tactic, and because Glen was a big kid, I easily began to identify him as a bully.

I remember thinking at the time that Glen's tackle was an important incident in my life, but not because it introduced me to violence. My father had already been brutal with me, so I already knew that violence and pain could be inflicted on another person. No. It made me realize that my mind was now open to ponder such things. My mother's kidney disease had done this to me—made every traumatic thing that happened to me feel like an epitomizing event.

I had the impression that the tackle was some sort of metaphor for my young life, that the shock and force of the body block exemplified the helplessness that seemed to be the motif of my life during my mother's illness. From my mother's body decaying in front of my eyes to my violent father at home to the surprise body block on the playing field—my life was being intersected with destructive encounters, and I always seemed worse off for these contacts. Even my asthma attacks surprised me as painful reminders that I didn't have control over even the most basic and essential thing as breathing; most other people generally didn't have to worry about performing so fundamental a body function.

My realization that Glen's body block had made concrete some existential impotence was indeed a poetic one for me. At age nine, I was already searching to find similarities among my various experiences.

One day after morning recess, my classmates lined up single file to walk back into the school. Glen, who was standing in front of me, turned around. *Ugh! What's that brown stuff on your teeth?*

I picked between my front teeth with my fingernail.

*No, not on your front teeth. It's not food. It's brown junk.*

I shot back defensively, *It's orange. I was just eating an orange. Ask Brian.*

Brian was behind me.

*Brian, take a look at Joe's teeth, behind his front bottom teeth. What do ya see? Show him, Joe.*

*No.*

*What? Are you afraid we're gonna think that you have shit on your teeth? Go ahead. Don't be afraid. Show Brian your teeth.*

I'd heard the word *shit* used before, by some of the boys in school, but no one had ever used the word when talking with me. I didn't appreciate that the first use of that word directed at me was associated with my mouth. I reluctantly opened my mouth for Brian to peer inside.

*Yeah, what is that stuff?*

I closed my mouth fast and spat out. *It's orange. Remember when I ate the orange, when I gave you a piece?*

Glen shot back, *It's not orange, so quit saying it is. It's dark brown and is all over your teeth, not just stuck between 'em.*

Brian agreed. *Yeah, Joe. It's not orange, and it's real ugly in there.*

I hated Glen. And I hated toady Brian for slavishly echoing Glen's insult. Brian had been my friend the year before; now he was casually siding against me. Brian had a slight frame and his face was irregularly lean. Two cowlicks made his hair seem angry, as if straining in various directions. Even then I understood that he was siding with Glen out of strict adherence to the schoolyard code. There were many recesses left in the year, recesses that would be spent with Glen the Pounder, Glen the Brute, Glen the Body Blocker—who could inflict as much grief on Brian's body on the football field as he had on mine.

I got a hall pass to go to the bathroom, and sure enough, there was a brown film behind my bottom front teeth. I tried to scrape off the stain with my fingernail but it seemed glued to my teeth.

Why did I have filthy teeth? The other kids obviously ate food as frequently as I did, but every time I was able to sneak a look at the backs of their lower teeth I never found any stain even remotely resembling the brown mess in my mouth. It couldn't be true that being Mexican, with our different diet of spicy sauces and dark brown mole dishes, would discolor my teeth, could it?

I was miserable, thinking, *Great, just what I need, another type of brown smudge to mark the difference between me and my classmates.*

Preoccupation with my teeth exploded into a full-blown, all-the-time awareness of my differences with the kids in my class. Suddenly I saw that Curtis, Randy, Brian, and Timothy all had thin, dirty-blonde hair that rested flat on their heads, while my thick, black hair sat on my skull like a helmet. I envied their normal, regular-guy hair. Their white-boy hair. I observed that blonde Becky Van Auken and Darcy Underwood liked handsome Curtis, athletic Glen, rich Brian. The girls liked the winners. I was smart, but big deal. I presumed they ignored me because I was dark and ugly and poorer than the other boys. The strict physical discipline I received at home made me feel easily defeated by my father, so I convinced myself that I was a loser who didn't deserve to be liked by the white girls, who had a pool of better stronger boys to choose from.

On the day we were supposed to take class pictures, I decided that I wanted my hair to look like the other boys'. I'd seen my father use pomade to straighten his wavy hair, so I asked him if I could use some. But I applied too much, flattening my black mop onto my skull so much that it looked like it was ready to slide off. My hair resembled that of black folks in 1940s photographs, the pomade caked on their Afros to make their hair straight and flat on their heads.

My dad laughed at my greasy hair. *You can go ahead and wear your hair like that if you want, but it doesn't look good.*

*Yeah, it does.*

*No, it doesn't.*

My father was right. I hate that photo to this day. I look goofy in it.

The only difference between me and my classmates that made me feel special was my father's brilliance (and the respect he was earning from esteemed white men at our church). I suspected that the skill and prizes he was acquiring would accrue to me over time. This translated into a confidence that told me that although I couldn't compete with the white boys in terms of money or looks, I would one day preach to them, however, and in that way regain some status, as the man of moral stature who was their link to God. Then I'd be able to use the church pulpit like a bully used the playground, and use God's Word to my advantage.

▮▮▮▮▮▮▮▮

Before he came out to teach at Brethren Elementary School, my fourth-grade teacher, Frank Biddell, was a young good ol' white boy from Texas who graduated from Bob Jones University. Mr. Biddell lived alone in the apartment complex at the back of the school property. Several nights a week, my brother and I stayed at his apartment after school and watched TV while we waited for our father to pick us up. Biddell left us in his apartment alone while he stayed behind at school to do his work.

Paul and I would watch cartoons and pilfer Cheez-Its and sunflower seeds from the large jar Mr. Biddell kept in his sparsely supplied kitchen pantry. I remember that the jars and cans were evenly spaced and lined up so that all the labels could be read in one glance at the shelf. On another shelf, boxes of crackers and cereals were organized by height.

I walked around the apartment and peeked in Mr. Biddell's drawers, surveyed his simple wardrobe of black and gray wool slacks with half-inch cuffs, his white button-down shirts (short and long sleeved), his pairs of black and brown wingtip shoes.

Drinking glasses stood flush with one another in his cupboard, each type next to its mate. The sink was always empty, magazines evenly stacked, shirts hung facing the same way, each piece of clothing folded neatly in its drawer. His bathroom was whistling clean. Nothing was out of place, like underwear out of the dirty clothes hamper or towels hanging askew. With such an immaculate apartment I wondered what Mr. Biddell's private life was like.

This single, meticulous, neat freak was also exacting with kids. I'd been a straight-A pupil in all my classes since kindergarten, but in Mr. Biddell's fourth-grade class, my perfect grades fell. The upheaval in our home made concentration on schoolwork difficult. Mr. Biddell seemed displeased. When the first semester was over, he called each student up to the front of the classroom to receive their grades.

*Joe Loya.*

I walked between the small desks to the front of the classroom. Mr.

Biddell sat behind his desk, eyebrows scrunched. He extended the report card to me over the desk but held on to it tightly as I tried to pull it from his hand. I looked into his eyes, curiously, like a dog whose master has offered it a bone but will not let go of the gift when the dog has it in its teeth.

I saw a stern face, a small grimace—a teacher menacing me, communicating that I had done wrong and that he was angry at my stubborn refusal to improve my standing.

I was withered by the look.

I returned to my seat. I'd swallowed the lesson that the favor of a teacher, like other adults in my life at the time, was fickle business. While events at home turned grim, I'd let my grades slip, and in Mr. Biddell's neatly arranged universe he could only interpret rebellion in my wandering attention and academic sinking.

Years later, when I wanted to dwell on humiliating moments to summon my rage, Biddell's aggression, his vivid displeasure at my scholastic performance, coupled with the clear pleasure he took from antagonizing a nine-year-old, was always my starting point. In prison I fantasized about meeting him in an alley and kicking him in the balls and then knocking out his teeth with a two-by-four.

▮▮▮▮▮▮▮▮▮

Around this time my soul turned gothic. I wrote a series of short horror-mystery stories starring a Joe Friday–like detective who was investigating a ramshackle house based on one that sat on the property next to our school. The house was dark shingled, which my playful eye saw as burned by a suspicious fire. The wildly overgrown yard in my nine-year-old mind was merely the neglect usual to haunted homes on TV. I was toying with turning life into fiction.

I ended these adolescent stories with the kind of interpretations Rod Serling gave at the conclusion of *The Twilight Zone*. *Submitted for your approval, the figure of a petty man in desperation, the morality tale of a little man made ineffectual by too much reading, blah blah blah . . .*

I was being raised on Bible stories, each one simplistic and with a clear moral at the end. (*Lot's wife was turned into a pillar of salt when she disobeyed*

*God and looked back to see Sodom and Gomorrah on fire.* The moral of the story is . . . drum roll and envelope please . . . the moral of the story is don't disobey God.) That was how I initially absorbed stories, with clean and tidy endings.

By the end of the school year my class had to write two reports about great men in history. My classmates wrote about Moses or King David or Thomas Edison or Abe Lincoln. I wrote about Beethoven and Genghis Khan—Beethoven because his fierce imagination grew in intensity as his hearing and sanity slowly deteriorated, and the scourge Genghis Khan because he was a cold Mongolian terror who swept down on unsuspecting villages and, like a merciless disease, annihilated them. Many things impressed themselves on me in those days, but I was mostly becoming seduced by darker themes like madness and disease and absence and extermination, while my classmates pondered the genial and predictable.

And I was beginning to associate my intelligence with mischief. I expected that Mr. Biddell counted on all the reports having some uniformity and that the kids would simply regurgitate what had been shoved at them. But I wanted to disrupt his orderly sense of the world, to use my intelligence in a mischievous, if not malicious, way.

What surprised and concerned me about this change in me was that my vision of things and what I placed value in—my developing obsession with the strange or wrong moment rather than the correct or coordinated moment—seemed not to affect others. For example, once I realized that I could smell my lunch turning sour in my mouth by two or three o'clock in the afternoon I began obsessively smelling it. But one day I was delighted to notice that I'd gone the entire day without smelling my own bad breath. I couldn't wait to tell someone, so I mentioned this odd and valueless observation to my uncle Tony. He looked at me as if I had three heads.

▮▮▮▮▮▮▮▮▮▮

My grades continued to fall. I hid one mid-semester report card from my father, hoping that I could recover by the end of the semester. I was sure my lot would change, even though the odds were against it. After all, that's what the doctrine of getting into heaven had taught me. I'd had the bum start of being born a sinner, destined for hell, but there was always the possibility of grace, that Hail-Mary pass to a well-covered receiver in the end zone, that possibility that I could recover from my moral missteps and with a well-timed miracle make it into the good book, by hook or by crook. And sometimes a literal last-minute recovery was what I prayed for.

A parent-teacher conference was all it took to expose me. After the conference I sat in my bedroom and listened to my father's car pull into the driveway. The car door opened and slammed shut. I heard the muffled sound of footsteps on the porch, then keys in the door. The door creaked open and then closed hard.

*Young man, get in here right now!*

(We always knew we were in trouble when he called us "young man" or "buddy.") I could only hope for mercy, which wasn't entirely out of the question. Periodically my father would surprise us by asking us why we did what we did—lied, stole, or deceived him. He could be charming with his curiosity and we could tell from the way he asked a question that even an honest answer that seriously incriminated us wouldn't be punished severely. Then he'd only make us drink Tabasco sauce, to punish our lying tongue. Those were the rare mercy days.

And we knew what mercy was because Sunday school teachers quizzed us on the difference between grace and mercy. We'd chant out to the teacher, *Mercy is* not getting *what you* do deserve. *Grace is* getting *what you* don't deserve.

My father's expression was stern when he asked me to get the report card. I couldn't figure out how he knew that I still had the incriminating evidence. I walked outside, behind the house, and opened a vent that exposed the dirt under our home. I'd first learned of this spot when my frog, Sam, died. I'd accidentally suffocated him by not making big enough breathing holes in his shoebox home. My dad had helped me bury him just inside the vent.

Now, before digging up the report card, I knelt and prayed, eyes shut tightly, imploring Jesus for special dispensation.

*Please Jesus, please rapture us right NOW!*

I opened my eyes. No rapture.

Evangelical Christians believe that one day Jesus will blow his celestial horn and all the true believers will be raptured to heaven, leaving nonbelievers behind to suffer seven years of Tribulation on earth, when the Antichrist is supposed to emerge as the false Savior of the world. Kneeling there praying, I was basically begging God to usher in the Apocalypse for my convenience.

I closed my eyes again.

*Okay Jesus, please, please Jesus. Rapture us NOW!*

I opened my eyes. No rapture. One more time. I closed my eyes desperately tight.

*Okay. NOW!*

I sneaked a quick one-eyed peek then closed it again fast, for one final time.

*Have the rapture RIGHT NOW!*

My selfish desire for last-ditch deliverance was not without Biblical precedence. Even Jesus in his most frightened state at Gethsemane had cried out to his Father in heaven, praying for the cup to be passed from his hands. Jesus got a little weak there in the end and wanted to save his own skin, too.

I opened my eyes. I was still kneeling in the soil. I'd been raised to believe that appeals to God were answered expeditiously. My own life (once saved from overdose) was a living, breathing example of the power of intercessory prayer.

I finally gave up praying for Armageddon, dug up the report card and walked inside to turn it over to my dad. I was hit with a belt that night. No whipping across the face. No punches. No kicks. Just a simple belt whipping across my naked butt.

■■■■■■■■■■

At the funeral parlor my grandma Nellie made Paul and me sit on each side of her. Reverend Sal Delgado spoke about life and death and how heaven was celebrating my mother's arrival. He invoked a verse to remind the faithful that my mother was *absent from the body, but present with the Lord.*

From where I sat in the front pew, I could see the top of my mother's face. When the service was over, my father rose and led Paul and me by the hand to the casket for a final visit with our mother's body. I looked at her dull brown face, made up in a phony, powdery way. I cried lightly. I hadn't seen a dead body before, so I was curious. My father took off his wedding ring and slid it onto one of my mother's fingers. He lifted us up a bit, and we leaned in to kiss her goodbye on the cheek. She was good and cold and hard and dead.

Grandma Nellie took Paul and me away, and my father remained standing at the coffin for his final moment with my mother's body. Later he told us that he swore to her that since he would never have been able to tell her in person again how much he loved her, he would go out of his way to show his love in verbal compliments to friends and strangers for the rest of his life. He would turn his private love for her into universal affection for others.

At the gravesite in Rose Hills Cemetery, we three "Loya boys" were again the first ones to stand up and walk to the coffin, suspended over the open grave. We each lay a single long-stem rose atop it. Then my dad guided us down the lawn to the mortuary limousine. I hated Mr. Biddell so much, in fact, that on the day of my mother's funeral, when I saw him at the grave site among the crowd of mourners, I remember thinking that on a day I could have been at school enjoying his substitute teacher, I had the misfortune of being at the same place he was.

# iv

The basement was a full house: Indian Early; No-Bet Stone Man; Wayne Bruce, whom everyone just called Batman; William Jurgensen, whom everyone called Hillbilly Willie; Belligerent Bey; Missouri Ron; and seven other men who weren't with us long.

In the late 1970s Stone Man was recruited by UCLA to be a running back. Then he and his twin brother decided to rob a bank. His brother was killed in the attempt and Stone Man was given a life sentence. He was six-foot-two with a physique like a fuckin' bronze statue.

Stone Man was considered by some L.A. boys to be one of the original street-gang Crips. He was also a major drunk, always making pruno (prison wine) in his cell. Every week we listened to football games on our Walkmans. Before a game Stone Man would get his testosterone all pumped up and challenge the other guys on the tier, shouting to us from out of the blue, "Early, you ain't got no heart to bet on the Colts plus three and a half," or "Joe, I dare you to take the Jets and the two and a half points."

And just as quickly we'd say, "I'll take that bet, now lock it in."

Then he'd back off real quick. "No bet no bet, we ain't got no bet." That's how he earned the nickname No-Bet Stone Man.

Batman was an old Golden Gloves boxer, initially in prison for a brief stint for drug trafficking. He was a humble guy in his early forties, the kind of prisoner who would open a bag of Tostitos chips or Oreo cookies and offer to have Indian Early, the runner, pass some down to you in an envelope bowl. You'd never have imagined that he murdered a bully in his unit who pushed him too far.

Indian Early started out in an Arkansas state prison, where he forged over a million dollars' worth of postal money orders. He was arrested in his prison cell wearing a Rolex and conducting a poker game with forty thousand dollars in cash on the table. He'd paid off guards, so the Feds finally had to nab him.

He'd been able to have all those money orders cashed by using lovers he'd met through the personal ads in gay magazines. His letters seduced the men, and they didn't see the harm in cashing what they considered to be legitimate money orders and then sending the money to Early through crooked guards. Early said that wooing those queers was the same as wooing a broad, except that a girl's panties get wet while reading the letters while a man's underwear just gets taut.

Hillbilly Willie was an escape artist. A guard had found a big hole in his wall, so now they searched his cell every two hours. He had a very thick Texas accent that made him sound effeminate, as if he spoke with a lisp.

Missouri Ron was a serious plotter, a white-supremacist, and a damn good explosives man.

Then there was Belligerent Bey, an older black prisoner. He was a large man, and by the look of his biceps and shoulders he'd once been a strapping young convict. Now he had a paunch. Bey's bulging eyes were magnified by thick Coke-bottle lenses. His head was bald with a bit of gray stubble around the sides. He was constantly running his sweaty palms over the top of his head when he spoke. And he spoke a lot. By the time I got down there he'd been locked in solitary confinement for more than a year.

The nurses came to his cell twice a day to give him drugs. He was a chatterer who fancied himself a jailhouse lawyer. He always interrupted other prisoner's conversations with legal advice, and on more than one occasion I'd hear him quoting some obscure legal case to prove to a guard that he had a right to have a larger cookie than the one he'd been served on his dinner tray. Bey loved to be in everybody's business. If he heard another prisoner complaining about a guard or a family problem, he'd offer advice like, "Mind over matter, bro. It's mind over matter. If you don't mind, then it don't matter."

The most earnest thing about Belligerent Bey was the way he told jokes to inmates on the way to the showers, jokes that he thought were tailored to the prisoner's ethnicity. To a tall, blond guy he'd tell a Viking joke, or to a brother he'd tell a joke about Africa. In my case, he once asked, "Joe, you know why were there so many heroes at the Alamo?"

I answered, "Bey, I don't give a fuck."

He said, " 'Cause there weren't no back doors. Get it? No back doors."

## Corruption

### 1971, Via Luneto, Montebello

I turned ten the summer after my mother's funeral.

We moved to the Hensel Gardens apartments in Montebello to be nearer to my grandma Nellie and grandpa Joe. This isn't to say that the two lived together. My grandpa Joe divorced my grandma for the second time in the late 1960s. (They first divorced in 1946.) They lived one block apart in the same massive six-block apartment complex.

At Montebello, my father often let Paul and me walk unescorted to the Garmar Theater, four long blocks away from home. (The Garmar Theater in Montebello looked like a giant tin centipede that had fallen from the sky and landed on a large lot on Whittier Boulevard.) He'd give us three dollars to share between us, an ostentatious amount of money for two boys back then. A movie cost only seventy-five cents—and that was in the day of double features—so we'd spend the remaining money on candy, two hot dogs, two sodas, and one medium-size popcorn. This was how rich people lived, we were convinced, as we gobbled our feast like gluttons.

My first visits to the Garmar were G-rated experiences. I saw zany Disney movies like *The Love Bug* or *The Computer Wore Tennis Shoes*, starring a very young Kurt Russell. I sang "Zippity Do Da" with Uncle Remus in *Song of the South*.

One day that year, my aunt Gloria took me along with some of her lesbian friends to see Robert Altman's film, *McCabe & Mrs. Miller*, starring Warren Beatty and Julie Christie, the first R-rated film I'd ever seen. At that time I was needy for any attention a female member of my family could give me—my aunt Gloria's attention in particular. At family gatherings I'd sit on the carpet next to where she sat on the couch and she'd scratch the back of my head, a tender touch that reminded me of my mother's gentle calming.

So I sat there in the butter-smelly dark of the Garmar Theater, my aunt's hands in my hair. I didn't know what to make of the scene where naked Chinese whores jump from one bathtub to the other, giggling, butts and big tits jiggling. I turned my head away in shock, afraid that viewing the scene constituted a sin. But the vivid carnality seduced my eyes back to the screen. If this was sin, no wonder I was supposed to avert my eyes. I was riveted. Until the point in the second feature (also a Western) when a rude, drunken cowboy burned his cigarette out on a harlot's fleshy breast. She screeched, and he laughed. The barbarism startled me. No one else in the theater seemed to care.

My mother's dying had turned me sentimental. I mythologized her, thought of her as a saint whom God needed in heaven more than we needed her down here. Sad memories swooped down on me from out of nowhere, for no particular reason, and on no special occasion, and I'd break down and cry. My imagination was tender, so I was repulsed by the sadistic frivolity of burning a woman's breast. I couldn't comprehend a world where people observed savagery seemingly unmoved.

Soon after that startling trip to the Garmar with my aunt Gloria, my grandfather took me and several cousins to see *The Omega Man*, starring Charlton Heston. Hanging out with Grandpa Joe was a rare occasion. He was an impatient man, stern and serious, who always seemed put off when I ran to hug and kiss him on the cheek.

But there we were in the Garmar Theater, five of his grandchildren, each with his or her own soda and popcorn and candy bar. I'm sure he thought that if he bought us food to shove in our mouths then we wouldn't be able to talk too much before the movie. But we were chatty and fidgety anyway.

*The Omega Man* was a remake of *The Last Man on Earth*, starring Vincent Price. Heston played a futuristic Robinson Crusoe in a world wiped out by plague. By day he'd tool around barren, debris-strewn Los Angeles, a ghost town, in a red convertible. (L.A. as the site of the Apocalypse didn't surprise me; I was already afraid of its shifting ground.) At night Heston lived in a fortress surrounded by white-hot spotlights to keep away the other "survivors"—what reviewers of the film called a "diseased pack of neo-people with pale white skin and bleached-out, light-sensitive eyeballs."

One day, Heston meets a small group of survivors, healthy like him, but who are on the verge of turning into the nocturnal neo-people. He falls in love with Lisa (Rosalind Cash), a pretty black woman with a huge Angela Davis afro. Unfortunately, one evening, on her way home from a day of pillaging deserted department stores, she turns into one of the creatures.

I was sitting in an aisle seat. The camera focused on her. There was an open sore on her face. Then she unwrapped the scarf around her hair to reveal a ghostly albino-white afro. Then she took off her sunglasses. I squirmed in my seat when I saw those familiar milky irises. Her ghastly pallor resembled my mother's dying face, which at the end of her life had turned into a gaunt, sinister mask.

An intense fear overcame me. I felt as if one of those corpse-looking creatures were creeping up on me from behind. I abandoned my seat on the aisle and scooted down the row to sit next to my grandfather. I didn't ask him if I could move down. I didn't tell him that I was scared. I just moved fast, compelled by terror. He saw me coming and told my older cousin Bobby, who was sitting next to him, to switch seats with me.

Rosalind Cash led her new night master into Heston's bachelor pad, and a javelin in the heart finally felled our hero. I sat petrified next to my grandfather, frightened, but also embarrassed at not being strong enough not to be scared. Perhaps my aunt and grandfather considered these kinds of films to be some sort of rite of passage. But I couldn't help but feel like a slow developer, panicking when the adults around me expected me to be strong.

Walking to the car next to my grandfather, I knew that my cousins considered me a sissy for being afraid. But I didn't know how *not* to be afraid. I felt helpless, without the skills to disguise my naked vulnerability.

▌▌▌▌▌▌▌▌▌

Soon what other kids thought of me became less of a problem as I began to lose status in my own eyes. I felt as if the world had conspired to alter the trajectory of my life. Once, I'd been the miracle boy, anointed. Now I was full of dread, a cowardly liar scuttling under the house to hide my report cards, a gutless wonder fearing celluloid zombies. I felt I was constantly being placed in ethical quandaries (like keeping my mom's salt secret or watching naked women on film), where my soul wasn't strong enough yet to help me control the tremors in my inner world, or to help me overcome the confusion of the material world where I was expected to be valiant. I felt that God was being unfair. He had inspired me to aspire to the higher things, yet at every turn He was whacking my legs out from under me.

▌▌▌▌▌▌▌▌▌

That same year, my father was asked to teach junior high kids at Camp Acorn Lodge. Since he would be lodging there, Paul and I came too. The first day, when we drove up to the camp parking lot, my father couldn't find a folder of notes he'd asked me to put in the car. He quickly lost his temper, threatening to thrash me. Furiously rummaging through our luggage, he finally found the folder. It turned out that he had missed seeing it when he first looked in his briefcase. I wasn't at fault. Silently we continued unpacking the car. Paul and I were completely uncomfortable, our bodies still roiling with the fear our father had instilled in us during his tirade.

On our last trip to the car my father asked us to sit with him on one of the logs surrounding the parking lot. He asked our forgiveness, and cried as he apologized for acting hypocritically. Then he asked us to pray as a family so that we could start the trip over again, on good footing this time. I didn't want my father to get upset again, so I said I'd forgive him, and pray with him, too. He hadn't hit us but he was behaving in typical post–volatile outburst fashion: Overcome with guilt for terrorizing us. He'd done it before. After using verbal threats and taunts, or after slugging my ten-year-old face as if I were an adult, he'd lie prostrate on the floor, crying and pleading for our forgiveness, moaning from the pit of his soul that he was a sinful man who needed God's mercy. His entire body would tremble, utterly overcome with grief and remorse. It was all very Old Testament, very sackcloth and ashes, that weeping and gnashing of teeth stuff. But Paul and I always took his ceremonies of disgrace seriously, bought into this catharsis of absolution.

Still, these breakdowns created an occasion for our most intimate time together, a time when we were united by the same grief—not unlike the time our father told us that our mother was dead. Then we'd folded into each other and cried and became one pile of emotionally exhausted bodies, conjoined in equivalent anguish, consolidated in our faith, a congress of dysfunction. I forgave him that first day of camp, but that was also the day I started to keep tabs. I couldn't go on forgiving him for the same infraction indefinitely. I knew that perpetual, mindless forgiveness wasn't in my best interest.

Paul and I were allowed to sleep in the cabins with the junior-high boys even though they were four or five years older. At the end of the week I was stunned when, during the final night's campfire session, I was told that I'd been voted "Outstanding Camper of the Week." The camp leaders and campers clapped for me as I walked down to the fire and received a wooden plaque with a shiny gold plate pressed on the heavily lacquered side of the wood. The adults patted me on the back. Older kids asked to hold the plaque, and I sensed their envy. But overall the event made me feel consequential, distinct. I loved the attention, the applause, and the validation of my moral superiority. After all, didn't this award imply that I was more than decent, someone to be admired as exemplary, with solid character, of finer cloth, perhaps a little bit saintly, a virtuous parable that other parents would tell their children?

That was the first time I recognized how a concrete, public award was tied to a positive interpretation of someone's works, although, I suspect that the loss of my mother only six months earlier had something to do with my getting the award. (You know, part pity vote.) Still, I secretly swore an oath to figure out exactly how the reward system worked and to meet its criteria by being sly and manipulative. I intended to win again. I never earned another summer camp award, but the plaque awoke in me an obsession. From then on, I measured the value of my behavior on a point system: The most points went to moral acts with the most public exposure—volunteering to feed paraplegics at Christmastime when the church had a special holiday dinner for them. The least number of points went to good deeds done in the dark, unnoticed and for their own sake—praying for missionaries.

I became obsessed with publicly presenting myself as living a correct life, playing to an audience, to the proverbial "they"—"they" think they are better than us; "they" don't like us; "they" wouldn't appreciate our behavior; "they" see right through us; who I perceived was out there observing me, gathering intelligence about the quality of my goodness.

There's a Bible parable that stresses how good deeds should be done privately, and with a humble heart. The right hand shouldn't know what the left hand is doing. I disregarded these passages and did the exact opposite. I took my hands into the street and started clapping them, drawing attention to all my virtuous deeds.

■■■■■■■■■

My father had earned his high school equivalency diploma through a correspondence course, while my mother was still alive, and then enrolled himself in East Los Angeles Community College. He took some time off from pursuing his degree during my mother's illness, but when he returned to school after her death he had enough credits, at age twenty-six to transfer to Biola College.

He often spoke to the college-age group at the Church of the Open Door. His younger brother Tony returned from Vietnam in 1970 and eventually became president of the church college department. Soon my father was dating the secretary, Brenda Joyce Seale, a twenty-year-old who also attended Biola College.

Brenda's father was originally from Texas, and her mother hailed from the Blue Ridge Mountains of Kentucky. Landing in Turlock, California, with Brenda's father, she'd traced the same immigration route as the couple in Janis Joplin's posthumous pop hit, "Me and Bobby McGee": "From the Kentucky coal mines, to the California sun."

A pioneer woman from dust bowl people, Brenda had been raised to milk cows, bake bread, can jams, make quilts . . . and prevail. In high school she thought she would like to be a nurse. A family friend named Jean, who attended Brenda's church, was the nursing supervisor of the Ob/Gyn department at the local hospital. But Brenda's family didn't support Brenda's ambition. Turlock was remote, and college was discouraged. Brenda's mother, Bertie, was a Kentucky mother. This was a huge deal in Brenda's imagination. Saying no to one's mother was looked down on in Kentucky country culture, and was tantamount to a stern rejection of country values.

So Jean encouraged eighteen-year-old Brenda to consider attending very conservative Biola College. The idea of attending a quasi-cloistered campus appealed to Brenda. A sheltered farm girl, naïve to the ways of slick city folk, she sensed that if she were thrown into the big world of a faraway school she would be distracted. But Biola sounded like a cushioned landing, a place where she could live on campus, learn about academic life, and get the lay of the land.

Brenda's church pastor had graduated from Talbot Seminary, which shared the same campus with Biola. He knew people in the administration at Biola, and he told Brenda he would help her get in. Brenda received scholarships, and everything looked good for her attending Biola. Then a last-minute surprise Memorial Scholarship disqualified her from getting five hundred dollars from her other financial aid package, and she lost her chance to attend Biola. She would have to go to a local junior college.

For a while during that summer after high school, Brenda worked as a waitress in the Woolworth's lunch counter in downtown Turlock. One night her father, Sam, a well-known local drunk, came into the Woolworth's a little tipsy. He mumbled something to Brenda about how he wished he could do more, assured her that she made him proud, and then handed her an envelope with five hundred dollars in it. He'd gone down to the Veteran's Administration and picked up the money that had been allotted for her to attend college.

My father and Brenda would sometimes meet for lunch at the restaurant attached to the local Carriage Inn. They became official boyfriend and girlfriend when my father invited Brenda to a holiday party at Ron Hathaway's home, less than eleven months after my mother died.

Small-town Brenda was easily impressed with what she considered the high caliber of my father's friends, like Ron Hathaway and Dean Dow. Ron Hathaway worked with my father at Quality Frame and Door. It was at his father's condo in Palm Springs where Brenda and my father stayed on their honeymoon, and Ron's in-laws lived in a wealthy enclave in Long Beach known as Bixby Knolls. Dean Dow was another one of my father's work buddies. His father was a dean at L.A. City College. In Brenda's new Southern California universe these men—with their nice houses and families who owned businesses or who were elders of churches, whom some might call "connected"—epitomized cosmopolitanism.

A photo taken on my dad and Brenda's wedding day shows Brenda in her lacy white bride's dress kneeling between my brother and me. Paul and I are dressed in our spiffy blue suits and ties and leaning into Brenda's face, each of us planting a boyish kiss on her cheek. With our dark *Indio* faces pressed against her pale face, we look otherworldly, like angels at a carnival.

I was an alert and superstitious boy, so I found it uncanny how my replacement mother had the same initials as my real mother: B. J. Basilia Jesus meet Brenda Joyce.

After the wedding, Brenda moved into our apartment and immediately began making it her own. She placed lacy doilies on the dressers and potpourri in the drawers. A large trunk at the foot of her bed contained yearbooks, photo albums, and the mementos, knickknacks, and posters of a girl at college. Candles sprung up on shelves everywhere. There was even a lantern, for earthquake blackouts, complete with wick and oil—the kind I'd only ever seen on period TV shows like *The Big Valley* and *The Rifleman*.

I'd never paid attention to the color of our living room couches until Brenda replaced them with lime-green recliners and a forest-green sofa. She bought thick curtains to match, curtains that you tied with a velvety rope to keep them open. She sewed red-white-and-blue, bold-striped curtains with matching window canopies for our bedroom. Our pillow-cases matched the curtains. Dark blue bedspreads and dressers, painted the same bold colors of the flag, rounded out the patriotic motif.

I aspired to please my new white mother who sewed the curtains in our room, who knew intimately the mysteries of food and fabric, who made provisions for natural disasters, and who smelled like a woman.

Brenda was of Irish descent. Her hair was reddish blond, long and straight like Marcia Brady's. Her flesh was so white it was light pink, and she had flecks of tiny, unusually light, caramel-colored freckles all over her face and arms. Her high cheekbones and sharp nose made her classically pretty in an angular Anglo sort of way. My father's term of endearment for Brenda was "white-skinned thing," as in, *Come over here, my pretty white-skinned thing, and give me a kiss.* My dad would often poke fun at her foam white calves and knees whenever she dared to wear cut-off jean shorts.

My brother and I were as fascinated by her white complexion as our father, acting like aliens who'd abducted a human specimen when we pressed our fingers gently on her forearm to watch with native amazement as a tiny bruise instantly formed on her delicate skin. She'd smile and turn again to running material through the sewing machine. We'd dash off to play.

I loved Brenda, loved kissing her goodnight, I loved what she'd done to our home. But I felt secretly guilty for my easy affection for her, as if I was betraying my mother by not fighting harder to hate Brenda. I was conflicted, so at first I was sometimes cool to her little efforts to earn my trust.

I was still haunted by the image of my mother at our final Christmas, in her robe and house slippers, gaunt, ugly and scared, but happy that my brother and I were playing and giggling over our new toys. I wished I'd been more aware to pick up on the fact that she was dying. All the signs were there: the long hospital stays, the obvious physical deterioration, the whispering adults, the generosity of spirit displayed to me by church-men not prone to treating children kindly. But as a nine-year-old boy I didn't know how to read the signs. I hated how my ignorance had al-lowed me to be surprised by my mother's untimely death, so I swore I'd never be that stupid and naïve again. I didn't want to love easily again.

▪▪▪▪▪▪▪▪▪▪

In the second year of his new marriage my father came home one day and handed me a calendar that charted out a schedule of daily readings from the Old and New Testaments so that the entire Bible could be read in one year. He told me I was to follow the chart.

I did so, for two years. Brenda devised another kind of reading sched-ule for my brother and me. With her schedule, within a few years I'd have read *Gulliver's Travels, Robinson Crusoe, Les Miserables, Jane Eyre, Dracula, The Adventures of Huckleberry Finn, Frankenstein,* and other books Brenda praised as "the classics."

Brenda wanted us to enjoy literature, but my father demanded monthly book reports from us. Sometimes substandard assignments were met with whippings.

Renfield, Huck, the Houyhnhnm and Yahoo, Friday, and Heathcliff all became characters I added to the stories I knew we humans liked to tell about ourselves. My reading made me aware of the hidden like-nesses in many narratives. The Houyhnhnm were talking horses en-dowed with reason in *Gulliver's Travels.* In the Old Testament, Balaam has a stubborn mule that won't go where it's directed, so Balaam beats the mule. The mule becomes filled with the Spirit of God and turns around to explain to Balaam why it will not budge. I recognized how Balaam's ass and Swift's Houyhnhnm were the equine forbears of Francis and Mr. Ed, talking horses in film and on television. And Transylvania, Wuthering Heights, the Mississippi River, and Brobdingnag all became localities in my imagination beside Biblical Nineveh, Canaan, Gehenna, and Golgotha.

When I was in seventh grade, my father enrolled at UCLA, where he double majored in philosophy and the other classics, Greek and Latin. He learned how to translate Sophocles and Cato the Younger with equal facility. While at UCLA, he was asked by local members of the Southern Baptist Conference to co-pastor *Iglesia Bautista Fundamental* (Fundamentalist Baptist Church)—a small, Spanish-speaking church on Ford Boulevard in East L.A. There he taught the fire-and-brimstone message that the wages of sin are death.

He asked our old family friends, the Garcias, to join the church board. Brenda and my dad would come home in good moods after some of those serious board meetings.

*Brenda, remind me again. What was the first one Lily said?*

*She said that she wanted to second the "emotion."*

*That's the one. Boy, she's funny to listen to. But my favorite one was when she apologized and said that she would have to "recline" the nomination.*

Like the Figueroas, the Delgados, the Lopezes and other Mexican families, the Garcias offended me with their lack of education or polish, and their Old-World belief that because they were the adults that made them right and we children weren't allowed to disagree with them. I looked at Mr. Lopez, whose son Matthew hated him, and I wondered at the peculiar world of Mexican Bible thumpers. They seemed to have an utter lack of skill to keep a family together with love, and instead resorted to whippings to keep their children in check. I had attended large churches run by white men, and I was pretty sure that those churches didn't become big and famous by having uneducated, petty men like Mr. Garcia influencing their direction. I was also pretty sure that *Iglesia Bautista Fundamental* was always going to be a small church of no spiritual consequence as long as they had a young boy from the ghetto like my father co-pastoring it.

There seemed something completely improvisational about our makeshift *barrio* church. Lacking the mystical polish of an ancient synagogue or an age-old storied European cathedral, *Iglesia Bautista Fundamental* sat on grounds that looked like a used car lot someone had decided to plant with grass. In fact, sometimes the parishioners were allowed to park on the grass. (If you drove down the mostly residential

Ford Boulevard you could see the same *barrio* ethic alive in homes where people parked their Chevy Impalas or Ford Trucks on their front lawns.)

The co-pastor with my father was a man named Ernie Withrow. He'd wanted to be a missionary, so the local Southern Baptist Board Conference sent him to our church. I knew even then that I never wanted to be a missionary. I didn't find anything quaint or romantic about a working-class community whose residents parked cars on their front lawns. In fact, I wanted to leave this proletariat place behind me, and never revisit it or minister to it. I felt like I deserved to turn into a pillar of salt if I looked back.

But I loved the potluck dinners that the congregation seemed to hold more often than Bible studies. The chicken *mole* and homemade tortillas. The cheese and chicken enchiladas. The chile rellenos. The large, deep trays of lasagna, Spanish rice and beans, and *carnitas.* The German chocolate cake and the ten or twelve different types of Mexican sweet breads. There wasn't anything amateurish about these church potlucks.

As embarrassed as I was about inviting my friends from Grace Church, in the San Fernando Valley, to my dad's new church, I didn't have any problem inviting some of my Mexican friends there. They were impressed by the very things that mortified me: The achievement of community among Spanish- and English-speaking Mexicans. The official-looking church property and chapel with pews and a pulpit. The men dressed in polyester suits and the women in smart Kmart dresses.

It wasn't merely the leisure suits, bad grammar, and ghetto accents that disturbed me. No. It was the continued waning of my faith that opinionated adults knew what was going on and were telling me the truth. I'd sit in the pew on Sundays and rub my hand over the bruise under my sleeve, the bruise that my father had given me during a beating. (Sometimes he'd have us get into the push-up position and hold it. When we collapsed, he'd smack our backs with a bat. Then we had to get up into the position again and repeat the exercise.) I'd look at one of the adults near me and try to send them ESP messages that a child was suffering nearby. I prayed to God to make their hearts heavy so that they would have to investigate the source of their discomfort and maybe take their heads out of the clouds and see the person suffering in their vicinity. If God spoke to any of the adults in that church, they must not have ever heard His voice, because they simply kept their eyes upraised and hallelujahed our neglectful Savior.

Eventually I became amused by these folks. They wanted me to trust their faith, their judgment in the spiritual realm—like how they knew when they were being animated by the will of God or that God had secured their Protestant salvation in the Book of Life, while sending Catholics and existentialists to hell—but they were absolute dullards when it came to concrete things on this earthly plane, like how to recognize the abused child seated next to them.

Sometimes I'd confide in a Christian aunt or the mother of a friend or an elder's wife that I was sad and missed my mother. They'd tell me to be happy for my mother, to rejoice because I'd be reunited with her in heaven one day. My grief and turmoil intensified, and no one seemed to care. They seemed not to be speaking to me when they tried to console me, and I suspected that adults might be lying to me about an array of things, both trivial and important. And their peasantlike faith that every ill could be dealt with simply by finding the right chapter and verse to explain it away seemed unintelligent to me.

▦▦▦▦▦▦

In our Montebello apartment, a bookcase was lined up against every spare wall. There were bookcases in the dining room, the living room, the hallways, the hallway closets, and in every bedroom. My brother and I shared a room; two four-shelved bookcases partitioned it into halves.

I still recall lying in bed, my head sideways on the pillow, facing the books. I looked directly at *The Washing of the Spears* by Donald R. Morris. I remember its unusually colorful cover: A Zulu warrior with spear and multihued shield standing opposite a red-liveried British officer. The politics and African location in the book seemed far away. Although that old war foreshadowed a modern race clash (Civil Rights marches, Watts riots), I couldn't relate to the explosive climate of war or picture myself on that South African landscape in the conflict between black Zulu and white British.

The book cover's imagery had resonance with my imagination because the film *Gunga Din* had been one of my father's favorites. (My father was always making Paul and me co-conspirators in his latest adventure. When he began his operatic voice lessons, Paul and I crooned Neapolitan love songs along with Mario Lanza on the turntable. When he studied Hebrew, we listened to Israeli music albums that helped him learn pronunciation, and we'd dance to the tunes. Or for a Saturday matinee, we three would drive downtown to the Music Center to listen to the L.A. Philharmonic Orchestra perform Tchaikovsky's *Pathétique* while a storyteller held us children in rapt attention. Or we would go to the Montebello City Library with him and sit in the children's section for hours while he studied Menander's plays in a private room near the back exit.) One Saturday, when I was in junior high, he requested that my brother and I sit down with him to watch *Gunga Din* on television. That kind of invitation was how I learned about Sherlock Holmes and Moriarty, Blondie and Dagwood, Mugs McGinnis, and the Bowery boys.

*C'mon, little fellas. You're gonna love this flick.*

A Kipling poem turned into a Hollywood history lesson: Brown Gunga Din at the battlefront, regimental *bhisti* (water carrier) for the fatigued British infantry under attack by relentless *thuggees*. Gunga Din wanted to become a soldier-bugler so badly that he actually shot a gun he'd picked up from a dead enemy as his troops retreated under heavy fire. The lieutenant in charge threatened to beat Gunga Din if he ever touched a gun again, calling Din names like " 'eathen" or "limping lump o' brick dust" or "squidgy-nosed old idol."

At one point, Cary Grant catches Gunga Din behind the barracks practicing marching with a bugle under his arm. Grant behaves more decently (he only calls Din "good old grinnin', gruntin' Gunga Din") and, on the sly, instructs Din how to march and salute correctly.

Poor Din lives under a constant barrage of insults and the perpetual threat of the whip. But in the end, when it looks like an entire battalion of British troops is going to ride right into a trap set by the *thuggees*, Gunga Din, near death, manages to climb atop a temple to the goddess Kali and blow his bugle like a true soldier. He saves the day, and the Brits rout their enemy. In the last line of the movie, as in the poem, a soldier looking down at Gunga Din's corpse covered with a sheet, says, "You're a better man than I am."

But watching *Gunga Din* I consciously desired to be like Cary Grant and Douglas Fairbanks Jr., both men suave under fire. They found time to take a civilized tea (and whiskey) break on the Empire's time, even though they were clearly in danger. Yet I also recognized that my real role model was Gunga Din—played by the manic actor Sam Jaffe—a gentle brown lackey in the British-Indian scrimmage. I surmised that he had sacrificed his life nobly in the service of the Empire, and had finally established himself on the right side of history.

For all my desire to be like my fellow white classmates—no matter how much I told myself that I was like them or was them—I was still ambivalent about who I was in their eyes. And in the pit of my soul I suspected that my attempts to be white were pulled off with the same lack of alacrity as clumsy Gunga Din's attempts to march with that bugle.

▮▮▮▮▮▮▮▮▮▮

While at UCLA, my father would read stories to us at bedtime from his thick *Norton Introduction to Literature* textbook. He'd walk into the bedroom, sit on the edge of my bed, and flip through the thin pages to Shirley Jackson's "The Lottery," a story about a town that practices a yearly sacrificial stoning; or to "Vanka," by Chekhov, about some abused kid trapped in servitude in nineteenth-century Russia; or "The Short Happy Life of Frances Macomber," by Hemingway, about a cuckold who is murdered on safari by his wife; or Kafka's "A Hunger Artist," about some literal starving artist cry-baby whining about how nobody appreciates his work. A few times my father read us the poem "Richard Cory," by Edwin Arlington Robinson, about a man whom the whole town looks up to, who thinks he has his life together, but who one night shoots himself in the head.

Being just a twelve-year-old boy, I found these stories a little difficult to decipher. Near as the words were, their meanings felt far away. But I had an inkling that one day I would understand the mysteries of the texts that surrounded me. I couldn't comprehend the themes, but something in them resonated with me. Was "Vanka" a tale about dumb faith or the story of an abused boy whose naïveté thwarted his efforts to return to the warmth of his grandfather's home? And was the hunger artist deluded? And who did the hunger artist symbolize to Kafka?

Literature seemed to imply that I needed to bring something of my own life to the reading. The themes and lessons of literature were difficult for me to decipher because I hadn't a context in which to appreciate them. (And I knew that my vocabulary was still growing. My father was beginning to use new words in the home. *Absurdity. Existential crisis. Despair. Nausea* was the title of one of his schoolbooks.)

I was nonetheless obliged to those short stories my father read to me at night. Tucked warmly in bed, in plaid flannel pajamas, being read to by the man I feared and loved most in the world, I suspected that one day I would be able to identify with, and give language to, the same tragic alienation resounding through modern short fiction. I was flirting further with the writer's detachment.

▮▮▮▮▮▮▮▮▮▮

Several times in our Montebello apartment I woke in the night unable to breathe. I'd get out of bed, walk down the hall, knock on my dad and Brenda's bedroom door and mumble the words "asthma attack." A loud commotion in the bedroom ensued as my father bounced out of bed, scrambling in the dark to locate his shoes, all the while talking to me in a reassuring voice.

*Mijo, I'm coming, just let daddy find his clothes. Don't worry, it'll be all right, just need to find my keys.*

I'd stare at the door until it was flung open. Then my father would scoop me in his arms as if I were a large sick dog, and lay me in the back seat of the car. We lived ten miles from the hospital so he'd race to the hospital, barely slowing down at red lights to make sure that no other cars were coming. He never fully stopped at STOP signs or waited for red lights to turn green.

The doctor would give me a shot of adrenalin as my father held my hand. After a half-hour of observation by the staff, I'd be released and my dad would take me to McDonald's, a mile from our home.

The sky would still be dark morning blue, the sun ready to rise on our car parked in the McDonald's lot. I was happy to be the first customer of the day. My dad would order us Egg McMuffins, hash browns, and orange juice. The Egg McMuffin was one of those peculiar foods I decided to try only because my dad said he liked the taste and he'd challenged me to take a bite. (When I was in high school he challenged me to eat raw fish at a Japanese restaurant, and I did . . . and loved it.) That first time eating the breakfast sandwich, I decided right there on the spot that this was my new favorite food, although I could barely understand or appreciate any of the flavors in my mouth.

At these times I felt a special bond with my father, that my time in his presence was an introduction into another way to experience the world, apart from the predictable daytime roles we played. There was something furtive about skulking around in the dark with him. And the large dose of adrenaline pumping through my veins made me feel vital, more acutely receiving pulsations from the world, wide awake while the rest of the sleepy world staggered out of bed. And there was something private and conspiratorial about eating an impromptu breakfast at an unorthodox time and place, with my father seated next to me, unshaved and sockless, wearing a wrinkled shirt and frumpy sweater, his hair disheveled.

Years later, more than a few times I'd chew on an Egg McMuffin as I sat in my car and cased a bank. On one morning, around nine o'clock, I drove by an outdoor mall and saw a bank nestled between a dry cleaner's and a Thrifty Drugs. It was one of those malls where every store could be accessed from the parking lot. There was a McDonald's across the street. I bought some food there and drove around to the opposite side of the bank and parked. After a few minutes, I finished my Egg McMuffin and hash browns, guzzled down the last of the coffee and orange juice, and got out of my car. Inside the bank I was shocked to see only two teller stations and one tiny desk in the dinky area trying to pawn itself off as a lobby. The tellers who had been talking to each other turned their heads to face me when I entered. I looked at both of them as I stood at the door. Then I said, *Okay, you know the drill. This is a bank robbery, so both of you give me the money or I'll blow both your fuckin' heads off! Now hurry up!* They started digging into their drawers ASAP. I walked over to the teller on the left. She'd placed her money on the counter first. I grabbed a pile of it and shoved it into my bag. Then I walked over to the other teller's station and shoved more stacks of money into my bag. I went back to the first teller. *Hurry up! And give me the big bills in the lower drawers.* The money kept flowing. I kept moving from one teller station to the other. *Good. Now get up and walk away and count to ten.* When I turned to leave a guy was walking in. He held the door open for me. I hit the bricks and started running. I turned right and saw my car in the distance. Within a few seconds I heard someone yelling for me to stop. I looked back. There was plenty of distance between me and the fat security guard chasing me. I got into my car and raced out of the parking lot. When I got home I counted my loot: $12,459.

■■■■■■■■■

Several times in the four years after my mom died I'd be startled awake by nightmares. I'd sit up and stare at the dark walls or I'd go over to Paul's bed and touch his face to check if his still body was cold like my mother's was the last time I kissed her cheek in her coffin. A lot of people turned cold in my nightmares. I never told Paul this but I had a persistent premonition that he would turn cold, too—so persistent, in fact, that I was ashamed of myself for such thoughts, for my uncontrollable dread.

I suppose I had much to feel anxious about. By the time I was in the fifth grade, I'd lived in seven different residences, I'd been enrolled in four schools, and was now about to go to my first secular school. (My mother's illness had left my father with a huge medical bill, and he could no longer afford private education for us.)

When I got to Montebello Intermediate School, I thought that the teachers must have thought their Mexican Eastside students less than bright because they showed us a lot of educational films and offered us classes like wood shop, print shop, and homemaking. (I baked my first peanut-butter brittle cookies in that class.)

My reading and writing levels as a transfer student from private school were so high that I was given "independent study classes" for half of the day. For independent study four Asian girls and I met with Miss Babcock, an extremely wrinkle-faced, sixtyish school counselor who dressed like a preppy grandmother and whose golfing buddies at the country club may have called her something like Bunny. In our meetings with her, Miss Babcock helped us design our own personal curricula and class projects.

When I arrived at Montebello Intermediate School, in the sixth grade, I heard rumors that Carla Vargas had had to abort Johnny Castillo's baby. Johnny was my classmate and a reputed gang member of VNE SP—*Varrio Nuevo Estrada, Espantos*—the Little Ghosts of New Barrio Estrada. His wardrobe was the perfect tough-guy uniform, baggy in all the right places, with perfectly sharp creases in his pants that showed diligence, if not obsession. I envied him, the way girls were thrilled by his rare smile and seduced by his roguish charm, how the other boys—sissies like me and tough kids like him—feared his hair-trigger anger. He was caught several times french-kissing girls in home-room, suspended for beating up other boys or smoking.

I knew that for all Johnny's worldliness, the world held more promise out to me. He was fun to watch, daring and swashbuckling in a "Pirates of the Caribbean" way, but we all understood where he would end up, in prison or an early grave—an outlaw either way. Johnny and I were headed in opposite directions. I was sure of it. Life for me was going to be a much finer story. (Last I saw him he'd graduated to continuation school, then gone on to juvie.)

I was bookish. For my independent study project in eighth grade I proposed making an animated film describing one implication of Einstein's Theory of Relativity. My father bought me a comic book that explained in cartoon format the part of Einstein's theory that suggested how if one twenty-five-year-old twin brother boarded a spaceship and took off into deep space at a speed approaching the speed of light, time would seem to pass as it always had. It would take him twenty-five seconds to tie his shoes or four minutes to brush his teeth, but when he returned to earth a mere three days later—having traveled the entire time at a speed approaching the speed of light—he'd find that his twin was now an eighty-year-old man. I drew still cartoons to illustrate this theory.

Beyond my nerdiness I was also a sissy, and the really tough kids knew this. Every year, Cantwell High School, the local all-boys Catholic school, hosted a carnival in Montebello. One late afternoon at the Cantwell carnival, my brother and I stood counting our money, a few bucks, trying to figure out which rides we could afford. We started bickering. Paul wanted to spend the remainder of our money on popcorn or cotton candy. I wanted to buy a stuffed animal or toss coins onto plates for a prize. As we stood there arguing, a boy not much older than we were swiped the bills out of my hand and nonchalantly walked away. He didn't run. He didn't turn back. It was painful to know that he'd accurately sized me up even before he'd robbed me. He knew me better than I knew myself because it was only as he was walking away that I confronted the hard truth that I would never have run after someone who robbed me, and fought them, if there was a chance that I could get my ass whupped. (This fact should have been obvious to me a long time before that petty theft in front of the House of Mirrors on the carnival grounds.) I suppressed a congested rage at how bitterly unfair the theft had been, blatant and unremorseful, committed in front of God and everyone, just like the beatings by my father that I sensed were a public humiliation that everyone knew about but dared not intervene in.

▮▮▮▮▮▮▮▮▮

I joined the school drama club and quickly became the class clown, always ready with a quip. I was willing to play any slapstick role and even brought a comedic edge to a villain named Murdoch. I was all yuk-yuks, embellished arm gestures, and exaggerated grins and smirks. I'd slink around the stage, my cape held over my mouth.

Ms. Chavez, our young drama teacher, and the first "Ms." I'd ever encountered, was also the girl's softball coach. She had a ten-year-old boy's body and wore her hair in a pixie. Her encouragement of my small talent and my theatrics was permissive, subversive even. Acting began to supplant my more durable knowledge of things, like the Bible and physics. I was seduced by the possibility that life could be less demanding than memorizing Greek on the weekends, that I could feel playful and a sense of abandon, as I did on the stage.

▤▤▤▤▤▤▤▤▤

For a few weeks each summer after my mother's death, my brother and I would stay with our aunt Maggie in Pico Rivera. I never really thought about my aunt Maggie's polio limp, her quasi-stumble when she walked. That's because she wasn't tragic or moribund about it, but instead laughed often with a loud cackle. We liked our cousin Terry, a tenth grader and wannabe ballerina. Aunt Maggie was a fiercely possessive mother. But sometimes she'd hit Terry with a metal clothes hanger. Fortunately for Paul and me she never demonstrated anything akin to discontent with us, so all we got from her was affection.

Aunt Maggie had been in Germany when my mother died, married to a serviceman named Rudy Guadarrama, so she hadn't been able to attend the funeral. Rudy moved back to the States and got a job at the Ford Motor plant down the road from their apartment. Uncle Rudy had the meanest-looking Adam's apple I'd ever seen. Knotted and protruding, the mangled lump looked ready to tear through his skin.

Rudy was a man with a simple routine. We'd pick him up after work in the family's burgundy Chevy Impala. He ate his dinner on a TV tray while watching *The Evening News* with Walter Cronkite. After a few beers, he'd doze in his leather lounge chair. The only time I ever saw him laugh was during *M\*A\*S\*H* or *American Bandstand* on Saturday afternoons.

He and my aunt Maggie had the kind of marriage where they had to taunt each other through a third party before they could take off the gloves and really get into a fight by themselves. We'd all be watching TV in the same room, my aunt on the couch, Uncle Rudy leaning back in his recliner, his feet propped up on the foot cushion.

AUNT MAGGIE: *Joey, ask your uncle Rudy why he only knows how to listen to the TV with the volume up so loud. Ah! Ask him if he wen' deaf or something in all those Vietnam rice paddies he's always bragging about?*

UNCLE RUDY: *Joey, tell your aunt Maggie that I didn't go deaf in 'Nam with all those guns blasting around my ears but that I went deaf listening to all her screaming and complaining in the house, always yapping like some kind of power drill.*

AUNT MAGGIE: *Tell your uncle that I wouldn't have to yell if he acted like he heard me when I ask him to get his lazy ass off the chair and stop watching cartoons for two seconds to clean the gutters or mow a lawn.*

At that point I wasn't needed anymore to act as their go-between. Uncle Rudy swiveled in his lounge chair and spoke directly to my aunt.

UNCLE RUDY: *Lazy? Lazy, huh? Let's see how long we'd have this apartment and our car and this ugly sofa that we still owe on if I stopped working and we had to rely on you actually contributing a dime to this cushy life that I give you.*

I never understood how two people who didn't like each other could stay together. I wasn't surprised when they divorced after their ten-year attempt to play house.

During the summer of '73, the *Los Angeles Times* featured an account of a chartered plane full of Uruguayan soccer players that had crashed in the Andes. Rescue efforts were cut short when the weather turned bad. When they realized that no one was coming to save them, the college-age survivors of the crash finally lived off of the flesh of their fallen teammates. (The story was later turned into the book *Alive!* and then later a bad film with the world's most improbable Latino, Ethan Hawke, playing a lead role.)

For two days I sat at the breakfast nook table and read the long article about the crash while my aunt Maggie made my all-time-favorite sandwich in the whole world: bologna and cheddar cheese on white bread with mayonnaise and mustard, lettuce, tomato, pickles, and lots of black pepper. (That was the sandwich I would dream of the most when I was in prison.)

When we arrived at aunt Maggie's apartment, my brother and I would barely unpack our suitcases before we quickly raced out on both of Terry's bikes to ride around the neighborhood. That we were boys of ten and twelve and the bicycles were little-girl pink, with bells and wicker baskets, didn't bother us at all. In fact, the baskets actually came in handy when at night my brother and I rode into a nearby alley and pilfered huge ripe peaches from a tree whose branches hung over from someone's property. My aunt Maggie encouraged us to bring back what we could, that there was no harm in taking fruit that was simply going to fall into the alley and rot anyway. One night Paul and I yanked on the peaches with such aggression that the wild shaking of the tree and the rain of peaches pelting the earth eventually drew the owner of the tree out of his house. We heard the back screen door creak open as a man's voice yelled at us, threatening to call the police. We hopped on the bikes we'd leaned against the wall and zipped away with our stash of peaches, made even more delicious by the thrill of larceny.

I liked this kind of prankish chase. I felt playfully hunted. An impish dread. On my way home from school I'd sometimes intentionally taunt Cantwell High School boys and get them to chase me. I was quick, in a nervous-rabbit way, and had great instincts for scaling fences and climbing over walls at just the right moment to elude capture. I'd draw the high school boys out and let them get close to catching me, and then I'd be gone.

The thrill of being discovered and getting chased, then the final reward of getting away with the petty thievery, was an adrenaline rush for me, a charge, a straight-up adventure of young scofflaw proportions that I would later recall with some amusement as I fell asleep on my prison bunk.

Later, as an adult out of prison, I joked with my aunt Maggie that she was the reason I'd ended up robbing banks. *You're the one who first made me imagine that I could be a good thief, by making me go into that alley to steal those peaches.*

She cackled, *Ay, Joey, no, don't say that.*

I laughed with her. Then she slyly added, *But those peaches were good, huh?*

I playfully blamed my dad, too. He used to walk in the front door and pretend that he was scared. He'd turn away from us, hiding something in his right polio-damaged hand. Paul and I would give him the bum's rush and he'd fall to the ground, where we'd wrestle our allowance out of his feeble grasp.

*You see that, Dad,* I'd later point out, *I'd never have robbed those banks if you hadn't first schooled me in the fine art of mugging the helpless for a reward.*

                                              ▌▌▌▌▌▌▌▌▌

I was a skinny four-eyed kid who got picked on a lot by neighborhood bullies. One day I finally decided to stand up for myself and challenged a kid named José to a fight after school. He said, *Cool.*

José brought along his two friends, Jerry and Mikey, to referee the fight. We all walked to Montebello High School, down the block, where we found a nice, private fighting space behind the gym. José pointed at the ski sweater I was wearing and suggested I take it off so that it wouldn't get torn. My grandma Bertie had given me the sweater for Christmas, and I thought that José was being mighty honorable to notice its value. But as soon as I got the sweater pulled over my head, all three boys pounced on me. They left me on the cement with a torn sweater and broken glasses.

When I got home, my father was studying his Bible at the dining room table. He looked at me—bruised, clothes tattered, broken eyeglasses in hand—and asked what had happened. I told him how the boys had beat me up. He was infuriated—not that I was hurt but that I'd lost. He walked over and slapped me hard. Then he said something about how he wasn't going to have his boy grow up to be a sissy. (He was like that sometimes, studying his Bible, close to God, pious almost, then I'd make some noise and he'd yell out in an angry voice, *Hey you kids, you better shut up! Can't you see I'm studying the Bible?* The power of his humility slayed us—positively inspired us to jump right into the text with him so that we could be good, kind, and thoughtful vessels of God's love, too.)

My father piled my brother and me into our Ford Maverick and drove us around the neighborhood to find José, Jerry, and Mikey. He told me that I had to fight all three of them independently, and if I let them beat me up again, he was going to beat me.

*Is that them?* My father asked as he pointed out three boys walking out of a liquor store.

I pieced my broken glasses together and raised them to my face. Sure enough, it was them. I slunk lower in the front seat and whimpered, *No. That's not them.*

He drove on.

I was numb, I was more than hurt, more than simply humiliated. I couldn't really feel what exactly was happening to me. Something folded itself into me, and I couldn't understand how I was supposed to feel. It was as if I'd been erased, as if I couldn't feel because something else had taken over and kept me calm, kept the tears from flowing, kept me from jumping out of the moving car. This submission to a force greater than me, that could shut me down so swiftly, compelled me to face the fact that I was beaten. And not simply for being beaten up and losing the fight, but also for being thought a sissy by my father, for being a loser in his eyes. I remember thinking later that night that the world had only two verdicts for guys: winner or loser. Winners were heroes who gained the respect of other guys. But losers could be treated any old way by the winners.

And for evidence that my sissy/loser instincts were spilling out of me uncontrollably, I had only to look at my crush on a sixth grader when I was in the eighth grade. The younger sister of a pretty and delicate class-mate named Diane Rivas, Tina was a cute, chubby girl with a bubbly per-sonality. She was sweet to me one day during nutrition recess, and I was smitten. Her affection for me was real and true, I believed, so I went home and made a card for her, drawing in bold letters on the front of the card "I LOVE YOU!" I drew flowers blossoming around the words, with a leafy vine snaking down both sides of the card.

The next morning I handed my work of art to her before school. She promised to read it during her next class. I thought that for sure she would surrender to my romantic charm by the next recess. Instead, she was cool to me. I was baffled. Then she asked me why I wrote "I LOVE YOU," as if to imply that this was completely impossible or, worse, untrue. But what I was feeling was LOVE. I was sure of it.

There she sat, this lovely lass, questioning the veracity of my affection. How dare she? Did Juliet impugn Romeo's love simply because he was too young? What was Tina doing to me? Why me? Sensitive and true me? A poet and lover, even one familiar with all three Greek words for three very different connotations of love. (*Agape* was God's love for man, self-sacrificing, as in *for God so loved the world that he gave his only begotten son; phileo* was brotherly love, as in Philadelphia, City of Brotherly Love; and *eros* was a lustier rendition than the other two.) I knew what love was, and there she was treating me as if my declaration were inappropriate. Why couldn't she understand that I'd lost my mother and now had an overflow of love that any girlfriend or wife would benefit from? I was nothing if not a bundle of frustrated and congested love dying to be released. Her rebuff made me feel pathetic, and the wounded dejection unleashed in me a fierce hatred for my desperate, clumsy need for female affection. Being open to so many sensations from the world meant that I was equally open to rejection. Betrayal seemed to lie in wait for me near all my desires.

Tina's rejection reminded me that girls were a mystery to me in ways I believed that they weren't to other boys. Back in fifth grade there were the scrawny Alexander twins, whom I'd known since I was a young boy at Church of the Open Door. Their father, Big Al, worked with my father at Quality Frame and Door, in Cerritos. Barbie-dollish and rail-skinny, Cindy and Cathy were goofy girls with long blond hair, freckles, and super-gawky, narrow faces—more homely than cute. But they were diffident toward me, and that's who I wanted to want me.

I was especially smitten with Cindy. I don't remember how I got the money, but one Sunday morning I walked up to her, said that I liked her, and handed her one dollar bill. After some relentless coercing, she took the dollar.

Later that night, Big Al called my dad and told him what I'd done. My father called me into the living room and confronted me. I don't remember his being mad as much as maybe a bit curious about what was going on in my head. He told me not to do that again, that it wasn't polite to give someone money like that.

I was confused. This made no sense to me. I for one was envious of the money that other people had. In fact, I was thoroughly impressed by their displays of wealth—the clothes they wore, the cars their parents drove, the homes they lived in, the things their families could afford beyond my own. So how was I going to get some of that covetousness directed at myself if I wasn't allowed to demonstrate some easy access to money?

I made a similar mistake many years later when I worked at the Crocodile Café in Pasadena, during the time that I was robbing banks. A bartender named Emilio used to have his wife bring their beautiful boy to the restaurant during his breaks. Julio would always run to me when he came into the restaurant. I'd play with him, lifting him and suspending him horizontally in the air to cruise him around as if he were Superman in flight. But one day I didn't have time to play with him so I just gave him a dollar bill. He was so excited, he ran to show his parents.

Emilio, who was usually very friendly with me, stomped over and scolded me. It was as if I'd slipped my hand into the kid's shirt and touched him inappropriately. Emilio shoved the dollar bill into my hand.

*Don't give my kid money anymore. What's wrong with you?*

I heard echoes of Big Al's dissatisfaction, and I wanted to slug Emilio in the mouth.

With Cindy Alexander I was getting the lay of the land, trying to see clearly the ethic of the world: I was only going to get a wife or friends, or amass prestige, power, and influence—in other words, get ahead—if I had money, or could demonstrate financial liquidity.

Seeing the world in such a naked and vulgar way could only of course, lead my immature mind to imagine an obscene exchange of money for female affection. Hadn't that been the lesson I was learning on the playground? Wasn't I simply being honest about the world? With my father's scolding I resented the duplicity of a world that challenged me to apply its instruction but became revolted by my application of the lessons. I didn't think that the adults around me were being intellectually honest with themselves, and I now began to believe that my intelligence was outpacing the puerile moralities that had enveloped me all my childhood.

▥▥▥▥▥▥▥▥

While I was riding around on a girly pink bike in my aunt Maggie's neighborhood, or getting beaten up by bullies, it was Brenda, my stepmother, who gave the striver in me new incentive to be more American than America, who made me feel that I could own the English language. It was Brenda who polished the ghetto's gutter stain off my English:

*You don't "win" your brother in a basketball game. You "win" a trophy. The correct way to say it is "I beat my brother in a one-on-one basketball game."*

*Don't ask your brother, "Where was he at?" It's sufficient to ask "Where was he?"*

*And don't ask, "Who did you go with?" Sentences aren't supposed to end with prepositions.*

I aspired to please Brenda because with her I had access to a smart and beautiful white woman's approval.

One day I came home from school and boasted to Brenda that I'd fought some kid who had said "Your momma" to me. I expected her to reward my chivalry with a smile or maybe a homemade brownie.

*Don't you ever do something stupid like that again. Words don't hurt me. Especially the words of a thirteen-year-old boy. I don't ever want to hear again that you're fighting for me. Do you hear me?*

*Yeah.*

*Yeah, what?*

*Yeah, I won't fight anymore.*

*Honestly. I've never heard of such nonsense.*

▥▥▥▥▥▥▥▥

I used to sit in my independent study class and daydream of one day owning the entire school, Montebello Intermediate, and converting it into a family compound. I'd draw elaborate schematics of the property and detailed floor plans of each building, remodeling them in my imagination into residences that I'd give to my family members. Only immediate family would be allowed to live in the recently constructed homeroom building. I would occupy the entire second floor, while my dad, Brenda, and Paul would each occupy a third of the bottom classrooms. The library, cafeteria, music room, tennis courts, and playing fields, would always remain open for the communal use of all compound residents. All the bathrooms were to remain open for communal use as well. I liked the idea of a commune, but for *others*. The bathrooms on the top floor would be out of bounds to everyone but me. I didn't think any of the other compound residents would complain. After all I had magnanimously provided them with their own large living spaces.

Like all utopias, I'd have to keep some family members out. In this case, my same-age aunt Lucy would be exiled. Banishing my grandmother's youngest daughter would be a thorny family problem, threatening to disrupt family peace, so I decided I'd appease my grandma Nellie by giving her the gymnasium, and I'd buy great big chandeliers to hang from the rafters.

There were plenty of male adults in the family—men like Uncle David and Uncle Tony, who were Vietnam vets—whom I could have looked to as future patriarchs of the family. My grandpa was still alive, too. But none of the men in my family excited anything resembling true submission in my heart. So I dreamed of being the shot-caller of the family compound, imagined myself Pa from the TV show *Bonanza*. The school was to be my Ponderosa. Family members would love me, praise my magnanimity, show me fealty, proudly affiliate themselves with me, and toast to my success. And Montebelloans of all stripes would point and whisper to each other when they saw me walking down the street.

*Hey, you see that boy? He gave his grandmother an entire gymnasium to live in.*

One day I was playing football with friends after school at Ashiya Park. My good friend Ronnie Tarrazas tackled me head on. When I fell, my head slammed on the hard ground and I got a concussion.

My friends knew I was dazed because I couldn't continue playing. Instead, I wandered around asking them questions. *Who am I? What were you saying?* They thought I was joking at first. So Carlos and Caesar teased me. Carlos told me a fantastic lie about Eleanor Nanci and Joanne Bogdanoff, the two most attractive girls in our junior-high class. Carlos and Caesar told me that Eleanor and Joanne were lesbians. "Lezbos," I think they called them. I was shocked, and they laughed at my extreme gullibility.

Whatever topic came up, I would fiercely attach myself to its suggestion for ten seconds before the flash just slipped away, as if my mind hadn't any traction and I'd never held the thought at all.

The game concluded, and as we walked home I continued repeating the questions *Who am I? What were you saying?* Each time they retold the lie to me I was both drawn to and repulsed by the idea of Joanne's and Eleanor's public and shameful lesbianism, and I responded as if hearing the story for the first time.

When I arrived at my apartment, Paul escorted me to my bedroom. But I walked to the kitchen and asked Brenda when she expected my dad to get home from the hospital, where his job was to rent TVs to patients. She answered, and I returned to my bedroom. Then I went to the kitchen and asked again.

She'd answer, and I'd walk back to my bedroom. Then I'd walk back to the kitchen and repeat the sequence.

Brenda became tired of what she thought was an attention-getting game. When my father arrived, she told him what I'd been doing. He called me to the dining room and asked me to sit next to him. He looked hostile. I thought he was upset that I'd been injured by local hooligans. (Paul had told Brenda about my fall.) I interpreted his tension as angry concern.

I was relieved when he asked me if I was faking my injury, lying about my condition. Lying was a bad thing to do in our home. There was always chile juice in our refrigerator that my father could make us drink if we lied. But I couldn't be lying about my condition, because I didn't know what condition my father was referring to. I felt safe when I answered no. I thought I'd cleared up his confusion.

Then he slugged me on the side of the face. *WHAP!*

I was knocked off my chair and onto the floor. Too scared to plead or protest, I placed the chair upright and sat in it when he demanded, *Get up! Are you lying?*

*No.*

*Whap! Get up! Are you lying?*

*No.*

*Whap! Get up!*

The next morning I awoke as if from some Kafkaesque nightmare. I vaguely remembered my father pummeling me. I had a crushing headache. I asked my brother to fill in my memory gaps from the night before. (When one of us was getting whacked around in the dining room, the other would sneak out of the bedroom and peek through a heater grate in the hallway.) Paul was the one who gave me the blow-by-blow account.

That was the fall of 1974. I'd just turned thirteen.

▓▓▓▓▓▓▓▓▓▓

If someone had asked me to write an essay about what I did that summer I couldn't have told them. And it was a whopper.

I hung out at Crawford's Market on Whittier Boulevard collecting shopping carts to run through a machine in the store that punched out green stamps that could be used to buy stuff like transistor radios or board games. I made it known to my Hensel Gardens neighbors that I was available to make quick grocery runs to the store. I would race to the supermarket to buy their tortillas, eggs, juice, or laundry detergent, and they'd give me a tip, which I'd spend on candy and soda.

Lorelei was a twenty-two-year-old neighbor who asked me to run to the store and buy her a dozen eggs and a loaf of Wonder Bread. Her husband was in the service and was frequently gone. When I returned to her front door, she called to me from deep inside her apartment. I entered. Her voice in the back room instructed me to put the groceries on the kitchen counter. Then she called me to the back bedroom for my tip. I walked down a short corridor into a shadowy bedroom. Although it was midday, she had the curtains drawn. I saw her money lying on the dresser on one side of the room. On the opposite side of the room she was lying naked on her stomach on a large unmade bed.

*Go ahead. Take what you want.*

*What?*

*Take what you want on the dresser.*

*Okay.* I walked to the bed and placed the bedsheet over her brown butt. *You're naked,* I said.

*Oh, I didn't know. Oh, thanks.* She squirmed under the sheets a bit.

I went to the dresser and put the change in my pocket. Then I walked back to the bed and unbuttoned my shorts and let them fall to my ankles.

*What are you doing?*

*I'm undressing.*

She pulled the blanket off her naked body and rolled around onto her back. I pulled off my briefs. Her nipples were dark and rubbery looking, browner than deep chocolate, almost black. And her pubic hair spread onto her inner thighs.

I mounted her like the good wannabe missionary I didn't want to be. She raised and spread her legs, then reached down and guided my slender penis into her hairy wetness. A sheet flew across my vision, and her face was instantly shrouded so that I couldn't conceive of kissing her mouth, and could only guess at her lovemaking expression.

I moved a little, mostly letting her grind up against me. At one point she reached behind me, grabbed my small ass cheeks, and pulled me hard into her. When she climaxed, she dropped her legs and lay still. All the bedspring noises went silent, like an earthquake's sharp halting, along with the awkward grunts and sloppy flesh slapping. This seriously frustrated my earnest efforts. I thrust into her a few more times, then gave up. (I once met a necrophile, in prison, and asked him how he could get his jollies from dead-muscled corpses. He answered, *How would I know. I wasn't trying to get pleasure for myself. I was only trying to please them.*) I didn't want to get Lorelei mad. I wanted her to love me. I needed to feel wanted. I had confused Lorelei's lust for love.

I walked out of the dimly lit bedroom and stepped into a dark bathroom. I turned on the light to investigate the phenomenon that was my glistening pink-tipped protrusion. I saw Lorelei's wetness on my puny, slightly throbbing, barely hard boy's prick. Something like a milky substance was caught in the thin, veiny folds of my already shortening length.

For the next eight years, Lorelei let me knead her big, full breasts in private. Sometimes we even role-played. I'd pretend to bump into her in the elevator, knocking her purse out of her hands. Then she'd pretend to show up at my apartment, randy, making herself available for casual sex.

Knock, knock.

*Who is it?*

*Hmm! You don't know me, but my name's Wendy.*

*Yeah?*

*We bumped into each other in the elevator downtown the other day. I dropped my purse, and you helped me pick up my stuff. I think you dropped something in my purse.*

I was desperate for a woman's love, for adult female attention beyond Brenda's. Instead, Lorelei gave me her warm sex, which I accepted, even though it was a dirty closeness, comfort attached to a stigma.

When she showed up at some of our family gatherings, I'd follow her around the house, in and out of the kitchen, through the hallway into the back part of the bedroom, and while everyone was outside she'd lift her blouse and let me suck on her nipples.

When we had more time, she'd allow me to inspect her vagina up close, down on my knees. I'd pull open the outer lips with my fingers to investigate those folds that always exuded a faint odor of pee (except one time, when she applied some strawberry sundae–flavored cream down there). She'd let me lick her as she ground her pelvis into my face. But even though she was generous with her flesh, and let me see her entire body—explore her pussy and her puckered anus—she never let me see her guilty eyes during sex.

That's when I began to admire Brenda's heavy breasts, the way their fullness pulled her sweaters down in the front, like on one of Russ Meyer's lusty vixens. (Brenda was the same age as Lorelei.) Sometimes I would examine Brenda's warm bras, fresh out of the dryer, to imagine the heft and swell of her generous bust. I always imagined spongy pink nipples that smelled of the bath oil she kept in a large yellow green plastic bottle near the bathtub. I wondered about the size and contour of her areolas. Silver-dollar circumference? Smooth and flush with the curve? Or tight, puny circles, dotted with something like goose bumps?

Her nearness to me was erotic. I would look for gestures that might suggest she understood my desire for her. But there was no erotic warmth in Brenda, nothing sexually animated about her movements. At night when my brother and I would say goodnight to her, giving her a quick peck on the cheek, we'd receive only a judicious "thank you" and a "goodnight" in return.

I yearned to be nearer to Brenda, to prove myself worthy of her affection. But since I would not have access to the taste of her sex, I recommitted myself to making her vocabulary and literary tastes my own.

▮▮▮▮▮▮▮▮▮

Growing up, I knew that my parents had been married at age sixteen. I knew my mom was six months older than my father. I also knew that they'd dropped out of Garfield High School, the school made famous in *Stand and Deliver*, a Hollywood film about a math teacher who turns intellectually lethargic Mexican students into math whizzes. And I knew that part of my father's Christian conversion "testimony" centered around what a bad kid he was in junior high, something of a thug with a heart of gold when he caught my mother's eye. I knew all the bad things they wanted me to know. (One of the convenient prerogatives of being a parent.)

But I didn't know the sly, wink-wink nature of the "you know what" my mother hinted at in my father's yearbook, that is, not until one day in Mr. Tolstrup's eighth-grade homeroom class I did the math and realized that my devout parents had got married exactly four and a half months before I was born. And when I did the math further, I realized that my parents had started having sex at roughly the same age that I did.

▮▮▮▮▮▮▮▮▮

The mixed messages from my father—the Gospel's "turn the other cheek" ethic versus the macho "don't let the bullies whip your ass" ethic—disoriented me. I dreaded cataclysm all the time. I was still waking up to touch Paul's flesh to make sure he hadn't turned cold. And if a teacher noticed my attention wandering in class, or if I wasn't getting my typically high grades, they'd hold me after school and exhort me to do better, as if my distracted performance could simply be chalked up to adolescent rebelliousness.

As a Bible-reading boy, I read and studied the great nineteenth-century evangelist and Bible expositors, Charles Finney and Charles Spurgeon. My Baptist upbringing brought into our home a daily King James Bible text and biographies of famous English missionaries. I swore a high oath to God when I read how his courageous missionary, the remarkable Hudson Taylor, set up, against terrible odds, the Inland Road China Mission to save a heathen China.

In public, I was a bright and pious boy who taught Bible classes to my peers at church and spoke about a future in the ministry. But in private I was tortured by my "adult affair"—good, secret sex that deeply satisfied me physically but made me feel guilty when I thought that my mother could look down from heaven and see me lying on top of Lorelei.

But I was becoming comfortable with the concept that some people could conceal or compromise the meaning of words, or otherwise commute the hard truth of language, saying one thing but meaning another. I didn't have a specific term for it, but I was toying with implementing sophisticated words like *duplicity* and *disingenuous* as my new ethic, without knowing their consequences.

My distrust of authority figures ripened. I continued to have nightmares and see vagina juices on my penis. And I continued to miss seeing my father's left hooks coming.

# V

Heavy D was so fat that a judge ordered the bailiffs to escort him to the post office and weigh him on a postal scale. He weighed 673 pounds.

On Heavy's court days a guard would enter the tier with a box full of newly sewn clothing, made to be worn only once. The guard would stretch his arms as wide as possible, like he was yawning, and unfurl a pair of lime-green boxers (the size of a flag that might fly over a government building) and say, "Heavy, we brought that sexy lingerie you asked for."

Each brown boot resembled a fully stuffed backpack. The khaki shirt looked like a small tent, with a chest pocket large enough to hold a regular-size binder. The khaki pants were almost a parody of pants, as if they'd been made to be worn by giant performing circus bears clumsily riding unicycles and banging tin drums.

Heavy was in solitary confinement because he'd socked a lieutenant in the mouth and broken his jaw. He was going to court and the U.S. Attorney was trying to give him ten to fifteen years for the assault.

Heavy D pleaded insanity. He even stood up in court, held his arms out, and said to the judge: "Look at me. Look at how fat I am. What do you think? This ain't normal. I'm not right."

The judge took pity and ordered the Bureau of Prisons to force Heavy D to lose weight. So he was moved to the hospital wing, where he was shackled to his bed and forced to go on a liquid diet. That's when they moved me into his cell.

# Stain

One spring morning, while prowling the school hallways before class, I yanked down the metal handle of a fire alarm and broke the thin glass bar that activated a loud buzzer. Ha! Ha! Big laughs all around. My friends thought I was cool. Over the next few days, I set off four more fire alarms.

A pretty blonde girl who'd never spoken to me before asked me to pull an alarm in the afternoon to interrupt a test she hadn't prepared for. I couldn't escape my classroom, so I simply yanked on the alarm in Mr. Tolstrup's homeroom class. The entire student body emptied their classrooms and marched out to the football field, where we waited for twenty minutes before we were told that everything was clear and we could now safely return to class.

Some of the student body was aware that I was the one pulling the alarms, and yet they kept their mouths shut. I appreciated this. I also enjoyed feeling like I was subverting authority. And I felt positively elated that I, puny little cries-his-eyes-out-like-a-little-girl-when-he-gets-his-assed-whupped-by-his-dad me, could make the entire school stop on my whim while the adults scurried about, worried about a true emergency. I loved agitating momentary terror in the staff.

Once we returned to the classroom and found our seats, Vice-

Principal Norton entered our room and explained that the glass bar in the fire alarm next to the pencil sharpener in our classroom had been broken, which meant that the culprit had been someone in our class. Mr. Tolstrup went around the room and asked every student where he or she was standing when the alarm went off. I said that I was standing next to Irma.

*Was he next to you, Irma?*

*No. No, he wasn't.*

*Yeah, I was. I was behind her.*

I looked at Irma with something like subtle supplication in my eyes: "*Don't do this to me, Irma. Look, I'm even giving you an out. Just say that I could have been behind you, that you're not sure.*"

*Think carefully, Irma. Could he have been behind you?*

*He wasn't anywhere near me. He's lying.*

*I was right next to her!*

Mr. Norton was a tall man, square-jawed. He could have been a college athlete but he walked stiffly, as if he wore a full-torso cast to keep his spine straight. He couldn't swivel his head, so if someone called to him from behind he'd have to turn his entire body.

Mr. Tolstrup harrumphed and briskly stated, *Well, this'll just have to be straightened out in Mr. Norton's office.*

I defied them to prove empirically—oh yeah, I was smarmy enough to employ words like *empirical* and *epistemology* at age twelve, mostly to embarrass Mr. Martinez, my P.E. coach—that I'd pulled the alarm.

*C'mon, Joe. This has your intelligence all over it. No wonder we couldn't figure out who pulled the other alarms. You're smarter than the other kids.* They were playing to my idiotic vanity.

Well, it was about damn time adults were taking note of my craftiness, my ability to dupe them like they'd duped me. So I broke down and confessed. Vice-Principal Norton took me into his office. He didn't praise me anymore when he told me to bend over his desk so that he could whack me three times with a thick paddle with six two-inch holes drilled through it.

Mr. Norton and the head principal, Mr. Monsour, were getting ready to telephone my father to explain that I'd be suspended for a week. I didn't have enough time to beg God to install the next phase of his eschatological calendar, so I begged and pleaded with both principals not to notify my dad. I said that my father beat me when he was upset. Ms. Babcock had joined us. She told me to sit outside while they conferred for a half hour in Mr. Norton's office. I stood outside and nursed a sore butt. Finally they called me back into the office and told me that they wouldn't telephone my father. Instead, I was to hand my father an envelope and ask him to call them immediately.

*Oh, by the way,* Mr. Monsour added, *you'd won the school's American Legion Award, but because of your little shenanigans, you better believe that the award will now go to someone else.*

This dig, piled on top of punishment and suspension, was gratuitous and offended my sense of fair play. I'd deviated from the rules, I'd got caught, and they'd punished me. That should have been that. But no, Mr. Monsour somehow took my "shenanigans" personally, as if I'd set off his *home* alarm. Taking it personally, being petty and feeling wounded all the time, was something that I usually did. But now here was someone, ostensibly an authority figure, someone who was supposed to be an example of how to behave in society, behaving with schoolyard petulance, a smallness that I recognized in my father.

My dad had an eerie habit of peppering our beatings with mocking words. He'd punch us and say, *Thought I wasn't going to find out, huh?* Or he'd slap us and instruct us, *See what happens when you lie to me?* Or he'd kick us on the floor and sarcastically ask us in a *tsk tsk* tone, *It's not fun getting caught, is it?* And he'd rhetorically coerce an admission that the beatings had merit, *Are you going to obey me next time?*

From my dad I learned the scary habit of taunting my victims, with verbal threats and demeaning comments, while robbing or assaulting them.

*If you have a God, you'd better start praying that I don't get fuckin' pissed.*
*See what happens when you fuck with me?*
*Merry Christmas, motherfucker!*

I went home and tucked the suspension notice under my mattress. Every morning, for four days, I walked to school before classes began, only to return home to watch TV when I knew that my dad and Brenda had gone to work.

I felt betrayed by Irma the Cossack. (My dad had read me a short story entitled, "The Most Dangerous Game," from one of his literature textbooks. There was a Cossack character named General Zaloff. I knew that Cossacks were Russian, and since there was a contingent of Russian-Americans in our school, I lumped Irma in with them, calling her Irma the Cossack behind her back.) In my opinion, Irma the Cossack was of the caste that was supposed to defer to and protect her schoolyard betters.

In most cases, I figured that white bested brown, that even white trash trumped generic brownness. But, according to the bizarre ethnic calculus in my imagination, I assumed that in this one rare instance my brownness trumped Irma's whiteness.

Yeah, she was white, but she had minuses that demoted her below my brownness. First, she was plain—homely and fat. Granted, she had pretty eyes, but her personality was sour. In fact, in our school a boy would often be ridiculed by being accused of liking Irma, as in *I saw you kissing Irma behind the gym*. Some guys said she looked like a boy so they called her Irmo. Her second strike against her: She wasn't particularly smart or witty. Also, she was a follower, with no real talent, not compelling in any way at an age when opinions begin to matter about the way you'll be categorized later in high school. The fourth minus against her was the fact that she had attended public schools all her life, unlike me who'd attended private schools for the first six school years. As far as I was concerned I was studied, and had hobnobbed with wealthy, smart, middle- and upper-middle-class white kids. Sure, her parents were steadfastly middle class, she was on her way to college, could or would marry into money, and was generally ahead of me in the bigger game, the grander scheme of things, but in my twisted arithmetic of color I didn't recognize that her whiteness was a privilege over me, because I felt that through my schooling I'd had my station elevated above white trailer trash.

She was my inferior, and she had upset the school hierarchy—the unpopular had rebelled against the gifted. This was as dangerous to me as it would be if all over the country the nerds became the popular kids.

*I was standing next to Irma.*

I'd given her an easy lob, right over the center of the plate. Even she could have hit that one out of the park. I thought of myself as some sort of Ferris Bueller, the popular kid giving her an opportunity to do me a favor, to lie in order to protect me, giving her an "in" into the realm of legitimacy. (I wasn't totally delusional: I was well liked and considered gifted by students and teachers. Hadn't the school staff voted for me to get the American Legion Award?)

If Irma hadn't Judas-kissed me like that, I would never have given her the name Irma the Cossack. In fact, I would have stood up for her, real chivalrous-like, if I had heard anyone else use such a name for her, even something that *sounded* like Cossack, like carsick or cod sack. I might even have told her how pretty she looked when I noticed that she'd spent a little more time getting herself dolled up for school. And you know what? Eventually—although this was a long shot—I could even have considered going out with her for a week or two, to smooch and maybe cop a feel, but also to give her some status, make her more mysterious and therefore more attractive to the other boys. The other boys would see that I liked her and figure that if Ferris Bueller liked her then she must be pretty good. That's it. I was upset with her because she couldn't see how I would have bestowed all this juicy ripeness on her if she'd only backed my play, recognized that I was giving her a chance to provide me with an alibi.

But no. She had to go and prize honesty and integrity over the virtue of doing the right thing by a popular kid.

*He wasn't anywhere near me. He's lying.*

She'd stabbed me in the back and forfeited all my phantom largesse. See what happens when a man casts his pearls before swine? That's why I needed to pay back Irma.

I wasn't allowed on the campus during my suspension, so I told Jessie, Sal, and Mark Mendez—we always called him Mark Mendez, never just Mark—to circulate a petition asking our fellow classmates to sign, promising to shun Irma the Snitching Cossack. Sixteen boys signed the petition on the first day. Four the following day. None by the third day.

▉▉▉▉▉▉▉▉▉▉

Brenda was church secretary, and the money she and my dad collected for their offering was kept at home, in their bedroom. During that week of suspension, I got a butter knife from the silverware drawer and set to work burglarizing the wooden chest where they kept rolls of ones, fives, tens, and twenties, tucked into small church offering envelopes. I'd pilfer one or two dollar bills from each envelope. The score was about twenty bucks, enough for me to take all my friends to Foster's Freeze for cheeseburgers, strawberry floats, and hot tortilla chips drenched in diluted guacamole sauce.

During my week of suspension, Jessie, Sal, and Mark Mendez ditched school and hung out at my place during the day. On one of those recreational school-suspension days, I walked into Thrifty Drugs and stole six *rad* lime-green and neon raspberry-colored flex skateboards, the rave of the day. I was handing the skateboards to the guys outside when the manager raced out of the store. We spun and zipped up a steep hill behind the store, but the manager was stronger and faster than we were, so he gained ground pretty quickly. He took to the hill, scrambling easily up the embankment. He would have caught me too, if Mark Mendez hadn't turned and tossed three skateboards at his feet so that he lost his purchase on the loose dirt and slid down the hill. We jumped over a low wall, into a parking lot, and dispersed into a large newly built community of condominiums.

After a few minutes we all found each other and laughed at the adventure. And just as in a movies—where criminals prematurely celebrate their getaway only to find a tenacious cop on their asses—an Orowheat bread delivery truck suddenly turned the corner, tires screeching, and stopped sharply at a curb. A big, athletic-looking Mexican fellow wearing a brown uniform, leapt out of the doorless vehicle and started chasing us. I recognized him as the man who was having the manager sign something as I fled the store. We took off running again. I yelled

"Von's!" We dispersed again and reunited at the supermarket five blocks away.

A few minutes later we shoplifted grapes, cigarettes, sodas, Twinkies, and donuts. Mark Mendez pocketed a few girlie magazines. The boys came to my place and drank booze from small airline bottles that our friend Walter had brought from home. (Walter's dad unloaded luggage at LAX.) As my friends were leaving my place drunk late in the afternoon, Mark Mendez tore pages out of the girlie magazines and shoved them into the mailboxes of the tenants in my apartment building. I laughed and thought nothing of this.

When my father came home, he became suspicious of the lewd material he'd found shoved into our mailbox. While Paul and I played outside, he went into our room and searched for pornography. Instead he found the suspension note under my mattress.

He yelled out the window for me to come inside. As I approached the house, I saw him at my bedroom window, peering down at me, cocksure. When I entered the kitchen he took one swift step toward me and slugged me hard in the solar plexus. I fell backward against the kitchen counter, then to the ground, gasping for air. He kicked me, punched me in the face, dragged me across the floor by my hair, and continued to beat me until my skin was a patchwork of purple bruises.

The suspension was over, but I couldn't go to school for several days. I stayed with my grandma Nellie for my father's enforced daily detention. My father gave me his college algebra textbook and told me that I had to teach myself a chapter a day and do the homework assigned at the end of each chapter.

*And don't look at the answers in the back of the book.*

The answers didn't help anyway. They actually sort of mocked me, the solution dangled just beyond my reach. *(Nah-nah, nah-nah, you can't figure me out.)* My dad intended me to write out the full problem, to show my work. I thought that I could somehow work backward from the answer, but my mind was too foggy, too full of dread, completely unable to focus or concentrate. I was punished for three nights because I couldn't figure out how to do the work.

I returned to school a week after my beating. I couldn't wait to graduate to the ninth grade. I wanted change so badly.

Ms. Babcock was hugely disappointed in me. After I was suspended, the faculty had to scramble to find another "best all-around student" to give the American Legion Award to. Bobby Estrada, an oddly mature kid with huge feet, got it. I wasn't too upset. Rumor had it that Bobby's sixth grade girlfriend had been abducted and her body parts were later found wrapped in plastic bags in one of the neighborhood alley dumpsters.

▌▌▌▌▌▌▌▌▌▌

Due in part to my Absalom-like rebellion, my father quit the pastorate, giving the elders the excuse that he couldn't minister to other folks as long as his house wasn't in order. What he meant was that Brenda feared him and sometimes his sons couldn't go to school because too many bruises on their faces and the backs of their thighs meant the risk of too many questions. He actually gathered Brenda, Paul, and me together and told us that he wasn't qualified to be a pastor because his own behavior in our home wasn't morally up to snuff.

After my father quit preaching at *Iglesia Bautista Fundamental*, we needed a church to attend. Grace Community Church in the San Fernando Valley was a forty-minute drive from our Montebello apartment, but after the C.O.D. congregation split, a large group of them began to attend Grace to hear a young upstart exegete named John MacArthur Jr. (Rumors had him related to General MacArthur.)

I.Q. tests administered in the eighth grade confirmed that my new church friend, Randy Wallingford, was a genius. (In the summer before tenth grade he attended UCLA and aced calculus and chemistry.) I used to hang out at his home, and in the summers I was often allowed to stay there for several days. Randy had a book in his library entitled *The Cross and the Switchblade*, written by Nicky Cruz, ex-member of the Puerto Rican New York gang the Mau-Maus. Nicky Cruz was now a Pentecostal minister, and his autobiography was one of those Christian testimonials written in the sensational style of "look how bad I was before God got hold of my life and humbled me." (My dad's own conversion testimony had been like that of a gang member who finds Jesus.) Nicky Cruz was Puerto Rican, and he was called a spic a lot in his book. I was happy that I wasn't a spic. Mexicans were called beaners. (I preferred the word *beaner*, rather than *spic*. *Beaner* sounded more elevated.) Anyway, my dad wasn't a spic, but I did think of him as the Mexican version of Nicky Cruz.

Nicky was a confused kid with a lot of rage, which I understood, but I had to put the book down when I read how he and his boys would hold an enemy's arms out like he was hanging on a cross and then stab their switchblades into his armpits. Such barbarity! How could God save such heinous youth? In church there were arguments that even Hitler could have gone to heaven if he had made a last-minute deathbed confession. But I felt that God shouldn't overlook any savagery.

A part of me liked the bravado of gang kids, and I tried to mimic the tough-guy stuff at school. But I also knew that kids like Danny Nuñez and his ilk would never see me as one of them. So, while I was attracted to the image of the Nicky Cruzes and Danny Nuñezes, I also resented that I couldn't be them. I secretly wished that they would get their comeuppance, would be brought low. If I wasn't brave enough to move beyond connivance and be a true lawbreaker, then I wanted the law to break all refractory boys who had the balls to act without fear, mostly the tough brown kids who I wanted to be but never could.

▓▓▓▓▓▓▓▓▓

In 1976 several elders approached my father and asked him to help start Spanish-speaking services. When the famous evangelist Luis Palau, the Billy Graham of South America, came to the States to speak at our church, my father was asked to ride along with the elders when they went to the airport to pick Palau up.

My dad's star soon rose in our new Grace Church community. He was the darling of the white elder elite, many of them ex-C.O.D. members. There was a sort of old-boy network that treated my father with deference. He had loved the Bible enough as a young man to begin teaching himself Greek and Hebrew, so he'd proved his devotion to God.

None of this was lost on me. I noticed who the important men were and how they sometimes huddled with my father before or after services. He was being groomed, which made me feel like a prince, afforded some privilege for my proximity to him—the inspiring speaker, the talented linguist, the strong-willed, self-educated, driven man, the real deal, the genuine article.

I also had a nagging feeling in my heart that his reputation was a house of cards. If the elders knew how he behaved at home, they wouldn't admire him so much. In my book, he was a fraud. I took two lessons from this: First, it was possible to be a good pretender if you could throw a lot of legitimate Bible knowledge around. This led to the second realization: The congregation could be impressed by the hype if only a few elders (with some spiritual clout) could be duped.

Thus the seeds of my religious disillusion were planted: Here was my father, acknowledged as an instrument of God, clearly deceiving men to whom I would otherwise have attributed spiritual insight.

There was a joke among the Mexicans I knew in prison. A customer walks into a fresh fish store and sees two buckets of water. Two crabs are inside the first bucket, while two crabs are crawling around *outside* the second bucket. The customer points at the free crabs and asks the owner, "What kind of crabs are these?

"Those are American crabs," the owner replies. "When one got out he helped the other one get out too."

"Well, then," the customer asked while pointing at the two crabs inside the bucket, "What kind of crabs are these two?"

"Them two are Mexican crabs. Every time one starts to get close to getting out, the other one pulls him back down."

I was beginning to feel like a Mexican crab. I couldn't stand to let my father get away with his canard so easily. If I had my way, he would not escape our dirty, sludgy family bucket.

▮▮▮▮▮▮▮▮▮▮

During talent contests at Grace Church camp, other kids asked me if I knew any Cheech and Chong stuff. My aunt Rosemary's boyfriend, a member of the notorious biker club, the Mongols, had several Cheech and Chong comedy albums that I'd listened to when she babysat us at her house. I'd replayed the albums over and over again to memorize their jokes. For two years in junior high, I performed watered-down Cheech and Chong skits at church camps, to an audience of a hundred and fifty white San Fernando Valley kids. I had them in stitches. But I was a brown Pagliacco (the tearful clown who disguised his sorrow by performing the funny role). Several fathers of the white girls at my church told their daughters that we could be friends, but under no circumstances were we allowed to date.

Cindy Smith liked me, but her father (a house painter) commanded her never to consider me as a potential mate. She apologized to me, and soon after her decision to obey her father, she and Randy became boyfriend and girlfriend. I was devastated. This blatant relegation of me to brown beta-male was a rejection I felt helpless to challenge.

I suspected that more of my friends' parents were bigoted too, but without the public gall or occasion of Mr. Smith who I began to fantasize about injuring. Not by simply excluding him from my future Montebello compound, but by sneaking up on him with a friend and hitting him with bats. Or maybe stabbing him in the armpits.

In the Old Testament, God once communicated to King Saul that he wanted to make the Amalekites pay for treating Israel badly when they were leaving Egypt: *Now go, attack the Amalekites, and totally destroy everything that belongs to them. Do not spare them: Put to death men and women, children and infants, cattle and sheep, camels and donkeys.*

There wasn't any need to blame literature or lax cultural mores or Hollywood's glamorization of violence in films for dementing my imagination and enabling me to fantasize about committing great bodily harm. No. I had the Bible for that. (Though no one in my church thought that this kind of cruel and vengeful God might be giving me ideas.) In the Bible, payback was as good a motive as any for men to commence a good day of civilian bloodshed. It was Bible stories that first taught me that shed blood is required for personal salvation. It was Christian theology that introduced me to the notion that the Kingdom arrives only after apocalypse.

▐▐▐▐▐▐▐▐▐▐

My belief in the sanctity of God's temple diminished rapidly in those days. I accepted the fact that the man of God in my home was a religious fraud. Could my faith also be false? I rebelled in small ways. I'd pass riddles to my friends in church while the pastor sermonized.

Q: *What stretches further: Flesh or rubber?*
A: *Flesh. The Bible says that Balaam tied his ass to a tree and walked two miles.*

At one church camp, we kids were told to write our greatest sin on a slip of paper. We anonymously tossed the folded notes into a hat being passed around. I wrote the word "Adultery." Only one other kid was more wicked than I. He wrote that he had committed the abominable sin of homosexuality. I didn't feel quite so guilty that evening.

I took sexual sin seriously, but I also knew that Southern Baptists were the laughingstock of many other denominations, with our hardcore Baptist prohibitions against living a life of drink, dance, and coitus.

The way I distinguished pre-marital sex and adultery in my head bothered me. Sin was sin in God's eyes, I was taught. But I always categorized sexual sins as more deviant and grave. Still, I knew that my conscience had been shaped by an insane religiosity, and that my ideas about human sensuality were absurd when I looked at them the way an unbeliever would. Soon, I was poking fun at my own puritanical community, at my dogmatic self, with more riddles passed down the pew.

Q: *Why don't Baptists make love standing up?*
A: *Someone might see them and mistakenly believe that they are dancing.*

## 1975, Mariposa Street, Burbank

I was told that we were moving to Burbank so that we could avoid the forty-five-minute Sunday drives to the San Fernando Valley. (The true reason for the move came out later.) Our new apartment was ten minutes from Grace Church.

My brother and I perceived Burbank as our move out of the ghetto. (Montebello was an ocean of brown. Burbank was a foamy white sea.) We unpacked our clothes and sang a modified version of the theme song to the popular TV sitcom *The Jeffersons*.

*We're moving on up, to the Northside*
*To a deluxe apartment in the sky*
*We're moving on up, to the Northside*
*We finally got our piece of the pie.*

Bob and Sharon Litts, friends from my mom and dad's Joint Heirs days at C.O.D., had purchased a home with five back-property apartments. We moved into apartment D. I was just starting the ninth grade.

My brother and I enrolled at Luther Burbank Junior High. Each morning we'd sit on a brick wall in front of the school and watch the students walk up or spill out of station wagons, distinguishing who belonged to what clique. We spotted the insecure kids like us and learned who were the popular ones. It was pretty easy to figure that out since the members of the Student Council wore green letterman sweaters with yellow collegiate stripes on the sleeves. Almost every girl who wore that sweater was blonde, except for Lisa Solis, a sweet, short gymnast who was also the best drama student.

I tried to make friends at Luther Burbank. In homeroom I sat next to a geeky-looking boy with an atrocious case of acne and thick plastic-framed glasses: Danny Shaw.

*How'd you get that scar on your hand?* I asked him one day.

He turned to me. He didn't speak for a moment, then he said, *A spic from my last school knifed me.*

Danny was also a transfer student. He and his younger brother, Larry, lived with their mother in a rented home on my way to school. By semester's end we became best friends. I'd phone him in the morning and let him know that I was leaving the house, and five minutes later we'd meet at the corner of Victory Boulevard and Buena Vista. He'd ride his ten-speed next to me while I walked.

Danny's father was a Vietnam vet. *Soldier of Fortune* magazines and corny paperback war novels littered Danny's room. He was a faithful reader of the Remo Williams pulp fiction series, about a rehabilitated tough guy who relies on his wit and the ubiquitous presence of a sly Chinese master to bust up bad guys. (Joel Grey later played the Chinese master in the film adaptation.) Danny, a Remo wannabe, studied the martial arts with a Korean teacher named Kim Soo Young. The dojo was a rundown storefront in a dilapidated Burbank mall.

During my first semester in Burbank, mock elections were held in Mr. Wasserman's government class, as a civics lesson about the electoral process. I'd become popular in class with my humorous interruptions, so I was nominated to run against my new friend, Pam Franke, one of the girls who wore the coveted green letterman sweaters of the Student Council. She and I courted delegates for the red-white-and-blue-bannered convention. The race was close, with one crucial holdout: nerdy Mary Lolonis, whom Danny and I badgered. I pestered her until one day she cried and called me insensitive. Then she broke down and cried to Pam. Pam made a scene near our lockers, accusing me of being coercive. She complained to Mr. Wasserman, who told me I'd been leaning too hard on Mary. You'd think I was a loan shark threatening to bust her kneecaps the way everyone scolded me.

The day of the convention arrived. Everyone had to vote out loud. Mary cast her vote for me. Pam voted for herself. To win, I needed only to vote for myself.

But I stunned my classmates and Mr. Wasserman—and pissed off my small election machine who'd worked so hard for me—by casting my vote for Pam. Mary's crying had made me feel embarrassed for my corrosive, Machiavellian approach to winning the election. Conceding the election was my clumsy attempt to behave nobly.

In the second semester I joined the drama department and was awarded my second "Outstanding Drama Student" plaque. I'd become a popular kid. When it came time for high school my father told me that I would have to enroll at a high school different from that of my closest friends. My friends composed a letter asking my father to reconsider and send me to John Burroughs High School. He relented. I felt as if the world were finally starting to give me my props. Like my father, I was being asked to join the club.

My neighbor Lisa Perez and I didn't get along well. I'd ignore her in the halls of John Burroughs High School, feeling superior to her because I was hanging out with what I considered prettier and more popular girls. But Lisa and I had peculiarly contentious crushes on each other. We'd sneak away to the apartment complex laundry room to make out. I was perpetually trying to slide my hand into her cute red gym shorts, grinding my pelvis into hers. She never caved under the pressure, but I didn't care. I could always count on sex with Lorelei if her husband was at sea.

▆▆▆▆▆▆▆▆▆

Paul and I had two friends from church named Charlie and Danny Sturman. Charlie was my age, Danny was Paul's. Charlie and Danny were wiry, athletic boys, as rambunctious and competitive as we were. When Paul and I stayed at their home, we held mini-decathlon competitions, racing the one-hundred yard dash, playing two-on-two basketball, and wrestling Greco-Roman style.

I'd gotten hold of a sketched diagram showing Asian men in gym shorts, tank tops, and white gym socks performing jujitsu moves on each other. Paul and I each independently tried to deceive Charlie and Danny, pawning ourselves off on the brothers as studiers of jujitsu. Since jujitsu was the exotic Asian art of foot jousting, the sparring was more mysterious; we wouldn't need to display any flamboyant hand movements or regular arm-jousting moves (like the kind displayed on *Kung Fu Theater*, the Saturday afternoon TV program we watched religiously with our father) to fool people. When Paul and I each found out that the other was making the same bogus claim, our collusion took the form of silence. Neither one of us ever challenged the truth of the other's claim for fear of being exposed himself.

The fantasy ended when, after we'd convinced Charlie and Danny with our quick foot movements that we were true students of jujitsu, their mother telephoned Brenda to find out where we took lessons, how much it cost, etc. Brenda informed her that we'd not only never studied martial arts but that she wouldn't allow us to study anything that promoted violent contact.

▌▌▌▌▌▌▌▌▌

I attended many church camps over the years—Acorn Lodge, Hume Lake, Westmont, Lake Arrowhead—but it was at Forest Home that I felt the most intense spiritual tug. The camp's chapel was nestled on a hill a little hike above the camp. At the rear of the chapel, in a private corner, was a bookshelf filled with large, three-ring binders, with years written in bold numbers on their spines. The binders were in chronological order, 1966 tucked between 1965 and 1967. Inside each binder alphabetical letter tabs catalogued last names. In the *L* section, I found one written prayer after another, hundreds of prayers, all written to God by campers whose last names began with the letter *L*.

For three years I sat in that chapel and wrote my prayers in those binders, genuinely pleading with God to make me humble. There was something about the mountain air and campfire music and constant Bible education that allowed me to acknowledge more readily my sinful state. I was fourteen, fifteen, and sixteen years old and preoccupied with the peril of my soul, of the width and breadth of my ego's rebellious state.

My prayers weren't without precedent. Ruth Burke remembers cautioning my father when, as a boy, he prayed for God to "break him." *Be careful what you pray for, dear. That's a dangerous prayer.*

My father told me the story of Ruth's caveat several times when he was trying to figure out why, in retrospect, his life seemed to have been one calamity after another. Perhaps his streak of bad luck was God's way of answering his prayer. And maybe my father thought that his ills would be easier to accept if he could portray himself as a modern-day Job.

▌▌▌▌▌▌▌▌▌

When I first attended John Burroughs High School, I had intentionally avoided joining the drama department because I despised my staggering desire to get attention, my overarching reliance on other people's good impression of me. I felt that the stage brought out my most desperate urge to solicit favor. No amount of attention could satiate my need for validation. No matter who praised me—teachers and school administrators, the cutest girl in the drama department, or the most popular girl in school—I felt a hollowness in theater.

I considered myself to be of sturdier material, imagined myself a budding, brooding poet, a boy-scholar, the athlete-aesthete. Surely acting was for the shallow person, incapable of anything more than a devotion to whimsy and the cosmetic, capable only of mimicry and disguise; fawning, ingratiating himself, succumbing to emoting and equivocation, lying to himself as surely as lying to others, unable to accept the hard truths about himself and therefore running into distraction, from the ignoring of truth to a mad self-delusion. As far as I could tell, illusion was all that theater offered me.

I thought myself more consequential than my peers, with more will than they possessed. Did I want my brilliant moment to arrive while I was onstage—a fop standing there in tights, a cape, and stage makeup, uttering lines of second intensity (because not mine)? Emphatically, *no!* I was God's instrument. He'd saved my life for great work, to please him and to minister to his flock, not to a secular audience. Theater was Satan's way of tempting me to low, self-indulgent themes. He wanted me to allow myself to get loose and sloppy with my feelings, to lose control, to trust my own instincts and rely on my intuition, my skills of improvisation, so that I would eventually be seduced to use my own subjective standard as a challenge against the hard, objective commands and truth of the Bible. Abandonment to the theater equaled eventual abandonment of my faith, abandoning the sacred for the profane.

I genuinely wanted to be better, to behave more consistently, to exercise more moral control in my life. I wanted to develop more skill at keeping my sins in check, but I considered myself wholly inadequate at reining myself in. The stage threatened to sway me. All that emoting felt good, was brief balm for the burgeoning grief in my soul. In a performance I could abandon myself to hysteria, anxiety, or rage. But the force and vehemence of the emotional turmoil roiling to the surface scared me. I was frightened of losing a sense of myself in that turbulence, surrendering so fully to expression that I would collapse under the weight of my sorrow and become a puddle of tears and emotion. I feared my vulnerability to this weakness, or more exactly, I feared that through drama my panic and frailty would become public, that someone might learn that I was spiritually anemic, unimpressive, and not really trusting in God. I assumed that people would ridicule the truest me, and I couldn't handle anything that would chorus my own self-ridicule.

So I quit the theater. I begged God to make me humble. I begged God to stop my being seduced by the vanity of the stage. The prayers I scribbled in those binders implored God to help me mortify my flesh. I was tired of being spiritually squishy. I wanted to be strong, unyielding. I needed to lean on God's rod and staff, that he might comfort me through my valley of the shadow of pride that cometh before a fall and leadeth unto temptation and death.

▓▓▓▓▓▓▓▓▓

Brenda and my father went to see the movie musical, *The Man of La Mancha*, starring Peter O'Toole as Alhonso Quiana and Sophia Loren as Aldonza. Then they surprised Paul and me by going to a music store and buying the soundtrack. We played the album on the record player during our chores on the weekends. Over time I memorized all the lyrics, even Sophia Loren's part. And since I'd arrive home from school before Brenda or my dad, I'd lie next to the record player in our Burbank alley apartment and lust after Sophia's image on the album cover, with her brown skin and her big breasts falling out of her peasant's blouse. Her oozing sensuality reminded me of Lorelei's heaving lustiness.

The flights of fancy in the character of Don Quixote stirred me. I found him to be a sympathetic character. The notion that someone must lay down his melancholy burden of sanity if he wants to hope for himself, or the world, sure made sense to me, intuitively. This idea took root in my imagination. Madness and eccentricity seemed like a legitimately alternate way to cope with the harsh facts of life. One had to be crazy to be a prophet or a man of God. All the great men of the Bible struck me as madmen.

It wasn't hard for me to think of my father as a sort of Don Quixote, and me as Sancho Panza—high dreamer and willing servant of the dreamer's delusions—as he continued to pursue spiritual enlightenment. I remember sitting on the couch listening to Peter O'Toole rant and rave like a soapbox evangelist with a musical score, the same couch that my father would lie on when he wept and cried for our forgiveness after he'd lost control and beaten us. We would bawl with him and wail out that we forgave him, and he would promise that there wouldn't be a next time. And we believed him because it was so beautiful to believe in an impossible dream.

▮▮▮▮▮▮▮▮▮▮

Brenda typed one hundred words a minute, so she quickly found a job in a typing pool at MacClaren Hall, a shelter for abused children. More than once she came home distraught, after typing up reports about children with bite marks or with broken arms after being thrown down flights of steps. One day I overheard her telling my father about a family of children brought to the shelter because their father had baked their infant brother in the oven. When my father severely beat us she'd angrily warn him that we might one day end up at MacClaren Hall.

▮▮▮▮▮▮▮▮▮▮

Brenda had a plan.

It was Thanksgiving, 1976, and we'd driven up to Turlock to see Bertie and Sam. (Grandpa Sam was a sixty-six-year-old Texas "fiddler" who'd given me my first violin. I joined the junior high orchestra at our school, proud to please Grandpa Sam during another Thanksgiving visit to Turlock. But within two years, I quit playing the instrument. The other boys always called me a sissy when they saw me carrying my violin case.) Brenda intended to have Paul and me stay behind with her in Turlock, but she had to figure out how exactly to accomplish that. She knew that my father wouldn't allow it if she asked for his permission. He was too suspicious. (Brenda wasn't allowed to have her own friends. She couldn't simply say, *I'm going to go with a friend to the museum today.*) So she decided to just come out and tell her mother that my father brutalized her and that she needed to stay behind. But before she could say anything, her sister Debbie announced that she was pregnant. Brenda couldn't very well ruin Debbie's great news by confessing her wretched state.

So she went to Plan B. She asked her mother and sister to ask my dad if she could stay behind for a few days to help Debbie plan her baby and help Bertie move out on her own, away from Grandpa Sam. My dad couldn't say no to Bertie and Debbie because he always wanted to appear accommodating, expansive, giving—a great guy. They loved him and thought that he was a loving father and caring husband. My father said okay. Good, Brenda thought. She would wait a few days, letting the joy of Debbie's pregnancy die down before she brought up her problem.

A couple of days later, Brenda and her mother were seated in the living room discussing Bertie's recent separation from Grandpa Sam. Grandma Bertie had finally moved out on her own after years of unhappiness. Brenda thought that now would be the best time to bring up the brutality at home and suggest the possibility of moving back in with her mother, maybe even bringing Paul and me with her. Bertie glanced out the window and saw Sam's pickup truck drive up and park on the street in front of the house. Brenda didn't have the same view of the front yard that Bertie had.

*Heere comes yur father.*

They braced themselves for his alcoholic anger, the vitriol of a wounded has-been yelling for them to open the door and let his wife come home with him where she belonged.

But nothing like that happened.

They heard Sam walk up and step onto the porch. Something scraped against the bottom part of the door. Brenda walked to the screen door and looked out.

*Dad, get up.*

Grandpa Sam was lying down on his back, the crown of his head against the screen, the soles of his cowboy boots facing the street. He'd lain down in an apparent attempt to block the screen from opening out. Bertie said that she'd go out the back door and come around to the front yard. There was movement around Sam's chest, inside his jacket. Brenda couldn't really tell from her angle, because of the screen's blurring, but she thought she saw him tilt his head up to look at her upside down.

Then *Blam!*

Bertie's first thought: *Sam's killed hisself.* She ran back inside and called the police and paramedics.

Grandpa Sam had shot himself with a handgun. His brains were splattered on the trim of the house and on the front porch. Not until later would somebody notice the red speckles of blood on Brenda's white pants.

My father raced up north and performed the funeral ceremony. He gave a rousing eulogy. He could do no wrong. Brenda was now unable to rely on her family for any kind of support as she tried to navigate away from my father. It was as if God had conspired against her.

Brenda came home with us after the funeral, but she was never the same after that. All I could do was watch as she cooked us dinner, performed the maternal role like a Stepford Wife *(Pass the butter, dear. Could you please give me some of those Brussels sprouts.)*, then excused herself from the dinner table with eerie composure to retire to our bulky early-1970s stereo, where she would place the headphones on her head to listen to music that would transport her away from us for the rest of the evening. She listened to radio music, or forty-fives, letting the sounds seduce her to fantasies of a different life in a better home with another man.

Brenda quit working at MacClaren Hall when my dad became an insurance salesman for the New York Life Insurance Co. (NYLIC). Dad told her that he needed her to be his secretary. Soon Brenda started talking about divorce. She was unhappy, she'd say. My father, by contrast, felt like he was moving on to a better place. Financial success had made him expansive. He was even preparing to move us into an upscale neighborhood in Pasadena.

One night my father beat Brenda to the point that she had to sleep in the car. In the wee hours of the morning she went to the NYLIC office in Pasadena. A secretary named Flora (who worked for Jeremy Kline, the salesman in the office next to my father's) happened to walk in the women's room as Brenda was washing up. Brenda tried to lie about why she was in the office so early, making an excuse about why she was wearing the same clothes that she'd worn the day before. Flora simply looked at Brenda and said, *Brenda, you can lie to everyone else but you can't lie to me. And everyone here already knows what's going on.*

Shame and relief competed within Brenda. She was ashamed that abuse had turned her into a scared little animal perpetrating a public lie, surviving only on denial. She implored Flora not to say anything to anyone. Flora agreed, but only if Brenda did something about her situation. Flora couldn't keep her mouth shut forever, especially now that she knew that things at home had escalated to a place where Brenda was now sleeping in the car in frigid temperatures.

Over the next few weeks Brenda received assurances from Flora that if she really wanted to leave my father, then either she or Jeremy would shelter her.

Brenda felt that she owed God and her marriage one last good-faith effort, but even if that failed, she couldn't see a way to escape.

My aunt Margie once noticed dark bruises on Brenda's thighs. She didn't care if Joey was her brother, she said, he had to be stopped. She told Brenda to talk to the pastor of her church, Brother Tom. So Brenda went to Brother Tom for marriage counseling. She accused my father of beating all three of us. Brother Tom told her that these were serious charges and that she should return a few days later while he figured out a plan. She returned, only to find my father seated in the pastor's office. Brother Tom had felt that it was theologically improper in the eyes of God to have a man of God not be able to confront his accuser, especially if, as in this case, the accuser was a woman leveling charges that threatened the stature of the spiritual head of the household. My father wept in front of Brother Tom, and asked Brenda for forgiveness. But Brenda knew what most battered wives knew: You don't humiliate a bully in front of men whose respect he craves and not expect vicious payback.

Four days later, after much brooding, my father's surface congeniality cracked, and he beat Brenda again. That's the real reason we moved to Burbank: to ensure that my father and Brenda would never have to go to Brother Tom's counseling sessions again.

▓▓▓▓▓▓▓▓▓

During the lulls in violence in our home, my father could be immensely protective of us, almost hyperattentive to our injuries. Sometimes his reaction was in inverse proportion to the level of bodily harm inflicted. Once, I dislocated my shoulder while playing football at Ashiya Park. When I arrived back at our apartment, Brenda offered me an ice pack. Three or four hours later my father came home from selling insurance ("underwriting contracts") and saw me in severe pain. Brenda had never shirked her responsibility as my mother, and was indeed alert to our woes and tended to us exceptionally well—everything from taking us to the dentist our first time to taking me to various doctors when it seemed in tenth grade that I had a heart condition. So my father had never had the occasion to step in and usurp her motherly role. Except this one time, when he got angry at Brenda for what he considered sheer ineptitude, a bad call, an almost irresponsible response to my pain. He piled me into the car and drove me to Burbank Hospital, where I was X-rayed. Along with the dislocation, the doctors found three fractures in my shoulder. And to make matters worse, the ice pack Brenda had given me had caused my shoulder muscles to tighten, locking in place the dislocation. I had to be put under general anesthesia and the doctor had to yank and jerk and pull my shoulder out of its torpor and into its proper socket. That was one of the few times in my childhood where my father was a true hero in my eyes.

▓▓▓▓▓▓▓▓▓

All the clues had been there for us to interpret. She lost a lot of weight and started paying more attention to her appearance, wearing more fashionable clothes. She withdrew emotionally, was quieter at mealtimes. Brenda bought the hokey forty-five record "Afternoon Delight" and played it over and over again in the months before I came home from school one day and found a note on the kitchen table.

*Boys, your dinner's in the crockpot. Love ya, Brenda.*

By the time I read the note that late afternoon, Brenda's closet was empty, the contents packed into her Dodge Dart, and Brenda was gone—with Flora and Jeremy at Jeremy's apartment, to powwow about what to do next.

My father came home that night and notified us that Brenda was gone for good. He told my brother and me to get in the car. We drove to South Pasadena, a ten-minute ride from our Burbank apartment. My father chewed his fingernails as he drove. He rolled down the window, rolled it back up again. Ground his teeth so that his jaw stiffened. But he was strangely tender toward us when he remembered our presence.

*You boys eat?*

That night we were *his* boys.

It was a Friday night. Eightish. Dark outside. We drove past big houses camouflaged behind leafy plants and other homes with flat, green lawns like golf course fairways. My father had once attended a party at Jeremy's place. He slowed down and tried to reacquaint himself with the neighborhood.

He parked in front of a modern-style apartment complex, the upscale southern California kind of swinging bachelor pad you'd find in Marina Del Rey, Brentwood, or La Jolla. Lots of stocky midget palm trees elaborately dotted the landscape of undulating mounds of deep green grass. Bushes and palm fronds lined a winding pathway to the glass door of a brightly lit lobby.

*This is it. This is the one.* He looked at the building. *Stay here. I'll be right back.*

He stepped out of the car and walked tensely into the building. I couldn't figure out what was happening. A few minutes later he raced out of the building and to the car like a man who'd just robbed a liquor store. He started the car, panting, weeping. Paul and I began to cry. My father muttered something about Brenda being an adultress, living in sin up there with Jeremy.

Her betrayal stung me. I felt a sharp stab in my groin, as if a voodoo doll of my likeness had been pierced with a long, thin needle straight up into the base of my balls and into my abdomen. I doubled over in the front seat, hugged my waist, and squeezed out a moan.

There is a sleazy scene in Martin Scorsese's film *Taxi Driver* where Travis Bickle (Robert DeNiro) picks up an edgy rider (Martin Scorsese) and drives to a spot where the man tells Travis to park. Travis turns off the meter and starts to jot down something on a clipboard.

Scorsese starts babbling: *Keep the meter running. Did I tell you to stop the meter? I said keep the meter running. That's right. What are you writing? Stop writing. And put the meter handle back down. I didn't tell you to stop the meter.*

His demands are unbottled hostilities. Agitated in the back seat, he leans forward to engage Travis in conversation. *You see that light up there? The one on the second story? See the woman in the window? Yeah, well, I don't want you to see that woman. That woman's my wife. And it's not my apartment. Know who lives there? Of course you don't know who lives there. A nigger lives there. I'm gonna kill [garbled]. There's nothing else [grumble, mumble]. I'm gonna kill her. What do you think of that? Don't answer.*

The guy's loopy. Even demented Travis Bickle—whom we know to be a sickass, whacked out of his gourd—even he knows that this guy in his back seat is behaving inappropriately. Travis, his wide-eyed expression caught in the rearview mirror—struggles to comprehend the rambling lunacy from his backseat. Meanwhile, Scorsese continues to talk about the way a face might look after a bullet has blown it off.

The first time I saw that scene I understood DeNiro's bewildered expression in the front seat of that cab, watching a contorted soul in fitful anguish. I understood that the naked emotional squalor of the cuckold is the most pathetic and unglamorous grief to witness.

▐▐▐▐▐▐▐▐▐▐

Brenda started divorce proceedings after five and a half years of a miserable marriage. She didn't turn cold in my nightmares, but I hated the feeling of abrupt abandonment, the way the pain made me feel needy.

I interpreted Brenda's leaving my father as also leaving me. You hear stories about this all the time. The child of divorced parents believes that their love wasn't compelling enough to keep the parents around, together, happy. My father's loss was also our loss. I'd fallen in love with Brenda's presence: her powders and lotions in our bathroom cupboards; the perfume in the glass bottle molded into the shape of a genie's lamp; the toilet paper–wrapped menstrual evidence in the wicker trash basket; her Weight Watchers food-portion scale; her bargain shopping at day-old food outlets for our sack lunch snacks; her sky-blue Dodge Dart; the forest-green Dutch leather clogs she wore on her wide feet, even though she knew my father despised them; and her warm kitchen, which sometimes smelled of gravy, dumplings, peach cobbler, ham hocks, fresh-baked bread, or homemade granola.

■■■■■■■■■■■

When Brenda left my father, her drastic step forced the church elders to get involved and mediate a possible salvaging of their marriage. But when my father learned that Brenda had had sex with Jeremy while they were separated, he balked and said no. He wouldn't take her back. He didn't have to. The Bible gave him permission to divorce her now that she was a harlot in his eyes. No matter the reason for her bad judgment at a time of great pain, vulnerability, and confusion, our church leaders concentrated only on the fact that they were now dealing with an adulteress.

The separation unmasked my father's violence at home, but now he was playing the contrition game *(Yeah, I was a bad husband. Yeah, I've hurt my kids, but I'm sorry and I'll do anything you ask of me.),* so the elders had no grounds to excommunicate him. If one had to get Torah-technical, my father was accepting responsibility for his sins. And he was even quasi-submitting to the elders. It was true that the Old Testament God told the prophet Malachi that he hated divorce (Malachi 2:16: *"I hate divorce,* says the Lord God of Israel"). But it's also true that New Testament Jesus gave my father specific permission not to take Brenda back when in Matthew 19:9 he said to the Pharisees, "I tell you that anyone who divorces his wife, except for marital unfaithfulness, and marries another woman commits adultery." Brenda handed my father the only excuse the Bible allows for divorce, her adultery. So the elders didn't push the issue of reconciliation. After all, they were males, and everyone knows that religious men will always hold fast to the theology of no "sloppy seconds."

Besides, the elders figured, it was better for us boys not to have that Jezebel around anyway. What we needed was for my dad to continue to submit to them and pray to God, and our troubles would dissolve into the grace of God who is merciful on high.

Like Shenandoah Street after my mother's death, our Burbank alley apartment became a haunted place where my father could no longer live at peace. Everything—from the green furniture to the kitchen utensils to the drapery and bed sheets—was soiled with memories of Brenda's disgrace, and the implication of her dirty absence. And because Brenda had conducted her affair with my father's co-worker, my father suffered the double indignity of working among men who knew that he was a cuckold. He'd also lost the security of two incomes. Soon he quit NYLIC, after his client base collapsed, and the bills accumulated. Creditors constantly called our house. Dad would say, *If that phone call's for me, tell them I'm not here. Tell them I went to the market.*

After his bankruptcy he brooded around the house like a drunk. And the violence escalated. We were perpetually nervous, not knowing what excuse he would find to hit us. Once, he tied his belt around my brother's neck and lifted him off the ground by yanking the belt up. As Paul choked, my father spat in his face. Another time, Paul and I were washing the dishes. (Paul was fourteen; I was sixteen.) We heard my father walk into the kitchen and we stiffened up. I heard a shoe scuffle on the kitchen tile and instinctively swung around, just in time to see my father pivot on his left foot and sucker punch Paul in the ribs. Paul winced and buckled over. My father grabbed him by the back of the hair and dunked his head into the sink full of soapy dishwater. He lifted Paul's head out of the water. Paul was gasping. Water leaked out of his nostrils and mouth. Just before being dunked again Paul looked at me. Ah, I felt like shit, like he was begging me for help. But I stood there, paralyzed, a wet plate and soggy dishtowel in my hands. I couldn't move. After two more dunks of this black baptism, my father raised Paul's head out of the water, leaned in toward his ear, and growled, *You should have died instead of your mother!*

I wanted to die. Literally. I wanted to lie down and have God take my wind. But God hadn't answered any of my desperate prayers lately, so I felt it was time I took things into my own hands. That's why that night was the first time I seriously contemplated killing myself.

I hated that I hadn't done anything to help Paul. I hated my helplessness. My instinct to preserve myself and stay away from my father's wrath haunted me. And my guilt was compounded by the fact that very early on I was trained to protect Paul. My father told me once that when I was eighteen months old he pulled me aside and let me touch my mother's pregnant tummy. I felt movement.

*Feel that? That's your little brother. He'll be here soon. Your mother and I aren't going to be able to raise him by ourselves, so we need your help. Like when you hear him crying, then you can come to us if we aren't around. Okay? You need to make sure that he stays safe. He's going to come out and look up to you. He'll need you. Do you think that you want to help us?*

The idea that I could ever have been the last line of defense for my brother is silly to contemplate. But my father was brilliant at appealing to my tiny boy nobility, painting all sorts of scenarios in which he and my mother wouldn't be around and I'd have to save the day by being the alert caretaker of my brother. When Paul finally came home from the hospital, I was completely prepared to see him as a positive presence in the home. I never responded to him with jealousy or as an infringement on the attention I was receiving from family members. Quite the opposite: He was an opportunity for me to win even more adult approval.

Now, fourteen years after that, the kitchen humiliation made me feel like I'd failed at my task. I didn't want to exist if I was forever going to be weak, helpless, a coward at the moment when those whom I loved needed me the most.

Over the next few months, I presumed to see the problem more clearly. I couldn't protect others if I couldn't protect myself. I hadn't made the rules that governed my life. Spontaneous violence was the world I'd been born into and I saw only one way out of that violent world: I had to be more violent than the force of violence that oppressed me.

Maybe my dad's deflation by Brenda's infidelity, and our elders lowering esteem for him, wounded him so that I could imagine jumping on the dog pile. Whatever the case, the solution, as I finally saw it, was to kill my father. The violent cycle had to be broken.

Murder sounds a bit drastic, slightly (or largely) outrageous. But I was familiar with death. I had kissed my mother's cool, stiff corpse. And I certainly knew the center of cold-blooded violence. But before that Burbank incident death and violence were separate traumas for me.

1) My mother died.
2) I got beaten.

Completely separate things. But by submerging Paul's head in the dishwater while telling him he should've been the corpse in my mother's place my father had merged the two traumas. Now, I grasped how,

3) I could get beaten to the point that I would die like my mother.

I was already disturbed by dreams about coldness. I sensed and dreamt that my brother and I would not survive childhood. The beating mingled with talk of the grave made me even more jittery, heightened my sense of impending doom. A beating was a beating, but a beating with death as a threatening undertone was a much more serious thing altogether.

I had been educated to see myself as a warrior and to accept that all spiritual growth and victory could be earned only through battle. Our brand of patriotic churchmen believed that American religious might made right, so they sent missionaries all across the globe, armed with military metaphors. That's why in Sunday school I sang martial songs that glorified jihad—Christian warfare—while I ate my milk and cookies.

> *I may never march in the infantry*
> *Ride in the calvary,*
> *Or shoot the artillery.*
> *I may never zoom o'er the enemy,*
> *But I'm in the Lord's army.*

The near drowning of Paul in our Burbank kitchen galvanized my will. The image of my brother gasping and choking for air, begging for help, would remain a nightmare image, terrorizing me for years. From that traumatic point on, whenever I saw someone struggling for air when they cried, I'd always associate their weeping anguish with the twisted face of Paul in helpless agony, begging for a deaf world to rescue him.

For the next five months, I dreaded the next time that my father would expose my cowardice, even though notions of revenge were growing and comforting me at night.

## Fall 1977, Fremont Avenue, Alhambra

The white world we'd moved into after leaving East L.A. had ceased to be impressed with my father. He was a failed preacher, a failed husband, and now a failed insurance salesman. And the elders at Grace Church learned a lot more about his bad behavior in the home when Brenda met with them to explain her story of why she left my father. He wasn't excommunicated from the church, but he was shunned.

My dad lurched back to his comfort zone, to an apartment in the city of Alhambra, less than two miles from the Maravilla housing projects where our family began. Now he'd get to be a big fish in the little ponds of Mexican Protestant churches. (Years later he confided to me that the move to Alhambra was the worst mistake of his life.) He easily impressed the small congregation at his new church with his sophisticated knowledge of Scripture. They knew that Brenda had left him, but they knew only what he had told them about the divorce. He never once mentioned beating Brenda.

A young neophyte Christian named Suzy fell in love with him, and they started dating.

One Saturday evening we visited my aunt Gloria's house, a mile from our apartment. My dad asked her for some money so we could buy beans, tortillas, and orange juice. Although my aunt Gloria had started out as a lesbian, she met my uncle Leo, a construction worker who looked like Eric Estrada from *CHiPs*, and they married. When we went over there that Saturday Leo was in the garage holding one of his famous poker games. My dad's youngest brother, Danny, three years older than I, said that he would loan me five dollars to sit in the game. I took the money and got lucky, parlaying it into thirty dollars within twenty minutes. My father called me out of the garage and said that we needed to go home.

My uncles were perturbed that I was taking their poker money from the table, but I had to go. I couldn't argue with my dad. Neither could they. We went to the market and used the money for groceries. The next day in church I surreptitiously dropped seven dollars in the offering basket.

Even as a sixteen-year-old my father had been a faithful provider. Even while my mother was in the hospital and the medical bills were soaring, my father somehow managed to provide for us. Now he was reduced to sometimes asking his sister for food money. No longer at NYLIC, he picked up the odd laborer job at construction sites where my uncle Leo worked.

A few months after that dishwater incident with my brother, my father's new girlfriend, Suzy, took Paul and me out for a steak dinner. I'd been beaten a few days earlier, so I snitched to her about the brutal punishment. She was shocked. I told her that my father was a fraud, that he led a double life. I said that everyone at church was easily fooled by his charm and phony Christian piety because of his expansive knowledge of the Bible.

As I explained the beating to her, I was suddenly embarrassed for painting myself as weak and helpless, incapable of defending myself or my brother. I feared Suzy would think I was a sissy, so I grabbed my steak knife and held it up like I was ready to stab the air. *I'm going to stab him the next time he touches me.*

*No, Joey. Don't even think like that. Revenge doesn't solve anything.*

I pleaded with her to leave my father. Told her that he would hurt her like he hurt us. I made her promise that she wouldn't tell my father that I'd revealed the beatings to her.

The following weekend, I accidentally reduced by half my father's already meager wardrobe when I placed some of his clothes in a dryer at the neighborhood Laundromat and they shrank. When we arrived home I was scared that he'd really give me a thrashing, based on how fierce his outbursts had been at the Laundromat. But he simply punched me in the face and told me to go to my room. I did, for an hour.

*Joey! Come to the kitchen.*

I turned the corner and saw him washing dishes at the sink, his hands in sudsy water. I stood behind the serving counter that separated the living room from the kitchen.

He told me that Suzy had told him all about our talk. Poor thing. I should have known I couldn't trust her. She wasn't a good actress. I knew that she wouldn't have been able to hide her sense of betrayal from my father. My dad had the keen senses of a con man, so of course he'd have known that something was up with her even if she'd tried to be shrewd and drifted only slightly away from him. I figured that he'd challenged her somehow, confronted her, and she'd cracked.

Now, standing there in front of my father, who was calmly washing dishes, I was petrified with fear.

He said, *Don't worry. I understand why you needed to tell her. I just wanted you to know that I knew what you said to her, and it's all right, you don't have to mope around feeling like you have to hide it from me.*

He caught me off guard by taking the high road. So I told him something like *I'm glad you understand.*

But I was as stupid as a sheep. He'd set me up.

*You did what?* he shouted.

That was the last time I'd ever confess to anything.

He chased me to my bedroom and started hitting me with a tea kettle he'd grabbed off the stove. He slugged me hard in the solar plexus. I fell on the rug and curled into a fetal position. That's when the kicking phase of the beating always began. People who've experienced severe beatings by adults on a regular basis know that there is a sort of unspoken, choreographed pattern to the beatings. You get knocked around till you hit a wall or bed. Then you fall, and that's when they get their last kicks in. And you only make it worse if you try to crawl underneath things, like a bed or a dresser, or try to hide in the closet. You've got to let them utterly humiliate you, make you whimper like a fuckin' dog, before they can finally feel like they're in control again.

After my dad wore himself out, he went to use a pay phone at 7-Eleven to break up with Suzy. (He hadn't paid the phone bill for three months so the telephone company had cut off our service.) When he left, I told my brother to lock himself in the bathroom. Then I walked in a daze to the kitchen, opened the silverware drawer, and took out a steak knife. Then I returned to my bedroom and sat on my bed. I hid the knife under my pillow.

*Damn those kids, snitching to Suzy like that I never complained when my father beat me Never once thought to betray them Took my lumps like a little man And I got beat ten times worse than these wimpy boys of mine Our generation knew how to respect our elders This is what happens when you spoil kids Spare the rod and they lose respect for adults and forget how to keep their mouths shut Got to blabber to strangers about a little rough discipline here and there This generation is selfish all gimmegimmegimme Refuse to obey authority and follow the order of things Think they got all the answers That life is supposed to be easy These boys haven't any appreciation for how tough it has been for me to be both father and mother to them I got their mother pregnant when we were sixteen years old but I did the right thing I married her Could've been like other irresponsible boys at sixteen who found themselves in the same situation But I didn't And when Bessie died I could have left the boys with her family But I stayed with them and worked hard to keep food on the table and nice clothes on their backs Private schools Bikes at Christmas Disneyland Church camps But do they care that it was a financial struggle for years to keep them in private school Ha And this is how they repay me Bunch of lousy ingrates I wish I'd had it as good*

This record of our family history leaked out over the years whenever we misbehaved and my dad wanted to indicate that we were of lesser moral heft than he was as a child. We'd hear patches and snippets of this history lesson, his private account, that had the most prominent events in our family always playing to his favor. He would never understand how the highlights of his life, as he saw and experienced them, were not the highlights of ours. Like a Southern plantation boss might highlight the Christian care and generosity he'd shown toward his slaves—maybe teaching some of them to read and write or giving them medical treatment on occasion—the slaves themselves would pass on a crueler, less flattering tale about their slave master when they gathered in their dark shanties at night.

I heard my father's key in the front door. The door slammed.

*So you sniveling boys thought you've had it bad up till now Well I'll show you what bad really is*

My father strode to my bedroom. He stopped just inside the door and glared at me. Everything about his posture—head up, shoulders erect, elbows bent, his body balancing on his toes—indicated that he was poised to spring into the next round of punches and kicks. He scanned the room and spotted a weightlifting set in the corner. He looked at me, then at it, then at me again. With his eyes still on me he walked to the barbells. I didn't know what he was going to do: Use the steel bar or the twenty-five-pound cement weight? He was improvising. This was a whole new level of savagery. When he picked up one of the weights, I reached under the pillow and pulled out the knife.

My father dropped the weight real quick. I'd raised the ante by pulling out the knife, so bluffing was out of the question. I rose from my bed and stood straight for a moment. He reached out, motioning for me to halt. He must have misread my hesitation as a lack of resolve, like I didn't really intend to use the knife, because almost right away his posture changed. You know, like if muscles had attitudes, then his muscles were saying, "*Oh no, you're in trouble now.*" Arrogant like that, even though *I* was the one with the knife.

He began walking toward me, demanding, *Put down the knife, put down the knife.*

I charged him. His eyes went big. Panic flashed in them as he turned his head away and threw up his left arm to deflect the knife. We wrestled a little bit, but finally, with one swift thrust, I was able to pound the knife hard into his soft neck. I twisted it, trying to break the blade off. Paul was crying out hysterically from the other room: *Joey, what's happening? Joey, what's happening?* His panicked voice was like a soundtrack to the combat with my dad.

He fell, reaching up to grab the knife. *You killed me*, he screamed. His voice was genuinely scared.

I was scared too. This man had been kicking my ass with impunity for sixteen years, so I was afraid that he would somehow get up and finish me off with that knife. That's why I left him to die on the avocado-green shag rug.

When I ran out of the bedroom I found Paul. He'd had unlocked himself from the bathroom and was standing at the front door, holding it cracked open, ready to run. I told him to *Go! Go! Go! Go!*

We ran to my aunt Gloria's house, running in the middle of the street all the way there. I was crying, telling Paul, *I killed him, I killed him*. Paul was crying too. We were a mess.

When we arrived I told my aunt what happened and she called the police. They sent a patrol car to our place, but my father was gone.

After my brother and I left the apartment, my dad pulled the knife out of his neck. He composed himself enough to stand up and get some bath towels to press against the wound. The medicine cabinet was full of drugs that he thought could kill him, so he swallowed all of them. He staggered to the dining room table and began writing a suicide note. As he hunched over the table, he fought passing out. He was extremely woozy. He got more towels to absorb the leaking blood. Then he walked outside to his car and drove to a secluded place near Legg Lake, in Pico Rivera. He parked and waited to die from the overdose. But along came the L.A. County sheriffs. When they saw him, slumped over the steering wheel, vomit in his lap, they thought he was high on angel dust. They said that he "resisted arrest," so they beat the shit out of him. Then they saw that he was bleeding, that his hair was matted with blood. That's when dad confessed that he was trying to die because his oldest son had stabbed him. They committed him to Camarillo State Mental Hospital for a seventy-two hour evaluation. A case psychiatrist finally released him, convinced that he was no longer a threat to himself.

(My dad knew several languages but his violence gave birth to the writer in me and the story of the home became mine. This is where my knife took his language and one of the first things I wanted to do in police custody was write down the details of that day's violence.)

One of the detectives at the police station noticed that I seemed calm, even proud, as I explained why I stabbed and killed my father. (At the time I didn't know that he'd survived.) This detective badgered me, asking me why I hadn't simply run when my dad left the apartment. He told me that I had had plenty of options, that I didn't need to stab my father. He said that my story sounded an awful lot like I had been lying in wait, plotting to kill my dad. He said that he could even see how I could be charged with murder. There I was, arrogant from the power of my victorious combat, and this cop was basically telling me that he sided with my dad.

Then I saw something quite clearly: This man probably beat his son. You know, roughed him around a bit. Taunted him for being a sissy, a crybaby. Told him to fight back, not to run from a fight. And I represented the boy who would throw all those macho lessons back in his father's face. The boy who had learned those male lessons far too well. I'd fought back.

I sat there, a bit afraid of this new rival, but also of the possibility of getting charged with murder. But I also felt some relief at finally seeing something clearly: that my dad wasn't my only enemy. It was authority— men with church collars, men with badges and guns, men in coaches' uniforms, men who treated me like I needed to listen to them—it was all these men I needed to be wary of. These men looked out for each other, turned a blind eye if one of them got a little rough with his kids. After all, didn't boys need to get cracked over the head a little bit if they were to be molded correctly? All these men were complicit in my father's beating me. Their silence was tacit approval of my father's abuse of me.

As I sat there stewing in my seat, I hated that cop. I wished that he'd been my father and I'd stabbed *him* in the neck.

A few hours later, after the adrenaline in my body subsided, my body ached fiercely. I complained to a female cop, and I was taken to a hospital. X-rays revealed that I had a fractured rib and elbow. The doctors also concluded that I had sustained a major concussion. There was no more talk of charging me with assault.

After my arm and rib were bandaged, a police officer drove Paul and me to MacClaren Hall, the very shelter for abused kids Brenda had warned my father we'd end up in.

No other juvenile in MacClaren Hall had ever retaliated against his or her abuser, so I was treated with particular deference for having successfully recovered some of my lost self. The band of abused little people who gathered around me in the yard that first day admired me and asked me to repeat my story. I stood among them and bragged that I could take care of myself. And I swore to them that I would protect all my friends at MacClaren Hall from bullies.

I had long been habituated to the grotesque in man. I knew firsthand the startling and jaundiced profile of parental evils, the same as the six-year-old boy whose back was broken by his barbarous father or the eight-year-old girl whose face was forever disfigured by a father trying to burn her mother's resemblance off it. But even though I was rib-bandaged and wearing a wrist cast, I did not feel like a legitimate victim anymore.

At MacClaren Hall, on my county cot, I bore my wounds as a badge. A "you-should-see-the-other-guy" kind of cockiness. In the wake of bloody combat with my father, I conceived my "torn body to be peculiarly happy." I was delusional, like Henry in *The Red Badge of Courage*. The normal effect of dull head trauma.

It was at MacClaren Hall that I first felt a sexual power, the eroticism of violence. It was with a girl named Ruby. She was a troublemaker before I arrived, highly sexualized, notorious for lifting her blouse to flash her massive breasts to the boys and the male staff. When I arrived and she learned that I'd "almost killed" my father, she became my girlfriend and immediately went docile on me. Always on my arm, she stopped exhibiting the overt sexual gestures that had made her infamous.

I told my story often. My attack on my father had transformed me in the eyes of others, girls especially, into a noble and violent protector, chivalrous like Don Quixote de La Mancha. (Ruby even gave me a hero's welcome to MacClaren Hall: a neck tattooed full of blotchy red hickies.) I was still sweet, but no longer was I pitifully ineffectual.

I felt a little uncomfortable with the power that had accrued to me based solely on the fact that I had acted out of sheer panic. The kids feared me. Abused children are very alert. Keenly aware of changes around them. Mood swings, voice modulations, the pace of steps coming up the drive, they can interpret whole tempers in the sound of one car door slam. I was changing in front of their eyes: The hunted was becoming the hunter. I was moving away from them even as I tried to live among them.

Nighttime was scary at the Hall. A kid or two would sniffle, then start to cry out loud for mommy or daddy. I'd hear the night counselor's chair scrape on the floor and listen to his footsteps as he walked to various rooms to comfort the frightened children. Some nights, several kids joined the chorus of tears, and other counselors had to be called into the unit to hold and rock these children to sleep.

Meanwhile, lying in bed, I'd replay the triumph I felt at the precise moment when my father screamed out in fear for his life. It felt good to have that bastard off my back. I'd felt righteous paying him back for the way he'd made me feel helpless at that kitchen sink six months before. Whatever else my attempt to kill my father would eventually mean for me, it catapulted me far from the miracle baby who was supposed to grow up and be an evangelist of Jesus's peaceful message of love and forgiveness.

When Brenda's former co-workers at MacClaren Hall saw our names on abuse reports and admissions documents they telephoned her to tell her that Paul and I were a mess. She contacted a church counselor and told him to have us call her. I did, several weeks later, when I left MacClaren Hall for a foster home in Pasadena.

■■■■■■■■■

After I stabbed my dad I began to receive immediate sympathy from friends and staff at Grace Church. I was torn between portraying myself to them as the meek boy who was forced into violence and portraying myself as the put-upon boy who was always supposed to be a tough guy and when given the chance had proved his mettle.

Four months after I stabbed my father I developed a huge crush on a girl at church camp. Ruth Blankenship was a pretty blonde who was also new to the group. Never before had getting a girlfriend been so easy, especially what I considered my *dream* girl, with blond hair so white she looked Scandinavian. I was frenetic in my devotion to her, holding her hand as we walked to chow, to show everyone that she was *my* girl, *with me*, and that they were to stay away. I'm not gonna let you get even close enough to hit on her. Between seminars Ruth and I would slip away on romantic walks to make out in private in the chapel, near a pond, by the tennis courts, behind the showers, the swimming pool.

Ruth had broken her left wrist while riding a horse near her home in Reseda, and the cast she wore made her seem vulnerable, in need of manly protection. She inspired chivalry in me. I weighed exactly one hundred and fifteen pounds that summer before my senior year—and that was right out of the shower, sopping wet, with all my clothes on, my pockets full of change, holding a sack of hammers in one hand, a bag of bricks in the other. I mean, my body looked like what my father constantly called *un sacko de huesos secos* ("a sack of dry bones"). During a Bible study session, seated on the floor all huggy and snuggly cuddly with Ruth, holding hands with my girl, I'd lean back and she'd lean on me. We'd sneak a peck. I'd rub her leg and she'd scratch my neck. And I felt as if I were living one of those Persian scenes as a sheik caliph, with women fanning me and feeding me grapes. One of the high school–age pastors would be talking about being sanctified, quoting verses from the Book of Hebrews, encouraging us to remain steadfast and faithful like Abraham and Joseph, and all I could think of was how to get Ruth to give me another hickie, this time below my collar, closer to my chest.

One day, after Bible study, a burly camp counselor named Woody walked over and said that he needed to talk to me. I told Ruth I'd meet up with her afterwards. We kissed, and she walked away.

Woody was a divorced businessman and after-school football coach who resembled Burt Reynolds, with his black hair and thick moustache. We attended the same Wednesday-night high school Bible study in Burbank. He'd never actually led a Bible study, so I'd never thought of him as a spiritual leader. He was just an adult presence. But as soon as the room cleared, Woody started scolding me for my lack of respect for God's Word, for my lack of regard for the pastor who'd worked so hard to prepare his homily. He said I should be ashamed of myself for the way I, who should know better, was keeping that girl from hearing the message of God that the Holy Spirit might be trying to send her. My out-of-control libido was being used by Satan to harass the girl and keep her from dedicating her life to God.

Two things happened in me at once: First, I wanted to smash Woody's face with my fist. How dare he talk to me like that. Didn't he know who I was? I was the kid who had become a man. I wasn't a boy anymore. He needed to be taught to respect his peer. (That was how idiotic I was. Something aggressive had been awakened in me, and I now felt it my right to inform that I was monitoring the level of respect they showed me, and that if I didn't receive my fair share that they should fear the consequences, like the kind my dad suffered.)

The second thing that happened to me was I realized that Woody was merely pointing out something important I needed to see, that he was helping me. I'd interpreted his rebuke as combative when I should have more reasonably read it as mentorship, a seasoned male showing a young buck how to hold up the true-grit male ethic.

My public display of affection revealed a major weakness: neediness. The boy Joe Loya had always desperately craved female affection, especially after his mom died. The new powerful Joe Loya required something new, a new attitude about how to conduct himself in the world. I had to take myself more seriously. (I'd done it before, when I stopped acting in junior high. But there I was seated on the floor with Ruth, all horny grubbing for attention like a starved and desperate kid. Woody was right. I needed to amp up my seriousness quotient. What had I been thinking? Real men don't betray emotion. Real men aren't touchy-feely. I needed to become stoic, to say no to P. D. A. (public displays of affection). I was a man now, and I needed to act like one. So, instead of punching Woody, I decided I'd follow his lead, try to control my body to make it behave like a man's. Reinvent myself. I'd become a solid man who wouldn't need other men to correct him. This would require all manner of contortions on my part, but I was up for the new challenge. I so drastically wanted to be manly.

From then on I committed myself to never betraying emotion. I wanted to be admired for my detachment. I wanted other Woodys to see me and find no reason to criticize, but rather find reason to celebrate our macho similarity.

The first place I thought I could demonstrate improvement was through sports. At the end of my junior year I was considered the number-one man on the junior varsity track squad at Alhambra High School. What I felt I now deserved was respect and true recognition from the varsity guys. So, with my new resolve, I decided to work out all summer, not only to make the varsity squad, but also to be one of the fastest guys on the team. I found a workout by the runner Billy Mills, a

1964 Olympic champion in the 10,000 meters. Every morning I'd walk to a local school to stretch and run sprint drills. Sure enough, when track season came I surprised all my teammates by being one of the fastest sprinters. The coaches had seen me practicing regularly four months before the season began, so they admired me for being such an on-the-ball kid, disciplined and self-motivated. They weren't surprised when I broke a school record in the 330 low hurdles event. I had made my body submit to pain to make a point to myself and others that I was different from them, that I was becoming a new person, somebody to be reckoned with and taken seriously. While other boys worried about girls and fast cars and Saturday night dates, I developed a loathing for the material world with its fascinations, for the easy and shallow life. While my classmates did their senior-year homework, I attended seminary classes with a friend.

This was the second place where I felt that I could demonstrate improvement: in matters spiritual.

Steve Alva was my favorite adult leader at my church high school group. He attended Fuller Seminary in Pasadena, where I was a guest several times for Philosophy and the Christian Faith, taught by Colin Brown, a professor of Systematic Theology. (From the class textbook's jacket: "Colin Brown surveys the thought of over 400 philosophies from the Middle Ages to the present day, showing how various thinkers and ideas have affected Christian belief.")

■■■■■■■■■

After six months in foster homes (Paul had moved home three months earlier), I moved back home to be with my father. He was reading Christian books about caring and sharing and sensitivity (after all this was the seventies), self-help books that ministered to the soul, turn the male into a feeler, teach the reader how to get in touch with his inner Jesus. I was pleased to see that his taste in Christian literature was changing from Old Testament law to New Testament emancipation themes.

Our family orientation toward God had changed. Our faith was to be more participatory now. We designated one weeknight as family night, when we went out to eat or stayed home and played board games, all three of us. We prayed together every night too—kneeling on the same bed where I had tucked that knife under my pillow eight months earlier—crying to God to heal our home, to rain his merciful love down on our family bond.

We also briefly attended family counseling. The church elders who provided the counseling wanted me to talk about how I was feeling, but the truth was, I didn't want to talk about how I had lost respect for my dad and was beginning to despise him. I didn't want to tell them that this whole God thing was beginning to feel like it wasn't big enough to accommodate the swelling in me that I could only identify as ego.

I still wanted to be humble, the boy that God had preserved for a special mission, and I wasn't ready yet to comprehend a new destiny for myself, one where all things spiritual were banished. In fact, I saw myself as a person acting in good spiritual faith when I came home to forgive my father. And I loved being seen as a spiritual boy. I loved it when I was called Christ-like by the adults who were aware of the severity of the violence in our home. But I was tired of petitioning God and getting nothing good in return. In fact, as I saw it, the best thing that had happened to me so far had been my father's stabbing. God was nowhere to be found that bloody day. My emancipation from Him occurred only when I stopped begging Him for relief, when I put aside spiritual principles, and picked up a material object to jam into my father's neck.

I didn't want to tell Elder Barshaw any of this, and in many ways these thoughts weren't completely formulated in me yet. They were only inklings, phantasmagorical notions hovering around me, nothing I could put my finger on.

When I returned home in September of my senior year I was absolutely earnest to mend the familial rift. But by the time Christmas arrived, I was becoming moody and hostile, really angry that I had returned from a wealthy middle-class foster home to a low-income blue-collar house—where Paul and I were rationed one small glass of Sunny Delight orange juice every morning; where we were so poor I couldn't buy a class ring, a yearbook, or any of the senior-year paraphernalia, or attend any of the senior-year events. The fury that was slowly churning in me made me feel like I was entitled to a better life, a kinder future.

# APOSTASY

# vi

eavy D lost fifty pounds after a four month diet, but he got so mad, so fuckin' hungry, that he threw his shit on an associate warden making his rounds that day, yelling, "Ain't no fun when the rabbit's got the gun, huh?" as the warden staggered back and wiped the wet shrapnel off his moustache.

For that infraction Heavy D was transferred back to the basement, and that's when I saw him for the second time. He was walking hunched over on his cane, not naked like the first time but wearing a bed sheet wrapped around him like a toga-wearing Roman senator.

When Heavy moved back onto the tier he had to wiggle a little bit before he could slide his body all the way through the door. As he was doing the cell-door shimmy, he yelled out, "Stone Man, check out how slim I am now. I lost fifty pounds."

Stone Man yelled back, "Nice new slim ass, but you still got a buffalo head, you fat fucker."

"I got a buffalo head between my legs too, Stone Man. Wanna see?"

I decided right then that I was going to make it my mission to help Heavy D fully outgrow his cell again. At every meal I would yell down to him, "Heavy, I can't finish my food. Want my dessert and the dinner roll with butter?"

Of course he was all for it. He loved to get his grub on. I'd yell down to the other guys, "Hey I'm sending my tray down to Heavy so why don't you guys pile anything you're not eating on top of it."

Indian Early would be released from his cell to pass the trays.

▓▓▓▓▓▓▓▓▓

Most of the time Heavy walked to the showers naked. His thighs and ankles were so fleshy that his ass crease started at his lower back and ended at the floor.

My cell was near the showers, so sometimes when he was finished with his shower and was waiting for guards to escort him back to his cell, we'd shoot the shit.

"Hey Heavy, who would you fuck first? Say Oprah and Whoopi both came to your cell and you could only have one. Who would it be?"

"Whoopi. It'd have to be Whoopi."

"Okay. Who would you choose to fuck, Esther Rolle or Whoopi?"

"Esther who?"

"Esther Rolle. The Mother on *Good Times.* J. J.'s mom."

"Maaan. Quit playing. Fuck that old broad? I'd fuck Whoopi and Oprah before I'd fuck that old broad. Maaan. You ain't right."

"Slow your stroll, big fella. No need to get hostile. I'm just askin'."

"Fuckin' Esther Rolle." He growled her name, sounding exasperated.

"I got it now. Who would you choose to fuck first? Weezy or Oprah?"

"Who's Weezy?"

"Louise on *The Jeffersons.* Remember, George used to call her Weezy, short for Louise."

"Yeah, yeah. Straight. I remember. She wasn't bad. But I'd still have to fuck Oprah first. Oprah ain't bad. She's got loot. Mad loot."

"Here's the real question. Who would you fuck first? Janet Jackson or Lisa Bonet?"

"Fuck Janet. That pussy is garbage."

"Fuck Janet? Pussy garbage?"

"Yeah. Janet's a fuckin' tramp. The bitch dissed my boy Tupac."

"Two packs of Coors?"

"Yeah, Tupac Shakur. She told him that for their love scene in *Poetic Justice,* she wanted him to have an AIDS test. Ain't that about a mutha' fuckin' bitch?"

"Janet's fine. I'd fuck her."

"Maaan. Janet is tired. I'd fuck light-skin Bonet before I'd fuck Janet. Shit, I'd fuck Weezy before I'd fuck Janet."

We were silent for a while. A strange silence. I could tell he'd been enjoying our talk of fantasy sexual conquests.

He broke the silence.

"Hey, player."

"Yeah, player?"

"How come you didn't ask me about that big titty broad from *Facts of Life.* What's her name? I forget her name. She's on that show, *Living Single.* Ooh-shit! I'd rub my shitty little dick between her fat sloppy titties quick fast and in a hurry."

"With a quickness, huh?"

"Yeah man, with a mutha-fuckin' quickness."

## Impersonation

*My name is Legion: for we are many.*

—Mark 5:9

### 1979

I told my father that I wouldn't attend my high school graduation. He said, *Your mother always talked about the day we would go to your graduation. If you don't want to go for me then go for her.*

I went.

Three days after that cockamamie ceremony I moved in with Tim Sullivan, an older friend from church. He was a manager at Marie Callendar's restaurant in Northridge and he'd offered me a job as a fry cook there and a mattress on the floor of his Reseda apartment. I didn't tell him that I'd never held a job before, but I was happy to finally be out on my own.

A month later I answered an ACCEPTING APPLICATIONS sign at a McDonald's around the corner from Marie Callendar's. I became the 6:00 A.M. opening-grill man, a genuine double-shift guy. I had to wake up at 5:00 A.M. to get to work on time. Most nights I didn't get home until midnight.

But I was feeling strong. I was finding that I had a lot of energy and self-discipline to push through the fatigue of working double shifts. And I saw that friends and family were proud that I had two full-time jobs. I felt like I was some sort of exception among my friends, and this made me feel superior to them. They'd ask me to go to a movie or a concert, and I had to decline. But I didn't feel left out. I felt more like I didn't have any time to waste. I sensed purpose in my life of sacrifice and deprivation, and I felt sorry for the saps that had to party to feel whole. I had a spiritual dimension to me that made me supremely different from them. I even thought I was superior to my roommate, Tim, who drove a Porsche and spent his money on music and concerts. I thought that his materialism made him a small man.

I'd be on the road by 5:30 A.M., speeding on my ten-speed bike in the cold. I turned that thirty-minute valley crossing into my prayer time. My prayers were a system. On a single sheet of paper I'd listed two columns of friends' and family members' names. The ones whose dedication to God was on the wane got two asterisks by their names. When I prayed, I would linger a little longer on them than I did for the others.

A new fanaticism overcame me in those days. I rededicated my life to God, gave salvation the old college try, put all my eggs in this Easter Savior's basket. I wanted to be a spectacular Christian, thinking maybe that I hadn't ever given Christianity a true adult effort, you know, as the new and improved Joe Loya with all my monstrous new willpower. I believed that I could be a dynamic Christian. God must've been prompting me to think big about my spiritual mission on this earth. How else to explain this desire in me to outgrow myself, this feeling that I could swallow the world? Finally my surviving the overdose of baby aspirin made perfect sense. I was going to be God's point man here on earth. He needed someone whose life was of almost epic proportions. And didn't my story have it all? I'd been preserved as a baby just as if I had been Moses himself, being carried adrift by the Nile's current to the right place. I'd been Daniel surviving the lion's den. I'd played Absalom to my Dad's King David when he cried. No, better yet, I'd played the shepherd David to my father's Goliath. I wanted to be near God like King David had been. In fact, my favorite Christian hymn lyric in those days was a refrain from the Psalms: *Create in me a clean heart, O Lord, and renew a right spirit within me.* I wanted to speak with Him and "walk" with Him the way Adam did in the garden.

I'd been asking church friends for rides to the supermarket, since I didn't have a car. My friend Dennis's mother owned a Plymouth Fury III that she was selling for six hundred dollars. She was nice enough to hand over the car keys and pink slip even though I'd paid her only two hundred as a first installment. My big work checks from the double shifts hadn't come in yet, so I promised to pay the rest of the money in a month. But the fees for registering the car and buying the insurance were costs I hadn't expected, so I didn't pay her the final installment. I ignored her phone calls. One time, Dennis came knocking on my apartment door. I pretended I wasn't there. I didn't want to give up the money.

I enjoyed my first car. It gave me the freedom of the highway. I could be lonely in my Reseda apartment on my one day off, but thirty minutes later I could be eating Grandma's homemade tamales in Montebello.

When my father learned that a Marie Callendar's restaurant was opening near where I went to high school (a two-minute drive from the apartment where I'd stabbed him), he invited me to return to live with him and my grandma for free in the Hensel Gardens apartments in Montebello. All I had to do was enroll full-time at East Los Angeles Community College (ELAC) in the fall.

Although I'd been deceiving my friend Dennis and basically stealing his mother's car, I felt that my dedication to God was still strong, had not yet fallen apart. That's because the car and my spiritual life were two different things to me. One was a financial responsibility issue, the other was my eternal future issue. And I didn't see taking the car as stealing. I intended to pay for it. And I must admit, a part of me felt entitled to that car, that Dennis's middle-class mom should've cut me some slack. I was barely coming out of my poor, troubled beginnings. I resented her and Denise making a big deal out of the car. They were putting money before me, their Christian family. We were brothers and sisters in Christ, and they were elevating private property above our communal spiritual bond.

So without giving notice, I left Tim Sullivan's apartment, left Marie's and Mickey D's. I finally paid Dennis's mom the rest of the car payment, but not before I used the car to haul all my stuff back to the east side of Los Angeles. I moved in with my father and grandma Nellie.

▮▮▮▮▮▮▮▮▮▮

One afternoon I drove to Montebello Intermediate School (my once fantasy family compound), on the prowl for a weak boy walking home. I knew that just as there are weak boys walking home from school every day, it is equally true that there are school bullies nearby. And sure enough, the male schoolyard ethic did not disappoint. I came upon a slight boy having his schoolbooks knocked out of his hands. I made a fast U-turn in my Plymouth, sped up to the curb, and slammed on the brakes like the *Rockford Files* hero I fancied myself. I leapt out of the car and ran into the ruckus. I was all crime-fighting attitude as I charged the bully and poked him hard in the chest.

*What's your problem? If you wanna pick on someone, then pick on me!*

Of course I had no moral authority accusing him of bullying while I was bullying him, a kid half my size.

*Get the hell out of here and I swear that if I ever see you pick on my friend here again then I'm gonna kick your ass and all these punk friends of yours.*

The kid whose life I felt I'd just saved was shaken up, but was nonetheless deeply grateful. I asked him if he thought he'd be all right walking home. He said sure.

I didn't offer him a ride because I didn't want him to fear me. He might have been worrying that my inappropriate behavior up to that point implied that there were other, more nefarious and inappropriate, ideas in my head, like trying to slip my hand down his pants. I told him that I'd be around keeping an eye on him, and that he should always re- member that bullies were just scared boys waiting to be exposed.

▮▮▮▮▮▮▮▮▮▮

I was beginning to fancy myself the Great Exposer of fraud, lies, and propaganda. I enjoyed knowing that I could unmask the enemy (e.g., Christians like Dennis's mom who was soiled by the world's lust for tem- poral things). This developing sense of confrontation made it feel good to blow bullies' covers. I was feeling my power. I thought the bullied boy would feel better knowing that there was a just force in the world, hovering over all human interaction, able to swoop down on a whim and correct a wrong.

That was the beginning of my minor-Messiah complex. I was starting to believe that I could use my newfound sense of power and justice as a good force in the world, that maybe I could be God's good soldier down here, a sort of crime fighter, like the Green Lantern, except that I would be the Brown Lantern. But what I should have recognized was how, in my mania for exacting justice, I more resembled Don Quixote.

That was also the fall that my grandmother cried when she learned I was going to vote for Ronald Reagan.

*Mijo, he's going to take away my Social Security.*

I became the first Republican in my family anyway. Being raised among white kids whose parents had money and privilege made me sense my inferiority in my class and the color of my skin. Poverty had been a humiliation that stung me, so I'd be damned if I was going to allow myself to be poor forever. My vote was intended to secure a good future for the eventual wealth I imagined for myself.

If I had thought Dennis's mom was guilty of chasing the golden calf by being greedy with her car then I thought that I was just being fiscally prudent with my vote. I felt that my decisions about money were always going to be morally superior to hers, or those of people like her, because I was being guided by the Holy Spirit.

▮▮▮▮▮▮▮▮▮

Joey Jay had been a friend from Alhambra High, a stoner kid. His Christian mother had hoped I could be a good influence on him. Like me, Joey Jay had gone to Christian schools, but he'd been kicked out, and now he was the only friend I had who periodically smoked marijuana. (He was one of the few people on my prayer list who had two asterisks by his name.) In high school I encouraged him to submit to righteous themes, to love God and himself, to become everything Jesus wanted him to be.

Brian Okada's father was Japanese-American and his mother was

Irish-American. (She had only four fingers on one hand, something about an ugly washing machine accident.) I tried hard to talk Brian out of Catholicism, to consider instead the Protestant message. He eventually gave in.

Brian and I got fry cook jobs at the new Marie Callendar's in Monterey Park, and a few months later Joey Jay and my brother were hired as busboys.

Joey Jay, Brian, and I enrolled in all the same classes at ELAC. Introduction to Psychology, Western Civilization, Philosophy, Anthropology. I was trying to do the right thing, conform, sacrifice, and put in my four years of college so that I could earn the benefits of education. I thought for a while that I was going to transfer to UCLA and major in Philosophy, to become either a lawyer or a theologian.

Halfway through his junior year my brother took the GED, and he enrolled at ELAC too, in all my same classes. Brian used to pick all of us up in his Blue Chevelle every morning before school. We'd listen to The Cars and Pat Benatar and Billy Joel's *Glass Houses* on cassette (though Brian still had an eight-track player in his car on which we listened to Rod Stewart sing about how sexy he was, asking us if we wanted his body).

## 1980

Leo Karlyn had known my father since my mother's death. He tracked down my father at church after he heard about the young man turned recent widow. Leo's wife was schizophrenic, in and out of hospitals, so in some ways he felt like his little children were also growing up without a mom. My father's and Leo's grief bonded them. He was a wealthy man who treated me like a godson. In 1980, when he learned that I didn't have a car, he gave me a 1966 Ford Mustang. Just gave it to me.

One evening after work I boasted to some cocktail waitresses and bartenders that I paid the lowest car insurance premium of anyone at the table. I lied. I didn't even have any insurance. That night, while racing down Atlantic Boulevard, I got into an accident and totaled my car. One of the bartenders had been taking the same route home so he stopped to help. He heard me tell the police that I didn't have insurance, and he looked at me with a funny expression on his face.

My lies were like that. Gratuitous. I'd lie for no reason at all. I was a pathological prevaricator. Most of the lies were in the service of puffing myself up, making me sound smarter than I was (*Yeah, I've read that book.*), more spiritual than I could be (*I pray an hour every day.*), braver than the next fellow (*I won my last nine fights.*), and more charming than my competition (*I kissed more than fifteen girls by age eighteen.*). I didn't re-alize this about my exaggerations at the time, but this invincible self-delusion was obvious to many adults. My deceits worked with my young, just-out-of-high-school peers, who themselves were trying to get their own footing in the world, but not with adults.

I was trying to impress people. I'd always believed that God had saved me to do some striking work. When he didn't make the road clear, I tried to be extraordinary on my own. But that was hard. Play-acting at being substantial was much easier than actually finding one path and sticking to it all the way through to the end, at a solid and consistent pace.

One conversation from that time in my life best characterizes how disconnected I was from the person talking to me. It occurred during a lunch break at Marie Callendar's. I was seated alone with a cocktail wait-ress. She was maybe twenty-three or twenty-four, but she may as well have been thirty-eight or thirty-nine, because the difference between this fresh eighteen-year-old boy and that twenty-four-year-old single mother was vast. And the way I looked at her made our differences that much more stark.

Like I said, she was a single mother, and this meant to me that either she'd never been married, which made her a slut in my mind for having premarital sex, or she had been married but then had got a divorce, which could mean two things: one, she was dumb for falling in love with an asshole who probably cheated on her, or, two, she was too dumb and emotional and utterly noncompelling a person to keep a man interested in her longer than two years.

She was a drinker and a cocktail waitress, and that placed her in the floozy category in my mind. She obviously hated her life without the Holy Spirit. This was the natural state of Mankind, forever to look for meaning in dead-ends, like liquor bottles and bars and premarital sex and drugs. This woman was to me at the time just one, maybe two steps up from harlotry. I mean, c'mon, is this the best she can do? Cocktail waitress? Not going to school to better herself or for that matter try to give her little boy a better life? Oh yeah, and did I tell you that she smoked Marlboros? A smoker, a drinker, a fornicator—that's definitely only one step away from being a whore. So I had no respect for her. Considered her stupid, my moral inferior. Essentially, a prime candidate for me to impress with my Christian compassion, since I knew her sinful state and was best poised to woo her to the soft forgiving and Jesus-loving themes of the Gospel. (Maybe she would be my Mary Magdelene.) She was clearly a sinner. With just the right amount of sincere identifying/sympathizing with her alienation from God—but also showing her how I'd been able to find obvious meaning in *my* life with the help of God—I was sure that I could convert her to Christ.

I steered (don't you dare say manipulated!) the conversation to the spiritual realm, asking her how she dealt with the stress of her job. I would have been too obvious asking her if she went to church on Sunday. No, that was for the impatient evangelist. I was too sophisticated for that. Then I stayed on the topic of stress and asked her how she dealt with the stress of being a single mother. This was so I could take the conversation to the home where I could then bring out my understanding about a rough home life, explain to her how I'd been able to overcome the severe fracture in my own home that occurred after my dramatic retaliation against my father.

When I finished telling my story, I told her how I had at first felt tugged away from my faith after stabbing my dad, how I felt that God had left me alone, had turned his back on me one too many times, making me realize that I had no one to rely on but myself. I kept telling her how that proved to be a lie, that every man needed God, that it was our natural state to look for meaning. That's what all philosophy teaches by its very existence, that we are looking to be reconciled with God, like Adam had been when he was in the garden, the Edenic state of mind, taking daily walks with his Creator. I shared with her how in my vanity I realized that if I continued on the road of denying God then I could lose my mortal soul. And the idea of spending eternity in the lake of fire mentioned in the Book of Revelations was too much to bear. I came to my conclusion: Finally, I told her, like Saul on the road to Damascus, I knew now that God had saved me, that my salvation was safe and eternal. I was grateful to God that he'd allowed me to have my own permanent life-altering experience at age sixteen so that I could now go on loving and walking with him without interruption for the remainder of my days.

And this is how I intended to get past the age issue with her. You see, seated there in front of me, most people would have deferred to her as the wiser of the two of us. She was older and had experienced more life. This dismissal by condescending adults was the hurdle I had to overcome. I hated the feeling of inferiority, so I wanted to show her that with my spiritual algorithm, I was able to make myself not merely her equal but actually more mature than she, if you factored in that I'd dismantled my future doubts and spiritual indecision and would never have to suffer from lack of faith ever again. Truth is, I believed that if God looked down at that moment He'd have recognized that I was the sage in that conversation.

She wasn't having any of it.

*Well,* she said, *sounds like you've been through a lot. But don't hold on so tightly. You are still young, and there is a lot of life for you still to experience.*

*No,* I interrupted. *You don't understand. I know, I know in my heart, know just as powerfully as I know that we are having this conversation, that this is it. I'll never doubt God again. And it doesn't get any more intense than this belief. I mean, I almost killed my father.*

*I'm not saying that you're a phony or insincere,* she said. *And I realize that this was a very important event in your life. But life has a way of throwing curve balls. You may change your beliefs two or three more times before you are thirty.*

I hated her for trying to beat me with worldly wisdom. I had God on my side, and with him I could not lose.

*I'm telling you, no, it isn't going to happen. I know. This is it. I won't turn fifty and have a mid-life crisis. God has made me immune to those cycles of life. I had my mid-life crisis early: the doubting, the wondering about purpose.*

She gazed at me with a look of bewilderment, like I had three heads.

Silently, for a second. Then she gathered her lunch dishes and stood to leave.

*Joe, okay, you're right. Who am I to question you? All I can say then is good luck. I hope that your beliefs stay the same as they are right now, for the rest of your life. Seriously. Good luck.*

And then she was gone.

## 1981

The Beatles were Paul's favorite rock band, an obsession for him since age fourteen. He taught himself how to play the guitar so he could perform their songs. He had a friend named Kris, and she and Paul memorized dates, studied concert attendance numbers, deciphered the codes in "I Am the Walrus," read all the Beatles mythology, and of course dabbled in the whole *Abbey Road*/Paul McCartney is dead necromancy. They'd go to the Rialto Theater in Pasadena and watch four Beatles films in a row (*Help!*, *Hard Day's Night*, *Let It Be*, and *Magical Mystery Tour*). They were buddies who shared the same obsessive view of their heroes.

Kris moved to Nevada before their senior year, and Paul joined the Air Force. Paul wasn't yet eighteen, so he needed my father's signature to sign up. When my aunts wanted to know why he was leaving the family, he said flat out, *I don't know what to do with my life. I need discipline, plus they'll pay for my education when I get out after four years.*

Reagan had recently been elected President, and the world and the press were calling him a cowboy, suggesting that he would nuke the Russians, "the evil empire." War seemed like a serious possibility for this warmonger with an itchy trigger finger on "the Bomb."

After my father and I dropped Paul off at LAX on his way to boot camp at Lackland Air Force Base in Texas, the forty-five minute drive home was silent. Back home I closed my bedroom door and played John Lennon's comeback album, *Double Fantasy*, and wept quietly. I didn't know exactly what I felt because the pain enveloped me, suffocated me. It wasn't located in one spot. Like I couldn't say my heart ached because my stomach and head and memory and future and present, all those things felt sore, beat up, like the pain I'd known during a concussive state of mind. The world seemed a nebulous thing, and if it resembled anything it felt like the numbness I felt when I thought of my dead mother. The tears jerked me the same way, my chest and throat lurched spasmodically, and my skin tingled. I wanted to fall on the floor and curl up and crawl into a hole and sleep forever. It was a grubby and graceless grief that I had no language to describe at the time.

▐▌▐▌▐▌▐▌▐▌▐▌

*The Official Preppy Handbook* was released in October 1980, during my sophomore year in college. The book promoted nicknames like Skip, Biff, Kip, and Winny for boys. It described preppy phrases, preppy code words, and preppy accessories (like a wool-plaid afghan to keep in the trunk of the car for impromptu picnics).

There were two films that brought the preppy fad to my attention: *Breaking Away* and *Ordinary People.*

*Breaking Away* was about a blond American kid who wanted to be Italian like his favorite bicyclists. He shaved his body hair to lower wind resistance, spoke with a fake Italian accent, cursed in Italian, and pretended to be a foreign exchange student at the local university. His nemeses were a group of frat boys who all wore the preppy uniform of Lacoste "alligator" polo shirts, wool sweaters tied round their shoulders, striped belts on wide-wale corduroy pants, and brown Sperry Topsiders. Even though the frat boys were the bad guys in that class-warfare tale, I liked their clothing fashions, the way they wore their uniform with pride. And I admired their bluebloodism. Yeah, I saw how badly they treated the eccentric blond cyclist and his townie friends, how they looked down on their working-class backgrounds, but I believed it was all a misunderstanding. It was easy for me to make excuses for the frat boys' elitism because they were who I wanted to be, who I identified with in the film. (Except, of course, I knew that I'd have been the compassionate one of the clique. A compassionate conservative who wouldn't pick on the poor working-class people.) And the preppies were clearly the Republicans in the conflict, and didn't I have solidarity with their political views? I didn't have sympathy for the boy cyclist, who was insecure and impersonating another nationality. Nah. I felt like I belonged with the privileged kids, who understood that the world is divided into *us* and *them*. They knew (and embraced) that they were superior to the plebeian who could only aspire to be like them.

The other film that influenced my fashion sense in those days was Robert Redford's Oscar-winning freshman film, *Ordinary People*. The location was a wealthy Chicago suburb, and the kids wore wool cardigan sweaters, wool scarves, and button-down shirts. Clothed in fall plaids, Timothy Hutton and Elizabeth McGovern made a strong impression on me.

I went preppy crazy. I wore loafers with pennies in them. There was a huge yearly clothing sale at a famous preppy store in Westwood Village. Friends of mine from church were getting into the preppy craze too. We waited outside on line all night so that we would be the first people in the store. Many of the people on line would be the same people who would line up with sleeping bags for a week to save a spot on the Pasadena Rose Parade route. This was my version of a rock concert.

The store was a madhouse scene during the sale. Red cotton ties with yellow geese in flight prints were discarded in favor of bolder-striped university ties. Khakis with normal-length legs were madly traded for a slightly high-water pant to be worn above a sockless ankle in penny loafers with pennies in them. I bought quarter-panel pants (just like it sounds: one half of one pant leg was blue from the hip to the pant cuff, the other half yellow; one half of the other pant leg was green, the other half bright red).

Soon every JCPenney was selling alligator shirts, Topsiders, and penny loafer knock-offs.

▐▐▐▐▐▐▐▐▐

After two years at ELAC my mind was absolutely distracted by the idea of getting rich. (I earned mostly As or Withdrawals, not many grades in between.) Try as I did, I couldn't get myself to consider the value of working hard today for a payoff tomorrow. I had only a fantasy relationship with the future. Like voting Republican because I "knew" that I was going to be rich. That belief wasn't based on anything concrete. I had a few hundred dollars in my bank account. I wasn't a saver. I lived at home. I was losing my self-discipline and I was without prospects. Nothing about my life choices was in the service of creating wealth.

I dropped out of college.

▥▥▥▥▥▥▥▥▥

I wanted to become a waiter at Marie Callendar's, but the manager—a coarse, fat-bellied, walrus-mustachioed man named Cary—told me that I was too good a fry cook to be promoted to the floor. He told me that the more I asked him the more stubborn he would get about telling me no. He pissed me off.

Brian and I became disillusioned as fry cooks, so we went up to the Marie Callendar's in Pasadena. We got hired immediately as cooks, with the understanding that if I proved to be a good worker then I would get promoted to waiter. Brian and I shined at Pasadena, and we got Joey Jay hired to be a cook there as well. We all lived with our parents then, but frequently all three of us camped out at each other's homes. We were like the Three Musketeers, faithful friends who always watched each other's backs, ready to pull the others out of a bind. We were twenty years old.

One morning, Rob Ott, our manager, needed to contact me to cover a shift. He phoned my home but my dad said that I hadn't come home the night before and that I was probably at Brian's or Joey Jay's. Rob called Brian's home, and his mother said that Brian hadn't come home and had probably slept over at my house or Joey Jay's. The manager called Joey Jay's, and his mother said that Joey Jay hadn't come home last night and had probably stayed at my house or Brian's.

A few minutes later, Brian, Joey Jay, and I walked in the back door of the restaurant. We were completely exhausted from staying up all night—powwowing at a cemetery, hanging out on the beach, going to all-night bookstores in downtown L.A., eating Tommy's burgers at 5:00 A.M.—and were now coming to the restaurant to use the head.

Three months after I started working at the Pasadena Marie Callendar's, I was promoted to waiter. Two months after that I was elevated to headwaiter.

## 1982

When I read the novel *The Razor's Edge*, by the British novelist W. Somerset Maugham, I declared to my family that I wanted to change my name to Winston Somerset Loya, or W.S. Loya. (I liked the whole W. H. Auden and W. B. Yeats and W. S. Merwin literary thing.) And I told my dad that I would allow my good friends to call me Winny or Win for short. When I became the headwaiter at Marie Callendar's, I'd post instructive notes around the waiters' stations and sign them "Winny." The girls thought the pretentious WASP wannabe was cute.

▮▮▮▮▮▮▮▮▮▮

Priscilla ("Prissy") Manley, ex–Miss Temple City, was hired as a hostess at Marie Callendar's in Pasadena. In her Miss Temple City photograph, she looks like Snow White on a Main Street Parade float at Disneyland.

The minute I saw her holding a stack of menus at the front counter I knew that I had to have her. She was the prize, the culmination of all my life's work to be viewed as a legitimate insider, not some poseur or wannabe conniving at the gates of whitedom. My dad had had his white beauty, so I'd have mine, too. And I knew exactly how to woo her.

Prissy attended Lake Avenue Congregation Church in Pasadena, and the college group pastor, Mark Neuenschwander, was an old student of my father's C.O.D. college department. I was connected. When I showed up to the group, I received a special welcome. This did not go unnoticed by Prissy.

When I looked at Prissy I thought of a burly driver I'd met the week I traveled with a church group on a camping trip. The driver of the camper was a wide, barrel-chested man, dark and swarthy, with a thick, black mustache. An ex-linebacker from Pasadena City College, he'd met and married the queen of the Rose Parade, the blonde waif who sat in the large swivel front passenger seat and knitted during the entire trip. A monosyllabic working-class guy, he nonetheless had been smart enough to hook up with a beauty pageant queen whose father invited him into the family business after he transferred and graduated from USC with a business degree.

And as I watched Prissy Manley flashing her pearly whites (*Welcome to Marie Callendar's. How many people in your party?*) I thought it might just be possible for me to snag the beauty queen, too.

I asked around (some of the waiters knew Prissy from school or church) and learned that there was a stigma attached to her family. Her father, who was considerably older than she, close to fifty years older, had been a prominent surgeon in the community until he botched a woman's surgery. It was discovered that he'd been high on drugs during the procedure. He was sued for malpractice. (That's how I heard the story.)

I could sniff all of Prissy's daddy issues. It was as if I were a lion in some nature documentary, watching a herd of wildebeest, looking for the small or infirm one at the back of the pack. I was on the prowl for the wounded, and Prissy had all the telltale signs.

After weeks of pretending only to want a spiritual relationship with her—to be her brother in Christ, available to pray with her any time she felt the Holy Spirit's power waning in her—I finally succeeded in getting her to open up to me, to confide in me about her difficult home situation: her rapidly declining and absent father. By then he was completely off the wagon, staying late at bars every night, and then stumbling home, rousing Prissy and her mother from their sleep with his drunken clumsiness—knocking over lamps, turning the stereo on loud, and eventually passing out on a Barcalounger with the TV blaring.

She invited me to her home one night. On the family fireplace mantle there was a photo of her as Miss Temple City, posed at a three-quarter stance. She resembled a crowned Snow White, with a white cape, preppy blunt cut, and cute upturned nose.

One night her father was arrested for drunk driving and forced by the courts to admit himself into a rehab center. That's when I stepped in and tended to both mother and daughter, praying with them for the peace that passeth all understanding, always using the language of the church around the mother, code for *I'm a spiritual man who has tamed his carnal appetites, mortified his flesh, therefore I can be trusted with the care of your daughter's soul.* I pretended I was a eunuch, when all I could think about was getting in her underwear.

For an entire week I spent the night at Prissy's home, sleeping on the couch, going to church and prayer meetings with Prissy and Mrs. Manley. I wanted to make sure that Mrs. Manley and her clutch of cackling God-fearing women friends—all divorced and burned by charismatic men (religious frauds)—saw me as a fine, upstanding, legitimate Christian lad.

My relationship with Prissy lasted a few months until finally, one day, she started crying and claimed she couldn't trust me. First was the five hundred dollars she'd lent me and that I had had trouble paying back. Then there was sex. She told me she couldn't continue having premarital sex with me—at church camp, under her parents' roof while they watched TV in the other room, in her mother's friends' swimming pools while mother and friends sipped ice tea twenty feet away. Prissy wept, adding with repulsion and betrayal in her voice, *And my mother and her friends all told me that I should go out with you because you're a God-fearing boy. Ha! If they only knew.* This statement stung me, but was also weirdly gratifying. I guess I understood that I wasn't really a fraud if my intention the entire time was to have her be my girlfriend so that I could get in her panties.

Sven Ilum was a waiter at Marie Callendar's. He was a graduate of Berkeley, where he'd studied Linguistics. I admired anyone who thought about language, mainly because I'd always associated language with power: He who controlled language controlled the flow and interpretation of knowledge, could manipulate his lessers.

Sven and I became friends, and I attended a prayer meeting at his home. He invited me to a new-style church in Santa Monica called the Vineyard, where Christian rock music replaced hymns (drums were set up behind the pulpit) and the congregation was made up of tattooed folks with long hair and body piercings—a church where gay men like Sven obviously felt comfortable. (Sven insisted that he was not gay because he wasn't giving in to the temptation to engage in homosexual sex.)

After Prissy Manley broke up with me I drove to Sven's apartment.

We prayed to God to give me guidance, to help me cope with the emotional distress. I wept for the loss of her and petitioned God to take away my self-pity. But after some crying, something shifted in me. By the time I left Sven's place I felt impenetrable. I was in strict control of my emotions, not sad anymore, more like pissed off, and charged with purpose. My rage had been ignited. I turned against Prissy.

Who was she to judge me, the slut. Hadn't we bumped into a fireman at the Rose Bowl Parade who, I later learned, had popped her cherry when she was sixteen years old? If it wasn't me in her underpants, it was gonna be someone else, you best believe that.

I sure did.

And that was the way I believed most things about women in those days. All women were Eves, easily duped with any talk of love or matters mushy. I liked the Christian ideas that insinuated that men were more gifted with rational thought than women. Females could be distracted by softer emotions, and then you got what happened with Prissy, who'd been hoodwinked by flattery and deception.

With Prissy I had wanted to fulfill my fleshly desires, and to hell with what she thought. I felt entitled to have Miss Temple City give it up for me, knock me off a little some-some. Whether she agreed to it in her soul or not didn't matter to me. Me me me. I was like that greedy little Pacman, relentlessly gobbling up everything in front of him. Me me me. Concerned only with having his own needs met, satiated. Me me me. Desires fulfilled, dick sucked, balls licked. Me me me. I didn't care if we just walked out of the Bible study tent and did it, with any one of two hundred fifty campers roaming the woods. I needed her naked body leaning against that tree at that moment so that we could do it doggie style. Me me me. Her and me making love like those crazed weasels everyone sees on the Discovery Channel.

With Prissy, my Christian self-delusion was quickly leaving me. I'd exploited my Christian knowledge and church connections to impress her, so that I could get in her pants. And I did so with little hesitation. Up until then, every time I'd strayed or showed signs of not having real faith, I simply chalked it up to mere backsliding. (*Backsliding* is a wonderful catch-all term that can work for anything, from the measly Jimmy-Carter sin of lusting in your heart to the more grisly sin of serial killing.) Hell, as far as I was concerned, most believers were in a perpetual state of backsliding, so before my tryst with Prissy, I didn't think or believe for one second that I really didn't have faith in God.

But by the time of my breakup with Prissy, I pretty much knew that any time God's name rolled off my tongue it would be a Ten Commandment violation, because to some degree, I'd be using God's name in vain. First John 1:6 said that, *"If we claim to have fellowship with Him [God] yet walk in the darkness, we lie and do not live by the truth."*

▮▮▮▮▮▮▮▮▮▮

My breakup and the subsequent anger brought me to a new level of fatigue and spiritual decline. I was tired all the time, incapacitated, as if some great inertia infected my nerves and muscles. No matter how badly I desired to accomplish a task, I'd find myself at the moment of truth—when I needed to lift a foot and take the first step to a job interview or move my hand to pick up the telephone receiver to make a call—I found that I just couldn't make the most fundamental first move. This was a crisis for me. I had so much responsibility at the restaurant, and now I was passing more and more of it on to my senior waiter.

The headwaiter duties at Marie Callendar's Restaurant and Bakery were relatively simple: I devised a weekly schedule for all wait persons; consulted weekly with managers, the head busboy, and the head cook; and trained all the new waiters, either hired off the street or promoted from busboys.

I was beyond tired. Some sleepiness descended on me that was almost narcotic. I'd get out of bed after ten hours of sleep, shower, and get dressed for work—then I'd already be exhausted, as if I hadn't slept for two weeks. My eyes felt heavy, my muscles listless. *There's no excuse for this*, I thought, *I've just woken up*. I called in sick a few days in a row. After three days of sleeping, then waking up for an hour or two, then going back to sleep for four more hours, I decided to get my ass to work. I didn't have a cough or any nasal stuffiness or the muscle aches and pains associated with the flu. Plus, I'd finally run out of waiters and waitresses to cover my shifts.

Between taking orders and dropping off plates of food at customers' tables, I'd lean on a pie-cutting counter and close my eyes for twenty seconds.

*What's the matter, Joe? Are you going to pass out?* Irene touched my shoulders.

*Nah. I've just been so exhausted lately. Beat.*

*Are you sick?*

*Nah. That's the thing. I'm not coughing. No sniffles. I think I might have mono.*

*Yeah. It could be mono. My friend Barbara had mono our entire senior year. It wiped her out. You feel drained all the time, right?*

*Yeah, and not just drowsy, more like dead tired. Like I haven't slept in a month. And the thing is, I can wake up after ten hours of sleep, I'll shower, get dressed, and then I'll get sleepy again, as if a doctor has just given me a shot of morphine. It's crazy.*

*Sounds like mono to me. You gotta go to a doctor and get yourself a checkup.*

*I hate doctors, so I've put it off so far, but this is the fifth day. Even I'm starting to worry.*

*Go get yourself checked. You sound pooped and you look burnt out.*

*I will. Thanks.*

*And don't forget. Suzie has me covered for next Saturday night.*

I was a classic faker. Later in prison, I'd refer to my younger self as a fake, a fraud, and a part-time broad. But I wasn't joking about this fatigue, wasn't playing for attention. In fact, my malaise was so intense that I thought surely when I got myself checked out by Dr. Anaradian he'd tell me that I was gonna die. I just knew that my life was being depleted and that I would die at a younger age than my mother.

I finally went to see Dr. Anaradian, and he told me that there was nothing wrong with me. He gave me a shot of something and charged me seventy-five bucks. I still wondered if Dr. Anaradian was partially responsible for my mother's death. Maybe he should have noticed earlier that there was something wrong with her, and then perhaps she would have gotten treatment sooner. I paid with a check and then promptly stopped payment on it. Family doctor, my ass. He was cut off. I never saw him again. After a few weeks, the fatigue passed.

▌▌▌▌▌▌▌▌▌▌

I needed a distraction. My rescue came in the form of Bob Litts, an old family friend from the Church of the Open Door. He worked for a bartering company in Palmdale, a desert community ninety miles northeast of Los Angeles. He telephoned and convinced me that I could make a lot of money by working for his company as their point man in Pasadena. So I quit Marie Callendar's.

Unfortunately, my beat-up Capri died. I got fifty dollars for it when I towed it to a local junkyard. Fifty dollars for the heap of doors and handles and rims and tires and car seats—each an item that the junk man could sell individually. I asked Sven if I could borrow his car to drive out to the training in Palmdale. Since he lived with his brother, Nick, and used Nick's car, since Nick mostly rode his motorcycle, he wouldn't be needing it anyway. He agreed.

The bartering company was set up to help businesses increase their sales while conserving cash flow, all by bartering goods and services within a membership network. Local businesses could save needed cash reserves by using barter dollars earned from selling products or services to other member companies. Frank, the tailor, could use his barter dollars to eat at Sandy's diner. Sandy could buy airline tickets from Diane's travel agency—all with barter dollars. In my capacity as point man, I was supposed to bring this tremendous opportunity and fantastically sophisticated system to Pasadena.

When I returned the car to Sven I asked him if I could buy it from him in five-hundred-dollar installments. I figured I could pay a generous sum for it since I was going to earn fistfuls of cash very soon. Sven agreed, and I proceeded to use his car without paying him one thin dime.

While Sven tried to track me down for payment, I zipped around to friends' homes and pretended to be this big-shot bartering agent who was going to take over Pasadena. I wanted to be perceived as Mr. Entrepreneur, but I was penniless, already desperately borrowing money to subsidize my happy-go-lucky lifestyle, telling friends that I had a big commission check coming.

After a few months with no income, I ended up sleeping in my aunt Gloria's garage, in a tight half-framed space that my uncle Leo hadn't finished constructing.

▉▉▉▉▉▉▉▉▉▉

As a last-ditch effort to try to get my life on track, I enrolled at the Logos Bible Institute. The professors were thrilled to have me in their classes— I was a challenging student who appeared to be deeply interested in the subtleties of God's Word—and I was thrilled when my plots to deflower their virgin female students succeeded.

Logos was good for a few weeks, but what the hell was I doing there? Christians were boring and certainly no longer the type of folks I wanted to hang out with. My arguments in class against the existence of God were becoming my truest beliefs. But I was tired, so I resisted disbelief, suspended my apostasy. I lasted one semester, pretending to believe.

Finally, I accepted that I was an active disbeliever, an apostate. I lost my faith. I called it quits. I believed no more. I couldn't lie to myself any longer. I was on the road to perdition.

▉▉▉▉▉▉▉▉▉▉

In our freshman year in college, my friend Randy Wallingford and I had been seduced by an elder in our church, John Bates, to join his multi-level marketing scheme to distribute Slick50, a magic fluid that supposedly would permanently protect a car's engine. With Slick50, car engines would run twice as long, since the fluid would prevent metal rubbing on metal for the first few minutes after a car was started cold in the morning. Randy and I each bought a case of the stuff to begin selling, and we attended several serious business meetings at Mr. Bates's home, in Glendale, where we were both touted as golden boys, future businessmen. Within two months we had to return the cases because we couldn't move them. This was my first unsuccessful foray into entrepreneurship.

Now I was living in my aunt's garage (she wasn't too happy) and conniving for each meal. I had no money and was running out of options.

I became inured to the disconnect between my talking about my big plans and never beginning them. So when a friend told me that he was about to make a lot of money with very little effort, I was obviously curious. That night I found myself at an Amway meeting, the perfect place to be if you want to talk about wealth in the abstract or hype yourself into believing that you are going to be amazingly rich one day without ever really doing much work.

I was familiar with the evangelism of Amway promotional meetings: the proselytizing, the message implied that Americans are God's chosen people, the marriage of the mission field with patriotism, mixed with the religion of the dollar—a moral message that the good need not be without cash.

■■■■■■■■■■

I quit the God business to make money, committed to multilevel marketing programs like Amway or Slick50 or other ventures, like Evelyn Wood Reading Dynamics and telemarketing firms. I wanted manna, not miracles or mysticism. Each time I was sold on the quick money I could make with the business projects, I'd throw myself into the endeavor with a convert's zeal. I'd open a business checking account, register with the city as a D.B.A. ("Doing Business As"), get business cards printed, and even improve my wardrobe. I'd attend all the meetings to impress the elder businessmen. I'd call all my friends to impress them with my new title and my vision of a wealthy and famous future.

I was finally and officially a full-fledged fraud.

And a huge mooch. I'd show up to Joey Jay's or Brian's and loiter until I was asked to stay for lunch or dinner. All I did was chatter, talk about how one day I would have the perfect marriage because I understood the Biblical principles of the marriage chain-of-command. I'd talk about all the possible ways that wealth was going to accrue to me. Talking about it to convince my friends and their mothers was really my way of trying to convince myself, to hype myself into a frenzy of belief in a future that I clearly was doing nothing to bring to fruition.

Finally, one night Sven Ilum tracked me down and took his car back, like some sly repo man.

## 1983

My father was shipping-and-receiving clerk at Premier Pool and Pump. He worked for the Haisman brothers (Bill and Harry), who knew my father from twenty-two years earlier when they offered him a two-week job sweeping up their tooling shop, only to have him stay for two years. That little tool shop was now responsible for making most of the pumps that were used for jetted tubs (like Jacuzzi) around the country.

As a shipping clerk, my father was constantly being wined and dined and wooed by myriad freight company salesmen. One of his favorite salesman was one Harry Gong who was young and enterprising, as I ostensibly was, and who had quite a talent for dressing like a model out of *GQ* magazine—suspenders, yellow power ties, two-hundred-dollar Italian loafers—a flair uncommon among the typical freight salesman.

Harry Gong told my father that he was quitting, to start his own company distributing video games in Los Angeles. Harry was Chinese but had a Korean partner who was paying Harry a ton of money for his panache and salesman's savvy. And Harry *was* quite a salesman, because he managed to persuade me to become a salesman for this company. (At this point, the bartering company gig was long behind me.) My dad agreed to let me use his Ford Granada during the day while he was at work.

But every day, after I'd awakened and dressed myself in my best preppy outfit (blue blazer and pressed khakis; white button-down-collar long-sleeve cotton shirt; red tie with a ducks in flight motif), I'd drop my dad off at his warehouse—unlike me he was actually living *inside* my aunt Gloria's house—and drive to Joey Jay's or Brian's and go to sleep.

I continued to borrow money that I knew I had no intention of paying back. I guess I secretly felt entitled to people's generosity in some weird way. If they trusted me, then they deserved to get burned. It was an outlandish logic, I know.

I asked Randy's dad to co-sign a twelve-hundred-dollar loan for me. After I didn't pay several installments, the loan defaulted and because I was nowhere to be found, Mr. Wallingford had to pay the loan back out of his own pocket. Randy had recently told me that if he knew back in junior high that my life would turn out to be such a fantastic mess, then he wasn't sure he would have chosen to be my friend. Our friendship, he said, was too hard on him. His remark wounded the hell out of me. So I guess I was getting back at him by not paying his dad.

I hated knowing that I could exhaust people, as Randy's comment implied, or that my charm wasn't convincing enough or lasting. Up until then I'd still pretty much seen myself as someone everyone wanted to have around. Randy's remark made me realize that maybe I wasn't seeing things correctly. Maybe everyone else was exasperated with me, too. At first hurt by Randy's remark, I quickly became overcome by a feeling of rage, a fuck-you kind of anger.

I began to imagine a world in which I wasn't beholden to anyone, a universe where I didn't care what people thought of me, where I never needed to borrow money from anyone or ask them if I could have a sandwich. But it was only a temporary thought. I'd return to it later, but at the time I could only wish.

So I did the next best thing: I began attending new churches. Fresh flock to exploit. In these new congregations of God's gullible groupies it was easy to perpetuate the fraud of spirituality and good faith. I knew the hymns by heart, the right verses to employ during conversation. I'd always ask a fellow parishioner, *How is your spiritual life?* While play-acting the pious role, I couldn't stop myself from looking at people I met as dollar signs. (*Hello Jim. Nice to meet you. I'm attending the Wednesday-night prayer meeting. Want to come along? Great. So what kind of work do you do, Jim?*)

I was good at sizing up a person's disposable income.

If I learned through a friend that another friend had received a tenthousand-dollar gift bond from his grandfather, then I wanted to get my hands on that dough.

I listened carefully when an acquaintance told me that he'd already saved six thousand dollars toward the condo he was planning on buying.

I'd spot the trusting gudgeon and go after his cash—like the time I asked a Christian acquaintance named Brad if he was interested in supporting my father's ministry in East Los Angeles. (My father didn't have a ministry. Brad unwittingly donated five hundred dollars to my wallet.)

Some of the people whom I borrowed money from I ended up paying back. I wanted to establish some credibility for the future, when I'd make a play for a larger purse. It was all very *The Sting*, what with my intricate intrigues to separate a man from his money, patiently cultivating friendship before finally fleecing him.

## 1984

I was tired. I couldn't work. I aspired to be and do much. I'd had so much opportunity placed in front of me, within my grasp, but I couldn't be a stand-up guy and just do the right thing. I couldn't work hard or tell the truth. The world, with its honest priorities and daylight responsibilities, seemed too far away from me, designed for others to function in. I clearly wasn't suited for the straight-and-narrow. I'd been trying hard to figure a way to fit into society, but I could only ever function on the margins, away from the light, conniving my way into the mainstream briefly, only to commit so much fraud that I had to scurry away into the shadows again.

I was as sloppy a sufferer as I was a fraud. I slobbered all over the place, wept after any tragic afterschool special (Kristy McNichol dying of cancer?), sentimental to a fault. I hated myself, this perceived weakness, this transparency that said, "Here I am, pathetic and needy. Watch me make a fool of myself as I bend over backward to win your approval. Playing it cool, like I'm my own man, certain of myself, in need of no outside validation because I have this really strong, genuine, committed, sublime relationship with God." Oh the bullshit that was my life! I was such a fuckin' phony. Phony, phony, full of fuckin' baloney.

Some drastic action was needed. So I finally started thinking about how to become who I really was.

Stabbing my dad was the only drastic thing I'd ever done in my young life. That was my only passion, born of genuine fear and loathing, desperation and concussion. That was the only believable part of me. By stabbing him I showed that if I was pushed hard enough, I would act like any animal once it found itself caged or trapped or cornered. I knew how to make one last lunge for survival's sake.

I quoted Nietzsche a lot in those days.

*God is dead!* And we killed him! *This feeling, of having killed the mightiest and holiest thing the world ever possessed, has yet to dawn upon mankind: it is a monstrous, new feeling! How does the murderer of all murderers console himself? How will he cleanse himself?*

I'd been living in a bubble all my life, an insular Christian world, and now the bubble had burst. I began to hate with as much fervor as I once tried to apply the Christ-like attributes of love and charity. I hated that my father and his church had trained me to aspire to the heavens as a young boy and yet every time that I had tried to reach up it seemed that God swiped my feet out from underneath me. I hated that he took my mother. I hated my elementary school teacher, Mr. Biddell, for ignoring my grief when my grades slipped. I hated my father for beating me. I hated Woody for not realizing my need for female affection was desperately related to the death of my mother. I hated that God had ignored my pleas for intervention in our home when my dad's anger exploded. I hated the church for telling me that all I had to do was pray to get well. I hated that it was so easy to fool the church. I hated that I knew how much I was suffering. I hated lying, having no option in my life but to be a fake. So much had been expected of me and I couldn't pull off God's holy mission for my life with anything resembling precision.

I had feared my father since the cradle, and by knocking him down, I'd knocked down God. And since I couldn't see or feel God anymore, I decided to become my own God—Nietzsche's *Ubermensch*, a moral authority unto myself, free to act with a god's caprice. I started to mock the notion of love and goodness as principles meant to keep me placid, weak, in check. I started to hate society for its moral imposition, and I took it as my honorable mission to act with complete contempt for its rules and moralities. I often took comfort that as far as sinners went I was a greater sinner than most, of a finer caliber, an extraordinary unbeliever, the Apostate—someone who previously believed in God but turned away from the truth once they knew it—and therefore worthy of greater punishment, a higher accountability on Judgment Day.

▌▌▌▌▌▌▌▌▌▌

Brian enrolled at Logos the semester after I did, so I moved into the house where he lived with other Logos students. For several months I lived there rent free. One day the fellows got six hundred dollars together for the rent. They left the money in an envelope on the table for the landlord to retrieve. They went to work, and I went on a shopping spree.

After that, I moved into a room rented out by Joey Jay's neighbor, seventy-five-year-old Charlotte. Charlotte's husband had recently died, and she needed the extra income. She drank a Manhattan every afternoon, and once in a while I drank one with her. My new job was in a factory, as a shipping-and-receiving clerk. Joey Jay's parents lined up the job and the living space to help me out. The job lasted only three pay periods though. I borrowed the company truck and didn't return it. My foreman had to come to my home and retrieve it.

I was still tired all the time, like I could sleep the sleep of the dead any day or night.

Pretty soon I bounced a check or two with the old lady, Charlotte. I felt a little bad. Seriously. I even kept a list of all my debts that were piling up, and I updated it too.

I still owed Mr. Wallingford that twelve hundred dollars. He could afford it. Again I felt entitled. And tired. I couldn't explain it, but it was wearying being around so many people who refused to recognize my entitlement. I owed Mr. Arrellano seven hundred fifty dollars; Roxanne had five hundred coming to her. And then there were the thirty- and fifty-dollar debts.

▌▌▌▌▌▌▌▌▌▌

Rob Ott, my old manager at the Pasadena Marie Callendar's restaurant, was hired by the management of the historic Griswold's Restaurant in Pomona, California. Griswold's owner was in the process of opening a new restaurant in Santa Barbara. Rob called Brian, Joey, and me and asked us if we'd join him in the project. The old team was back together again.

Unfortunately, Rob could offer us only $5.50 an hour, a minuscule amount of money. But the job appealed to me. I needed to get out of town, and Santa Barbara was one hundred miles north of Los Angeles. I hoped that I could start all over again there, no more shiftiness or using people, and maybe my faith would be reanimated.

Once there, the long hours, low pay, and Rob's receiving all the accolades—even though he couldn't have pulled off such a lavish re-opening without us—made me resent him and hate the job. The only thing about it I liked was my new girlfriend, Jennifer.

One day the kitchen ran out of an item, and I was asked to drive to Ventura to pick it up (a forty-mile drive south). Rob let me use his car. I enjoyed the late afternoon drive. I didn't own a car, so this was a special treat. I loved the freedom of the road. It cleared my head, took me away from my problems. On the way home, I stopped at a mini-mall and made a copy of Rob's car keys.

A few days later, on my day off, I walked to the parking lot behind the restaurant and used the duplicate keys to drive Rob's car down to Los Angeles. I parked the car one block from my aunt Gloria's home, next to the air and water pumps at a gas station parking lot. I told my dad and aunt that I'd taken the bus from Santa Barbara.

I honestly hadn't thought this through at all. Rob's car was eventually going to be found, so I needed to get rid of it, but instead I left it parked in the same spot for two days. When I went to pick it up, it was nowhere in sight.

The car's getting found a block away from my aunt's house was re-markably incriminating, but I decided that no matter the force of the accusation I would plead innocent against all evidence. And there was plenty of evidence.

1. I was the last stranger to use the car.
2. I had had plenty of time to make a copy of the key.
3. And they knew that a key had been used, because there was no broken

glass at the parking stall where the car was stolen, and the ignition had been started by a key, and had not been hot-wired.

4. The car came up missing on the day I left for Los Angeles.

5. I had no alibi.

6. And, finally, the car had been found one block from my aunt's home.

I had fancied myself a *Ubermensch*, but instead my criminal retardation was supreme.

I figured that all I needed to do was get up to Santa Barbara and walk into the restaurant as if nothing had happened. Deny. Deny. Deny. Like Nixon. That would be my tactic. Make 'em prove it. But something else came up. I didn't have enough money to pay for a bus ticket, so my mind quickly turned to stealing another car.

I thought, I'm already a criminal, why not riff with this? Go where my madness would take me. Because in this madness lay my emancipation. I wouldn't think small anymore. This could be my *Ubermensch* moment. I wouldn't need to be kind. I could think outside the box, for myself, without referencing some other person's moral code.

I'd been tired and wanting to detach from having to please people, to conform to the norms and mores of my upbringing and my religious community. I wanted to rebel against sanctimony, I needed to develop and nurture disdain for certainty, for dogma, for rules, and regulations and systems and authority. I needed to break away from my dad and Woody and that cop who wanted to charge me with attempted murder and whoever else demanded utmost earnestness from me—and this crime then would be a perfect way to do it. Finally, my big break had arrived. I would become a true criminal, acting against God and society.

First I walked to a main street in Alhambra and started to take note of the people and car traffic. I watched a car wash to see if it was possible to just jump in a car and take off. Nothing looked promising. Too many men ready with towels to dry the cars as they came off the rollers.

But the supermarket across the street was full of possibility. I'd never actually physically robbed anyone before. You know, stuck a knife in their ribs and asked them for their wallet. My criminality had always been deception: bounced checks, basic defrauding, defaulting on loans.

Rob's car was my first real theft, but even that had been subterfuge, not overt robbery. But what I was imagining—grand theft auto—was considered strong-arm robbery and carried more time. But it was what I wanted to do, *needed* to do, if I was going to lay to rest my ethics forever.

Ever since I stabbed my father I'd felt a power growing in me. I'd used that power to stick up for that kid being bullied after school, and I'd used it to turn away from God. Embarrassed that I'd fumbled the Rob thing so obviously, now I wanted to use it to commit an anonymous theft, where the victim wouldn't be able to identify me and I could feel strength again.

I was taking things up a notch. To commit this crime I was going to have to summon my strength to physically overpower an adult to get something from them. Naturally, I could only imagine attacking a woman first, an older lady, if possible. And then I saw her; maybe sixty years old, pushing a cart. Her car was parked at the edge of the parking lot. I walked up to her as she was fumbling with the keys to open the door.

*Excuse me*, I said.

She turned slowly, but my hands were already on her hands and the keys. She struggled to hold onto them.

She muttered, *What are you doing?*

*I have a knife in my bag, so don't fight. Give me the keys.*

*Help me! Help me! Stop! Stop!*

I yanked the keys from her and pushed her away from me. I unlocked the car and got in. She pounded at the window.

A car drove up behind me to block my leaving. Other men had seen what I was doing and had rushed to help the old lady. They banged on the windows.

I shifted into reverse and punched the gas pedal. I smashed into the car so that it moved out of my way. Then I drove out of the parking lot and jumped onto the freeway not far from the store. That's when I heard a loud pop sound and the car swerved a little bit. I had a flat tire. (The police report said one man punctured my back tire with a screwdriver.)

I pulled over to the side of the road and began to wipe off the stick shift, inside door handle, and steering wheel with my sweater sleeve. I got out and I scaled the freeway wall. I landed on the other side, in Joey Jay's neighborhood. I ran six blocks to his place (he'd quit the restaurant and returned to his parent's home the previous week) and explained to him that I'd just tried to steal a car and had barely got away. I told him that I needed an emergency ride to Santa Barbara. I didn't tell him about the old lady.

I lay down on the back seat of Joey Jay's car and wept. I didn't know what was wrong with me. Why was I making these choices? All that puffed up philosophizing wasn't anywhere to be found in that pitiable back-seat ride to Santa Barbara.

When we got to Santa Barbara I walked into the restaurant. Brian saw me and went to the back of the restaurant. He returned with Rob at his heels.

Rob asked me *Why?*

*Why what?*

*Why'd you take my car?*

*What are you talking about?*

Joey Jay looked at me. He hadn't known about any of this.

*Don't lie, Joe. The cops found my car down the street from your aunt's place.*

*I didn't take your car.*

*Listen, Joe, I won't press charges if you just admit that you took my car.*

I started to cry.

Joey Jay told them about the car I'd stolen in Alhambra. All I remember is that I lay in a booth for an hour and wept like a baby. Phone calls were made. At one point I knew that the Alhambra Police Department had been notified.

Rob came to me, speaking to me in a low tone, like a doctor to a sick patient. *Joe, we've arranged for Joey Jay and Brian to drive back down with you to Alhambra. They'll pick up your dad and turn you in to the Alhambra Police. If you agree to turn yourself in then, I won't press charges up here. You need help, and this will force you to get counseling. You're sick, Joe. You need some help.*

I turned myself in.

I wrote the judge a letter and told him that my crime was actually a symptom of a deeper issue. I used the metaphor of the red indicator oil light on a car's dashboard. When it lights up, we don't hammer the dashboard and smash the light and think that we've solved the problem. No. The light is merely an indication that there is bigger trouble under the hood. The red light is meant to prompt us to pursue the problem elsewhere. I wrote that I had committed a crime, but that the crime was due to some mental instability on my part. I promised to go to counseling after serving whatever sentence he felt was just.

He gave me a two-year suspended sentence, but I had to serve a ninety-day work furlough.

I felt like I'd gotten away with the crime. My charm still worked and had duped the entire judicial system. Sure, it was a close call. I could've been judged more harshly and made to pay for my entire crime, but instead I had been judged to be a decent person who had made a bad error in judgment. Then this impression they had of me started to fuck with me. Did they not take me seriously enough? Did they see me simply as an adolescent vandal, a pathetic excuse for a lawbreaker? Couldn't they see that I was an evil genius?

Well, work furlough was something. For two months (two-thirds of the jail sentence) I slept in the county jail and was let out for work during the days. My father was still working for Premier Pool and Pump, and they'd just acquired NFC Industries, a fancy title for the work of one man named Richard. Richard's junction boxes, with their various speeds, complemented Premier's pool pumps. Among Richard's many cultivated personae was a juvenile delinquent who'd been saved by entrepreneurship. Capitalism had set him straight, got him on the right track, and now he was a Christian man who would hire me and set me right with the virtues of good old manual labor.

The job was easy work. I stayed even after my work-furlough sentence expired. All I did at first was assemble PC boards with diodes and transistors and transformers and lots of soldering of wires and cables. I then packaged and shipped them. As grateful as I was to Richard and my dad, and no matter how rapidly the company expanded (to thirty workers) or how much my stock rose because I'd essentially been the number-two guy in the company from the start, no matter all that good stuff, I was still unsatisfied with the money and promotions. And I was still irresponsible with my money. I couldn't stop living paycheck to paycheck. This was made harder because I was still trying to keep my relationship up with Jennifer in Santa Barbara. Every other week, when I got paid, I'd get on a Friday-afternoon bus for a four-hour trip north, where I'd spend money on food and films—all to make Jennifer think I was a man of leisure and means.

I really hated returning to Los Angeles on Sunday nights. It seemed that the trip came and went so fast. Plus, returning at all hardly felt worth it. After all, what was I returning to? To a stinkin' job at NFC Industries? To a boss who was a fuckin' joke of a man, who didn't fool me with his juvenile-delinquent narrative, which had to be patently false because he was still nothing but a momma's boy? And my dad, what did I care what he thought, since he was only a lackey at the job, he who had once held so much promise. It's for these guys that I'm bustin' my balls to get back to work in a hurry when I'm having such a great time in Santa Barbara with a woman who gives me the best sex of my life and who is beautiful and loves me like crazy?

So after four months of brooding over this resentment, I stopped returning to Los Angeles on Sundays and instead showed up to work an hour late each Monday morning, after taking the early-bird bus. A month after that I started calling in sick on Mondays, essentially giving myself a three-day weekend. And in the end I just quit NFC Industries altogether, convinced that Santa Barbara was my future.

The thing about Santa Barbara was that every other weekend I was essentially shacking up at Jennifer's mother's house without paying for rent or food, unless we went out to eat. I was invited to stay the first weekend, but after that I just acted like I was both wanted and entitled to be there. I'd finally found a place for which my delusion was best suited: the home of an ex–flower power single mom and her Pollyannish daughter.

True, I was like a big brother to my girlfriend's smart twelve-year-old younger brother Jimmy, but that didn't change the fact that I was still a big mooch. I had no savings and no prospects. For Jennifer and her family, it was as if a hobo had decided to move in. Jennifer's mother, Tammy, was the sweetest woman alive, but after only two months of my not showing any initiative, she finally asked me to find my own place and get a job.

I was offended. Her request made me sound insensitive, poor, and pathetic. Couldn't she recognize how special I was? I was becoming something, someone important, and I'd given her the privilege of under-writing this massive shift in my soul.

But I had to get out of the house, this much was true, and I had to get out fast.

First I had to find a room to rent in someone's house. That wasn't too hard. I could be charming. And I had a checkbook. Not much money in the account, but my prospective landlord didn't know that. I rented a nice room near the University of California at Santa Barbara. The older guy who lived in the house liked me. He thought I was a grad student at UCSB. Once my living quarters were set up, I got a job selling clothes at Loring & Co., a traditional clothing store. My preppy fashion sense helped me dress the right role for the interview.

In the beginning I was a hard worker. (I always worked initially really hard to impress my new employers. But that would last for only a few months, or weeks, and then I'd be gone, in search of a better deal, an easier hustle. After every job I quit I felt entitled to more money for less work.)

At Loring & Co. I had clothes all around me, and knowing that you could fool people by the costume you wore, I wore button-down shirts, prep-school ties, worsted wool pants with cuffs, and Cole Haan loafers. I even carried a burgundy Cole Haan man's purse. I bought and smoked a pipe. I wore a wool vest, right out of the Brooks Brothers fall catalog. The only thing missing was the duck hunt.

Once, some of the other salespeople and I were chatting about the billion-dollar bailout of Mexico. As a proud, card-carrying member of the Republican Party, I read the *Wall Street Journal* every day.

*We should annex them,* I said. *Make Mexico part of the U.S. and you'll see an immediate increase in their average household salaries.*

A woman out of sight behind a high shelf of button-down shirts chimed in. *I agree.*

When she walked around the shelf to join in the conversation, she looked at me, startled for an instant by my brown skin. Then she quickly recognized that she was in safe company. In my blue blazer, silk bow tie, pink button-down Oxford shirt, seersucker pants, and saddle shoes, I was a dark caricature of a preppy. (The film *Gandhi* opens with Mohandas Gandhi as a young lawyer, dressed in Western garb, clean cut and optimistic, telling his brown children at play to be good Englishmen.)

*Yeah*, I continued, *we need to save Mexico from herself.*

My quick allegiance with the woman's own opinions on foreign policy made her feel at ease, so she spoke frankly. *My husband and I lived there for a while, and those people's work ethic isn't what it is here. They don't have the same relationship to initiative and hard work like we have here in America.*

That's what Mexico was in my imagination, a siesta and a tourist trap, where you could get the clap if you weren't careful. For a while, when I was still a good little Christian boy, I thought about one day going to Mexico to convert orphans. Maybe even be in a position to sponsor one of the true converts in their application to become a citizen. I wanted to help. I thought that Mexico needed my help. I thought that Mexico, poor Mexico, desperately needed my patronage.

▮▮▮▮▮▮▮▮▮

Golf was becoming an obsession. Jennifer's brother Jimmy turned me on to the game. I still didn't have a car, so Jennifer would pick me up and drop me off everywhere. One day on the course I met two fellows named Robert and Oliver. We hit it off immediately. We played well together and liked each other's jokes. They were in business together, buying and fixing up homes. When I heard that Robert was selling his 280Z, I offered to buy it with cash and clothes. I told him he could go into the clothing store and pick out fifteen hundred dollars worth of stuff, and I'd sneak it all out the back door for him. So he did.

A bomber jacket: $380. Two pair of dress pants: $325. Two dress shirts: $175. Silk ties: $90. Three pairs of loafers, size 9½: $450. One man's leather purse.

The 280Z was mine, and I looked good in it. I was zooming around with a car, cash, and clothing now, feeling my worth. Plus I had a cash generator: the back door of the clothing store.

Oliver wanted new clothes too, so I told him that he could have fifteen hundred dollars' worth for nine hundred bucks.

Oliver drove a 250 SL Mercedes and he couldn't have been older than thirty, so I knew that this white kid had money. Still, he was interested in getting some free duds. The deal was consummated, and now I had two crime partners, each equally larcenous at heart.

Then I pushed things to the next level. I told Robert and Oliver that as my crimeys (fellow criminals) they were eligible to be let in on the other criminal money-making ventures I was a part of. I told them that my uncles in Mexico (of which, in truth, I had none) ran a stolen-car ring. As family, I'd give them cash and they'd invest it for me in their business. Last month, I told Rob and Oliver, my ten thousand dollars returned me fifteen. I told them to think about it. I didn't need their cash, I assured them, and I wouldn't bring it up again. I simply felt that I owed them the chance, since we'd committed other crimes together. Both Robert and Oliver were eager to see that kind of money in a one-month return. Within a week each man came to me with ten thousand dollars in cash.

When I started to commit fraud, I had a greater incentive to assume a false identity. I printed business cards for Loya, Richards, and Associates. My friend Zach Richards and I called ourselves business consultants. I was the president of the bogus company. He was my VP. These were the Reagan years.

Jennifer's father, a businessman told me that he'd read my D.B.A. announcement in the newspaper. I sat there, straight faced, and told him that I was doing business consulting.

*Be careful*, he said.

Be careful? What gall that man had to think that I was doing something shady. What a fuckin' racist way to think! But he had an M.B.A. from Stanford, and he knew that I didn't even have a B.A.

A week after Oliver gave me his ten thousand dollars, he approached me for a five-thousand-dollar loan.

*I have a bunch of money coming to me from my father's probate. It's all tied up in court, but I'll put up the Mercedes as collateral. You and I know that it's worth more than five thousand. If I don't have the money to you in ten days, the car's yours. That's how sure I am that this thing is close to resolving itself. Okay? Deal?*

I loaned Oliver the five thousand, and in ten days, when he didn't show up with the funds, I owned the Mercedes. I gave the 280Z to Jennifer, and I drove the Mercedes. I moved closer to downtown Santa Barbara, into a guesthouse behind a nice home. Crime was paying pretty well. For a reason. Christmas came to Loring & Co., and I was making out with fistfuls of cash. Anything that I sold for cash—not check or credit card—went straight into my own pocket. I tampered with charge tickets to make the theft look like it was coming from work shifts other than mine.

In fact, at one point Mr. Loring called me into his office and confided in me that the thefts had occurred while every other clerk had been working, and I was the only clerk whose shift turned out clean. I promised to keep an eye out for any of the tricksters.

Feeling uncatchable, I became greedy, I overreached. One day a man who had bought a suit from me returned it for tailoring during a shift that I wasn't working. He had his receipt, but no corresponding ticket could be found. To make matters worse, a ticket for other tailoring done on the suit—tailoring paid for in cash, which went into my pocket—was tracked down. There was evidence galore that a sales transaction had taken place on my shift but for which no money or house ticket existed.

I pleaded innocent. *I don't know what could have happened,* I said, *I know how it looks and I'm sorry, but there is a misunderstanding here. Please know that I'm not that kind of guy.* This was what I usually did: denied the facts vehemently, ignoring the empirical evidence. I treated my accusers as if they were superstitious to believe what was right before their eyes, as if they were wrong even to perceive me as able to commit such an act. And I suggested—not overtly, mind you—that maybe there was even an undertone of racism in their accusations. And boy did this work in my mind. By the end I'd almost convinced *myself* that I hadn't done the crime.

Sleepiness returned for a few days, and my stomach started acting up. Diarrhea all the time. Headaches too.

The police were called in. I failed a polygraph. (My excuse to them: an abusive childhood had made me nervous under any form of interrogation.) Two detectives badgered me, told me they knew I'd done it. In desperation to get a confession, one of them even told me that one day I'd be walking by a clothing store window and I would be racked with guilt that I never copped to this crime at Loring & Company. Swear to God. They tried that one on me. Straight out of *Dragnet*, when police officers could shame confessions out of suspects.

I was unmoved.

Mr. Loring liked me. During a dramatic conversation, after the failed polygraph, I pulled the store key out of my shirt pocket and slapped it on the desk. My honor had been besmirched. I'd rather have no responsibility, I told him than be thought a man who could betray his boss.

He refused to accept the key. He said that he was checking with his lawyers about how to proceed, and in the meantime I could keep the key. Then I made a mistake: *I don't want to sound conspiratorial,* I told him, *but maybe one of the other workers had a grievance with me and set me up.* He smiled. I knew instantly that I'd overplayed my hand. I left his office after telling him that I, too, was checking with my lawyers.

Then a weird thing happened. Someone burglarized the houses in front and behind mine on a day when I was in Los Angeles. The homes were burglarized five hours apart, and it appeared that the burglar had used my home as his resting area between burglaries. Sitting and waiting, maybe watching *Days of Our Lives* or *General Hospital* on my TV. Odder still, was the fact that as far as the homeowners could tell, the thief had stolen only a few brushes, some combs, and several jars of coins, but nothing that could be called valuable.

Secretly I assumed that my friend Zach Richards, whom I'd let stay at my home while I was away, had allowed his drunk girlfriend to trespass in the homes, and she'd merely dabbled in thievery.

When I returned from Los Angeles, detectives came to visit me. They knew that I was being investigated for the clothing store crime. They also knew that I had a lot of disposable income and a very extensive wardrobe, especially after I allowed them to come inside and look around.

*Like shoes?* one of the officers asked, after spotting my fifteen pairs of loafers on the floor of my closet, their value ranging from one twenty five to two fifty a pair.

Later that afternoon I defrauded a Christian surfboard-maker out of his BMW. When I showed up to buy the car I brought along with me as a gift a book about the *Christian Heroes of the Faith*. Believing me to be a credible Christian, the young Hawaiian's blond wife encouraged her husband to give me the pink slip and keys to the car without waiting for the twenty-thousand-dollar check to clear.

Saps. I immediately stopped payment on the check.

But I was a sap, too. When the police officers arrived at my house with more questions, I now had a top-of-the-line Beamer and a not too shabby looking Mercedes in my driveway, so I now looked more than a little bit suspicious to them. In their eyes I was a petty criminal. They just weren't sure of which variety. But they took a stab at it, bluntly accusing me of running a burglary ring that had been terrorizing homes along my stretch of road for as far as six miles. They had no facts tying me to any burglaries, but they said they didn't need any to have my probation officer call me back to live in Los Angeles. And that's how the Santa Barbara sheriff's office made me an outlaw in their city.

I promised my probation officer that I was leaving for L.A., but instead got a room at the Santa Barbara Sheraton Inn, where President Reagan held his news briefings when he was in town.

The noose was getting tighter and tighter, and my life felt more out of control, even down to the little things. The surfer guy figured out that I had burned him, and he reported the theft to the cops. I was hitting on Jennifer's best friend, Sandra, and when she turned me down I hit on her sister. I was tense all the time, with headaches and stomachaches. I was still falling into deep slumber at inopportune times. Once on a drive down to Los Angeles, to visit friends, I pulled over and slept at a rest stop for two hours. And twice during sex I had to stop mid-thrust because the crown of my skull felt like somebody had hammered a railroad spike straight into my brain. The anxiety over that incident made me revisit earlier suspicions that I was going syphilitic mad, like Al Capone. There was no logical way to explain how I could be behaving so erratically, so obviously to my detriment, ignoring all inhibitions, as if red stoplights were flashing warnings of a danger and I was just driving right through them toward an inevitable crash. How else to explain this suicide drive? Sandra's father was diagnosed with Epstein Barr, so then I thought that maybe I too had that illness. Something was seriously wrong with me. I could sense it, but all I knew how to do was create more chaos for myself. Finally, in a desperate moment—tired of conniving, of getting close to people to win their trust and approval—I quit. I told my girlfriend that I'd call her in the morning, and I told my dad that I'd see him in a few days when I drove down to Los Angeles. Instead, I packed some clothes in the Beamer, (I'd sold the Mercedes) and drove to Mexico to blend in with the morass of brown on the other side of the border. I was now a full-fledged fugitive, ready to start over again, maybe as a more so-phisticated criminal, but certainly as a man of mystery.

# vii

Heavy's voice sounded like Mike Tyson's voice, a bull on helium. And, boy, could he scream, I mean really shriek.

One night I was sleeping peacefully when all of a sudden I woke up to a loud, blood-curdling plea for help. I thought someone was being stabbed to death. Then I heard the screams more clearly.

"Help me! Help me! I can't breathe!"

I disliked Heavy and wouldn't have crossed the street to piss on him if he'd been on fire.

I heard walkie-talkies crackling, boots stomping, keys jangling. The grill gate to the tier was squeaking open. I heard a guard yell "Open cell fourteen. Hurry up! Cell fourteen. Hold on, Heavy. Here we come. We got you. We got you."

He'd fallen off his bed and couldn't get up.

The funny thing was, even though Heavy was so fat and greasy and smelly, and none of the guards really wanted to touch him, they nevertheless worked hard to save him. And the whole time we could hear Heavy saying, "Don't be afraid of getting your hands dirty, motherfuckers."

Big Man—a guard on the tier whom we kinda liked because he was a turnkey—didn't take the job personally. He just did his work and went home. Later he told us that it took seven men to lift Heavy, while he accused the guards of copping a feel of his nutsack.

Heavy was disgusting. We'd pass him on the way to the shower and peek in his cell. There he'd be, like a brown Michelin Man, sitting on his bunk. His belly looked like a monster truck tire wrapped around his waist. His tits were as big as extra large watermelons. Sometimes he'd be asleep and there'd be a massive trail of drool on his tits. When he was awake, we'd say, "Heavy D, let me see you suck your fine-ass titties."

And with both hands he'd lift one tit and put it into his mouth.

We'd say, "You're one fine motherfucker, Heavy."

He'd say, "Fuck you, punk."

He was the only man on the tier who was allowed to have his food trap open all day. The cells were stuffy and he had more trouble breathing in them than we did. He was also given ten or twelve clean bed sheets a day, unlike us who were given two clean bed sheets a week. Every few hours, he'd roll up the sheets, stick them out of the food trap, and drop them on the floor outside his cell. Indian Early would be let out of his cell periodically throughout the day to sweep the sheets to a dirty laundry basket designed specifically for Heavy's linen. Heavy would hear Indian Early moan and he'd say "Pick up my shitty diapers, bitch." Heavy went through the sheets like they were tissues, because he sat on them naked, and his slimy ass leaked all day long.

Bey would tell Indian Early, "You ain't gotta pick up his shitty diapers. BOP can't make you do that. You catch viruses and other sick shit from handling them there shitty sheets. That's unsanitary. If you want, I'll help you file a lawsuit against the warden."

# License

*From good to evil is one quiver.*

—Russian proverb

drove to San Diego, sold my stolen BMW for fifteen thousand dollars, and decided to buy another car. I went to a Chevrolet dealer at Mile of Cars with all the cash I had, about thirty thousand. I walked up to a young salesman, opened the bag of money, and showed him the cash.

*I'm gonna buy a car today, right now.* I could see him get real excited. I pointed at a shiny blue car and said, *I'd like to start by test-driving that Cutlass Sierra.*

He asked for ID. I gave him my driver's license, and he went inside to photocopy it. He came out smiling, thinking he was gonna make a quick bundle.

*I have to drive it off the lot though, for insurance purposes.*

I said, okay.

He drove us to a bank parking lot, parked, and got out of the car. I pretended to get out of my side, but when he started to walk around the car I closed my door again and slid over to the driver's side. He stopped and looked at me through the rear window.

I turned and shouted, *I'm just scooting over,* but I closed the driver's side door, too. Then I automatically locked all the doors.

By then, he was at the passenger window banging on it. I put the car into Drive and took off. He was banging on the trunk of the car, yelling at me, and he was pretty fast because he stayed with me for about fifty yards. Finally, I started to pull away from him. When I looked at my rearview mirror, he was standing defiantly in the middle of the road with both of his arms in the air, giving me the middle finger. I laughed and nonchalantly raised my right arm and gave him the bird too.

Twenty minutes later I was in Mexico, driving down the coast to Ensenada.

When I arrived in Mexico as a fugitive, it was predictable that the people I would hang out with would be Marines from Oceanside who had driven down to Tijuana and Ensenada on the weekend to get drunk and maybe pick up a lusty Latina for the night. I was as belligerent as they were, the worst kind of American—the patriot fugitive, drinking Corona beers in the cafés and waxing eloquent about how all Mexico needed was a benevolent dictator.

I was living large in Mexico, for a while—playing golf every day, clubbing every night, and trying real hard to make friends at the local Papas and Beer restaurant. I even rented a nice-size condo on the beach, where I threw a lot of parties.

Then, I returned to the condo one night to find that twelve thousand dollars in cash had been stolen.

This theft drove home the reality: even though I thought I was becoming a bad-ass, I was too nice. Even though my philosophy of life had led me to crime, I still wasn't hard enough, and the real bad-asses had seen this. I still had too much decency in me, a holdover from my early Christian days. I'd been a nerdy, bookish boy, trained to love language, to appreciate the classics, to be aware of obscure theological arguments. When I lost my faith I was forced to move toward the world, and that's when I discovered that I didn't know jack shit about its customs and cues.

On the night of the theft I got good and drunk, and put aside forever my childish preoccupations with soft words and sissy ideas. I wanted to become a brute; a mumbler; a grunting crotch-scratcher; a primitive, uni-brow public spitter—rude, crude, and lewd, and able to employ poker-table code, the pimp stroll, pillow or gutter talk. I wanted to be skilled at ordering a man's drink. I wanted to be a man of action. Not to think, but to act. Thinking, I believed then, was an impediment to action—so fuck books and ideas and language! I wanted to dumb myself down. Only then could I become a real man, a doer, a take-charge guy.

I sat back and thought, *Okay, I just lost a chunk of change. But I'm a fugitive now, so everything is open to me. I don't have to think about replacing the money legally. What are the criminal possibilities of this situation?*

I was tired of having to get close to my victims. Having to earn their trust was too time consuming. And I didn't have the time or the patience. I was too impulsive. I needed quicker victims. Better not to know them personally. Somehow it made me feel more principled to think that I wanted a realer relationship with people, truer, more honest, less fraudulent, not based on insincerity or phoniness. I couldn't be faulted for wanting to establish right up front that they were the mark, the victim, and I was the man who was there to rob them. No pretense. *Blam!* Right there. The truth of the moment would be beautiful and ferocious, and in that way my vehemence wouldn't have to disguise itself in passive-aggressive ways. I wouldn't have to lie. And my crime could be more ethical than lousy petty deception—not as ethical as getting a job, working hard, and spending my own hard-earned money, mind you—but in the world I lived in I would elevate myself from a bottom-feeder, to seize some moral high ground over the low-level criminal who scavenged for crumbs at the expense of his family and friends. I liked this idea of trying to be fairer with people by not being nice to them before I stole their shirts. Yeah, this would be better for them, and clearly easier for me, since I needed money like pronto. That twelve thousand dollars was a hell of a lot of money to lose in one wallop. I imagined as reckless a life as possible. Maybe being in Mexico, my mind was being romanced by the notion of the *bandido*, of Pancho Villa crossing the border and stealing money from the Feds. So I decided to rob a bank.

I'd never held up a liquor store or anything like that before, so this was a big leap. I really didn't know what I was doing. I just thought that I would go full-fledged into bank robbery. Fuck the bullshit. No more having to rip people off with cowardly deception.

I drove back up to San Diego.

I walked into a bank at nine in the morning, the first bank that opened up. I wrote a note on the back of one of the deposit slips: *We have a bomb. I have a gun. Give me the money NOW!!!* I underlined *now* twice. I waited in line for a minute, but then I got nervous, so I walked away and ripped up the note. As I walked out, I noticed that there were two cameras on me. I'd written the note right there in the lobby, at the customer station, and either one of the cameras could have zoomed in on me while I was writing it and deciphered my threat. I could have been busted even *before* I'd robbed the bank.

You can see how stupid I was.

The next time I wrote the note at Mickey D's. Then I walked down this long ass boulevard in Old Town San Diego. I walked in and out of banks for hours—B. of A., First Interstate, Great Western, Security Pacific, even a few Savings and Loans—but I didn't rob one of them. I was too chicken shit. I caught the trolley downtown to another big street with plenty of banks on it. But first I got lunch at Wendy's.

It was 2:00 P.M., and I was feeling like a fuckin' idiot. I knew I had to act like I had a pair and just do it. But I kept walking into banks, desperate and panicked, and then walking out again. I'd pretend that I was filling out a deposit slip, then I'd go and stand in line. But then I'd leave. Sometimes I couldn't even finish pretending that I was filling out the slip before I walked out. I was afraid, a total coward. I couldn't overcome my fear. But I kept trying.

I entered another bank and I stood in line with my note. It was 4:45 P.M. THIS WAS IT! I had to rob this bank right then and there because in those days, banks closed at five.

It was my turn. The short female teller said, *How are you doing, sir?* and I was like, *Fine, thanks.* Then I slid her the note. *We have a bomb. I have a gun. Give me the money NOW!!!* She looked down, and she would not look up. Ten seconds passed. She was still reading. Fifteen seconds. She was still pretending to read. I moved the note around the counter a bit like, *Hey, hey, look up. I'm over here.* She merely reached for the note and pulled it to her. I pulled it back. We were having this tug of war with the note, but she refused to look up at me. I murmured, *I'm not fucking around, I'm not fucking around.* I even patted my waistband as if I had a gun. Then she raised her head and roughly passed some money over the counter, pissed off, like I didn't scare her, but more like I irritated her. Her eyes were saying, *You fuckin' knucklehead.* I believe she knew that I was a beginner. But there was some energy coming off me, enough wildness to alarm her. She may have figured, *He's so scared that he might just do something really stupid.*

I took the money, left the bank, turned left, and start running down the street. I crossed the street and I looked back. People were looking at me, but I was far enough away so that there was no catching me. Near the train station I jumped into a taxi and told the driver, *Take me to the border.* We were on the freeway when and all of a sudden two CHP cars whizzed by on their way to close the border. I got dropped off in San Ysidro, but I didn't cross into Mexico. Instead, I walked to a Motel 6 and got a room.

And there I counted my take: $4,300.

▓▓▓▓▓▓▓▓▓▓

I'd gotten away with so much in San Diego already, so I got cocky, I thought I was slick. The next day I tried to drive into Mexico but I was caught at the border by CHP, who were checking for stolen vehicles. I was still driving the car I'd stolen from the sales lot. They ran a check on me. Five warrants showed up, and I was hauled into custody. They didn't know anything about the bank robbery, so I was sentenced to three years in state prison for all my other frauds.

▓▓▓▓▓▓▓▓▓▓

I served my time at the low-medium security prison in California. Two hundred men lived in dorms designed for the military. We all shared one large open bathroom area. In one corner of the bathroom, five shower heads hung down from one thick pipe spanning the ceiling near five freestanding sinks; thirteen toilets were lined up against a back wall, one and a half feet apart from each other, no partitions. (We sat close enough to wipe each others asses if we'd wanted.)

I showed up to prison unaffiliated with any street gang. I was kind of thin, wearing tortoise-shell glasses, not looking like anybody tough from the streets. No tattoos, no prison pedigree. Other prisoners could tell that I was a "fish," that this was my first time in prison.

So the Mexican prisoner powers-that-be assumed that I was a straight-up pussy, a sucker. They sent this kid Froggy after me. He was supposed to have helped them stab another prisoner but hadn't shown up. He gave them the lame excuse that he got locked in another part of the prison. They told him that he could get right with them if he stole my stuff. So Froggy tried to become my friend. He came and talked to me, walked with me to chow.

I was leery of him but not too concerned; it was too early for me to see his angle. As far as I could tell, his move wasn't sexual; a sexual come-on would have been wordier. Froggy and I discovered that we'd grown up in neighboring cities. We mostly talked about things as they were back in the day.

About a month later a friend of mine sent me my first thirty-pound prison package: cans of tuna, cartons of Camel cigarettes, Cup o' Noodles, Taster's Choice coffee, jalapeños in a can; a bunch of dry goods, like Doritos, Ritz crackers, Oreo cookies, and Snickers candy bars (stuff we called "zoo-zoos" and "wham-whams"). My friend also threw in *Playboy*, *Penthouse*, and *Hustler* magazines.

I carried my zoo-zoos and wham-whams from the property receiving room and put them in my locker. I decided that I'd only open the locker at special times: early-early morning, when everyone was asleep, or midday, when everyone was at work. I didn't trust anybody. I certainly didn't trust shady Froggy. I actually felt a little bad for him. The guys he hung around with teased him, treating him real greasy because he wasn't Mexican. He was a wannabe from El Salvador.

One day Froggy came in from working out and said to me, *Hey, I heard you got a package. Why don't you bust out some of those zoo-zoos?*

*Nah. I ain't hungry.*

He badgered me and badgered me.

I told him, *Hey, check this out. I ain't opening it, and you ain't got nothing coming.*

He left empty handed, but later that night he returned and whined, *Hey, man, at least kick down some of those cookies.*

Give him credit because he was trying hard to connive his way into my locker, but I just wouldn't cave in. It was a matter of will, and I was thinking Froggy had a weaker will than I had. He was so passive-aggressive about his connivance that I realized he wasn't *physically* going to take anything from me.

The next morning he started in again.

*Hey, man, why don't you at least let me look at one of your titty magazines?*

My thinking was that I would let him check out one of the magazines since I didn't care much for softcore pornography anyway, so I loaned him the *Playboy*. Two days later when I asked him to return it he looked up at me and said, *I sold it. What are you going to do about it?*

Somebody must have pumped up his heart to pull the power play.

Now, having been raised in East L.A. I know enough about the male ethic to know that this was my test, to find out what kind of man I was going to be. Plus, when I was in the county jail some older convicts told me that there would come a time in prison when someone would try to take my stuff, and I wasn't to give it up without a fight, or the rest of my prison stint would be horrible. People would then take all my property and feel that they could take my ass, too. That's why I translated Froggy's words as a direct threat to my manhood. Was I going to bend over and let someone take my defeated asshole or was I going to fight?

I told him, *All right. Wait right here. I'll be back in an hour.*

He kind of panicked thinking that I was gonna get a knife or something. *No, no let's do it right here.*

And I said, *No. Fuck you. I'll be back in an hour.*

Then I walked to the prison chapel.

I entered and immediately spotted the bruised and bloodied body of God's son dangling on the cross. Staring at Jesus, I wondered if this test would be my downfall, my Golgotha. Or would it be my resurrection? I bowed my head and summoned my rage. I conjured humiliating childhood memories. I remembered stuff like the time my dad almost drowned my brother, and the time I got my ass whupped by three bullies on my way home from school when I was twelve. And I recalled the exact fear I felt right before I pulled out that knife to stab my father.

I pulled out all those bad memories and held onto them for strength, as if they were some sort of religious medallion that I could rub to give me faith and power. And it worked, because the powerlessness subsided, and a rage started swelling. Soon I had all this fuckin' surplus anger, so I started to plot what I had to do.

First and foremost, I needed to draw a lot of blood—by either biting him, or smashing his face on the porcelain sink or against the mirrors, or kicking him so much in the face that I'd bust open his nose or his mouth. No matter what, I needed him to see a lot of his own blood. And I needed a lot of other guys to see his blood. That was the number-one thing I had to do. The other thing I had to do was make sure that nobody else jumped in. I had to make sure that the match stayed between the two of us.

There's a sort of prison ethic about fair one-on-one fighting. It is encouraged as a way to test your manhood. But like all mores, prisoners played fast and loose with that ethic. Like if you kicked a guy's ass then it was expected that the defeated opponent would return with one or more of his homeboys. I couldn't do anything about the future, but I desperately needed to establish that nobody was going to jump in for the kid if I started kicking his ass. That was my plan.

I finally emerged from the chapel, a dark, unholy spirit, all purposeful and shit.

I walked back to the unit. An older guy named Chupey was watching *Phil Donahue* in the dayroom. Chupey was short—five feet one, a quasi-midget—but he was a *veterano*, been doing time forever. He had a huge chest and big sixteen-inch arms, deformed big, fuckin' freak-show big.

I approached him slowly. *Dispensa?* I got his attention.

*Check this out man. You don't know me, and I don't know you, but there's this guy named Froggy over there.*

*Yeah, I know Froggy.*

*Yeah, well, I lent him my magazine and he sold it, which puts him in the wrong, so I'm going to go check him right now. I'm going to call him to the bathroom for a fist fight. And what I want—and I know you don't have to help me out here—but I think the beef should be between me and him, but I don't know anybody else around here, so I'm wondering if you could make sure the fight stays just between me and him.*

Chupey jumped up from his chair. *Fuck Froggy and the horse he rode in on. Yeah, come on youngster, go do what you gotta do, and I'll make sure nobody jumps in.*

While Chupey walked around telling people, *Hey, these two guys are gonna fight, so don't nobody jump in,* I went to call Froggy out.

Chupey went to the fellows who I thought might have been behind my extortion. But no matter how vehemently he cursed Froggy, for all I knew, Chupey could even have been in on the extortion. But I was deferring to him, showing him honor and respect as I handled my business. I had confidence that Chupey had my back.

I found Froggy seated on his bunk. I knew he'd been waiting for me. He had his boots on and he was wearing a thick jacket and weightlifting gloves. *Hey, let's go to the bathroom.*

He said, *Okay, all right.*

A crowd had gathered in the huge bathroom. I walked in first, my hands in my pockets. Chupey was saying, *Nobody jump in. Nobody jump in.*

A voice behind me whispered, *Take your hands out of your pockets. Take your hands out of your pockets.*

But I was trying to play it cool, play it cool cool cool.

Froggy finally walked in, and he said *All right.*

*All right.*

He put his hands to his sides and curled his fingers into fists. I took my hands out of my pockets and walked up to him very casually, like it was my Sunday stroll. Then I took one quick step toward him and kicked him as hard as I could, right in the nuts. I mean I carried his scrotum on the tip of my boots, straight up into his stomach. I kicked him that beautifully in the balls.

He bent forward. Then I punched him in the face, and he dropped. When he went down I proceeded to beat the shit out of him. I kicked him over and over again, but I felt like I needed more personal contact, so I leaned down and punched him several times. But that wasn't good enough either, so I turned him over on all fours and straddled him like he was a donkey, and then I reached around to the front of his face, grabbed his chin and lifted it up, and I came around with my fist, pounding, pummeling his face. He was defenseless. (When I was seated on his back, I felt something like a back brace on him. He'd taped books and magazines—prison body armor—over all the kill spots of his body.)

I picked him up and smashed him up against the wall. I was so mad I kneed him in the balls again. I was choking him and choking him. I was so angry that when I saw his ear I leaned forward and bit it. I was yanking and yanking on his ear, chewing and gnawing on it. When I pulled away I saw his ear all bloody red. Then I felt something in my mouth. I spat it out.

Then I screamed out *AARRGH!!* I was Mike Tyson and *Lord of the Flies* all rolled into one. I was having a fuckin' religious experience.

Then I heard somebody yell *placa placa* (slang for "police"). Somebody grabbed me and said, *Come here, come here.* I was out of control, my body was going crazy, I was amped, as amped as I could be. As we walked out of the bathroom, a second guy said, *Sit down, sit down.* I sat on a bunk and he sat right across from me. He set up cards between us like we were playing spades. Then he told me to take off my T-shirt. I did. A third guy grabbed my bloody T-shirt and tossed me a clean one. A fourth guy handed me a towel 'cause I had the kid's blood on my face and I was breathing hard, wondering what's going on, totally enraged, furious. All this stuff was surging through me—rage, violence, and now I was having to come down. It was kind of shocking. Then I realized that all the guys who had helped me escape out of the bathroom and were now cleaning me up on the bunk were the same guys I suspected of prompting the kid to extort me.

It ends up that the guard warning had been a false alarm. Froggy was in the bathroom splashing water on his torn ear, trying to clean himself up. The guy who handed me the towel, Tiny from Long Beach, addressed me respectfully:

*Dispensa, but hey, uh, we thought you were a lame, so we sent this guy after you, man. But we were in the wrong, man.* (Tiny had a habit: when he spoke he'd cup his right hand in his cupped left hand and repeatedly lift it and then gently drop it back into his palm again. It was a prison habit of many men, but Tiny had it to the extreme.) He told me that he had broken into

Froggy's locker and that I had first dibs on anything in there. I walked over to the kid's locker and took a pair of jeans, a carton of generic cigarettes, some colored pencils, and my own *Playboy* magazine.

▓▓▓▓▓▓▓▓▓▓

Later that evening, after chow, I sat on my top bunk and pretended to read a book as the other prisoners walked through the unit, on their way to the yard or to the evening service at the chapel or to a visit. When our eyes met, they'd nod at me to let me know that I was now respected as part of the mainline. Chupey walked up to me. The top of his head barely reached the bottom of my top bunk.

Orale, te aventastes. *You got off youngster. Where you from anyway?*

*I'm not from anywhere, no gang or nothing like that. My family moved all over L.A. but I was born in Maravilla.*

Chupey said, *Is that right?* Being from the Maravilla housing projects already put me in good company. It was as close to a pedigree as I got.

Chupey looked at me with his head tipped to the side, suspicious like. He paused for a moment then said, *I'm from Maravilla. Who are your peeps?*

*My dad's name is Joe Loya, like me. My mother's name was Bessie. She died when I was nine years old.*

*Nah?*

*Yeah.*

*They got married real young?* Chupey asked. *Went to Griffith Junior High, then Garfield High School?*

*Yeah: My mom was the Tower queen at Griffith. They dropped out of high school and got married when they were sixteen because I was coming.*

*I know, man. I know your peeps. My sister Esther, rest in peace, was supposed to be your godmother. Bessie and her were best friends. But Esther died of an overdose a few weeks before you were born. I didn't know your jefe or jefita very good. My brother Booby knew your mother better. Hey, you need a haircut?*

*Nah, not now. But soon, I think. Why?*

*Let me know. I'll hook you up. My brother Booby is an inmate barber here. We got busted together. I'll fix you up and get you to the top of the list. There's a waiting list. He usually charges a pack of Lemacs, but you ain't gotta pay. You're our homebody and you made us look good when you kicked that motherfucker's ass. You got long heart, kid.*

*What are Lemacs?*

*Man, you are a fish.* Lemac *is* Camel *spelled backwards. Lemacs are Camel cigarettes.*

*Oh, all right.*

*So, man, your peeps are the Loyas? Ain't that some coincidental shit? Wait a minute. Didn't your brother have a sister—*

*You mean my father?*

*What?*

*You mean didn't my father?*

*What'd I say?*

*You said, "Didn't your brother have a sister?"*

*Oh, right, dispensa. Didn't your* father *have a sister named Gloria?*

*Yeah, my aunt Gloria.*

*Fuck, she was fine. No disrespect, youngster, but she was the finest lesbian in all of East L.A.*

*Wait, you mean my aunt Gloria?*

*Yeah, youngblood.*

*Nah, couldn't be my aunt Gloria.*

*Youngster, look at me. I ain't bullshitting. Your aunt Gloria had long blond hair and a rack out to here. And she hung around with some other dyke,* buena chula. *What was her name?*

*Damn, I didn't know that my aunt Gloria was a lesbian.*

*Yeah, you didn't know that?*

*Nah. But that explains a lot. She had some really butch women friends who looked like* vatos—*you know, dressed in khakis and Pendleton's—who used to show up to all the family parties in the seventies.*

*What's she up to now?*

*Well, for starters, she goes by the name Sister Gloria and she belongs to New Kingdom Church, over there by Santa Rosa Hospital, off Brooklyn Avenue.*

*Cut it out? I know that church. That's where everybody calls each other brother and sister, and I'll tell you, I ain't that desperate for family.* He rubbed his hand down over his walrus-brush mustache, pensively staring into the air. *How 'bout that. She found Jesus?*

*Yeah, and like you know, it's one of those Pentecostal churches, so she attends Bible studies six nights a week.*

*Fuck, she went out like that?*

*Like that.*

*Man she was so fine. Hey, do me a favor.*

*Awright.* ·

*Tell her I said hello. Tell her Chupey sends his best.*

*No problem. I should be calling her soon. She'll probably tell me to tell you that she'll be praying for you.*

*Yeah, whatever. Just let her know I said* orale.

■■■■■■■■■■

Brian and Joey and other Christian friends from Logos Bible Institute wrote to me and asked me where I stood with my relationship to God. I told them that behind bars, among men of action, not men preoccupied with the theoretical, I had begun to conceive of God much like that one-time Archangel Lucifer must have conceived of Him. If God could be one, then so could I.

All through my early religious education the idea that you bent your knee either to God or to Satan had been pounded into my head. So now that I was done with God, He became my foe. I adopted the Maoist view that the enemy of my enemy is my friend. I could comprehend my loss of faith only as a need for a new allegiance. And I was ready to offer my allegiance to another higher power. Now all I wanted was to be the same rank in Satan's army as I had been in God's.

I was playing catch-up to my prison peers. Some of them had been dedicated to the lower themes since age ten, talented at full-throttle pettiness, skilled at killer gossip, giving in to their cruelest impulses, acting out and injuring others just for the rush. I wrote to my Christian friends and told them that I had no time for weak superstitious-minded boys telling me how to live. I was bitter, and all their theories about God's goodness did not survive contact with the hard material world I was now a part of.

■■■■■■■■■■

I got out of prison in 1988, hard muscled, with a hundred and fifty dollars, hard muscles, with a tough heart, and a plan to become a bank robber, and never to get caught again. I didn't want to be merely a good criminal. Like my hero Prometheus, who stole fire from Zeus on Olympus and gave it to mankind—a criminal with balls, a Robin Hood who wanted to open shit up, spread the wealth, take some of that power from God to poke Him in the eye—I wanted to be a demi-god: observant, detailed, ruthless, and ready.

■■■■■■■■■

An accurate accounting is always confusing business. Let's just say I robbed a lot of banks in a fourteen-month span. The FBI estimated between thirty and forty. The *San Fernando Valley Daily News* reported twenty-four. Even I lost count. It was easy to do. Sometimes I robbed two or three banks a day.

During that period of robbing banks, between 1988 and 1989, my fatalism operated at full tilt. No surprise really: I was the same age as my mother when she died, and I'd always figured that I was doomed to die young, like her at age twenty-six. I used to tell friends that any year I lived beyond my mother's age was a bonus.

On the morning of one robbery, I stood naked in front of my bathroom's steamy mirror. I wiped off a circle big enough for me to stare at my image—at my dark, sexy face, my clear complexion, my collegiate haircut, the small scar on my left eyebrow, my full lips, my deadened eyes. I dared my hard self to flinch. My mouth opened slowly and murmured an erotically morbid demand: *Don't return without fifty thousand dollars.*

That's the day I walked into the lobby of a Bank of America, straight to the manager, and casually explained that if he didn't take me to the vault I was going to blow his fuckin' brains out. He led me to the vault. To my surprise, two women were standing at the door of a huge open safe, white canvas Brink's bags at their feet. The women seemed to be logging and loading a recent shipment of money. I commanded them to face the wall at the end of the vault, get on their knees, and place their hands behind their heads. They obeyed. I loaded my pillowcase with bricks of the new bills I pulled from the open safe. To keep the employ-ees frightened, I told them to start praying to their God and ask him not to let me get fuckin' pissed. When I turned to look at them, I noticed a puddle of urine between one whimpering woman's legs. I felt like God, with trembling vassals at my feet.

I walked out of that bank with thirty-two thousand dollars, my largest heist yet.

I was a long way from the "Kumbaya" Christianity of my youth.

■■■■■■■■■

A little known fact: Stalin began his political life robbing the czar's banks. But unlike Uncle Joe, I didn't rob banks to help finance some great social cause. I never used the idiom of political ideology to justify my theft. I was simply a hedonist out to have some fun.

And I did what most poor people do when they acquire a bunch of money through crime: I played Daddy Warbucks. I picked up checks at pricey restaurants, like Citrus on Melrose; paid for a block of Shubert Theater tickets when I took ten friends to see *Les Misérables* and *Miss Saigon*; took my dad to Pink Floyd and Bruce Springsteen concerts; kept a Chinese tailor in San Marino; bought several cars; and played eighteen holes of golf five times a week, sometimes twice a day. I entered a Beverly Hills mall and left four hours later, six thousand dollars lighter.

I have a photo of myself shot during the late campaign days of 1988. I'd invited friends of like cynical mind to come to my house to watch the Dukakis vs. Bush presidential debate. In the photograph, we are all on my porch. I, the only brown man, am seated at the front right edge of the group, in khaki shorts, sockless ankles, casual loafers, and a T-shirt em-blazoned with an American flag and the slogan NIXON IN '88—a slogan that spoke to the crude truth that it took a crook to admire a crook.

I suspect my big, shit-eating grin in those photos had much in com-mon with O. J. Simpson's or Ollie North's or Charles Keating's. There was in it a hint of wry knowledge. It was the smile that says *Yeah, that's right, I did it. And you know I got away with it.*

I admired Republicans because, in my imagination, they were the wealthy caste playing wolf to the Democratic party's sheep. I also believed that, fond of robber barons' avarice, they would surely have admired my greedy initiative. It was my conviction that, like me, Republicans would do anything to get money and protect their power. (For a while I always kept thirty or forty thousand dollars in a duffel bag under my bed.)

For proof, I needed to look no further than Reagan's deregulation and the bundle Charles Keating and others had made in the Savings and Loan scandal. Tricky Dick had been resuscitated to elder statesman status by the late eighties. Ollie North became a hero for his complicity in an illegal fight against Latin pinkos in jungle parlors. Watergate criminal G. Gordon Liddy was reincarnated as a political commentator. Lee Atwater, the malicious man who dug up a grubby prison photo of Willie Horton and turned the 1988 presidential race into race baiting, was my favorite political operative. The Republican party looked like a book that might be titled *Let Us Now Praise Infamous Men*. All I wanted was a single chapter for my audacity.

Whether women liked me for me or my money didn't matter because *I* liked myself—for the ease of my life, which had been born out of fierce will, naked grit, and pluck. I had been tired of being poor, so I'd gone out and done something about it. Fuck whining. No more blaming others for my sense of inferiority. I now felt utterly superior to the mousy people who could only ever be passive players in the dramas of their lives. I developed contempt for them, people who couldn't cough up a nut sack and change their lives, lift themselves out of their ruts. The country was full of opportunity.

Bank robbery appealed to me philosophically. I enjoyed the notion of being an agent of hazard who'd introduce people—bank tellers or anyone else who got in my way—to terror whenever their lives intersected with my violent whim. Something about that exchange made me feel alive. I know it woke their asses up. I wanted people who otherwise felt safe in life to feel the stinging fear and shameful helplessness that I had felt crawling across the floor as my father or school bullies kicked and taunted me.

"Intersected with my violence" is a great phrase because it perfectly describes a car crash, where two moving bodies collide. But in my case

I'd cut across a person, halved them, cut them into two, reduced them. I'd run right over and through them thoroughly. I loved watching their faces. I loved watching the shock. They didn't know what to do. They were stunned, paralyzed by fear, in the grip of the real thing. This was not a mere hint at threat but the real, tough experience where all they could do was whimper or sniffle or mumble or fuss with their fingers. My collision with them made those tellers experience a different life than the safe one they were accustomed to. It made them smell the moment, and all the usual things that were their sedate existences, that mattered in that moment—whether they watched *Good Morning, America* or not, whether they drove their children to soccer practice or not, whether they went to Mendocino with their husbands for their honeymoons—none of it mattered. No story they told themselves mattered. And that was what I wanted to happen. I wanted them to know the humility of being victims to an all-encompassing greater narrative, which squashed their meager hopes and dreams, which ran roughshod over their puny aspirations. I wanted to make my narrative a boss over their lives. I needed to let them know that my existence trumped theirs.

I narrowly escaped capture a few times.

One afternoon, in 1998, I was driving around Riverside, prowling for the right bank to rob. (By that time, I had ten or so bank robberies under my belt.) I came across a red-brick bank building on a corner. There was a park across the street from it. I drove around the block and parked on the other side of the park, facing the bank. I'd run the two-hundred-yard dash in high school, and the bank seemed approximately that far away.

I sat in my Mazda RX7 and listened to Pink Floyd on my new CD player. I unwrapped a stick of gum and cased the area.

It was as if I had stepped into a George Romero horror flick. There were old people everywhere, shuffling around like zombies. The men were in golf clothes. The women wore their blue hair in sort of bouffant styles. Their sweaters were draped around their bony shoulders, buttoned at the neck like those of schoolmarms. Men in wheelchairs played chess at tables. Some women used walkers, and at least one shriveled sack of dry bones sat in his wheelchair with a portable I.V. rolling next to him.

A fat nurse in a tight, white polyester uniform and comfortable hospital shoes pushed another geezer to a crowded bocce court.

I figured maybe some old fuck was having a birthday party with his cronies. Then I realized that I was parked in front of an assisted-living high-rise.

I got out of my car and walked to the bank, through the park. I entered the bank and stood in line. There were three tellers, each with a customer.

The teller on my left was an older white woman, preppy looking with a gray blunt cut and wearing a sweater with a scene of geese in flight across her chest.

The central teller was a skinny young Mexican woman wearing a lot of makeup. She looked like a younger version of my aunt Maggie.

The third teller was a thick-boned black woman, maybe thirty-five years old. And I mean she was black, uncut black. In prison men that black were usually nicknamed Blue or Tar Baby.

Her window was the first to come open. I had never robbed a black woman before.

As I walked up to her, I was smiling, and she was smiling at me.

*Hello, sir. How can I help you?*

I said, *Yeah,* as I propped my fanny pack on the counter as if I was going to rummage through it for my checkbook. *This is a robbery. We have a bomb. I have a gun. Give me the money now or I'll blow your fuckin' head off!*

I punctuated the last word by stabbing the bag with my middle finger. My other hand rested halfway in the bag. As soon as the woman realized that I was robbing her, she froze up. Her eyes got large. It almost looked like she was ready to pass out. She started shaking.

*Ah shit,* I think, *this bitch is gonna faint on me.*

I never had anyone do this to me before. She looked like she was ready to shit on herself or run or faint—which one, I couldn't tell. But she was in heavy distress mode. I was ready to lose her, so I locked my eyes on her and spoke low but firmly. *Open the drawer.*

Her hands shook as she slowly slid them to the key in the drawer.

*That's right. Now open the drawer and give me the big bills first.*

I never looked down at the counter because if I broke eye contact I knew I'd lose control of the situation. So I was gazing into her eyes like Rasputin, trying to mesmerize her with my intensity. (That's what I always did, treated them like they were robots and I was their programmer. That way there was nothing for them to improvise. They just had to follow my orders. That's how I used their fear to my advantage.)

I continued sliding the stacks of what she was giving me into my bag.

*OK, good. Now the fifties.* She paused and sneaked a glance at Suzie Chiquita next to her. *Don't make me jump over the counter. Don't make me.* I put my hand on the counter like I was ready to bound over it. *Just look at me and give me the fuckin' money.*

She moved again, but slowly. Getting this money from her was like pulling fuckin' teeth. Every time I commanded her to do something I'd have to focus so much energy to get her attention that I barely had enough energy to convince her to obey my commands.

My eyes were locked on her. I didn't want to take them off her, so I just kept shoving the money into my fanny pack. But I didn't know what she was giving me. I had no sense of what she was giving me. You know, large or small bills. And she continued to look like I might be literally scaring the shit out of her. I saw small tears. I heard a whimper.

I zipped shut my bag and smiled. *Good. Now lock the drawer, turn around, and walk away. Don't look back.*

When she gave me her back, I watched her walk away, and I felt triumph, like *Oh my god, I didn't think that was going to end.* Then I spun around and started walking away. I saw that nobody was looking at me, so I walked out nonchalantly (typically that's the way it works), really feeling ultra triumphant now as I exit the bank and step out onto the sidewalk. I looked both ways, stepped into the street, and . . . about three steps into the street, I hear *BLAM!*

The bag I was holding flew out of my hands and landed on the road.

I turned around, stunned. A plume of red smoke was billowing out of a two-inch hole in the fanny pack.

*Damn!*

Then the bank's alarm bell went off.

*Fuck!*

I had to think fast. I had to pick up the bag (you know, evidence and all). The red smoke was blowing away from me, so I bent down for the bag real fast, completely unaware of the invisible tear gas.

I immediately pulled back, jerked back with my catlike reflexes, but not before tear gas soaked my eyes. Now I was blinking, blinking, blinking, and I was looking at the bag on the ground. I couldn't leave the bag, so with my head turned I reached for it and I yanked it up. Then I start trotting away. When I hit the park I start running. I was ready to go blind any minute. I mean the tear gas was powerful when it hit my eyes, and I had this bag behind me and there was this huge trail of smoke billowing out of the bag, and I was running with my eyes focused on the car, blinking, blinking, blinking. I swear to you that one millisecond longer in the tear gas I would have gone blind. With every blink I thought *this is the last blink, this is the final blink, I can't open my eyes again, I think I'm ready to go blind.* It burned so much I could barely focus on the car. My eyes were shutting fast. Ta-Ta Ta-Ta Ta-Ta. Like a camera shutter on speed.

I finally reached the car and opened the trunk. I was in complete panic mode, acting by instinct. I unzipped a canvas sports bag, threw my smoky fanny pack in it, and zipped it shut. When I got in the car I tore off my boots, jeans, shirt, sweatshirt, and jacket. Underneath it all I had on khaki shorts and a blue UCLA tank top.

I watched the bank as I put on green Sperry Topsiders. Two squad cars pulled up to it. Several officers ran to the wall of the bank with their guns drawn. They surrounded the building, approaching the bank's front door with caution. And I had the gall to think while I'm sitting there in my car blinking, blinking, blinking, *What a bunch of dumb fucks.*

I drove off in the opposite direction. I blinked, blinked, blinked my way onto a main street. A motorcycle cop looked hard at me as he passed me on his way to the crime scene. I tried to stay cool, even though my eyes burned like hot piss. The cop turned left at the next block. I suspected that he might be turning around for me, so I turned left and zigzagged through a few neighborhoods on my way to the freeway.

When I got to the next city, I stopped at a 7-Eleven. I bought Perrier water and washed my eyes out with it. Once I got home I tried to scrub the dye off the money, but every bill was permanently stained.

I'd heard about those exploding dye packs while I was in prison. One robber put the wad of money down the front of his pants, and the explosion blew off his left nut. He tried to sue the bank. I just threw the $7,658 in the garbage.

▆▆▆▆▆▆▆▆▆▆▆

People ask me, *"Didn't you know you were gonna get caught?"* As if I was motivated by logic. I mean, criminals are impulsive, that's who we are, and we really don't care about future consequences. I don't go along with the theory that we all want to get caught. I didn't want to get caught—I know that—but I just couldn't stop. I had a respectable fourteen-month run as a bank robber.

Stephen Crane describes a "delirium that encounters despair and death and is heedless and blind to the odds." I knew that altered state. I'd surrender my fear of death to the bathroom mirror, pick up a gun, draw a deep breath, and walk into those banks fully prepared for a final shootout with the law, if destiny deemed it.

But destiny never did.

▆▆▆▆▆▆▆▆▆▆▆

I got about a mile away from this one bank in Norwalk, then pulled over. I undressed in the car and threw all my clothes in a bag: a baseball cap, baby-blue windbreaker, a loud red-plaid shirt, and a heavy XXL brown sweatshirt. I tossed the bag out the passenger door and down a drainage ditch carved into the curb. I peeked into the moneybag as I pulled away from the curb, and saw many small stacks of money wrapped with rubberbands.

When I got on the next freeway on-ramp, I quickly moved over to the fast lane. All of a sudden I had to jerk the car back to avoid sideswiping one of the three sheriff's cars that were zipping by me, red, yellow, and blue roof lights swirling. I looked ahead. A helicopter was hovering above the traffic about a half-mile up. It appeared to be headed my way. The traffic was flowing pretty well, but I suspected that a roadblock was being set up ahead, so I quickly clicked on my turn signal and got off the freeway at the next off-ramp.

I turned right into a mass of herky-jerky traffic, where cars from the off-ramp and spillover from two side streets were all angling to make the light. Making matters worse were the cop cars nudging between civilian cars. They'd stop beside a vehicle, look at the driver, then pull up and repeat the procedure at the next car. One patrol car scooted up next to me. I turned and looked at the young blond cop in aviator sunglasses, a Jan Michael Vincent look-alike with a butch haircut. He stared at me then proceeded to the car in front of mine. I figured I was safe from detection. The cops were looking for a fatter man, one in a red windbreaker and a bright red Madras cotton shirt (the costume I had worn in the bank). I was wearing a white tank top and Ray Ban sunglasses.

The light turned green, and the traffic moved awkwardly down the boulevard. I continued driving straight ahead, checking off in my head the things I needed to keep clear about. My registration tags were current. There were no outstanding warrants for failure to appear in court for traffic citations. My blinkers were in working order; whenever I made a lane change, I used them.

At one point the helicopter was right overhead, able to see through my open sunroof that I was wearing shorts and that no gun or moneybag was visible. And nobody lay scrunched up on the floor below the dashboard.

But as I passed cop cars coming to the chase from side streets, they slowly began to drift in behind the clear caravan of sheriffs' cars forming behind me.

My funeral procession. I'd been singled out.

I still tried to play it cool, still using my blinker, etc. The Jan Michael Vincent look-alike pulled up on my left side again. I looked at him, then back at the road. He dropped back into formation. Then another cop drove up on my right side. Same thing: I looked at him and he dropped back. In the end, at least twenty cop cars were behind me. When I saw their lights go on and when the helicopter hovered low in front of me, I knew I was screwed.

*Pull your car over and put your hands on the steering wheel.*

I was surrounded. I pulled over. I knew that they didn't stop me because I fit the description of the thief. There was just no way they could have caught me by sound police work. I was too gifted. No, they were making one of their notorious racist rushes to judgment. I thought, *These fuckin' fascists can't treat a brown man like this.* I swear to god. I was actually offended! *Fuck it,* I thought, *I'm going to make a big deal of this stop so I can use it against them in court.*

My rearview mirror showed deputies out of their vehicles, kneeling behind their patrol car doors, their pistols and shotguns aimed at me. Like Hollywood would do it. A bullhorn blasted directions.

*With your left hand, reach for the keys, pull them out, throw them out of the car, and keep your arm outside where we can see it!*

*WHY'D YOU STOP ME?!?!*

*Shut the fuck up and reach out the window with your right arm and open your door from the outside! Slowly!*

*WHY'D YOU STOP ME?!?!*

*I said shut the fuck up so shut the fuck up! Now step out and face away from us! Put your arms in the air!*

*WHY'D YOU STOP ME?!?!*

*If you don't shut the fuck up . . . put your hands behind your head and clasp your fingers together. I said clasp your fingers beh—*

*WHY'D YOU STOP ME?!?!*

*Stupid motherfucker, better shut the fuck up before you get shot! Now start walking backwards to us. Slowly! Keep walking*

*WHY'D YOU STOP ME?!?!*

*Keep walking. Keep walking.*

*WHY'D YOU STOP ME?!?!*

*Keep walking. Okay. Stop! Now take two steps to your left. Freeze!*

*WHY'D YOU STOP ME?!?!*

*You'll find out. Now get down on your knees, yeah, down on your knees. Now lay down and lay your arms out away from your body.*

As soon as I lay down on the hot-afternoon asphalt, they rushed me. One sheriff, hyped up from the adrenaline of the chase, fell hard with his knee on my back. I felt gun barrels on my arms and legs and a shotgun barrel on my neck. One cop yanked the back of my hair and raised my head back so that I thought it was going to break. Then he leaned down close to my ear and said, *You wanna know why we stopped you, you piece of shit? We stopped you for being so goddamn ugly in Norwalk.*

From the back seat of a patrol car I watched a group of deputies creeping up on my car with their guns drawn. No one was inside, so they searched the vehicle. One of the deputies stood up and held my money-bag up in the air like a prize fish. *I got it!* The deputy in the front seat of the cruiser I was seated in looked at me in his rearview mirror, through the bulletproof glass between the front and back seats.

*You fucked up. You decided to rob a bank in the wrong city.*

I couldn't know it at the time, but there'd been a transmitter in with the money. Smaller than a checker piece, inside a small wad of fives. The technology had been imported from Nevada, the deputy told me, and could be traced by every law enforcement car and copter in the vicinity. That's what their patrol cars were doing when they were driving up on both sides of me. They were verifying the coordinates with the red indicator lights on their dashboards.

*We're the city in California that got to test the transmitter first. And guess what? You're the sixth bad guy we've caught in two weeks.*

The deputies held me at the scene, in the back seat of the patrol car, because they wanted to do a sidewalk lineup. About twenty minutes after I was caught, I was told to get out of the car and stand on a spot on the sidewalk and not to move. Another patrol car drove up to the curb. Two women were in the front seat.

*Don't look at the passengers in the vehicle. Turn to your left and stand still.*

I turned to my left and glanced at the people in the car.

*If I have to tell you again not to look at them, then you're gonna be in big trouble when I get your smart ass to the precinct. Now turn to your left again.*

I once again did as I was told. A call from his walkie-talkie distracted the deputy holding me. I looked at the women trying to ID me and was relieved to see them looking at me but shaking their heads, as if saying to the deputy in the vehicle that I wasn't the man who'd robbed them.

On our way to the station a call came over the radio: a 211 in progress. Another bank robbery. The chase was on for the next schmuck. White male. Late fifties to mid-sixties. White hair. Approximately five foot eleven. Beige pants. Blue windbreaker. A description of almost every retired white man on golf courses from Pasadena to Miami.

The cop looked at me again through his rearview mirror.

*Watch. I'll bet we get grandpa too.*

▓▓▓▓▓▓▓▓▓▓

Special Agent Cordes and his partner, Agent Shriver, were placed in charge of my investigation. After he interviewed my family and friends, Cordes realized that I wasn't part of any criminal milieu. I didn't belong to a notorious gang. I wasn't a drug user like the typical bank robber in Los Angeles. I was more like a seminary student gone awfully awry. One day, while escorting me to court, he turned around in the front seat of the car and looked at me, seated handcuffed next to Agent Shriver.

*Joe, I got to tell you that you baffle me. You're not like anyone I'm used to arresting for bank robbery. And I've been at this for eighteen years. Ask Agent Shriver next to you. The guy who usually sits where you are right now next to Agent Shriver has tattoos, is a junkie, and most of the time is a gang-banger. And now there's you, the anomaly.*

*Special Agent Cordes, here's a bit of advice for your philosophical soul. Don't get tied up in the mystery. Too much analysis can cause paralysis.*

His voice got excited. *See what I mean?* He smiled and looked at Agent Shriver, then back at me. *And how does that go again? The mystery of analysis causes paralysis?*

*No. TOO MUCH analysis causes paralysis.*

*I know some people who could use that advice. Right, Agent Shriver? In fact, we should get that phrase bannered and hang in it our office for our boss.*

Agent Cordes liked the friends of mine he interviewed. There was my shy, sweet girlfriend Jennifer at UCLA; Brian, the future Promise Keeper—those Christian men who gathered in football stadiums in the early 1990s and hugged one another and cried and prayed and swore to God in a public oath that they would be better husbands to their wives by taking more control of the home—Joey Jay, who, while I was robbing banks, had been attending Bible college. (We'd both come a long way from the days when he had two asterisks near his name on my morning prayer list.)

Cordes told my father that because of my instinct to surround myself with good people, he trusted that I would one day get out of the mess I'd created with my foray into crime. Then he confided in my father that at the time of my arrest, his own son was beginning to go through a rebellious phase, not wanting to get a job. Cordes was clearly beginning to mellow. Taking a view on crime now that wasn't so gung-ho. He'd commiserate with my father about how strange it was that fathers could do so much for their boys and yet their good sons could stray nonetheless. Thinking about his son persuaded Cordes to recommend to the court that I be released on bail.

▮▮▮▮▮▮▮▮▮▮

I was released on one hundred thousand dollars bail. Completely ungrateful for the gesture of goodwill on Cordes's part, and to prove to myself that I was truly without conscience, I absconded on the bail and robbed five more banks, placing my aunt Gloria's home at risk of forfeiture, since she had put it up as collateral for my bail. Of course, Cordes revoked my bail. A bench warrant was issued for my arrest. And I was gone, in the wind.

I was about to flee to Mexico when I decided to call Jennifer and make plans to rendezvous with her at the UCLA campus. I wanted to give her some money.

*I don't know what time exactly. But I know your class schedule for Friday. I'll scoot up to you sometime during the day and give you some money. Just walk your regular routes from class to class. Okay? I love you. Everything will be all right, Jennifer. I'll see you on Friday. I miss you.*

The FBI had copies of Jennifer's bank records that proved I'd given her big sums of presumably stolen money. They told her that while they didn't believe it, the U.S. Attorney would have a hard time believing that she wasn't an "accomplice after the fact" to my robberies.

Agent Cordes had a careful chat with Jennifer. *You know I like him, Jennifer. He's a smart kid. But he's listed in the law enforcement computers as "armed and dangerous." The LAPD or highway patrolman who pulls him over will only go by what is in the computer, and that's no good for Joe. There could be gunplay. Tell me where he is, or tell me when he gets in contact with you, and I'll be sure to bring him in unharmed.*

The UCLA campus was like my backyard. On Saturdays when I was in eighth grade, my father would take Paul and me to the campus with him. He'd lock himself in a private library for classics students and translate whole texts of Plato's *Republic*, Plutarch's *Lives*. Paul and I would run around and play army by Pauley Pavilion or hide-and-seek by Royce Hall.

The day I was to meet Jennifer, I found a seat in a busy student quad behind the library. I sipped a cappuccino while reading the *Wall Street Journal*. I kept a cautious eye out for acquaintances, held the paper up and peered over it. Several old friends from Grace Church attended UCLA and held a large Bible study on campus on Fridays. I didn't need to have someone say they saw me hanging around campus.

Several students seated around my table jabbered on about this or that professor who was too strict, and this or that teacher's assistant who spoke barely comprehensible English, and this or that block party that they had heard was a blast but had regretfully missed, and this or that frat party they'd attended where they'd fortunately got laid.

Then I heard a male voice inquire, *Joe?*

I thought, *Oh shit! And I was trying to avoid these nuisances.*

I turned to the voice out of reflex.

When I saw that the bookish, boyish person behind the voice was a stranger wearing tan shorts, wire-rimmed glasses, and a gray UCLA sweatshirt, I pretended he wasn't talking to me. I turned back to the page.

*Joe? Joe Loya? Is that you?*

I turned again to look at him as he walked toward me. His eyes shifted, and I sensed someone behind me too. I bolted upright, and the young man lurched forward. Someone behind me grabbed hold of my right forearm. I yanked my right arm up and into a cocked position, so that the person holding my arm was lurched toward me. Then I snapped my elbow like a compact hook punch and hit the person holding my arm. *Whap!* A ponytail whipped past my vision. The person who'd grabbed my arm from behind was a female FBI agent, also in casual shorts. I'd caught her on the chin.

Meanwhile, the boyish-looking agent was trying to grab hold of my flailing left arm. *We're FBI agents! You're under arrest!*

I didn't hear any footsteps running toward us, and I didn't hear anyone yelling for me to put my hands up. I quickly assessed that these two
agents were on their own. They'd been foolishly wrong to assume they
could simply approach me, pull out a badge, and scare me into handcuffs.

In the commotion several Valley girl students screamed out a few *Oh
my God's!* Metal chairs scraped on concrete as the students jumped up
from their tables to make room for our violent squabble.

*You're under arrest! We have guns drawn on you!*

*No, you don't.*

I pummeled the male agent until he was finally under me, sprawled on
his back on the table. The female agent, still dazed on the ground, clung
weakly to my leg. I knew that with a few more blows to the man's head I
could escape their grasp. The male agent could feel me, and the situation, slipping away. So, he surrendered all his pride and shouted to the
circle of stupefied students watching this mad group of people grappling
and grunting, *Help us!! We're FBI agents! This man is a bank robber!*

*No, I'm not. Stay out of it! I don't know these people!*

I knew I sounded stupid the moment I spoke. I continued gouging
and punching.

*Help us!!* both agents pleaded.

Next thing I knew my body was enveloped by a mass of bodies. I
couldn't budge. I felt a feeble hand throw a handcuff around my right
arm. She'd "pinched" me. I was yanked to the ground like a rambunctious calf finally dragged down by a rodeo cowboy.

The students who'd jumped in and aided the FBI were pleased with
themselves. Excited. This was the stuff of *America's Most Wanted.* Reality
TV made really real.

The concrete was cold on my face. The male agent was kneeling on
my spine with one knee and holding tightly onto my wrists, which were
handcuffed behind my back. Catching his breath, he asked someone to
find his glasses. He pulled out a walkie-talkie and called for backup.
Then, like a field trip professor, he fielded questions from the students.

*Is he really a bank robber?*

*Yes. He sure is.*

*Fuck you, bitches!* I yelled.

*Be quiet, Mr. Loya. You've been caught, and we're in control now.*

*How many banks did he rob?*

*Suck my dick, you fuckin' sissy pricks!* I screamed.

*A lot. I'm not sure. But more than twenty.*

*Wow!*

*What's his name?*

*You punks can call me your big dick daddy!* I said.

*He's called the Beirut Bandit.*

*The Beirut Bandit?*

*Yeah.*

*Why?*

*Someone at headquarters gave him that nickname because tellers misidentified him as Pakistani or Lebanese or Indian.*

*You all can go to fuckin' hell!*

*So, how did you become an FBI agent?*

*Yeah, tell the boy how many nut sacks you had to lick to get the job,* I said.

*Just ignore him.*

*Fuck! Fuck! Fuck! Fuck all you sorry motherfuckers!*

*Well, I went off to college thinking I would become an accountant. But, you know, I changed my major a bunch of times.*

*You're all a bunch of fuckin' momma's boys!* I yelled.

*I attended one of those work fairs on campus. The agents who spoke with me were really professional. Decent. So I said, why not?*

*Why not jack each other off while you're at it?*

*Wow!*

▮▮▮▮▮▮▮▮▮▮

I was taken to a holding cell in the tiny campus jail. Agent Cordes had pulled together a twenty-person team of collegiate-looking agents from around southern California, fresh out of the academy. Then he had them dress like students and wander around the campus in pairs, my photo in hand. With news of my arrest, they started trickling into the station.

*Where is he?*

*In the back holding cell. Go take a look.*

Two heads would stare through the small window cut into the steel cell door.

*So, this is him? That's it? You're not so tough now, are you buddy?*

I spat at the window. Told them to give me head. And when they left, I banged my head against the wall.

When all the FBI agents had gathered in an office down the hall I heard several of the young agents asking the ones I'd fought to describe the altercation.

*So, what happens to him? What's the charge? Assaulting a federal agent?*

Cordes spoke up. *That's what it's called, and he could get another ten years tacked on to his sentence for it. But I'm not trying to send him away forever. He's a good kid. He just has some problems to deal with. So, I'd appreciate it if you two wouldn't press the charges.*

*He's back there pounding his head on the wall. Is he crazy?*

*No. I'm telling you, he's usually not like this. He's just going through a wild phase right now.*

Agent Cordes walked to my cell and asked me to stop banging my head against the wall.

An hour later I was on my way to the Metropolitan Detention Center in downtown L.A. Before we left the campus, Cordes told me that Jennifer was somewhere in the vicinity and wanted to see me.

*It's no problem, Joe. I'll take you to her. It would be nice.*

*Nah.*

*You sure, Joe? It's no problem. She's been worried sick about you.*

*Nah. I don't want to see her. Not like this. Not the way I feel right now. I might say something I'll regret.*

*Fair enough.*

On our trip to the courthouse the following day I asked Cordes how many years he thought I'd have to do behind bars.

*Joe, you have to go away for a while. But we're not going to wash you up. Maybe you'll get twelve years and then get out in ten. You'll still be a young man in ten years. You're twenty-seven right now, right?*

*Yeah.*

*Then you'll be thirty-seven when you get out. And believe me, that's still young. Right, Shriver? Agent Shriver there would give anything to be thirty-*

*seven again. Yeah, you've been a bad boy, Joe. You made things hard on yourself when you skipped bail. The U.S. Attorney wants to throw the book at you. I talked him out of it. Again. No thanks to you. But we told him that you have a future ahead of you. We don't want to take that from you. But you have to go away for a while. You've been a bad boy.*

That's what I admired about Cordes. He didn't take things personally. I'd jacked him around, but his principles were more important than his ego. He wasn't petty punitive. He needed to lock me up, but he wasn't going to be mean about it and wash me up with a thirty-year sentence. Cordes's ethic was real and true, bigger and stronger than my small, angry self. When he meted out discipline Cordes was simply firm, not vindictive or heavy. By offering to let me meet Jennifer, he proved to me that all authority figures weren't bad. Some, I could now see, were actually compassionate.

▓▓▓▓▓▓▓▓▓▓

Two months later I telephoned Jennifer at around seven o'clock on a weekday evening. No answer. I telephoned Luke Vega, one of my best friends at the time.

*Luke V?*

*Yeah, Joe?*

*Let me speak to Jennifer. I know she's there.*

Long pause.

*Go on Luke. Wake her up. I know she's there.*

*All right.*

*Hello?*

She sounded tired and nervous.

*You're a fuckin slut.*

*Don't call me that.*

*I'll call you anything I want.*

*What about you? Luke told me about Kim.*

*What about Kim?*

*He told me that you went out with her and that you'd been sleeping with other women the entire time we were together.*

*Is that right?*

*Yeah. And Sandra told me that you hit on her. My best friend, for Christ's sake. And you always put her down in front of me.*

*Luke told you about Kim?*

*Yeah.*

*Yeah, well then you guys deserve each other.* I slammed down the receiver.

It wasn't the first time I'd been caught at something and had tried to turn things around so that I ended up feeling like the offended party.

Four months later, after pleading guilty to three bank robberies, I received an eight-year sentence.

Two days after that I was awakened at 4:30 A.M., fed breakfast, handcuffed, and escorted down to the basement, where a van waited for me and four other men.

Four flak-jacketed men in baseball caps (Bureau of Prisons emblem on the front), with automatic weapons on their laps, followed us in the trail car as we pulled out of the Metropolitan Detention Center for the three-hour drive north to Lompoc Federal Penitentiary.

I was twenty-seven years old when I entered my first maximum-security penitentiary.

I was un-handcuffed, stripped of my red transport jumpsuit, and searched. Then a guard took my photograph and laminated it to make my prison ID. He issued me the standard federal inmate uniform: khaki pants, a long-sleeve beige shirt, a green army coat, and black boots. The other men and I were then given bedrolls—two sheets, one wool blanket, and one towel—and pointed to a door.

*Go through there. Turn right. Go all the way to the end of the corridor, to K Unit. That's your housing.*

The door opened onto a corridor the width of a two-lane highway. The corridor was bustling with men in motion. I immediately saw Terry, a green-eyed black man who'd been in my unit at the Metropolitan Detention Center in Los Angeles. He'd arrived at Lompoc two weeks before me.

*Hey, Loya.*

*What's up, Terry?*

*You're gonna love it here. It's wide open.*

*Oh yeah?*

*Yeah. So what unit do they have you in?*

*K Unit.*

*K Unit? Damn. Killer unit. That's what the convicts call it. A body was pulled out of there just two months ago. It's down thataway. Follow this corridor all the way to the end, where it forks, then go into the door on the right.*

*Good looking out, Terry.*

*Ain't no thing.*

*I'll holler atcha later.*

▮▮▮▮▮▮▮▮▮▮

Jennifer had hooked up with Luke, so I couldn't expect affectionate visits from her any time soon. The disconnection was better for me, I thought. That way, I wouldn't be distracted with the affairs of the free world for a very long time. I'd use my time in prison to jack my criminality up a notch or two. After all, it was 1989 and I couldn't expect to be paroled until 1996—seven years.

▮▮▮▮▮▮▮▮▮▮

MacClaren Hall had been the most densely confined space I'd ever been in. Not because we didn't have enough room to move. We had plenty. We were tiny bodies, and the facility was relatively new and therefore large and wide open. No, the density had to do with our pain, with every kid's woeful inability to express his misery.

Very few experiences have altered me so permanently as what I recall about the nights in that hall, when the abused kids used to cry for their parents. It was madness, the pain so fuckin' palpable. I'd never seen human vulnerability so naked. I used to lie in my bed and not cry. These kids were being offered emancipation from their traumas, from their abusive homes, and all they could do was piss on themselves and want to run back to their abusers! Sure, positive change was hard to get used to. And liberty comes with a price. These kids preferred going back to what they knew rather than move forward into uncertainty.

I had vowed to turn my MacClaren Hall experience into my personal existentialist ethic: I would push through my fear and not look back, fuck Lot's wife and her anemic trust in her hazardous future.

While I served my time at Lompoc, I intended to continue to embrace my freedom from morality. Fuck picking up a Bible to lurch back into the Christian world! Decency had proved to be a bondage I could not bear. I wanted to press on toward an immoral life. Sure, my style of independence offered me nothing but greater anxiety and incarceration. But I would learn to thrive behind the stone and steel, among all the edginess of my new milieu. I felt as if those weepy kids at MacClaren Hall had revealed to me the core insecurity of the human condition. I felt as if their fear of change could be extrapolated to our species in general. I wanted to be superior to everyone. I wanted to be fearless as I changed into a monster.

I swore to myself I'd make serious criminal connections in the joint. I'd listen and learn the prison lore, the convict ethic, and pay close attention to the words spoken to me by wiser prisoners, who'd teach me how they had failed. I would again be the best pupil—hearing how criminal men talked, dreaded, imagined—just like I once listened to church elders and Bible lectures on cassette tapes, how I studiously learned how to navigate myself in the modest moral universe of Christian slogans like:

*We don't smoke, and we don't chew,*
*And we don't go with girls that do.*

I would fantasize about future heists and plot other criminal ventures. *I'll show them,* I thought. *Society will regret placing me in prison. I'm not done with this crime run. Not yet.*

# viii

O ne morning a guard told Bey that he was getting transferred to another prison and that he should have all his property packed up in half an hour. When the guard left the tier, Bey hollered out for us to send him anything that could help him jam his door shut. Within five minutes he had four dictionaries, three thesauruses, several Robert Ludlum and Jackie Collins novels, a broken broom handle, and dozens of magazines to wrap and tie around his body like body armor.

This was gonna be his Alamo.

When the guard returned and asked Bey to "cuff up," Bey refused. This set in motion the prison protocol for extracting an inmate from his cell.

A few minutes later the unit lieutenant walked very seriously to Bey's cell with a guard holding a huge camcorder on his shoulder, filming the entire conversation:

"Ernest Williams, are you refusing a direct order to 'cuff up'?"

"Yes, I am, and if you will let me—"

"Tell it to someone who gives a shit."

The lieutenant quickly left the tier.

Five minutes later, the warden knocked on Bey's cell door, the window pasted on the inside with newspaper.

"Bey, come to the door. We need to talk."

Bey peeled back some newspaper to reveal an eyeball bulging behind one of his black-framed glasses' lenses.

"Sorry I had to do this, Warden. You're a good man."

"Thanks, Bey. I try."

"That's why I'm trusting you to do the right thing. Here, you'll understand this." Bey peeled back more paper and held up a court document. "This is a writ of habeas corpus filed in the local court."

The warden placed his spectacles on and peered through the smudged bullet-proof glass.

"See that? Right there?"

"Yeah, I see it, Bey."

"Under the law that means ain't nobody supposed to transfer me outta of the court's jurisdiction. Nobody can go against that. It's my constitutional right. God bless fuckin' America. Ain't much good about this country, but sure as shit my constitutional rights is one good thing. Hear what I'm saying, Warden?"

"Yes, I hear you, Bey. Now will you listen to me?"

"But—"

"But nothing, Bey. I listened to you. Didn't I listen to you?"

"Sure you did, Warden. Yeah, you did. Damn straight, you did."

"Okay then. Now, you know I have a job to do."

"Of course, Warden. I can appreciate that."

"So, when I get paperwork from Washington saying you are supposed to get on a bus to go to Terre Haute Penitentiary, that means I've got to move you—one way or another."

"But what about the habeas corpus?"

"I don't know what to say about that, Bey. I can't speak to your legal situation. I'm responsible for the security of this prison. I do what the Bureau of Prisons tells me to do. Fair or not."

"But you know that ain't right."

"Sorry, Bey. It may not be right, but you'll just have to take it up with your lawyer. All I'm asking, Bey, is that you cuff up now. And since you have a legitimate beef and you talked to me good right here, I promise not to write an incident report on your initial refusal to obey a direct order."

"Fuck that, Warden. I'm doing a hundred years in this mutha fucka. You think I give a fuck about a write-up for refusing a direct order?"

"Bey, listen. Are you going to cuff up or not? I'm asking you nicely. I don't want to have to have this end messy. We don't want that, Bey."

"Ah, shit now. You gonna have to turn this messy and extract my black ass out of this cell, because I ain't just gonna lay down and lick my nut sack, give up all my fuckin' constitutional rights. I'm in the right here." He ran his palm over his head as he stepped back to quickly regroup. Then he stepped back to the door and continued. "And ain't that about a mutha-fuckin' bitch that the goddam government will lock me up for breaking the law, then turn around and break their own fuckin' laws. Nah, that ain't right."

"C'mon, Bey. Let's do this peacefully. We've always got along well. Don't ruin a good run."

"Warden, you are a good man, but I'm done talking to you. Go on and do what you gotta do. And I'll do what I gotta do. I ain't new to this. I'm true to this."

He re-pasted the newspaper on the inside of the cell door window, and the warden walked away.

Five guards wearing football helmets, thick baseball catcher's boots, umpire's vests, and hockey gloves—so much stuff that they walked like *Star Wars* storm troopers—marched onto the tier and stood one behind the other facing Bey's cell door. One guard filmed the event while another guard stood by so that he could yank the door open faster once it started moving on its rollers.

It was real tense there for a moment, then the lieutenant yelled, "Open cell seven!" But all anyone heard was the door jammed on the rollers, going ah-ahahahah.

"Stop!" yelled the lieutenant. "Clear the tier."

The guards marched off.

The door couldn't be opened electronically or manually because Bey had braced it shut with a broken broom handle and jammed book bindings into the door's roller.

One of the guards tried to hand-crank the door open. No luck. Finally, a welder had to be brought in to remove the door. When the welder lit the bright spark, Bey splashed toilet water out of the speaker holes in the cell door and extinguished it. A guard turned off the water in Bey's cell. When Bey tried to flush his toilet to replace the water he was throwing out, he realized what they'd done. That's when he went wild.

"Oh, gonna turn off my water, huh? Gonna turn off the mutha-fuckin' water! And you think that's gonna stop me? Ha! Well, I got something for your asses!"

A few minutes after the welder resumed welding, the spark was doused again.

"Ha! Ha! How you like me now? How you like me now?"

The welder jumped back as if he'd been doused with acid.

"Ah, fuck. He's throwing his piss."

"Ha! Ha! Come on Mister Welder. Step to this. There's plenty more where that came from."

An hour later five guards dressed in riot gear, rushed into the cell and beat Bey into submission. For the first few seconds we could only hear feet scuffling and Bey screaming out, "I can't breathe. Don't kill me!" When they finally dragged him out of the cell, he was hog-tied to a long pole. He couldn't speak.

I'd sent Bey some books to use, but I hadn't done so for altruistic reasons. I was in the mood for entertainment, and Bey was a train wreck waiting to happen. Yet, when he was carried past my cell and I saw his tongue dangling from his bloody mouth, his left eye already swollen shut from the beating, I felt sorry for the old man. I wasn't a complete asshole. This was some scary shit. Until then, I was fierce in my cell—up front, aggressive at the door, verbally harassing Keating, throwing shit at the guards—but this incident was a turning point for me. I realized then how vulnerable we all were in there, how little control we had in reality, in the end, over any part of our lives in there.

And I realized that I didn't want to end up like Bey.

When Bey was carried past Heavy D's cell, we heard Heavy chuckle and mutter in his characteristically falsetto voice, "Mind over matter, Bro. If you don't mind, then it don't matter."

Several weeks later, Stone Man got a letter from Bey telling us that he was all right but that he was suing the warden and wanted to use everyone but Heavy D as witnesses.

# Hazard

*To what end will your unbridled audacity display itself?*

—Cicero to Cataline

I met men in prison like me, guys who had been the golden boys of their family, holding the promise of the next notch up the social ladder for their families. Much had been expected of them, a future beyond the barracks or housing projects. You'd see such a prisoner and know that an aunt had played with him on her lap; a mother had dressed him in red corduroy pants and suspenders with a matching red bow tie (like the one I wore in a photo taken with my parents in front of our apartment door when I was one year old). Such a guy would tell all the assembled extended family at a reunion that he was going to go to college. His mother would think Harvard or UCLA, never South Central Community College or its extension program—the school of hard knocks or Youth Authority or a prison classroom studying to get a GED.

Our hero, on whom his family heaped so much praise and virtue, probably once sang in the church choir or was an altar boy and maybe even donned the Baptist robe and preached once or twice at a youth camp. When he was young, he impressed family, teachers, school counselors, coaches, even the periodic monster—dope dealers, gang girls, the ex-con in the family (home for a brief stay)—and every sort of community leader.

Then our boy-man found drugs, and his moral compass got broken. He misplaced God and he lost his family, too. Before he lost his teeth to heroin overuse or crack abuse, he took to stealing checks from his mom's pocketbook, stole her TV and the VCR-DVD that he'd bought her when he was "up"—briefly clean and working hard—to replace the one he'd stolen from her the first time. He stole his grandma's Social Security check.

He talked his way into every alternative sentencing program, got a spot in a lenient drug treatment halfway house, from where he promptly escaped within a few days. When we meet up with him, he's on our prison tier begging for "shorts"—the last pathetic puff of your cigarette before you toss it to the ground—and wondering if you could also kick down to him your used Walkman batteries before you throw them away. He curiously knows that we read a lot, so he tries to impress us by quoting Sun Tzu or Socrates. You say sayonara as you tell him to spin, that you don't have anything to give him today, so he should quit wasting your time.

Sun Tzu. He, submitted for our disapproval, is the sort of person who passes for prison intelligentsia, always uses the same old recycled quotes from what must amount to the prison's list of classics: The white boys read and quote passages from separatist manifestoes, like *The Turner Diary*. Blacks read and quote obscure Koran verses or passages from *The Elders of Zion*. Mexicans quote passages from the broken Treaty of Hidalgo. All the usual resentnik manuals.

And every racial group is an equal opportunity offender, equally misusing Lenin, Sun Tzu, Mao, Marx, and Machiavelli. Fox and sheep allegories are an obsession with this literate prisoner.

▮▮▮▮▮▮▮▮▮

When I entered prison the first time I was a fish, an easy target, a mark. But by my second prison stint, I rode high because I had found new family in my second cell mate, Creeper.

I loved Creeper like he was blood because, after I'd told him one of the stories about my dad kicking my ass, he was like, *Man, that punk needs to get touched up. Where does he live? I'll go out there and ring his door-*

*bell, and when he comes to the door I'll kick his ass for you. Want me to? I'll
do it, Bro. I'm serious.*

I dug the way he leaned into my pain. And it worked the other
way, too. Like I knew that when he was six he was hit by a car and had to
have some metal plate put into his head. He had to learn how to walk,
talk, and shit again. He even wore diapers for a couple of years. He
told me that at age thirteen he was still playing with firetrucks for toddlers. He was barely literate, but at night he tried hard to read *The God-
father* out loud. He pronounced Michael Corleone's name as "Mitchell
Coloney." Homeboy had had a long, tough road, so I figured I wouldn't
correct him. I left him alone and didn't use that part of his history against
him. Why? Because he was my new family. He trusted me.

▥▥▥▥▥▥▥▥▥▥

Incarcerated men find their intimacy in the silences.

When Creeper and I were just becoming friends at Lompoc Federal
Penitentiary, we'd stand outside of my cell and barely talk for the first fifteen minutes. We'd mostly just watch other prisoners. After the last five
minutes of near-silence, I'd say *"Al rato,"* then walk inside my cell. He'd
walk back to his cell (this was before we were cell mates). Neither of us
was ever offended. We knew that we'd be back to hang out the next day.
Creeper was one of my favorite people in prison, precisely because he
wasn't afraid of silence.

In prison I prided myself on being able to live six months next to
another prisoner and never utter *"Hello"* or *"What's up?"* to him, even
though we practically bumped into each other several times a day. I
didn't need to play well with others anymore. As my body and heart got
meaner and harder, so did my ethic on silence. I had begun to associate
talking with babbling, and babbling with weakness. I considered silence
strength.

The great carnival promoter P. T. Barnum said that there was a sucker
born every minute. But the silent male ethic says that you can be suck-
ered or hustled only if you listen to the carnival barker. In prison, that's
the guy pimping his boy toy for a carton of cigarettes to get into a poker

game upstairs, or the guy offering to get you high for free so he can shove his johnson in your drunk mouth at the end of the night.

Prisons are notorious for housing these talkers, hustlers, flatterers, and toadies. Like all good confidence men, they use words to confuse, to toss up dust as a ruse, to wear as a disguise to connive their way into a space otherwise not permitted to them. To avoid the hustle, the safest thing to do is tune out the chattering class of prisoners and let them know that they can't insinuate themselves into your world with blather.

One of the first things you learn not to do in prison is turn around when someone shouts, "Hey you!" even when you know that they are calling out to you. You got to make them call you by your name or you keep walking, make them come around to address you from the front. Turn your head too fast, and you display a weakness for being taken off your stride by words. Being silent makes you a small target. You can't be hustled, humiliated, or sucked up into someone's intrigue.

▮▮▮▮▮▮▮▮▮

Creeper was fearless. He was six feet tall and very slender. Slight, almost. By the time I met him there were rumors that he'd already been involved in two prison homicides during his thirteen years there. When I started to lift weights he mocked me for being too dependent on obvious force.

If a new prisoner in the unit irritated Creeper, he would walk into the guy's cell, unannounced, and throw a knife at the guy's bunk, saying matter of factly. *Check it out, I don't like you and you don't like me, so pick up the knife and I'll pull out the one I have in my pocket, and the last one standing wins.* Of course it never mattered how big or tough the guy was, that knife stayed on the bunk and the guy begged Creeper to pick it back up himself and put it away. He knew that in order for Creeper to have the balls to confront him like that he must have already made peace with his maker, which made him fatalistic, and hence, better prepared for a death match.

My friendship with Creeper gave me pedigree because Creeper was affiliated with the Mexican Mafia prison gang. So he worked with the big boys, the mobsters. So I got to victimize others while getting to the top of my game.

Creeper and I ranked high in the prison, which really meant that we could participate in the capital end of the prison economy. A mule brought drugs into the prison for us, and we sold them. I played on a high-stakes poker table with serious Mafia men, and I was advanced a twenty-five-hundred-dollar credit line, payable at the end of the month.

I'd finally earned all the benefits of a successful criminal life in prison. But being at the top of my game also consisted of being extremely "dominion minded." I took my skills of concentration and observation to a new level. I could detect the scared convicts by looking at their fingernails. If they were chewed down, then I knew that no matter how tough the façade, the man was really a *tenderoni*, nibbling his nails in the shadows of his cell at night.

If a man squirmed in his seat often, then I'd ask him when he'd injured his back *How'd you know?* they'd always ask. I just knew. I'd look at the guys who walked into the unit from playing basketball and I'd memorize who had a thigh or ankle wrapped with an ACE bandage.

That's how I knew that Fat Boy wouldn't do anything when I confronted him by the telephones.

On Thanksgiving Day, during a strip search, I'd bent forward, grabbed both butt cheeks, and coughed. When I started to stand, the guard told me to bend over again because he hadn't got a good enough look. That really pissed me off. Whenever I got real angry on the streets, to dispel some of that surplus rage, I'd go rob a bank or find a victim to assault. So on that Thanksgiving Day, I daydreamed of hunting for a victim to fuck up.

Fortunately, I didn't need to go scouting far. A two-hundred-sixty-pound inmate walked up to the phone bank and declared that he was going to use the phone next. Objectors could take it up with him if they wanted trouble, he said. He wanted us to know that he didn't care if we were offended. I was next in line for the phone. But I stayed seated, waiting for the heavyset man-boy to look at me. Then I firmly stated that I'd been waiting for twenty minutes, so I intended to use the phone next. He was only a bit surprised. He paused for a few seconds, moved in place.

Then, loud enough for the twenty or so inmates loitering nearby to hear, he directly challenged me. As far as he was concerned, he said, I wasn't going to be next on the phone.

This slob of a man, weaned on contest-living like me—life as a competitive match with other men—had drawn a clear line in the sand. But I had been trained in the first principle of prison existence: If an inmate lets a bully take anything from him—like gym shoes or a place in line—then he may as well surrender then and there, pull his pants down to his knees, lay belly down on his bunk, butt wiggling in the air, and offer the conquering man free access to his defeated asshole. All threats in prison, small or great, are really interpreted by convicts as tests of how well a macho man cares for his virgin anus. Fear of rape, or being ridiculed as weak, is what governs most prison posturing.

Fatso provided me with a ripe chance to display my nerve in dramatic fashion, to assert my will, to recover some pride, to feel in control, to expel some of the congested humiliation I was not handling well. I stood up, totem-pole still. Said nothing. I gathered myself, felt the poise rush through my veins. I was in my element again, ready to be the prisoner who didn't give a fuck. I waited ten seconds and then stepped up to him.

Standing eight inches from his face and staring stoically into his eyes, I whispered, *If you want to take my phone, then come upstairs with me and I'll let you try and take it from me in the privacy of the shower room.*

I had spoken clearly, but quietly, so only he heard me.

*No. No. Let's do it here. We don't have to go upstairs.* He yelled loud enough so all the men looked at us. All my efforts to keep it a stealth, a private, man-to-man conflict, evaporated in his one cowardly gesture. I tried to calm his histrionics so that the unit guard wouldn't come rushing in.

*Keep it quiet, bitch. You want the man to come in here and protect you? If you really want to take my phone, we can settle this like men upstairs.*

*Nah. Nah. Fuck that. Let's set it off right here.*

*What are you? A coward? A pussy? C'mon, you fat bitch, let's go upstairs if you aren't afraid.*

*I'm not afraid.*

*How can I tell? All I see in front of me is a punk. A broad. What you got to say about that?* I made a quick movement toward him and reached for my back pocket. *C'mon, you fat piece of shit, come and take that phone you were talking tough about a few minutes ago.*

My abrupt gesture scared him. His arms shot up into the air. He looked like the victim of a stickup. I saw panic in his eyes. He back-pedaled slowly. *Nah, you come at me. You're the one with the knife. And you'd better make the first shot count, because that's all you've got. One shot.*

*One shot is all I need. Now you need to ask yourself if you are willing to lose an eye for the phone.*

Blindness was more than he had bargained for. *Shit. I didn't even want the phone that bad. Fuck that.*

I leaned forward and sniffed. *What's that I smell? Did you pee on yourself? Look at you, standing in a puddle of your own piss.*

The room roared with laughter.

*Fuck that. It would be different if you didn't have the knife.*

*Shut the fuck up, you stupid fuckin' pig. You couldn't bust a grape. I don't even have a knife.* I reached back with my hand and patted the pocket. *I'm scaring you with a plastic spoon in my pocket. I bluffed you with plastic. So now that you know, will you please try and take my phone like you promised?*

He was beaten. I'd exposed him as a huge cowardly windbag. He was too easy to humiliate. I went and stood next in line. He went to stand by a wall. He was too stupid to be ashamed, so he kept looking at me with a menacing look in his eyes. I smiled at him and told him to go rest his neck.

*Lay down and lick your nut sack, you sloppy piece of shit.*

He mumbled, grumbled, then finally walked upstairs when his friends told him to quit acting stupid.

It felt good to exile that pudgy poseur to a sort of no-man's land where the defeated dwell—where I'd just been when that guard asked for a double peek. The fat youngster didn't know that I'd been sizing him up for weeks. I'd noticed that his knees were always wrapped with ACE bandages. This meant that his getaway sticks wouldn't hold up well in a fight, especially if I kicked them hard several times.

I also familiarized myself with a man's emotional vulnerabilities, his insecurities. I did this for two reasons:

1. I wanted to identify a person's emotional insecurity so that I would never engage it, never enrage it.
2. I also wanted to know it so that if I needed to I could exploit it to my advantage when the shit hit the fan. So, let's say that I know Shorty hates Franky as much as I do. And I know Shorty hates it when people refer to him as Little Fella. Then I might set up Franky by telling Shorty that Franky is going around referring to him as Little Fella. Blood will be spilt, and whether it's Franky's or Shorty's, it doesn't matter to me.

Creeper was as pissed off with religion as I was. Mostly pious Mormon foster parents in Salinas had raised him. He appreciated my level of blasphemy. And I was a true vulgarian, a blasphemer of the first rank. When a friend expressed fear that we were in danger of getting caught by the administration for doing some crime in the prison, I'd grab my crotch and quote the Old Testament: *Fear not, for I am with thee. My rod and my staff shall comfort thee.*

And Creeper and I were often at risk of getting caught, because we committed *a lot* of crimes in prison.

For starters, we worked in the prison's sign factory, which was responsible for making all the federal government's wood forestry signs, a lot of military base signs, and all the signs for veterans hospitals (from the big signs outdoors on the lawns to the little Men and Women bathroom signs indoors).

Creeper and I smuggled everything. During football season, we'd smuggle small quantities of paint, which we'd sell to guys who'd use it to silkscreen football team logos on T-shirts. Each T-shirt sold for five packs of Lemacs. (I'd proudly wear my Raiders T-shirt on Sundays.)

Sometimes we smuggled flammable liquids from the sign factory to our unit. Some prisoners liked to squirt their enemies with acetone, then set them on fire.

Or we'd smuggled thick pieces of Plexiglas, which were molded and sharpened to look like Bowie knives. Mexican and Italian Mafiosi paid us fifty bucks worth of cigarettes or products we bought at the canteen for those "bone-crushers." The thing about Plexiglas was that it could be transported undetected through metal-detector checkpoints throughout the prison. Sometimes the knives were buried in the prison yard, so when the guards nightly ran metal detectors over the surface of the ground, nothing would be set off.

The wealthiest smuggler beyond the sign factory is the prison drug trafficker. Creeper and I did that too. We'd use a guy named Mike. Mike resembled every picture of fair, fine-featured Jesus I'd ever seen. During a visit, Mike's girlfriend would go to the ladies' room, find a stall, pull down her panties, retrieve the balloons of heroin she'd stuck up her vagina, and pop them into her mouth like breath mints. When she'd return from the bathroom, Mike would stand up and they'd start "bustin' slobs"—kissing using those sexy, mouth-all-the-way open kisses—and the merchandise would be transferred. Then Mike would sit down and drink some Dr Pepper to send the balloon down his gullet. (The dope was wrapped two times in tiny party balloons, then plastic wrapped once again. Stomach acid always burned through the first layer of wrap. More than one man had died of an overdose when a contraband balloon burst in his stomach and gave him one helluva final jolt.) Mike would end the visit and walk straight to my cell.

On more than one occasion, Our Holy Warden Who Art in Heaven witnessed the farcical spectacle of Creeper and me holding scrawny Mike upside down, his body suspended over a toilet bowl that had been thoroughly lined with a pillow of toilet paper five inches thick. We'd shake Mike while he stuck two fingers down his throat and threw up watery bile and five small balloons the size and color of peanut M&Ms, each packed with two grams of "Mexican tar" heroin.

We'd give Mike a third cut of the dope, the going rate for a mule. Many times I'd stand in my cell doorway, the lookout man for Mike and Creeper, while they shot their first fix with a dull needle. Mike had to shoot into the vein in his ankle because his other veins were so shot to hell. Creeper usually shot into the veins in the back of his hand.

Then Creeper and I would work our portion, either by selling match-head size fragments—called "papers" because of their packaging—for fifty dollars worth of canteen: five big bags of nacho Doritos, a case of shrimp Cup o'Noodles, ten cans of tuna, three bags of Tang, some stamps, and packs of cigarettes.

A lot of men who worked for the prison industries (the print shop, the cable factory, the paint shop) made a full-time salary of two hundred fifty dollars a month. To buy dope from us they'd fill out a form requesting to send some of their hard-earned paycheck to one of my friends or to a family member outside. The prison required that we give a reason for sending money out, so they'd write, "transfer of funds to pay a phone bill," since we could only call out of the prison collect.

Drugs were everywhere in prison. And not just pharmaceutical drugs. The same drugs in there as out here: Food. Sex. Religion.

Many a man got fat in prison eating food, food, and more food. They'd buy zoo-zoos and wham-whams from the canteen or fat sandwiches smuggled in from the kitchen. In my unit, Fruitman, a Jamaican who worked in the prison kitchen, was the man to see if you wanted extra food. Creeper and I were his favorites. He'd started by selling oranges and apples, but then he added fried chicken, cinnamon rolls, and, periodically, steak-and-egg sandwiches to his menu. For a paper of dope, we established a credit line. Fruitman would stroll into the unit from the kitchen and holler *Cussy-cus*, a signal that he had a surprise for me, his number one CUStomer.

*What you got, Fruity?*

*Cussy-cus, who always look out for you?*

*You do, Fruity. Papa Fruitman.*

*Dat's right. The man try and he try but he can't keep the Fruitman down. Jackboot on my neck, almost strip-searching a motherfucka, but Papa Fruitman brings back the biggest egg-and-bacon sandwich for my Cussy-cus. You tell Creeper I bring him two gigantic grapefruit he aks for. Make good wine. Sheet, Papa Fruitman know.*

*Okay, Fruity. I'll tell him. Now kick in those sandwiches. I got a ferocious appetite.*

*Cussy-cus, ain't no joke with that food jones.*

That was the food deal. For sex, Creeper would sometimes barter some "Mexican tar" for a blowjob from Sandy, Puerto Rican Al's "girl." Al was Sandy's pimp. He had an irritating habit of calling everybody "B."

*C'mon, Creeper. Best blow job in the world, B. I'm telling you, B, she can even make me cum standing up. Now, B, you know that's good head, B. And for one paper, you can have her three times. B, I'll send her to the showers in ten minutes. What stall will you be in, B?*

Then there was Filipino Rich, who had a stable of dirty magazines that he pimped for a pack of unfiltered Camel cigarettes for a single night's date.

*Young Joe, I got a new* Assmaster. *Killa* Assmaster. *Series seven. Or I got* Girls Who Crave Big Cock *number thirteen. Nothing puny in here, young Joe.*

*Nah. I think I'll try that* Tales of Two Titties *again. That's my favorite.*

*You know the deal, young Joe. All I ask is dat you give 'er a shower and brush 'er teet before you give back to me.*

Over time I accumulated quite a collection of hardcore porn magazines. One Friday night, around count time, an older Argentine gentleman from the third tier came down to the second tier looking for a date with one of my magazines. Creeper handed Eduardo the stack and told him to pick what he wanted.

Eduardo was in his late fifties, but stayed in pretty good shape by running a few miles every day. He looked like an aging Mexican soap opera star, except for the ridiculously obvious hair weave that showed a clumsy stitch job through his thin dove-white hair. We never talked about his criminal case. He reminded me of those genteel bankers from Peru or Uruguay who worked for the Latin American cartels and who'd been lured to the United States, arrested as drug traffickers, and handed two hundred- and three hundred-year sentences. Buck Roger dates, we called them. Eduardo was too nice and refined to have been a street thug, but he clearly had done something serious for the government to have locked him with us in a maximum-security penitentiary.

Eduardo's young wife had moved within five miles of the prison, where she got a job with a local church. All the religious Spanish community in the prison knew who Eduardo's wife was, because she came to visit him all the time with their young daughter. I never felt sorry for her. Her love for Eduardo and God was equally gullible. I never hated Christians more than during those years, and I always enjoyed playing a part in their corruption with my pornography.

Creeper liked to fuck with guys like Eduardo, guys who didn't belong there, guys he called "out of bounds." One young prisoner once made the mistake of asking Creeper what Creeper was doing time for:

*What, are you writing a book? Well, leave my chapter out. Better yet, let me fuck you in the ass and we can turn it into a love story.*

Eduardo didn't know what he was in for.

*What do you jack off with, Eduardo? Baby oil? Regular lotion?*

*Baby oil, of course.*

*Oh yeah, of course. Like you're some kinda expert, huh? Okay, Mister Expert, have you ever masturbated with Ben-Gay?*

*Ben-Gay?*

*Yeah, Ben-Gay. See, I knew it. You never tried the real-deal love lotion. Tell me something. Have you ever used Ben-Gay on your muscles when you've hurt yourself?*

*Uh huh.*

*Well, what did it feel like? Hot, right?*

*Well, I guess so. Vibrating on my muscles.*

*There you go. When you rub Ben-Gay on your dick, the medicine in it makes your hard-on feel like it's wrapped by a hot, vibrating pussy. I'm telling you that it's the best sensation. You gotta try it.*

Eduardo tried the real-deal love lotion ten minutes after we were locked in our cells. He sat on his stainless-steel toilet, pants around his ankles, one fist wrestling with his testicles, the other hand holding my magazine, entitled *The Island of Dr. Porneau*. Thirty seconds later he was pounding on his cell door, screaming for the guard to open his cell so that he could run to the showers and rinse the Ben-Gay off his gonads.

In those days, my disgust with the correct world was dark and furious. I especially despised Christians. I even started collecting newspaper clippings of Christians dying: Christians in a burning church, or in a van accident on the way to save heathens in San Francisco, or getting shot in a church when an estranged spouse came to kill his ex-wife. My notebook full of these clippings was proof that God, like me, was not only wickedly cruel, but had an appreciation for the morbidly ironic twist in a story.

▓▓▓▓▓▓▓▓▓

Mail call in prison is the most exciting time of the day. Or the most painful. Men congregate at the guard's station hoping to hear their names called out. One day, as I stood at the back of the crowd, my name was called. As it started making its way back to me, over the other men's heads, I could see that it was a little booklet. When it got close I realized that it was a religious tract, a monthly Christian wannabe *Reader's Digest.*

A friend asked me, *What did you get Joe?*

*A fuckin' Christian rag. I don't know who sent this to me, but it's a sick joke. Everyone knows that I can't stand Christian bullshit.* I tore up the magazine and threw it in the trash. *I'm gonna make sure that this doesn't get read by anyone. Make sure that it's been wasted time and money to send me this kind of shit.*

A month later I received another one, and I realized that someone had ordered a subscription for me. I tore off the return address then did the same thing as before, tore the magazine into small pieces and dumped it in the nearest trashcan. Then I went to my cell and wrote a letter to the magazine's subscription department. I was firm, even angry, as I told them that I was in prison, was an unbeliever, and that they should contact the person who'd paid for the subscription and tell them that I'd been tearing the magazine into little pieces and throwing it in the garbage. So whoever they were, I suggested that they just cancel the subscription. Tell them that if they really wanted to be charitable then they should have sent the subscription refund to my prison account in the form of a postal money order so I could buy soap, pens, paper, toiletries, and stamps.

A week later I received a letter from the magazine notifying me that although they appreciated my situation, they had contacted the subscriber and that person had advised them to continue sending the magazine to me. I was livid.

▓▓▓▓▓▓▓▓▓

The next day my life changed forever.

I walked into the unit, after lifting weights outside, and Officer Sorenson, the day guard of our unit, told me that I had a new cell mate.

When I walked into my cell, I immediately saw that the new guy had rearranged the single shelf on the wall above the three coat hooks. I'd had ten books up there, now half of them were gone and he'd replaced them with toiletries and a thin Bible. I looked around for my books and finally found them in a box under my bunk. I also saw that he'd haphazardly thrown them into the box so that two of them were lying open, their spines clearly stressed, and one book's pages were folded over at the edges, risking a permanent crease.

I stood outside my cell and waited for this guy to return from wherever he'd gone. When he did, he walked up to me like a tough guy. He was wearing Ray Ban sunglasses on a really pockmarked face.

*Orale.*

*Orale.*

*This your cell?*

Yeah.

*I'm your new bunkie. My name's Chato.*

We shook hands.

*Yeah, I'm Joe. They call me Gafas.*

We stepped into the cell.

*Sit down. I need to talk to you.*

He looked stunned. But he sat down without question.

*For us to get along in this cell we need to respect each other. You know, consult each other for every change made in the cell.*

*Did I do something wrong?*

*Yeah. I came in and saw that you didn't wait to ask me which books I wanted to move to make room for you. For some reason you decided to just arbitrarily choose books to sloppily dump into a box before shoving it under the bunk. One of the book bindings was all fucked up. What's up with that? If you are going to touch my shit, you could have at least handled it better.*

*Hey. Don't you think you are making a bigger deal of this than it is?*

*Listen. I don't know you. And you don't know me. So that's all the reason in the world to make living together in the same space a big fuckin' deal. We have to sleep in here together at night when they shut the door. If we have a beef with each other, we need to talk about it.*

*Yeah. Okay. It's just that there are more important things in the world to worry about. That's why I didn't trip on the boxing the books shit.*

*Some quick advice: You are in prison now. This place is all the world you need to worry about.*

Chato was thirty-five years old and short (five foot five). He wore sunglasses indoors and had a *veterano* stroll, despite never having done time. He bought into the first-termer's sense of criminal romance, the glamour of walking the corridors among the elite members of every infamous Mafia, posse, cartel, and prison gang in the country. He assumed that he was tough by his proximity to them.

It was that first night, locked in our cell, when I heard about his two sons.

*The hardest thing is knowing that I will be away from them for eleven years. I love those boys. Stevie, the ten-year-old, is real smart. You should hear him talk. He's gonna be smarter than his mom or me. Do you have children, Joe?*

*Nah. I knew that when I chose this life of crime that I was going to eventually get busted. I lost my mother when I was nine years old, and I wasn't going to have children only to leave them when I came to the joint. Nah. Couldn't do that to them.*

*But you'd love them once they were in your arms, right when they are newly born. I was in the delivery room when my last boy was born. He didn't make it. He was born dead. I told the doctor I wanted to hold him. When he was in my arms I swear, and believe me, this is the God's honest truth, I looked at his tiny face and I saw Jesus.*

*You mean he was peaceful like Jesus?*

*No, I mean that it was like a miracle. I saw Jesus's face, you know the one hanging in churches where Jesus is light skinned with a beard.*

I shook my head in disbelief. Angry, in fact, that I had to listen to this nut.

*En serio, Joe. You don't have to believe me, but I know what I saw.*

*Hey, no disrespect right, but I just can't believe that Jesus would come down here and mask your kid's face with his quote glory unquote.*

*Yeah, but I know what I saw.*

*Awright. You know what you saw, and now I know that I got to get to bed. So I'll holler at you in the morning.*

What a sissy, I thought. A "sensitive" man moonlighting as a bad-ass. Why the hell did I even stay in the conversation as long as I had? Two weeks later he moved out of my cell. Good riddance, I thought.

■■■■■■■■

A lot of guys pick up a Bible or the Koran when they get to the penitentiary. They spend every night at the chapel away from the intrigues of the unit where they live. Kinda like the chapel is protective custody. Old-fashioned sanctuary.

Cletus was that type of prisoner. He was a bank robber who had escaped from the Metropolitan Detention Center in L.A. after he was first arrested. A few weeks later he was caught in a motel with a prostitute. She said that he'd kidnapped and raped her. He was given some outrageous sentence, like forty years or something like that. He'd sat next to me on the van ride from MDC to Lompoc Penitentiary.

Now, in the hierarchy of criminals in prison, the child molester and rapist are the lowest caste. So the prison ethic has it that the other prisoners are allowed to rape the rapist without being labeled rapists themselves.

Cletus was long waisted. It made him waddle like a duck. He had a big bubble butt that jiggled provocatively when he walked. Word came down the pike that Cletus had raped a prostitute, so he was marked even before he got to the prison. When he arrived at Lompoc he picked up the biggest Bible he could find. I mean, literally, the biggest Bible he could find. One of those thick, monstrous Catholic Bibles that you could use as a weapon to bludgeon someone. And he carried it with him everywhere he went. To the yard. To work. To the movies. He even ate chow with the Bible on the table right next to his food tray. I guess that was his version of a cross and garlic.

But eventually seven guys ran into his cell and hit him in the seat anyway. He couldn't snitch on them because after his breakout he was such a high security risk that he would remain at the maximum-security level. That meant that he would always be rotated within the same system, where he would end up doing time with these guys or their friends at other prisons. He couldn't escape them.

I felt bad for the kid . . . for about two minutes. That's because when my ex–cell mate, Chato, was murdered in his bunk, Cletus told the FBI that he had seen me near Chato's cell with a rolled-up newspaper. A total lie. In exchange for this information, Cletus was escorted out of the prison and transferred to a medium-security prison, and permanently away from his rapists.

A prison murder sets in motion a frenzy of opportunism by prisoners. Everyone wants things better for themselves, and because murder is such a severe crime, that's the time when prison administrations hand out special dispensations to guys who snitch. Guys can get reduced sentences, transfers to lower-level prisons or prisons nearer their homes. And some guys can get their bookies locked up so that they don't have to pay their gambling debts.

▓▓▓▓▓▓▓▓▓

On the morning of December 19, 1990, an intruder (or intruders) dashed into Chato's cell around nine o'clock, and only God witnessed the violent splash of blood made on the wall next to Chato's bunk. Chato had been sleeping, having worked 3:00 to 7:00 A.M. in the kitchen. Boiling water or hot oil was probably splashed in his face, so he would have gasped hard, in shock and tremendous pain. Then, while the unit's two-hundred men milled around outside the sheet-draped cell door, one or two men jumped on him and silently choked him unconscious. The prisoners who loitered outside Chato's cell, waiting for the prison to authorize them to go to work, to the gym, or to the yard, were utterly oblivious to the death match in the first-floor cell.

The killer probably plunged a pointed metal rod into Chato's chest, popped his ribs open like a can of beer, stabbed and twisted the weapon in his heart, then violently stabbed him through his eyes. One thrust would have pierced clean through to the back of his skull and punctured the pillow under his head.

A half-hour later, God surely didn't miss seeing a panicked male medic frantically shoving gauze into the shredded gash of Chato's chest wound and another trying to keep attached (and out of the way) the eyeballs that had been torn from their sockets and were resting on Chato's cheeks.

A female medic foolishly attempted to administer mouth-to-mouth resuscitation into Chato's gasping throat gurgling up blood. Some moments later prison nurses scrambled to place Chato on a gurney and in an ambulance waiting to race to the nearest emergency room. When Chato was discovered carved open, edgy guards locked the other prisoners in whatever area they happened to be at the time. The kitchen. The gym. Library. Chapel.

The Warden said he would not stop hunting until he caught the brutal perp. He assembled his disciples and commissioned them to go and do likewise. Go into every cell and preach the saving gospel of strip search and seizure. His flak-jacketed elect accepted their calling, mobilized in Captain Grulowsky's office, and planned their mission. They departed like sheep among wolves (*shrewd as serpents and harmless as doves*) to turn housing block K upside down. Seek-and-ye-shall-find evidence—on the sole of a shoe, or smeared on a doorway, a porcelain toilet, or on clothing dumbly tucked into a laundry bag. With luck, the assailant had been interrupted while covering his tracks, so the murder weapon might be lying around just waiting to be found.

At the time of the discovery of Chato's body, I was doing pull ups in the prison yard. Through the chain-link fence I saw guards racing from various parts of the prison toward the housing block where I lived. The yard guard ran to the door of the gateway leading into the prison building, quickly locked it, then ran off in the direction of the radio call. *Code blue in K Unit.* We unlucky prisoners were stuck outside in a drizzle that soon turned to rain.

About an hour later, the group of us, drenched and shivering in the cold, were told that we'd be escorted to the auditorium, where we'd stay until further notice. I was glad to get out of the rain. In the corridor leading from the prison yard to the auditorium, we were strip searched in groups of five.

The auditorium was colder than outside, and the seats were hard, flat wood. I sat next to Creeper. We said little, while the blabbermouths around us tossed theories back and forth.

*I overheard a voice on a guard's radio say something about K Unit.*

*Yeah, and I saw some medical staff goin' that way with a gurney.*

*Someone must've been stabbed.*

*Nah. It's gotta to be worse than that. We've been locked up too long, and the guards are going too slow at this. They're looking for something.*

*Drugs?*

*Hell no. Gotta be more than that. You saw how they responded to the call.*

*Maybe a guard was attacked.*

*Could be.*

*Serves 'em right, those sunzabitches.*

*Whatever it was, you better believe it's fuckin' serious.*

The mood among the prisoners was uncharacteristically docile for a maximum-security prison. Criminals drenched, corralled into an auditorium, and anxiously anticipating a longer wait, we were helpless, hungry, and confused, left only to imagine.

*Damn.*

*What?*

*Today we're supposed to have burgers and fries for lunch. Now they'll probably just give us sack lunches.*

A sack lunch was a punitive measure, and typically consisted of one elementary school half-pint carton of homogenized milk, a bruised apple or brown banana, a slice of pink bologna between two slices of Wonderbread, and a second sandwich, a dollop of peanut butter pressed between two more slices of bread.

It was two o'clock or so by the time we were told to get up and walk single file to the dining hall. That meant no sack lunches. The chow hall smelled of burgers.

I walked to the chow line, grabbed a watermelon-red tray, picked up a flimsy plastic fork and knife, and tossed them, along with some mustard and ketchup packets, onto my tray. Reaching for my burger and fries, I needled the man behind the counter nicknamed Chino to sneak me extra french fries.

*They're cold, homey.*

*No me importa. Pasa.*

He looked both ways. The coast was clear. He quickly dropped an extra handful of fries on the tray.

*Orale.*

I walked over to a table where Creeper and two friends sat.

About halfway through my meal, forty or more guards rushed through the chow hall doors—a parody of one of those cowboy movies where an outlaw gang busts through swinging saloon doors. A dark-haired guard, perhaps a Mexican, with a hunched-over gait and a paunch, led the way, walking down the center aisle while the others fanned out on the sides. Each had a small card in his hands: copies of a prisoner's ID.

One guard walked up to a seated inmate, told him to look up, then compared the photo in his hand with the face of the puzzled prisoner. I could tell they were hunting a brown man by the color of the men's faces they were investigating. They walked to where we Mexicans had segregated ourselves.

The first one through the door approached my table. I read his name tag: Sanchez. At five foot nine, he and I were approximately the same height, and we had the same native features: black hair, full faces, dark brown skin. But that's where the resemblance ended.

Sanchez looked at the photo in his hand, then at me, then back at the photo again. Then he asked me if my name was Joe Loya.

*Uh huh.*

He lifted his walkie-talkie from its leathery case on his hip, pulled it to his mouth, and mumbled something into it. Then he scanned the room like a company scout wearing night goggles in one of those commercials for joining the Army. *Be all that you can be.* He put the walkie-talkie back in its case, backed up a few paces, then asked me to stand.

I rose.

The other guards stopped their searches and converged around my table. We were perps or punks to them. To us, they were lames and momma's boys.

Sanchez's jet-black hair was straggly, but I could tell that he'd tried to comb it back that morning. It was so greasy that it appeared ready to slide off his scalp. Later, when he bent to pull my chair out for me, I saw that a halo of skin was beginning to peek through the thin hairs on the crown of his head. His complexion was Edward Olmos complicated, crater mounds of sand at the bottom of a shoebox, a child's lunar landscape school project. His thick, gray-plastic–framed glasses kept sliding down his nose. His pants were tight around the waist but sagged around the ass. And his black cowboy boots were so shamelessly scuffed that he reminded me of a homeless man. I couldn't imagine him with a woman.

*Please turn around, Mister Loya.*

Handcuffs were tightened on my wrists.

For a while my boss was this young Mexican guard. I wondered if he thought of me as a mediocre Mexican, a low-class criminal, shaming our name. I'd heard stories about that prison phenomenon when I worked in the prison kitchen. My boss confided to me that some racist guard on the night shift was making crank phone calls within the prison, targeting the Mexican guards in the other housing blocks, calling them dirty spics and stupid wetbacks, then quickly hanging up. He'd never been caught.

To assimilate, some Mexican guards chose to prove their solidarity with the white guards by being harder on Mexican prisoners, hating in us what others seemed to hate in them. For all the talk about racism in prison, men behind the walls learn that it's always your own kind who treat you the worst. Guards or fellow prisoners—same difference.

Shackled and escorted from my lunch table. I offered Creeper free rein over what remained of my cold french fries and half-eaten soy burger.

*Orale, Gafas. Buena suerte.*

I nodded goodbye.

*Come on, Loya.*

His hand gripped around my upper arm, Sanchez escorted me out of the chow hall. A real piece of work, this one. A regular super hero. All he needed was a crime fighter's cape, a Zorro mask, and the bold letters *S C* on his chest: Super Chile.

The other prisoners glanced up at me as I passed them, then turned away and went back to their burgers.

The chow hall led into a gigantic corridor that connected to every housing block and administration building in the prison. But for the guards and me, the corridor was empty. Handcuffs and dangling keys echoing, we walked down the corridors. I walked head straight, shoulders back. Okay. I would play along and let this crowd of Dudley Do-Rights get their kicks, pat themselves on the back for rounding up the bad guy.

*Turn left here, then left again. Into the next door.*

The captain's office could have been intimidating. He and eight other prison honchos were cramped behind a desk. They looked lined up for a group photo, or a firing squad. Three guards stepped into the room with me.

And then there were twelve.

A guard shut the door and then guided me to face the seated men. Then he backed away and blended into the larger group of guards. I kept my composure. It was time to take stock. I was clearly in deep, deep shit.

There wasn't a sound in the room. Fifteen or twenty seconds of silence swelled and assumed the dimension of several hours.

I shifted my gaze from the yard-sale paintings hanging on the wall (friendly quail in flight, dull landscapes in late fall) to the stern eyes of the men staring at me, totem-pole still. Four associate wardens, a captain, a duty lieutenant, the on-duty sergeant, a special prison investigator, an FBI agent, and three low-level guards—presumably in the room to protect the other prison officials from me. They all looked like they were judging my capacity to commit the crime for which I was being detained. Perhaps they'd compare notes afterwards.

A short, hairy, barrel-chested Mexican lieutenant, in polished black pointy boots, stepped from around the table to take charge of the strip search. He stretched white plastic surgical gloves over his hands. I knew him as the investigator despised by most prison guards because he tracked down and busted rogue guards. His name was Gomez.

He stood in front of me and stared up into my eyes through those silly lenses that are permanently tinted. Above his upper lip was a slim attempt at facial hair, the thin, buffoonish kind of mustache popularized by Cantinflas, Mexico's Jerry Lewis.

Cantinflas un-handcuffed me, then told me to take off my clothing, one article at a time. Shirt. T-shirt. Belt. Shoes. Socks. Pants. He held up my boxers and shook them, then cautiously checked for drugs or razor blades in the stitching. In that cold room I dreaded the inevitable: They'd eventually have to check out my anemic penis, now turtle necked.

Finished with my clothes, Cantinflas asked Sanchez to put the clothes into an evidence bag. *Seal it with the FBI tape.*

Super Chile did what he was told.

Done with my clothes, Cantinflas turned to examine my body. Pulling out a long law-enforcement flashlight, he barked directions in the terse clip of a drill instructor. The flashlight shone on whichever part of my body I was instructed to expose.

*Shake your hands through your hair.*

*Turn your head left and show me behind your ear.*

*Now the other side.*

*Okay. Open your mouth.*

*Stick out your tongue.*

*Lift up your arms. Show me your pits.*

*Bring them down and stretch them forward, palms up.*

*Now the back of your hands.*

*Lift up your balls.*

*Peel back the skin of your penis.*

*Okay. Turn around. Hands on the wall.*

*Show me the bottom of your right foot and wiggle your toes.*

*Now the left one.*

*Bend over, reach back and grab your ass cheeks.*

*Now spread 'em and cough.*

I coughed twice as the light lit up my twice-opened then pinched anus slit.

*Okay. Stand up and turn around.*

The light went to my hair, where Cantinflas meticulously inspected my scalp with his gloved hands, looking for the smallest sign of a scratch. He found no indications to satisfy him that my body had been involved in a death struggle that morning.

His stubby finger bluntly jabbed my shoulder blade, checking to see if I winced. I suppose he was trying to distinguish some body discoloration from the type of bruises usually incurred during hand-to-hand combat. Fortunately, my body was free of scratches and bruises.

*Put your clothes on.*

I took my time.

While I dressed all the warden's men dispersed.

▓▓▓▓▓▓▓▓▓

I was handcuffed again and led out of the room to the FBI office down the hall. The office was sparsely furnished, with one desk, a decrepit file cabinet, and a dry potted plant. I bumped into a metal coat rack while squeezing through the door with Super Chile's fist clasped around my bicep. He un-handcuffed me and told me to sit down. A fair-skinned, elderly FBI agent walked into the office, sat behind the desk, and dismissed my escort. The agent was one of the men who had witnessed my striptease in the other room.

On Sunday evenings when I was a child my father would turn on the TV in time for us to see Tinkerbell's magic wand sprinkling gold dust on Sleeping Beauty's castle, while the title *The Wonderful World of Disney* faded out at the end of the broadcast. A couple of commercials would pass—perfectly starched shirts, shiny General Electric toasters, and pearly white Colgate teeth. Then, for the next hour, my mother, brother, father, and I would gather on the cushiony couch, drink hot chocolate, and admire Hoover's boys as they tracked down the bad guys on the popular TV show *The FBI*.

My whey-faced FBI man had the same Technicolor earnestness as Efrem Zimbalist Jr. And he wore the requisite uniform: white shirt, plain tie, brushed-silver FBI tie clip (perhaps a gift from the Missus for graduating Quantico, the FBI training facility), a rumpled charcoal gray wool suit with one-and-a-half-inch pant cuffs, and well-worn, but polished, black wing tips. But he was not the complete well-groomed G-man. His whitish hair was wispy and disheveled, as if he had been running his exasperated hands through it for hours. His skittish veteran's hands trembled like a Parkinson's patient's. Maybe he had the jitters or was excited to proceed. More likely, he felt the pressure to solve a homicide that would not be solved easily if the murderer wasn't apprehended in the first couple of days.

The on-duty captain, a sea lion of a man, entered the office, pulled up a chair next to mine and wedged himself into it. *I'm Captain Grulowsky.*

Put Ben Franklin's spectacles on the grizzled face of veteran actor Wilford Brimley, TV spokesman for geriatric high-fiber cereals, add eight inches and a hundred and twenty pounds, and you'd get the grotesque picture of the captain. Orange stains on the tips of the thumb, middle, and index fingers of his right hand and in the center of his gray walrus mustache meant that he smoked filterless cigarettes.

Although working together in this tiny office, the two men were really at odds. The captain worked for the Federal Bureau of Prisons (BOP), and was a company man. Any blunder on his part, any finding that was an embarrassment to the prison administration, could certainly affect his promotion in Corrections. He knew who buttered his toast, and he had no incentive to aid any inquiry likely to reveal culpable prison staff. The FBI man, on the other hand, was a federal overseer, answering ultimately to Washington. Any aggravating evidence that the FBI agent uncovered could be used against the prison without the agent fearing reprisals. Such a usurper role meant that the FBI was always viewed suspiciously—as rivals or, worse yet, interlopers—by any federal prison fiefdoms.

The FBI man introduced himself as Mr. Foster and read me my rights. To remain silent. Attorney present. *Blah. Blah. Blah.*

*Mister Loya—may I call you Joe?*

*Sure.*

*Okay, then, Joe, this sheet of paper is just a technicality for us to cover our asses. You know how that goes. It says that you've heard your rights, that you understand them, and that you aren't waiving them right now. Which is fine with us. That's your basic privilege. You don't have to sign it, but the captain and I do.*

He slid the paper across the desk to the captain, who was already operating at the limits of his wakefulness. Grulowsky opened his eyes and made a gruff noise as he leaned forward and scribbled his name on the line reserved for "Witness."

*Again, it's not mandatory that you sign it, but we just like to give you a copy of this affidavit for your records. So, would you just sign here at the bottom and we can get this simple formality out of the way.*

Most men don't think twice about signing this piece of paper, which they believe absolves them of complicity with the cops, the FBI, the "Man." But to do so automatically, and in front of law-enforcement witnesses, reveals whether a person is right or left handed, crucial evidence for forensic experts.

I signed with my correct hand.

*Okay, then. I'll just tell you a few things. Remember, you don't have to answer back if you don't want to. The captain and I are investigating an incident that occurred this morning in your unit. By the way, do you know why you are here?*

*I haven't a clue.*

*You really don't know?*

*Why am I here?*

*Do you know Saul Dominguez?*

*No.*

*No?*

*That's right.*

He looked down at a piece of paper. *He went by the nickname of Chato.*

*Oh yeah, of course I know Chato. He was my bunkie for two weeks. I didn't know his first name was Saul.*

*He was murdered this morning.*

*Fuck!*

*Yeah, we found him at nine o'clock. Right after everybody in your unit was released to work or to the yard.*

*Shit! I just talked to him last night.*

*You did?*

Speaking to Chato the night before he was killed was a provocative piece of intelligence and could speak to Chato's state of mind before his next morning's surprise. The FBI agent wanted to check if the captain had caught the relevance of the remark. But the captain's eyes were closed, head slightly nodding, his left arm hanging lifeless, over the side of the chair, like that of a gallows-limp corpse. I could tell that Agent Foster was shocked by the captain's drowsy indifference.

We turned our heads back to each other.

I continued. *Yeah. He got his new cell about a month ago. I subscribe to the* Los Angeles Times *and pass it along to friends after I'm done reading it. I dropped it off with him last night. We talked about his oldest son, eleven years old, I think, a big USC fan. He wanted Chato, who's a relatively good artist . . . uh . . . er. Damn—WAS a relatively good artist—to draw him the USC logo. Tommy Trojan. I told Chato I was a 'SC fan from way back.* I slung my head down and looked at my hands, folded in my lap. I took a deep breath. *Damn. That's a fuckin' shame about Chato. Did you notify the family already?*

*We're working on it.*

We. That word embarrassed him. He shifted his eyes to his sleepy partner and desperately labored to will him awake with a glare. The trick failed. The captain could not be shaken from slumber from a distance. Apparently Grulowsky had been the night-watch captain whose shift was almost over when the murder occurred. Which meant that our time in that office was usually his bedtime.

Foster came back to me. *So, you said you talked to him last night? Did he seem bothered?*

*Not at all. In fact, he seemed to be in pretty good spirits, since he'd just talked to his sons. He loved them a lot. They sound like good boys. I think they still attend a private school. As a matter of fact, I talked to his youngest son last week.*

*You did? You talked to his son on the phone?* Quick glance at the walrus, then back to me.

*Yeah. I was waiting in line for the phone. Chato was already on one. All of a sudden he turned around and waved me to him. Chato gave me the receiver and asked me to talk to his youngest boy, keep him occupied while he ran to get his address book from his cell.*

Foster was clearly distracted by the Sandman show next to me.

I only turned my head to the captain a few times. My embarrassment for the poor slob was excruciating. I wanted to burst out laughing. Or clap my hands to startle him out of his stupor.

*Did you talk to the boy's mother?*

*No. But she knows I talked to him.*

*How do you know?*

*Because Chato told me that she was curious to know who that strange man was talking to her baby.*

*So, she knows who you are?*

*Call her up and ask her yourself. I'm telling you, yeah, that's what Chato told me.*

He listened, but, like me, he was a pathological doubter.

*Do you have any idea why this happened to him?*

*Well, he must have really pissed someone off.*

He became animated, leaned forward in his chair, wasted a glance on Grulowsky, then latched on to my comment as a possible break in the case.

*You know that he pissed someone off?*

*Well, what do you think? He was murdered wasn't he? You gotta be pretty pissed off to go through all the trouble of murdering someone. I don't need to know any secret plot to figure that one out.*

*Well, of course. I just thought that maybe you may have heard something.*

For a split second I was suspicious of the whole interrogation. I couldn't believe that these men were the adversaries my friends and I plotted against whenever we devised elaborate crime schemes in the prison. There I was, in the defining moment of their critical interrogation, and one man was asking inane questions while the other was fast asleep. A ruse? But Grulowsky's wheezy snore and narcoleptic twitch debunked all doubt.

*I heard nothing.*

*Okay. Well, Joe, we have a problem. You're here because someone said they saw you near Chato's cell with a rolled-up newspaper early this morning. It may mean nothing, but we also found some clothes in your cell that appear to have bloodstains on them. Would you like to talk about the bloody clothes now and try to clear up what may be a simple misunderstanding? Or would you prefer to exercise your right to have an attorney present for that line of questioning?*

If my curiosity could have spoken, I would have asked Special Agent Foster what supervisor he pissed off to earn his post in bumfuck Lompoc. His bare office (in a basic prison located in a boring town that advertised itself on a Main Street banner as THE FLOWER CAPITAL OF THE WORLD) struck me as FBI Siberia.

*Please don't be offended, gentlemen* (the Captain was stretching in his tight chair, slowly awakening), *but since you tell me I'm a suspect in a homicide investigation, I think it would be wise for me to exercise my right to have an attorney present.*

This concluded my interrogation.

Hands cuffed behind my back, I was taken to a security housing unit (SHU) commonly referred to by guards and prisoners as "the hole." There I was placed in a cell that was comprised of three stone walls and a barred front. (Some cells are completely enclosed, with a solid steel door and a little five-by-seven window for guards to look in.) The guard who escorted me yelled out to another guard at the front of the tier controlling the levers. *Open cell eighteen!*

The cell door opened. The guard threw a bedroll on the stained mattress. I stepped in.

*Close cell eighteen!*

The door slammed behind me. The guard pulled a key chain from his belt. *Back up to the bars.*

I did. He reached through the bars and unlocked the handcuffs. Then he turned and walked away.

I untied the bedroll and went to work on my cell. I made my bunk with the clean linen and thin blanket they'd given me. Then I ripped off a bottom portion of the sheet, sudsed it up with the small square of hotel soap I'd been issued with the bedroll, then, as best as I could, scrubbed the inside of the sink, and the inner and outer part of the toilet bowl. I ripped another piece of sheet, sudsed that up too, and got on my hands and knees and wiped clean the entire floor of the cell.

I had come to view prison as a microcosm of the whole world. I was in prison, but so was everyone outside. They weren't wearing handcuffs or confined behind barbed wire, locked down physically by concrete and steel bars, but they had to conform to social pressures, and that clearly was a sort of confinement of their imaginations. And it struck me that God was very much like a prison administrator, and earth his penal colony. If so, then God would have reported that for most of my first twenty-nine years on this planet, I hadn't been a model inmate.

That first night was a sleepless one. I paced the cell for hours, four steps from back to front, a space smaller than a parking spot at a mall.

I remembered times when I was on active duty in God's army, fighting evil, all the time secretly envying the freedom those unattached to religion seemed to enjoy. In Sunday school I used to joke that if there was a vacancy in the Trinity, then a fundamentalist must get the nod to join the other two to set things right.

Now I was alone in my cell, beginning what I clearly understood was an indefinite stay in solitary confinement, the central suspect in a prison homicide investigation.

# TOMBS

# ix

There was no love lost between Heavy D and Hillbilly Willie. Hillbilly Willie and Heavy were locked in the hole at the Leavenworth SHU together on the occasion when Heavy did a shit drive-by on the Puerto Rican runner of that tier. On the day that Heavy was to be transferred to Lewisburg, the runner came up to Heavy's cell and offered Heavy four ice cream cups, the kind with little wooden spoons. A peace token. Of course Heavy was delighted.

Then, a few hours later, as Heavy was sitting handcuffed to two other inmates on the plane ride to Pennsylvania, he started feeling sick. The Puerto Rican runner had laced the ice cream with Ex-Lax, and Heavy shitted all over himself. Hillbilly Willie (who was on that flight) told us that the entire plane stank for hours, that a few guys even threw up on themselves, chained and unable to move away from Heavy's stench.

The entire time that Hillbilly was telling us this story, Heavy had his mouth up to his food trap and was saying over and over, "I can't hear you, Hillbilly Willie. Pull your pants down, you're mumbling."

Missouri Ron and Hillbilly Willie looked similar, with their shaved heads and thick black goatees and pale, white skin. Coincidentally, they both had those comedy and tragedy theatre masks tattooed on their chests—one on his left pec, the other on his right pec.

One day, on the way to the shower, Heavy mistook Missouri Ron for Hillbilly

Willie, and threw shit on him. Talking about, "Oops, sorry Ron, my bad," but laughing while he apologized.

A few weeks later, Indian Early went to court, and Missouri Ron asked the guard to let him be tier runner for the day. When he was released from his cell, he walked over to the broom closet, took out a broom, and broke the handle with his foot so that it had a sharp end. He put some light bulbs in the mop bucket and sneaked up to Heavy's cell door with it. As Heavy slept, he squirted baby oil on Heavy's cell floor. Then he laid the broom handle on the trap door and shoved it hard into the cell so that it harpooned Heavy awake. *Aaah!* Then Missouri Ron started throwing the bulbs into the cell. We could hear them shattering. Then he lit pieces of cloth and threw them into the cell. Heavy didn't care about the broken glass at that point. He jumped up and trod on the glass with his Paleolithic feet to block the food trap door with a pillow.

When the guards came, Missouri Ron was already back in his cell. When they locked him in his cell, he started pounding on the door like a madman, yelling over and over again, "Heavy D, the same thing that'll make you laugh will make you cry! The same thing that'll make you laugh will make you cry!"

## Solitary

S ome men are in the hole for stupid reasons. Like the prisoner who was served too small a cookie on the chow line. He complained to the inmate who'd served him the cookie. *C'mon. Give me another one. That one over there. It's bigger than this one.*

A nearby guard forbade the server from exchanging the dinky cookie for the bigger one, so the prisoner with the grievance Frisbeed the cookie at the guard's torso.

*Fuck you, then! And rub this cookie in your fuckin' chest!*

That'll earn you a trip to the hole every time, and probably a beating by the guards once they have you in handcuffs and behind doors.

Other men, like me, ended up in the SHU under investigation for assault or murder.

By federal law, a prisoner in an SHU must be allowed three showers and five hours a week out of his cell for recreation. A stay in the SHU can last one month to one decade. Some men have been confined in SHUs across the country for more than seventeen years. When they first enter the SHU, every prisoner goes through a standard strip search, like the one I went through in Captain Grulowsky's office.

When a prisoner goes to the hole, all the property in his cell gets locked up, and he usually can't ask for any portion of it for a month or two. That means that a prisoner can go without toothpaste or deodorant or shampoo for a long while. It is forbidden for prisoners to pass things like toiletries from the general prison population to men in the hole. But often men tried to get some necessities to a friend in the hole via a friendly guard.

Creeper assembled a bag of goodies for me—what we call a "care package"—and approached Officer Sorenson about delivering them to me. Sorenson had once been a day-shift guard in our unit, and we got along with him well. After working in K Unit, Sorenson became a "rover," which meant he mostly patrolled the main corridor and randomly patted down prisoners who were loitering suspiciously.

Sorenson had recently been discharged from the Air Force after four years of dutiful service. Since my brother had been stationed at the same base with Sorenson in England, he and I would shoot the shit. Paul and he didn't know each other, but the coincidence gave us a point of reference, something to talk about. Sorensen was the sort of guard who periodically colluded with prisoners or, more frequently, cut us a lot of slack. He admitted that he hated his job, but said he really liked the medical benefits and the job security. He used to sit in the guard's office, leaning back in his chair, feet on the desk, spitting sunflower seed shells into a stained coffee cup. Creeper and I would bust his chops.

*Wipe your mouth. You got something on your upper lip. Yeah, right there.*
He'd wipe his mouth several times, then examine his hand. *Where?*
*There. Right there. Can you see it, Creeper?*
Creeper chimed in. *Yeah, right there.* He'd point to Sorenson's face.
He'd continue wiping. *Did I get it?*
*No, it's still there. Oh wait.* I'd lean forward and feign closer examination. *Oops. I'm sorry. I mistook your flimsy mustache for lint. Sorry, pal.*
*Fuck you, Loya.*

Creeper and I constantly asked Sorensen to bet us that we'd get laid before him, even though we were going to be in prison for several more years.

There are some guards who can be turned, made to bring in drugs, or liquor, or even guns. Sorenson never went that far. However, he once gave Creeper and me a beef burrito from his lunch pail, to split between us. Periodically we'd get glazed donuts.

(I once worked for a lieutenant in the prison who would walk into my room, which was next to his office, and declare, *I hate those enchiladas my wife packed in my lunch so I placed them in the garbage can next to my desk.* Then he'd wink. *Nicely wrapped, resting on top of a box. And I'm going out, Loya. When I get back in one hour I don't want to find them in the can. I can't stand the smell.*

The guards weren't allowed to give us food, money, gifts—not even a little plastic comb, so that was the lieutenant's way of passing food to me. I ate fried chicken, homemade cookies, and some decent enchiladas that way.)

Sorenson asked one of the guards assigned to the SHU to do him a favor and pass Creeper's "care package" along to me. One day, a short guard named Olivares walked up to my cell with a bag in his hands. He looked at me, then he stepped back to check the number above my cell door. My name was no doubt being thrown around the prison, among staff and prisoners, as Chato's possible killer, a bad guy. But in my boxers and wearing glasses, I hardly looked like the tough man possibly responsible for the mayhem in K Unit.

*Loya?*

*Yeah.*

*You're Loya?*

*Yeah. Why?*

*This is for you. Cuff up.*

He placed the bag on the tier floor outside my cell and pulled handcuffs from a pouch on his leather belt. I got off my bunk, walked to the bars, and turned my back to him. Olivares reached through the bars and handcuffed my hands. Then he yelled out, *Open cell number eighteen!*

The door opened. He slid the bag into my cell with his foot.

*Close cell number eighteen!*

After he un-handcuffed me, I rummaged through the bag and found a note: Gafas. *Here's some zoo-zoos and wham-whams. Stay strong. Call my sister.* Tu camarada con un chingo de respeto. *Creeper*

My care package consisted of six bars of Irish Spring soap, two bottles of Head & Shoulders shampoo, three Mennen deodorant sticks (musk scent), one toothbrush, and four tubes of Colgate toothpaste. Creeper had also tucked away a pad of paper, some pens, envelopes, and a book of stamps. Then he topped it off with two bags of Tostitos, a bag of Oreo cookies, a few Snickers bars, and a brand new pair of white athletic socks.

Sorenson was a lucky draw. And Olivares was a bonus. They hadn't worked in the prison long enough to have become jaded.

▉▉▉▉▉▉▉▉▉

News of my investigation trickled back to me via men like Dead Eye, my poker buddy in K Unit—who ended up in the hole, in the cell next to mine, for "refusing to follow a direct order." Dead Eye had a milky marble embedded in his right eye socket. He'd been smoking his breakfast cigarette, drinking coffee, and leaning on the second-tier rail when the unit guard discovered Chato's body that day.

*It was fuckin' hilarious. This hack. I don't know if you remember him or not, but he was a new Baby Huey–looking Chicano guard, only two or three days in our unit. Anyway, he locked the unit door after the nine o'clock movement, picked up his clipboard from the office, then started to make his rounds. Chato's cell was the third or fourth cell from the front. A blanket was draped across the open cell doorway. So the screw walked up to Chato's doorway and knocked on the outside wall, kinda meekly. "Take down the blanket," he said. No answer. "I said take down the blanket." The blanket didn't come down, so the guard got annoyed. He checked the clipboard to find out who lived there, then he continued, except he reached in and pulled the blanket back a bit, just enough to peek inside, "Mr. Dominguez, you can't have a blanket up like this." He must've not seen anything major because he stepped inside, curtain still up. I heard metal scratch on the floor. Like he was kicking the foot of Chato's bunk, trying to roust him awake. I could hear him telling Chato to get up, that it was past nine o'clock and all inmates were supposed to have their beds made by then. Whoever killed Chato probably pulled the blanket over him because the screw obviously didn't notice anything for a few seconds. Then there was a shrill "Oh my God!" I swear he sounded like a fuckin' broad. The metal screeched again, hard this time, and the bitch ran out from behind the curtain and threw up right there on the floor outside the cell. Of course, we thought he was a pussy, so Paddy and me and the other guys still in the unit started to laugh, called him a punk. We told him to go home and suck on mommy's titty. Then all of a sudden he reached for his walkie-talkie and pushed the panic button. The alarm went off. We thought he was calling back-ups because we were treating him like a lame. He ran to the unit door and opened it. Then he led the first guards on the scene to the cell, and they took down the blanket, sidestepping the puke. Nurses and doctors rushed to the unit and tried to revive Chato, I guess. By that time some of the guards that responded to the emergency call were telling us to get back into our cells. That's when they locked us all in. I could still see a little bit through my cell door window though. They were wheeling Chato out on a gurney. I knew he was dead. I never saw so much blood. I'm telling you it was bad. The papers later said that he died at the hospital, but the ambulance left the prison with only the lights on, moving slowly, no siren. He had to be dead before he hit the front gate. Two days later Mister Kristoff asked me to go in and clean the cell. But it needed more than a cleaning. I had to repaint the whole cell. That's how bad it looked.*

*When I first walked in there I saw a fuckin' bizarre stain, a streak of Chato's blood sprayed up the side of the wall, all the way to the ceiling. Fuckin' chilling. I never saw anything like that. There's no way that kid was alive when they took him out of that cell.*

▮▮▮▮▮▮▮▮▮

I used to stay up till three or four A.M. to write letters in solitary. I loved the stillness. A guard patrolled the tier every hour while most inmates slept.

One night, while I was writing a letter, I heard keys jingling down the tier. A guard was ambling my way. I stood to lean against the bars. The guard hesitated at my cell, surprised to find my cell light on and me just standing there. He looked at me, and I recognized him. He nodded and made a move like he was going to continue his rounds. I spoke low.

*They got you in here now, huh?*

He stopped again, in front of me, hesitantly. He hadn't remembered me, and he was wondering how I knew him. So he stopped out of courtesy. The sign of a new guard.

*Yeah. Just for the week.*

*K Unit too much? Had to get the late-night shift, huh?*

*Yeah.* His grin was weary. A bad memory.

*I was pulled out of K Unit for that mess a few months ago. I'm Loya.*

*Oh!* You're *Loya?*

*Yeah. And I heard you took the discovery pretty hard.*

He looked away from me, down the still tier. He hesitated for a moment, then muttered, *Yeah.*

*Wasn't it like your first week or something?*

*My third day. I'd just finished training the Friday before.*

*The guy you found dead was my old cell mate. A friend. I heard they did a real number on him.*

*I'm still having nightmares. He was pretty messed up.*

*It was that bad, huh?*

*You know what? I think I'm going to have to quit. I don't think I'm cut out for this job. That was too much to see in my first week.*

*Too much for anybody to see, no doubt.*

He rubbed the side of his face. Grimaced and mumbled, *uh huh.* He looked down the tier again. Trying to forget.

I pressed. *Do you think he suffered a lot?*

*Oh yeah. Yeah. I think his eyeballs were on his cheeks.*

*Ah. Nah. That's fucked up.*

*Yeah.*

An inmate somewhere coughed. And a toilet flushed.

*So what'll you do if you quit?*

*Something. Anything. Maybe go back to school.*

*School. That'll work. It's too bad you had such a fucked-up experience, but I can't say I feel bad that you have to go. This is a fucked-up place for anybody to work. So, good luck.*

He chuckled timidly. *Well, good luck yourself. With this mess.*

*I'll be out soon enough. Don't worry about that.*

He smiled and walked away.

I went back and sat at my desk. I was burning with something like pure contempt for that sissy guard. You weak-stomached bitch, I thought. Puking your guts on the ground. What the fuck? Could a man be more "softer than cotton candy" than him?

▐▐▐▐▐▐▐▐▐▐

There are always at least three battles going on in a solitary confinement cell:

1. prisoner versus prisoner;
2. prisoner versus guard; and
3. prisoner versus his own imagination.

## Prisoner Versus Prisoner

Before any inmate is released from his SHU cell for a visit, or to take a shower, he is handcuffed through a slot in the door. Then the door opens, and the shackled inmate is escorted to his destination by a guard. But that doesn't mean anybody is safe from bodily harm.

The old-fashioned cells have bars, but the newer cells are enclosed rooms. If you're in a cell with bars, you've got to always be awake when prisoners are walking on the tier. A prisoner can fill up an empty shampoo bottle with dissolved shit from the toilet and squirt you in the face on the way back from the showers. Or someone can throw a handmade grenade into your cell—a small V-8 juice can full of thousands of match heads compacted with metal zippers and jacket buttons and tiny blades from disposable razors.

In the hole there aren't conventional ways for a prisoner to prove he's a bad-ass. But everybody still watches to see who shows signs of weakness. Some prisoners act out by throwing their piss on guards or starting fires. Others do it by picking on weaker inmates.

If you get taunted and can't mete it out, then you become prey to everyone on the tier.

Mostly what you get are verbal aggressions where the match is even. Like the exchange between an Italian named Tony and a South Boston Irishman named Sean.

Italian Tony: *Hey Sean? If a husband and a wife from South Boston go to New York to get a divorce, are they still brother and sister?*

South Boston Irishman Sean: *Fuck you, Tony. But answer this one: Do you know the difference between a blowjob and a ham sandwich?*

Tony: *No.*

Sean: *Wanna go on a picnic?*

Once, on my way to Lewisburg Penitentiary I was temporarily incarcerated at an SHU, in Los Angeles with Charles Keating, Savings-and-Loan swindler extraordinaire. The first time I heard of Charles Keating I knew we wouldn't get along. A woman visiting me in prison, a former Lincoln Savings employee, told me of a Christmas party she'd attended at the posh Beverly Wilshire Hotel. (The orchestra was rumored to have played for then President Reagan.) Timex watches were passed out to all the employees as Christmas gifts, along with two-hundred-dollar bonus checks.

The day before the party, Darla was notified by her branch manager that Keating and his family would be in attendance at the party. Keating had passed the word down the chain of command: Employees were not to bother him with conversation. So the branch manager advised Darla and her co-workers merely to shake Keating's hand, smile, nod, and say only "hello" or "thank you."

I hated Keating and what he stood for. He'd just gotten a ten-year sentence in Arizona for his billion-dollar scandal. There were two guys on my tier who were serving twenty years for two bank robberies; one of them had netted only six hundred dollars. And there was Keating, a mega-million-dollar robber, getting off almost scot-free and allowed to keep some of his fortune.

On top of everything else, Keating was a religious hypocrite, like my father—the high rectitude kind I despised. He'd started out as an anti-smut crusader in Hamilton County, battling *Hustler* magazine's owner, Larry Flynt. But now he was just another phony Christian moralist I wanted to fuck up. The first time Keating walked to the showers he was naked except for a white towel wrapped around his waist—maybe thinking that the camaraderie on the tier would be military barracks–like. He was tall, lanky, and gaunt in the face, with short reddish-blond hair parted on the side. An aged frat boy. I considered him a fuckin' interloper. That he wasn't more timid that first day, didn't display more deference, was an affront to our serious company.

*You are one fine mutha fucka, Charlie. Come over here to the bars and let me place the tip of my shitty little dick on your tongue. You don't even have to suck it. Just let it droop there for a quick second.*

Someone else chimed in, *Yeah, Chuck, give the man a quick droop. Don't be an asshole, Chuck!*

The guards laughed as they escorted Keating to the showers. Ten minutes later, when he hurried back to his cell scurrying like a small scared animal across the jungle floor, we catcalled, pleading with him to give us a show of his ass. For the next several days whenever he walked to the showers, we continued to treat him as if he were a young plump virgin, launching into him with intensity.

*Chuck, I want to fuck you to a hardwood finish!*

His ass cheeks would visibly stiffen as he exaggerated his straightness. He didn't know what to do with his eyes, so he stared straight ahead. His pinched stride, presumably meant to indicate taut manliness, gave off the reverse effect. It made him appear as if he were trying real hard to fight off a natural swish.

Prison officials placed Keating in solitary confinement for his own protection. But the maximum-security regulations weren't strict at MDC, so when I was taken out of my cell sometimes I was able to shed my escort and I'd pivot to the back of the tier to hassle Keating. I'd walk up to his cell and startle him while he was exercising or reading or just lying silent on his bunk:

*Hey, bitch! You got a nice round ass. Is that all you back there or did you get a new wallet?*

The guard who was supposed to be escorting me would catch up with me, grab me by the arm, and escort me to the showers. He'd feign angry concern with my lascivious remarks and my having slipped out of his grasp.

*C'mon, Loya. Quit bothering Mister Keating.*

*I'm not bothering him. I'm just trying to get to know him.*

*Yeah, right. A welcoming committee, is that it?*

*You got it. A welcoming committee. Welcoming a view of that fine ass.*

Roars of laughter from the other inmates on the tier. The guards would also chuckle. (Guards always laughed when one prisoner verbally bullied another. That's why a prisoner could never expect a guard to watch his back.) And all the while Keating would stay as quiet as a church mouse.

It pleased me to think that as he sat in his cell he probably worried about what would happen to him if one of us got our hands on him.

## Prisoner Versus Guard

The ennui of solitude unhinged many of us locked in solitary confinement, lowering our thresholds for inhibition.

One morning I woke up to an angry, raspy old voice yelling from behind his cell door to a young clean-cut guard on the tier:

Old man: *I fucked your mother.*

Guard: *I don't have a mother.*

Old man: *What happened? Did she die while you were fucking her? I know I fucked her. She was a cheesy broad. Whenever I was finished fucking her, I wiped my hog off with her thrift-store blouse.*

▨▨▨▨▨▨▨▨▨

In the SHU there was nothing to lose. Almost. And if a person was serving a life sentence or something similar then there really was nothing to lose. Some guys would throw their shit on the guards or spit on them. Some would refuse to "cuff up" (get handcuffed before leaving their cell for transfer) and then threaten to stab any guard who crossed the threshold of their cell. Sometimes prisoners would light small fires to set off the sprinkler system. Anything to disrupt an obnoxious guard shift.

▨▨▨▨▨▨▨▨▨

A guard didn't have to commit a crime to make a prisoner's life miserable in the hole. There were a million ways they could fuck with your head.

A typical exchange goes like this: An inmate knocks on his cell door to get the attention of the guard. Even though it's the guards' duty to bring prisoners the phone at our allotted time or toilet paper, soap, toothpaste, etc, sometimes they don't, instead remaining at the end of the tier, playing cards and snickering, or ignoring us, or sometimes yelling out, *You're on your own. Get it yourself.* They ignore a prisoner's knocks for ten to fifteen minutes. Then the prisoner of course gets riled, furious really. Then he starts pounding and kicking his door. Then the guards yell, telling him to quit pounding on the door. Then the prisoner yells back that he wouldn't be pounding if he'd gotten some sort of answer when he knocked for the first ten minutes. Then the guards snidely remark that he won't get anything at all now since he was banging on the door. He calls them cowards. The guards call him a cry baby. They make childish sniveling noises. He calls them motherfuckin' bitches and dares them to step into his cell like men.

This is how the tension on a tier can escalate in one minute into tremendous pressure.

Some guards will tie a small noose outside a troublemaker's cell to indicate that they could rush inside and hang him and make it look like he'd hung himself.

Sometimes guards will search a prisoner's cell when he's in the shower and leave letters out of their envelopes, family pictures on the floor marred by fresh boot marks, or the mattress shoved against the wall.

The worst is the way some guards mess with a prisoner's sleep by shining flashlights in his eyes during the late-night count. They tamper with sleep because, as I once explained to a young inmate, we aren't really doing time when we're snoozing since we'd be asleep on the streets too. Some guards can't stand the idea of giving the wicked any rest.

When I first arrived at Lompoc Penitentiary, I'd sit in my cell and remark to friends that our jailers sure looked a lot like us. This wasn't really surprising. By choosing to go to the slammer eight hours out of every day, they spent a third of their lives in jail.

I saw a lot of new correctional officers come into the prison: fresh faced, young, eager, and sometimes a bit idealistic. We prisoners referred to these green guards as "fish" (the same word we used for first-time offenders unaware of prison etiquette or of what awaited them). I suppose it derives its meaning from the idea of small fish in predatory waters.

One "fish" guard at Lompoc was a momma's boy when he first arrived to the penitentiary. Officer Cronk took his job as a guard seriously, but he didn't seem to care much about his appearance. He showed up to work in half-pressed clothes, wore his hair parted down the middle and long around the ears. He'd bring his lunch to work, a sack with an egg salad sandwich and a thick slice of momma's fresh-baked apple pie.

At first, he was uncomfortable with his power. He wouldn't yell loud at mail call. If an inmate talked nicely to him, he tended to cut the guy some slack, on the premise that kindness deserved a just turn.

But soon the boy realized that he was living among hard-core men who considered him gullible and a sissy. Like many men before him who'd transformed their lives, he woke up in prison. Except his change went the other way.

He began to wear sharply creased clothes—convict style. He cut his hair and began to comb it slicked back—again, convict style. He grew a thick "walrus-brush" mustache—convict style. And he became obsessed with muscles the same way convicts were. (It never worked the other way around: Inmates didn't try to look like the guards, those fresh-faced boys recently discharged from the military and excited to apply for work in law enforcement.)

He began to pepper his conversation with guttural profanity. He'd lift weights after work and compare his workout techniques with those of brawny inmates, referring to those with smaller bodies as less than manly. He'd behave like veteran convicts expected wannabe tough guys to behave: watching how real mobsters behaved and then mimicking their pose, swagger, and speech habits.

Such changeling-guards often also adopted our contemptuous attitude toward the "good guys." They would use words like *rat* and *snitch* to describe the men whose job it was to investigate rogue prison guards. They talked about Internal Affairs with venom, as if those investigators were subversive agents seeking to undermine, rather than uphold, the law. They missed the irony when their insults sounded like the ones criminals used to describe all law enforcement officers.

Whenever I or one of my friends came across a really sadistic guard, we'd gather together and find consolation in the notion that he would succumb to the hazards of his job and become a mere statistic.

*Don't worry about him. He'll get his. He doesn't know it yet, but he will soon be a lonely and miserable fuck. Law enforcement guys have the highest rate of spousal abuse and divorce of any profession. If they don't kill themselves fast, they become huge boozers and kill themselves slowly. Oh yeah, these guys are real pieces of work. They will eventually hate life and themselves so much that their wife and kids will hate them too.*

We always used one particular case in Kansas as our example. Phillip Shoats was known among prisoners at Leavenworth Penitentiary as a "kick ass now, take names later" sort of guard. One day the police were called to his home for a shooting. When they arrived, they found that his fourteen-year-old son had shot Shoats dead with a shotgun, in fear for his life. Apparently the kid had got tired of his father kicking his ass with impunity.

Prisoners loved that sort of dark irony. *It ain't no fun when the rabbit's got the gun,* is one of the prisoners' favorite retorts.

Prison guards eventually showed the same signs of stress as the prisoners, precisely because the idea of becoming like us was inconceivable to them.

## Prisoner Versus His Own Imagination

Nietzsche wrote, "In solitude, whatever one has brought into it grows—also the inner beast." He knew that solitude could dement and wither a man, drive the psyche mad. No matter how tough you think you are, time in "the hole" is designed to make you go through some serious changes. That's because after being with your body in a tight space month after month, inevitably you succumb to aberrant thoughts.

The pressures of long-term solitary confinement made one prisoner rub his own shit all over his body.

The mind plays tricks.

Then there was Manetti who one night, while playing with himself, got a capless shampoo bottle stuck up his ass because the suction from his stomach was sucking the bottle up into his colon. They had to surgically remove it. He almost died in the hospital.

After many months in solitary, another ugly tattooed convict I knew walked to the showers with his grimy briefs rolled up above his ass cheeks, a grotesque attempt to make them resemble thong panties. He'd smeared colored pencil on his lips and cheeks to give them a cute blush. And his T-shirt was knotted in the front like a girl's bikini top.

▏▐▏▐▏▐▏▐▏▐

They say that astronauts in space spend the majority of their days in their capsules monitoring the gauges and systems concerned with their own safety, making sure the cabin pressure doesn't decrease and asphyxiate them. Their survival depends on their perpetual vigilance.

To maintain the tenuous balance of cabin pressure, for survival's sake, was the same goal I had when I was in a solitary confinement cell. The majority of my day was generally spent monitoring the pressure around me so I didn't suddenly succumb to it. I'd check and regulate my mood. On occasions, when I wasn't vigilant, the pressure cracked. I'd begin to feel tired, physically ill. Fortunately, I'd done enough time to be a sort of survivalist guide through solitary. I was as susceptible as the next guy to caving in under pressure, but having survived through these episodes before, I knew a few tricks that helped me recover quickly.

The trick of mental survival in the hole is to release as much madness as you can in your daily routine. Exercises like push-ups and handstands are good because they keep your blood flowing and release a lot of pent-up energy. Also helpful are concentration games. For example, I'd try to see how long I could last without uttering a word. Every day I'd sit on my bunk and focus my eyes on one spot for as long as I could. And each time I'd try to last longer than the time before. After several weeks of two- and three-day warm-up silences, I was finally able to remain silent for an entire week. I had mastered the art of silence. That's when I fell in love with the texture in the labyrinth of my solitude.

Most important, every day when I got out of bed in the morning, I'd make my bunk and force myself not to lie down on it until after lunch, and even then, only for a nap. In solitary confinement, the bunk is like quicksand. Once you lie down in it, your mind gets sloppy. That's when strange thoughts control your imagination.

But despite all my efforts, solitary confinement started to mess with my head after eight months.

Once, while in solitary, I asked a guard for some toilet paper. We were each given one roll of toilet paper per week, but, as I explained to the guard, I'd had a bout of diarrhea and had gone through my roll in only four days. The guard laughed and said, *Sorry, Loya. You've got to wait three more days, like everyone else.* Then he walked away, giggling. Later, when he opened my food slot to hand me my dinner tray, I threw a cup of my wet shit on him.

But my derangement manifested itself in other ways too. Soon after that, I started hearing loud scratchy noises, as if a volume dial for the static in my head had been turned up high. And more than once the surface of the wall in my cell began to slowly swirl into the shape of a galloping horse, then a man being chased, then a Buick driving down the road. During one concentration exercise, I was staring at a spot on the wall when it started to move and grow, becoming some sort of ghoulish mask of death. I looked away. When I looked back, it was still there, and then it started to morph into the faces of strangers—a man with a hat, a woman wearing a bonnet, a black man with a huge afro—old and young faces, black and white faces, fat faces, skinny faces. I closed my eyes, but the image stayed with me underneath my eyelids. I worried that I'd finally lost total control of my mind, that I'd be stuck looking at those faces forever. But when I opened my eyes, they were gone. This happened several times.

Then, for a long time, the faces of my victims haunted me in my sleep. I'd see their mouths contorted in pain and begging for mercy. I'd see myself standing over my father with a knife, him holding the wound on his neck. I repeatedly saw the face of that one frightened teller who pissed on herself when I faced her up against the wall of the vault and taunted her to settle things with her God. After such dreams, I'd awake and spend the entire day wiped out on my bunk with a headache or stomachache.

■■■■■■■■■

I got bad news. Word trickled back to me from the West Coast that Creeper had been arrested for a prison murder. Within a week he was found in his SHU cell with a needle in his arm. He'd OD'd on heroin.

Another friend of ours, Santos, didn't make it either. Once upon a time he had been heavily involved in prison life, one of those men to be feared and admired. But when I met him, he was reformed. I asked him if he had had to do things over again what he might do differently. He immediately said that he would never have tried heroin. (When I first met him in prison he'd already given up the drug for several years.) He also said that he would never have gotten tattoos. I took his words to heart and never tried heroin. And even though the urge to get tattoos was strong, I refused to betray Santos's wished-for ethic. If he couldn't go back and get rid of his tattoos, then I would turn my skin into a blank canvas as a testament to my respect for him.

Santos told me that when he left prison he was going to pick up a lunch box. We laughed. Then he added: *A see-through lunch box, just so people won't think I have a gun in there.*

He got out and met a woman, got a regular-guy job as a dispatcher for a towing company, and even became a dad for the first time. But one day, he put down the lunch box, picked up a gun, and robbed a bank. He was caught and taken to the county jail. There he shat out the bag of dope, the spoon, and the lighter he'd stuck in his anus as a contingency plan in case he didn't get away. He OD'd in his holding cell.

My two favorite people in prison had faced odds that they couldn't accept, so they cashed in their chips. I feared that my attraction to these men, the thing that we really had in common, was our inability to cope with despair.

Losing control of my faculties and deeply depressed over my two friends' deaths, I intentionally played back criminal scenes that reminded me of a time when I was much ballsier, more in control, cocky even. Like the time I robbed a Home Savings and Loan in San Diego.

When I got outside the bank I flipped through the wads of cash in my bag and instantly became perturbed by the chump change the teller had given me. So I walked into the Bank of America, next door, and robbed it too, knowing full well that the police were already on their way to answer the first bank's alarm.

And I still wasn't done: I robbed two more banks before calling it a day.

On the way home I hopped onto Interstate 5 and proceeded north to Los Angeles. I'd borrowed my uncle's BMW 320i and, enjoying its sportiness and the ease of the handling, I contemplated making him a cash offer for it.

I got to the part of the freeway approximately five miles before the immigration checkpoint—the Pacific Ocean was on my left and the rolling hills of Camp Pendleton were on my right. It was one o'clock in the afternoon, and I was feeling exalted with a little more than thirty thousand dollars in a satchel in my trunk, hidden under five separate changes of clothes. Everything had gone my way.

Then, all of a sudden traffic stalled drastically and came to a complete stop. There was traffic for at least a mile ahead. The freeway now resembled a stadium parking lot. I couldn't figure out what the backed-up car traffic meant. I'd been arrested before in a stolen car by an impromptu highway checkpoint, so I was immediately concerned.

I had to stay cool, but I also had to plot a getaway strategy. Then, right when I felt some sense of control by having come up with a contingency plan, a red indicator light on my dashboard flashed *HOT!!*

It was the gauge for the car's temperature. Smoke was puffing out from the hood. This fucked-up little BMW was overheating. I muttered: Fuckin' hoopty-jalopy motherfucker.

Now I had a new problem.

There was a lane to my right, between my car and the side of the highway, but there was no car movement. I didn't give a fuck about gently nudging my way through, so I turned my wheel and edged sharply between the two cars to my right. Horns beeped, steering wheels were pounded, tops of dashboards was slapped. I pointed to the smoking hood of my car, which by then looked as if it could be on fire.

I wedged myself between two cars and then looked back quickly to make sure no cars were coming up on the shoulder lane. All clear, I made my move into the lane, put the car in park, and turned off the engine. Then I looked in my rearview mirror. Far, far behind me, but coming my way were lights flashing on the shoulder lane.

*Fuck!*

CHP.

*Shit!*

Motherfuckin', god-damned buzzard luck.

My conundrum: An overheating engine and hot criminal justice colliding into each other.

I had to let the CHP pass, but there wasn't any room on the narrow lane to move out of his way. And I couldn't get back into the traffic. I started the car and drove forward slowly, trying to find a place where I could pull even farther to the right.

I found a small patch of dirt and pulled over, just in time too, because the CHP had slowed down behind me. For sure his stopping next to me, rolling down his window, and motioning me to lower mine was going to be his opportunity to thank me for my effort to clear the way.

*You're fucking lucky that there's an officer down ahead 'cause if I wasn't needed up there then I'd haul your fucking ass in for driving on the emergency lane.*

*My car is overheated. I had to pull out of traffic.*

*I don't give a fuck.*

Then he was gone.

Two overwhelming feelings swelled in me. First fear. Then satisfaction. I was the bank robber who was unstoppable, mostly because I was uncatchable, invincible even.

Fuckin' idiot, I thought. I was right here. In your grasp. But your emotion blinded you. Hysterical like a woman. Piece of shit. And another cop lying injured on the highway to boot. Damn, I was on a roll.

But I was still stuck with my problem: How to proceed? An overheated car can be fixed only with coolant, so I needed to get some. But what to do with the stolen money in the trunk? Do I carry it with me in a backpack or leave it behind? Thirty thousand bucks is a large piece of loot.

I got out of the car and opened the trunk. I filled a large fanny pack with all the money then strapped it around my waist. I was wearing Top-siders, khaki shorts, a UCLA tank top, and a baseball cap.

I wasn't in the mood to walk in the direction of that irrational cop up ahead so I walked in the direction I'd come, hoping to find a call box where I could wait—several hours if I had to—for a tow truck to come and bail me out of my predicament.

The reason for the traffic was still a mystery. The cop had said some-thing about an officer down, but that didn't quite explain the parking lot of traffic. But, whatever the cause, I figured that everything should be moving within two hours. Unfortunately, every call box for a mile back had a mesh cover with a neon orange $X$ slashed across it. I started to think "conspiracy."

*Smart sunzabitches*, I thought. *They knew to take care of all exit routes of the guy who would drive into their trap. Damn, they are clever.*

I was actually arrogant enough to believe that the covered boxes were an attempt to trap me somehow. So I did what came instinctively: I turned around and started walking straight back toward the den of the lion, toward the Highway Patrol, where the cop had been headed.

A mile ahead of my disabled car, the traffic problem became clear to me: The freeway had been completely closed off, and five lanes of traffic were being funneled into one lane and then diverted through Camp Pendleton. When I caught up with my obnoxious CHP officer he was standing in front of his car at the bottom of the Las Pulgas off-ramp, directing cars to go inland and follow the road into Camp Pendleton.

The CHP officer wore mirrored sunglasses, but I could tell he was scowling at me as he watched me walking toward him. He held his left arm out like on a cross, while making small circles with his right arm, telling people to go in the direction of his left arm.

*Hey, I'm sorry for being in your way back there, but my car was legitimately overheating and all the call boxes are out of order.*

The cop continued waving cars inland.

*Anyway, do you know if there is a gas station I could walk to in there?* I pointed to where the cars were driving.

*No, you'll have to go back toward San Diego.*

*Should I walk on this side of the freeway or the other side?*

*The other side. Go under the freeway here, then up the on-ramp, then walk three miles to a Shell station. I believe they can help you.*

*Thanks, Officer. I'm sorry for blocking your way, really.*

*All right.*

I could smell swine all around me, but the swine couldn't smell the stolen money on me.

Walking away felt triumphant. The cop was a man of power, so his reactions could be predicted. He needed people around him to defer to his power status. Insecurity tormented him, so he couldn't distinguish feigned reverence or deference from the real thing. They all served his ego equally. My performance convinced him that I feared him, that I was the good citizen who needed to fawn over his badge and gun and big, fast car.

Walking up that freeway on-ramp, puffed up with triumph and wearing a rich fanny pack, I scarcely heard the vehicle creep up behind me. I flinched when two cops in their squad car flicked on their *boo-OO-wooh* switch.

I say flinched, but what really happened was that I leapt forward a little bit and nearly shitted on myself. The CHP in the passenger seat, a young guy, rolled down his window. I'd made him laugh, and now he was just smiling big. *Where you headed?*

*My car overheated on the other side.* I pointed across the way in the general direction of my car. *And the officer at the bottom of the off-ramp directed me this way, to get help at a gas station a few miles down the highway.*

*Hop in the back. We'll take you.*

*Okay.*

I opened the back door to their cruiser, threw my fanny pack in, then climbed inside and closed the door.

*Ah,* I said. *It's nice and cool in here.*

They chuckled, and one of them said, *Nobody has ever said that when we put them back there.*

*How 'bout that.* I continued, *I've never been in the back seat of a police car before.*

The driver asked, *What were you doing in San Diego?*

*Well, a few weeks ago I met a girl at a USC party, and she goes to UC San*

*Diego, so I came down to see her for two days. But believe me, I was ready to go home after the first night. Too much drama.*

They nodded.

Good. Solidarity. I'd play to every misogynistic stereotype that came to mind. But I still had to play the citizen, and they were a power over me. I knew how this game worked: I needed to give them their due, some incentive not to feel like they needed to remind me who was boss in their car. After all, I had money to protect. It was always about money and power.

*The officer at the bottom of the ramp mentioned that there was an officer down. Is that why you closed down the freeway?*

The passenger cop spoke. *Well, we were chasing a bad guy, and there were gunshots fired, and he crashed, and the pursuing officer crashed as well.*

*I hope he's all right*

*Oh yeah, he's in the hospital. But he'll be okay.*

They chuckled then the driver spoke, *He's doing a lot better than the bad guy.*

Their low laughter sounded morbid and sinister.

*Does the officer have a family?*

I was pouring it on thick. They didn't know how far they were from that money at that point. Clean off the scent. They'd never suspect me.

*Yeah, a wife and a new baby girl.*

A sign for a rest stop flashed on the side of the road.

*Hey you know what, why don't you drop me off there?*

*Are you sure? It's no problem to drive on farther.*

*Nah, it's my uncle's Beamer, so he can drive down and pick me up. I'm tired of hassling with that car.*

*Okay then.*

Once we were off the ramp, the car rolled to a stop.

I reached for the door handles. *Hey, there aren't any handles on these doors.*

We all laughed. The driver said, *Yeah, my partner has to let you out.*

Once I was out of the car I leaned toward their open window and said thanks and to give my best wishes to the wounded cop in the hospital.

Then they were gone.

Fuckin' dim-witted mental midgets, cogitatively crippled, absurdly predictable Keystone Cop motherfuckers.

I got on the phone and called my uncle, who told me that the car's fan didn't move while the car was idling. I told him that I was thinking about offering him money for the car, but he was shit out of luck 'cause, after that harrowing turn of events in the back of the cop car, I would never rob a bank with his shitty car again.

That evening I got a telephone call from an ex–cell mate whom I'd met in the San Diego jail. He told me that a bank surveillance photo of me was being flashed on the evenings news as well as on the late-night *Crime Stoppers* program. He said there was a thousand-dollar reward for my capture. The local police thought that I was Lebanese or Pakastani, and they thought that I lived in Tijuana. I was nicknamed the Beirut Bandit.

I wondered what those smug CHP officers felt like the next morning when they figured out that I was the serial bank robber who had terrorized their community the day before.

▩▩▩▩▩▩▩▩

I tried hard to keep sane with these memories of victorious bank robberies. But one night, I was sleeping and I was startled awake by *JOE!!* No guard was at my cell door and nobody was in the cell. It was just me. But the voice had sounded real, not like voices in your dreams, you know, like murmurs in your head. No, this voice felt like a voice outside of me, as if a man had spoken my name. The vibrations had shot out of his mouth and traveled through the air and entered my ear and slammed my eardrum. *JOE!!* Like that. This happened to me three times. By the fourth time I was like, *Okay, here it comes. Madness in the house.*

Then came the nightmares.

In the first one, I was wandering down a lush tropical island path when suddenly a volcano erupted and I found myself running as fast as I could from a thirty-foot-high lava flow. It was gaining on me. The dream ended with the lava flow crushing through the prison wall and chasing me around the housing units toward the far corner of the prison, where I finally stopped and huddled with other prisoners while we waited for our inevitable annihilation by lava drowning.

The nightmare on the following night was actually two catastrophes compressed into one. It started with me standing in a phone booth on the side of the road. All of a sudden I heard a roar. I looked up in the sky and saw an airplane flying toward me, ready to crash into me in about fifteen seconds. I raced out of the booth, and at exactly that moment an earthquake started. I was shaky but able to race around a building for cover. Sure enough, the plane crashed across the street from the phone booth. I heard a loud *boom* and saw wheels and torn metal and glass whipping all around me. But the drama wasn't over. The ground around me began to convulse and lurch. Walls of granite suddenly erupted from under the soil, and I was thrown ten feet in the air. There was nowhere safe for my feet to gain purchase so I just sort of leapt from one undulating patch of ground to the next. And then the nightmare ended. I woke up and thought for sure that the meaning of the nightmare was that my mind or my self was fracturing.

But all of the noises in my head and the faces on the walls and the nightmares were only escalating to one key bout of psychosis.

One night I felt compelled to open my eyes after a troubled night of sleep. A young white boy was standing in the corner of my cell. He was wearing a little boy's striped T-shirt, like Opie on *Mayberry R.F.D.*, except this boy was completely bald. Somehow I knew that he was seven. His expression was blank. No pain, no anger, no guile, no judgment. He gave me nothing except his presence. He looked so innocent. And he was so pale. He wasn't moving towards me, or fidgeting like a little kid. No, he was actually a bit stiff, like a standing corpse. His presence was disturbing. He was there long enough for me to begin to wonder why the hell he was there at all. Was it bring-your-kid-to-work day? Maybe he was the son of a guard and he'd wandered away from his father. But I couldn't comprehend how he'd got into my cell. And what was up with his shiny, bald head?

I closed my eyes again. When I opened them later, he was gone. As I lay in my bunk staring at the ceiling I thought about the boy. As much as

I believed that I was alive on that bunk I believed that the boy had actually been there, standing in that corner. I was chilled by how his presence had felt so vivid. It couldn't have happened, I know, but he'd felt so fucking real. If I thought enough about it, I believed I could even convince myself that I'd smelled his milky breath. I lay in bed fully believing that a supernatural presence had haunted me. This meant that the rational part of me, the part not usually given to a belief in ghosts, now believed in them. I was starting to break. I was losing it.

I began to get deeply worried. I'd been seeing faces, hearing voices, having nightmares. And now this boy. It all added up: if my mind wasn't already broken, then it was breaking fast. My whole delusion of control was shattering.

I was scared shitless, and worried, that the next time the boy appeared he might talk to me, and I knew I'd have to answer him. I lay in bed all day, scared that I was finally unable to tell the difference between reality and fantasy.

In that hour of dire need, I wasn't visited by God or his burning bush. Jesus didn't call to me like St. Paul claimed he did to him, on that road to Damascus. No horns or trumpets blew. No angels in bright lights came to give me heavenly messages.

I merely saw a very pale little boy.

But my dad's theology was half right, and I can invoke him at this point in my story because after that haunting I believed in sudden personal changes again—the Pauline moment, the crucial turning point of redemption, the deathbed confession. That's because the boy's presence seemed to be urging me away from a vulgar future, calling me back to more pristine days of summer bike rides and bologna sandwiches in clubhouses and the bygone days when my mother was still alive.

At around noon the following day, it dawned on me that the boy who'd haunted me in my sleep was my seven-year-old boyhood friend from Deland Street, the kid who died of leukemia, Bobby. (He'd been my first occasion to learn about death.) I couldn't get him out of my head. It was his eyes. They were so piercing. Looking at me, longing for contact. His face was so innocent, so fragile. I realized how far away from this boy I was. How dark and disturbed and depraved my life had become. But I realized also that the bald boy was me, too. I mean, the part of me that had once connected with him, a part that was on the verge of extinction. My innocence was dying, flat-lining after all these years of systematic degradation. It was like I had one last chance to nurture the innocence still left in me, to embrace it, to bring it back to life. That little boy's look was telling me, *Please do it soon, or it may be too late.*

Remembering him brought up recollections of my life when my mother was still alive. For two days the memories of those earlier times rushed in on me in a strong way. It was odd to recall that I was once a sweet kid, a good student, a momma's boy. Here I was filthy mouthed and blasphemous, battling the FBI, throwing shit on guards, stabbing Griffith. But once I'd been innocent. Soon I was remembering a bunch of other stuff too, like my mother's funeral; like being bullied in the schoolyard; like writing mystery stories in the fourth grade; like Brenda's peach cobbler. There I was crashing my bike and permanently scarring my left eyebrow. And there I was taking my first sip of coffee with my mother on our way home from Mario's taco stand. There I was drinking Orange Julius drinks with my dad and mom after church. And there I was going to Saturday matinee symphonies for children at the Music Center in Los Angeles. Then there was the old story about God preserving me for his special purpose. My comforting my frightened brother with Bible verses. The random memories were like going back to another incarnation altogether.

My submerged past surfaced with full force, forcing me to confront tenderness I once displayed, but no longer claimed. I was embarrassed and terrified to be in possession of such sensitivity to my past. But by the second night, I felt like shit, ashamed that I had turned out so much worse than I'd begun. I couldn't help responding with some loathing to the images of my innocent child-self. The image of me comforting Paul with Bible Scripture could only mock me. There was part of me that still believed that introspection was a sissyish endeavor. It reminded me of the weak early years, when I admired abstract thinkers and optimistic believers. I was a doer now, so I felt that thinking before I acted would be a step backward into victimhood. I was torn. To stay the same or press on toward a thawing.

The realistic features of the haunting—the way I felt as if I'd smelled the boy—coupled with the usual violent dreams and phantom noises in my head, already had me believing that my mind was quickly fragmenting. This was the only metaphor I could grab onto to describe the phenomenon. A tectonic-like shift had occurred in my interior world, and the memories of my childhood were bursting through some sort of perforated seam in the landscape of my soul, forcefully released like hot geysers or dangerous gases no longer content to stay below the earth's surface. The initial crack in the ground had made the shadows pine for more light. So the suffocated soil erupted.

I suppose a sensual reaction to loneliness is as it should be: We are never more naked than when we feel our loneliness most acutely. Was that, perhaps, why I sensed that the boy had touched me? Hadn't the dream had a musky smell to it? In spite of the boy's calm, I'd reacted to his expression as if it were an accusation.

The apparition of madness finally released language. I picked up a pen and wrote out the story of the bald boy. Afterward, I lay on my bunk and felt high, lightheaded, relieved. The writing had opened me, had freed me to begin thinking again. I had toyed with writing since childhood. Raised as I was among the Bible and books, among dread, hermeneutics, and the dead languages, I couldn't help but inherit my father's obsession with the meaning of words. And his influence in this area came to the fore most intensely in my solitude.

As a child I'd spend days comparing myself to characters from the various stories I'd acquired. Now I remembered that when I was in eighth grade, my father read to us at night from his college literature textbook—stories like Kafka's "A Hunger Artist" or Faulkner's "A Rose for Emily." I used to tell teachers that I wanted to grow up and be a short story writer. And back in 1978 I told Bob Storm, my foster father in Pasadena, that I wanted to write a book about my battle with my father. He encouraged me to get started. And later, during several rough relationships, I scribbled sentimental poetry about tortured love and loss.

So in that cell, when I turned to the blank page for relief, poetry flowed first and easiest, but short memoir pieces soon followed.

My body would always become disturbed during those writing sessions. I'd get headaches or the runs, or suddenly become fatigued, as if I'd shot up a dime bag of heroin. But by the time I was done writing, I'd be in a better mood. Soon I recognized that my rage was somehow connected to these very simple stories of my childhood, even the good memories—*especially* the good memories. That's when I figured that writing could somehow help me learn to manage my temper, possibly to dismantle my sadism altogether. My mind, lighter and less fettered, flirted with transcendence.

I'd glimpsed an Easter moment with the boy's haunting, and I swore a small oath to myself: I would reconcile the refinement and barbarity in me. I was free when I thought of myself as a little boy on a bike. I wanted more of that emancipation. So I dedicated myself to learning to be more like him, to being the me I'd once been, the child who once laughed and cried and believed in resurrection.

Eventually the image of myself as a child dancing around the living room—happy that Jesus had risen from the dead—altered my imagination. I began to entertain ideas of my one day being free from prison, free from viciousness, free from the lie that I was evil, free from being antagonistic with my sweet earlier self.

I was fatigued by my loneliness in that poorly lit cell, and I yearned for peace in my life, a sophisticated passivity that would feel more like bravery than weakness. My writing was an unmasking of myself. No more hiding behind a façade of bravado. I was committed to disarming my rage so that I might eventually have a chance to live a normal life and stay out of prison. Organizing my blemished narrative on the page allowed me to grasp how my anger and violence had always disguised immense wounds, and had been mostly a profound grief for a life gone terribly awry.

I also thought a lot about killing myself in those days. It was odd how, when I began to imagine hope, I would be overwhelmed with thoughts of suicide. I know some of it had to do with not thinking myself strong enough to change. The thought of getting out of prison only to fail spectacularly and end up back in prison was too dreadful a possibility to conceive. I decided I would kill myself before I'd let that happen again. And I had inspiration for suicide. When my father realized, after I'd stabbed him, that everybody would know that he'd failed as a father, he popped a bunch of pills in his mouth, in hopes of croaking.

Change and a struggle for life did finally occur, however. On one of those lonely nights in my cell, while my memories and my future taunted me, my thoughtless life of crime ended, and my life of remorse was born.

# X

eavy D was pissed that Missouri Ron had gotten his revenge with those smashed lightbulbs. We'd all laughed at him for screaming "Aaah!" like a little girl. The next time Heavy was let out of his cell to go to the showers, he roared and twisted in his cuffs real hard so that they snapped. We peeked through the cracks in our cell doors and saw two guards fleeing the tier, and Heavy standing straight up like a bear, waving his cane in the air. We watched as he proceeded to use the cane to smash the phone jacks on the tier.

Whenever it was time for one of us to make his weekly fifteen-minute phone call, a guard would bring the phone to our cell and plug it into the phone jack located above the cell door. The phone was our lifeline. Guys set up their visits through the phone; they called their girls; drug deals were fixed. By fucking up the phone jacks Heavy knew that he'd be punishing us too; the guards would punish everyone by not expediting their repair. It could be another two or three weeks before we got to use a phone.

But Heavy was not only fuckin' up our phone connections; he was bringing big heat to the tier. After Heavy's "escape," the administration might feel so pissed off that they'd show us they still had the upper hand by searching our cells for contraband. And at that time, we all had contraband in our cells, and we were expecting a shipment of more drugs later in the day, through Indian Early who was bringing drugs from a visitor to give to Stone Man.

Heavy was pooped, so he walked to the back of the tier and sat on a step in front of mine and Stone Man's cells. He was huffing and puffing, all worked up. Stone Man and Heavy powwowed. Stone Man pleaded with Heavy to stop his tirade. He even told him that he would be cut in on the drugs and pruno if he mellowed out.

"Heavy, don't do this man. We got dope and shanks and pruno up in these cells, man. Whatever you want, just let me know, you got it. Just don't do this."

"What drugs you got now?"

"A little bit of weed right now, but tonight we got a good shipment coming in."

"Coke or heroin?"

"Both."

"I don't like heroin."

"Whatever you want, Heavy. I'll have Early slip you some weed when he gets back from court, okay?"

"Heavy, get back in your cell," a captain yelled out.

"Wait a minute, bitch. I got to talk to my boy Stone Man." He turned to Stone Man. "Are you sure you got me covered tonight?"

"You got my word, Heavy. Man, that's a trick, Heavy. You just busted those handcuffs like they were made of straw. And you a big gorilla motherfucka, Heavy, when you stand up straight. I didn't know you had it like that."

"I got a big dick, huh?"

"Ah Heavy, how come you got to go there?"

Heavy laughed like a girl. "All right, Stone Man, I'm going back to my cell now."

"We got your back, Heavy. You'll see. Don't worry. When Early comes back."

Heavy stood up to leave. As he was saying his goodbyes, Stone Man and I noticed a brown pellet the size of a large marble where Heavy had been seated.

"Heavy, what's that?"

Heavy turned around and moved closer to the pellet, clearly curious. Then he realized what it was. "I don't know."

"Heavy, you didn't shit on my porch did you?"

"Nah, that's not shit. It's a present." Then he waddled down the tier and into his cell.

▌▌▌▌▌▌▌▌▌▌

The government wanted Heavy to get ten to fifteen years for breaking the lieutenant's jaw, but the judge gave him only two years. He was already one year to the gate and since the sentence would run concurrently, Heavy would have to serve something like only eight extra months more than his original sentence.

The judge ordered the BOP to send Heavy to Springfield, the prison hospital center, to lose weight. The judge knew that the guards would be pissed. They wanted to punish Heavy with Marion. Marion was where they sent all the really fucked-up hard-core convicts who'd raped or assaulted staff, killed guards or fellow inmates, or were big-shot mob bosses, like John Gotti. Marion was where prisoners were greeted with the "finger wave"—a full-body search where a doctor put on a glove and checked your asshole for drugs or a weapon.

Despite the judge's ruling, Heavy was transferred to Marion. Stone Man got a hold of Heavy's lawyer and told him that they'd screwed Heavy. His lawyer went back to court and forced the BOP to put Heavy on a plane to Springfield. As much as we hated Heavy, we couldn't wish another prisoner's mistreatment by guards. That's bad juju.

Two weeks after Heavy left, Big Man was passing out our dinner trays when I overheard him telling Stone Man that Heavy had died of a heart attack on the plane ride to Springfield the day before. I thought about what bad luck Heavy had had on planes.

After a few seconds Big Man said, "You know what, Stone Man, I keep wondering, how the hell did they get him off the plane? I mean, when we tried to lift him in his cell he was so fuckin' heavy, and he was desperate to get up so he was trying to push himself up, and still it took seven of us to get him up. But on that plane, he was dead weight. I don't know how they got him off. Maybe some kind of forklift."

"Yeah, he was dead weight all right. Damn, he was a fat motherfucka. He went through those sheets like diapers."

"My four-month-old girl doesn't even go through that many diapers in one day."

"Yeah. Big-ass, own titty-nibbling, no clothes-wearing, shitting-on-himself Heavy D."

"Stone Man, I have a feeling I'll never meet a guy like Heavy for the rest of my life."

"Yeah, yeah, let's not get all weepy. The fat fucker is dead, and you know how that goes. You know what they say: Same thing that'll make you laugh will make you cry."

▮▮▮▮▮▮▮▮▮

The guards eventually came to take Sone Man to Marion the same way they took Bey to Terre Haute: Alamo style. Stone Man threatened to stab any guard who came to extract him from his cell. He held up a crude but sharp prison shank to make his threat real. But he was finally yanked out of his cell by five guards, and just like Bey, he was carried out hog tied, then shot full of Thorazine. When they brought him back to his cell for one night (his delay tactic had worked enough for him to miss the plane to Marion that day), he could only salivate on his cheek as he lay on his bunk. Indian Early couldn't stand to look at him and refused to go back on the tier until the next day, when Stone Man was escorted off the tier to catch his plane.

# Autopsy

*All that the rest forget in order to make their life possible, we are always bent on discovering, on magnifying even.*

—Rainer Maria Rilke

St. Aquinas listed writing as an act of prayer. But still I never thought that one mere handwritten letter to another writer could miraculously alter the trajectory of my life so forcefully.

I was finally released from solitary and into the general prison population after the murder investigation stalled. I was thirty-three. A few months later I was transferred to a medium-security prison in Massachusetts with three years of my sentence remaining.

One day while watching the *MacNeil/Lehrer NewsHour* program on PBS, I saw the dark-skinned essayist Richard Rodriguez, his face Indian like mine. I was intrigued by his smooth, soothing voice and the way he used words elegantly to describe his experiences.

I'd been working on my writing for two years now and was feeling itchy to have a correspondence with someone on the outside for the final two years of my sentence—preferably someone who would recognize the ambition in my sentences and encourage my writing.

I wrote a letter to the local PBS station and explained that I wanted to get a letter to Mr. Rodriguez and asked if they knew a way I could do that. They gave me a New York address for the *NewsHour* program. I sent a letter to him on July 27, 1994, exactly two years before I was due to get out of prison, addressing it to the New York City address. In it, I simply asked him if he had written any poetry. I was taking classes at the prison through Boston University but I told him that I was a student *enrolled* at B.U. (I didn't say I "attend" or I "go to," nothing to suggest that I was on the campus. I didn't want to lie. I just didn't tell him that I was a prisoner.)

He answered back by telling me that he was a journalist who wrote for the *Los Angeles Times* editorial page and was sometimes published in American magazines. He told me that I could catch up with his work by reading his two books, *Hunger of Memory* and *Days of Obligation*. Then he gave me his home address.

Our correspondence almost died there.

I asked my brother and father to find these books and send them to me. I obviously couldn't shop for them myself. (There is no Amazon.com for inmates.)

Some time passed, and I never received the books. I was embarrassed to write Richard back and tell him to give me the name of a bookstore where he knew for certain that his books could be found. But eventually that's what I did. He responded with a curt note.

> Dear Joe Loya:
> I am sorry you have had such terrible trouble locating my books. My first book, *Hunger of Memory*, is published in paperback by Bantam Books and is now in its 15th printing. I am astonished that stores in the Boston area do not stock it since it is assigned in university and college courses all over the country.

I felt like shit. Like he thought I was a poseur, someone only conniving at being interested in his writing, someone false, maybe looking merely to hang on to his celebrity. He did however give me the name of a bookstore in the Bay area that he knew for certain stocked his books.

I immediately sent out a letter to the bookstore and asked them how much money it would cost to ship *Hunger of Memory* and *Days of Obligation* to me as first-class mail. I explained to them that I was a prisoner and that the money exchange would be a little tricky. They would have to tabulate the total cost and send it to me, and then I would have to have the prison administration cut a check from my inmate account and send the money to them so they could send the books to me.

A week and a half later I was shocked when I was called to the property room and handed a small package with the bookstore's name on it. Inside were the two books. What the hell? I thought. Maybe they just sent me the books for free without our having to go through the rigmarole. The kicker came when I opened one of the books and found inscribed on the title page, "Courtesy of the Author." (Richard's best friend owned the bookstore.)

My mission that weekend was to start and finish both books so that I could write back small critiques. And show off a little bit.

> Your books did not disappoint my expectations.
> I made quick work of *Hunger of Memory*, finishing
> it by lunchtime the day after I received it. Your
> prose was intelligent and austere. Your friend
> commented that your work was full of "all that
> Spanish angst." Hmm. Maybe. I told myself early
> in the reading that I sensed a sorrow and some-
> thing like a relentless depletion in your work; as
> if the writing was a chore that distressed and
> wearied you . . . Which makes sense if it is true.
> We do lose something of ourselves whenever we
> volunteer biography . . . There is something of
> the anthropologist's sentience in your perception.
> While I read your books I was reminded of a
> remark by C. Lévi-Strauss: "The anthropologist
> is a man in control of, and even consciously
> exploiting his own intellectual alienation . . ."
> Alienation has been said to be the distressing

> by-product of intelligence. Perhaps that accounts
> for your revelations reading as an author's joyless
> self-discovery.

I came clean about the prisoner thing and asked if it was possible for us to have a correspondence for the remainder of my stint.

> I want to establish a reason for you to continue
> this correspondence, yet I don't want to rudely
> insinuate myself into your life. To find the tonal
> balance in this letter was delicate and awkward
> work: Too much desperate self-deprecation and
> I'd have sounded like that classic toady, Dracula's
> sniveling Renfield. Too much urgent solicitation and
> I'd have sounded like a slick televangelist with my
> hand already halfway in your pocket. You can see
> my dilemma . . . I know you value your privacy
> and solitude. If you are willing, I would like to
> develop a pen-pal relationship with you. (Right
> now Renfield would begin carrying on about what
> an honor and privilege it would be to have his
> master throw some crumbs his way.)

Richard started his lengthy reply with an apology for his curt response in his earlier letter. He answered yes to the idea of our corresponding.

And so I began to share with Richard the stories of my life: the early aspirations to love Jesus; the abuse that crushed my faith; my subsequent cynicism and antagonism with society. I told him about the terrible nightmares I was experiencing. I shared with him how I wanted to be more peaceful when I got out, but how I struggled daily to arrest my violent tendencies.

The language of redemption had been mine since childhood, the higher themes part of my early training. Hope emerged as the strongest theme in my letters to Richard.

My reformation had been tough, complicated work. For two and half years I hadn't committed a single act of violence in prison. I avoided the hot spots. I exercised and meditated regularly. I promised myself that once I left I would never return to prison again.

I told Richard that I would use our correspondence as a way to look back on the slow suffocation of my soul for clues to its demise, like a good coroner.

I am a "pure" reader. I read everything from Plutarch to pornography; Luther to Le Carré; Beckett to biker magazines; the law-technical Torah to tacky tabloids. I have an obsession with vocabulary. A linguistic affliction. In prison, where good reading material is sparse, I have a penchant to find and read all poetry, essays, and fiction. My appetite for written language drives me to devour the words of newspapers, pamphlets, magazines, fix-it manuals, whatever is available.

My grandpa Joe was a reader too. The Korean War veteran who commanded his home by a barracks' ethic, demanding of his boys a soldier's discipline. Beat them if they stepped out of line. My martial grandfather Joe loved war history. My father's first readings came from *his* father's library: Russian history and the Bolshevik revolution.

Grandpa Joe was also a drunk. His friends would hang around out back of the Maravilla projects and drink and brag to my boy/dad about their drinking partner's—his father's—intelligence. Grandpa gruffly bristled under those braggart's claims. He was a soldier. A grunt. Reading was his private effete endeavor.

My grandpa Joe, that "smart" soldier, who gave me a chemistry set for Christmas when I was eight,

but who gave his other grandchildren toys.
Grandpa Joe who visited me in prison at age 71
and told me to learn Japanese or Chinese since
they would soon consume the Pacific Rim. We ate
Fritos, moist turkey sandwiches on white bread,
and drank Dr Pepper, bought from vending
machines. That's when he told me about his
war years married to my grandmother.

*She knew how to push my buttons. I'd come
home late and drunk, or early the next morning
hung over. My head pounding. And she'd start in
on me. Nag. Nag. Nagging. Shut up Nellie, I'd say.
But she'd keep it up. So I'd tell her again, louder,
you know, to warn her. GODDAMMIT NELLIE,
SHUT UP OR YOU'RE GONNA BE SORRY! She didn't
stop. So I'd slap her hard, you know, to shut her
up. I didn't always realize how hard I hit her.
Sometimes I'd hit her to the floor. I was drunk, you
know. But your grandmother was tough. She'd
wipe her mouth and her eyes would get real mean.
She'd look straight at me from the floor and yell in
Spanish that I hit like a woman. After she told me
that I'd go crazy. I'm telling you. Nellie was tough.
She knew how to push my buttons.*

As I explained to Richard, our correspondence wasn't simply communi-
cation. It was a hermetic exercise, an emancipation for me. And more
than ideas were involved. My vulnerability felt like I was tearing a patch
of my soul out and throwing it down on the page.

I described to Richard how I wrote—feverishly, densely packing the
words in each sentence. I told him that once I believed I was mad, but
then I took up a pen and wrote, and I found that I could use writing as exorcism. Whenever I had a transgressive thought, I told him—like stabbing another inmate in the throat—I'd sit down and write instead (for
example, about a knife fight). If I thought of heaven as a bonfire where all

regrets were consumed by a pure flame, then I'd write a poem about a pyre. Slowly, I told him, I began to mellow. Slowly I began to rely on the blank page for therapy.

I told him about my obsession with words, how they filled my head, and how I used to get massive headaches—skull aches, really. Doctors gave me steroids and adrenaline in my occipital nerve. CT scans revealed nothing peculiar. Then, when I began to write, when I put the racket of words down on paper, my headaches left me.

And I assured him that I wasn't looking for fame through writing, that I could, as Henry James wrote, "work in the dark."

▮▮▮▮▮▮▮▮▮▮

Right around the same time that I began my correspondence with Richard, I was assigned a book in one of my college classes that radically revised my impression of the world and how I understood my place in it. The book was entitled *Metaphors We Live By*, and it was written by a University of California at Berkeley linguistics professor named George Lakoff, along with another academic named Mark Johnson.

The world as I knew it, the one I'd inhabited in maximum-security prisons, was a culture of dominion and violence. Everyone was constantly being sized up as weak or strong. I knew the rules of dominion well. For starters, in the early part of my prison term, a guy named Heriberto "Herbie" Huerta moved onto my tier. The head of the Texas *EME* (Mexican Mafia), Herbie was well known in the federal penitentiary system. He knew all the California *carnales* (Mexican Mafiosi) really well.

Creeper had done time with Herbie during a previous stint, so they were good friends. That's how I got inside the circle, through my affiliation with Creeper. Anyone on the tier could see that I had clout. Creeper had been doing the *carnales'* dirty business for many years—making knives for them, keeping point when they made their moves—so my friendship with him was a strategic alliance. I was perceived as a player, an insider, someone to be wary of.

One day a kid came to me and told me that some guy was leaning on him for a three-hundred-dollar debt. He asked me if I could take him under my wing—you know, squelch the debt and have him pay me off instead. I liked the kid because he was a hustler, constantly brokering deals—buying used sneakers low, then turning around and selling them high, stuff like that—always out to make a quick buck. His money was good, and I trusted him. Plus he had a great porno collection. He was merely having a little cash-flow problem. So I told him, yeah, I'd help him, but he'd have to pay me ten bucks a day. He said okay. So I went up to the uptight guy who was sweating the kid for the three hundred bucks and I told him that I was now in charge of the debt and that I didn't want the kid hurt. The guy was reasonable and we worked out some drug deal to pacify him.

Then, as promised, the kid came to my cell every night and gave me ten dollars worth of property. Canteen, photo tokens, cigarettes, and any combination of things. I'm telling you, he was one of the best hustlers I ever met in prison. All day long making moves.

Anyway, one night while Creeper, Herbie, and I were hanging out in my cell, the kid showed up and plopped ten dollars' worth of goodies down on my bunk. He was smiling real big.

*Why you got that shit-eating grin on your face?* I ask.

*That's the last payment. That's my thirtieth payment. We're even.*

I looked him square in the face and said, *Nah uh, we ain't even. I told you to bring me ten bucks' worth of shit every day. I didn't say for thirty days. The books are still open, indefinitely. So keep up the good work.* I pointed at the goodies and said, *And good looking out with tonight's issue.*

All he could do was look at me and sort of smile.

*I see you smiling, but I ain't joking. So spin, and I'll see you tomorrow night.*

He left, and Creeper and Herbie start to laugh.

The kid had no clue that with me he'd jumped out of the frying pan and into the fire. You see, he'd made the mistake of thinking that since we seemed to get along so well, that we were friends. But I was all business at bottom, and he was a white boy from the Northwest, so I had to play him way out of pocket to teach him that we weren't friends, what he considered equals. Poor kid didn't know how to act. The next day he gave me the cold shoulder, like he'd got his feelings hurt. I didn't care. I was waiting for the evening to see if he stepped right. Sure enough, the evening came and went, and he didn't pay me a dime.

Morning came. When the cell doors opened at six thirty, Creeper and I walked into the kid's cell. He was still sleeping, on his stomach. I jumped on him and held him in place while Creeper pulled the blankets down and yanked the kids' pj's down too. I leaned into his ear and said, *You thought I was joking, so here's how it's gonna be. Creeper is just gonna spank you right now with the broom handle, but next time the handle is going smooth up in ya. Get it?* Creeper gently spanked him three times. Then we walked out.

Dominion. By the ninth chapter in the Bible, God charged humans (through Noah) with dominion over everything on the planet. So should it surprise us that humans are dominion minded?

Needless to say, the kid paid me my money every night after that. Didn't raise a stink. And I'd seen the kid fight before. Once, he tangled with a bigger guy and did pretty well. Long heart, the kid had. But he knew that he was in the grips of more violent instincts than he owned. He knew that going against me was going against Creeper too, and by extension every other scary Mexican in our unit.

I'm ashamed of the way I acted with the kid. For several reasons. One, he was decent. He really was. I could see why he thought we were friends. We could shoot the shit for hours in the print shop where we worked. Two, he was funny. Unfortunately, we met when I was in a very competitive and ambitious frame of mind. All the alliances I was looking for were those that moved me into higher circles, those that would give me entrée into the inner sanctum of prison treacheries and intrigues.

I'd learned my ideas about the weak and the strong from my father, who schooled me that you were either a winner or a loser, the hunter or the hunted. As a boy I could only see myself as the hunted. But by 1992, I was clearly a skilled hunter in the toughest of environments. I felt in control of my life, as if I were making all the right choices to achieve a name for myself.

The kid, on the other hand, was weak. He'd let me take ten dollars a day from him, and he didn't do anything about it. And by the prison ethic that I was governed by, you are not supposed to let anyone take anything from you, nothing. That means that you can't even let a man cut in front of you in line.

One time a black guy cut right in front of me in the medicine line. Right in front of me, as if nothing had happened. He was a cool customer. But I didn't hesitate. I leaned into his ear and said, *Listen, you can cut in front of all the other lames in this line, I don't care, but you got to get behind me 'cause I ain't gonna let you cut in front of me.* He nodded consent, and we traded places. It was that easy. He knew that if I had the balls to confront him, then I had the balls to back my play. And I didn't begrudge the guy. He'd tried the power play. But it didn't work with me.

I'd learned the don't-cut-in-front-of-me ethic from a guy named Sharky. One day, we were standing in a long canteen line when a prisoner cut in the line, maybe twenty people ahead of us. Sharky brooded for a few minutes, then got out of line and went back to the unit. When he returned, he walked right up to the guy and stabbed him. The guy went to the hospital. Sharky went to the hole.

Territory. I read in a book once that there are few human instincts more basic than territoriality. Nation states do the same thing that men in prison do: Set boundaries and monitor them. They call them borders. Everything on this side of the line is mine, and everything on that side of the line is yours.

One time some guy stood outside my cell on the first floor and yelled up to his buddy on the third floor to throw him down some dominoes. I got up off my bunk and told him to go yell in front of someone else's cell. You see, in my mind, he was violating the three feet around my cell door that I considered part of my cell's space. It wasn't literally my cell, but an extension of it. Nation states with ocean borders don't say that their border ends where the sand meets the water. No, they push it out farther, twelve miles or so. And that's what I did with my cell. I made an arbitrary three-foot boundary outside of the door and monitored it as vigorously as if standing in that space was the equivalent of stepping into my cell to use my sink. Needless to say, the guy moved down the tier.

And it could get worse. If a guy in the cell next to mine made too much noise, and I was tired and he was keeping me awake, I'd have to check him. You might say, *But Joe, he's in his own cell. His* space. And you'd be right. But that wouldn't be his violation. He was in violation of my AIRspace. His noise was wafting over into my cell and disrupting me. (Again, nation states have the same ethic with their ideas about airspace.) Many men in prison have gotten into a lot of trouble for night-time airspace violations.

I was steeped in a culture where everyone and every move was being scrutinized in the context of a weak-strong paradigm. (It is even crazier, more intense in some ways, in lower-level prisons, where guys haven't yet made it to the top of their game, and are trying frantically to prove themselves.)

So I used to keep up my guard and measure people's reactions to me. Were they speaking to me with enough respect? Were they giving me enough room to walk by them when we passed in the corridor? Was the guy standing behind me in line crowding me? I was always measuring my satisfaction with life based on what other people were doing to me. And if someone didn't behave in a way that I deemed respectful, I could get mad in a split second.

Fast forward to solitary confinement: One day, I was lying on my bunk when all of a sudden I felt enraged and started fantasizing about hurting someone. But nothing, I mean absolutely nothing, had occurred. I'd been lying motionless on my bed for hours, and yet my mood had drastically altered, as surely as if someone had walked into the cell and called me a pussy.

I retraced my thoughts and I found the origin of my rage three or four thoughts back, in a remembrance of being chased by bullies. It was just a brief thought, as far as thoughts go, and I'd casually skimmed over it on the way to my next thought, but my reaction to it was fierce, as if I'd been meditating on the age-old wound for hours.

I learned then that my rage didn't need to be triggered by someone doing something to me—standing in front of my cell and insulting me, or not giving me a wide enough berth in the corridor—by active disrespect, but could be triggered by a simple brief thought, which could set my mind ablaze with images of mayhem. This was a huge insight for me. The next time I felt angry on that bunk I again retraced my thoughts, and

*Annie*

ANNIE

again I saw that the momentary remembrance of an old wound had brought on the most fantastic change in my personality. From Dr. Jekyll to Mr. Hyde. For months I retraced the turmoil in my mind. It was almost a game that I got good at playing.

I'll give you some examples of what I'm talking about: One time, my rage was triggered by remembering that my old restaurant manager was an asshole to me at work the day after I'd slept with her. I still held a grudge against her for that. Another time, it took only a brief memory of a man who wouldn't lend me money to get me full-throttle mad. That man had treated me as if he thought I was a liar. I'd hated his impertinence, even though he'd been one hundred percent right about the chances of my not paying him back. My memories were like that— small, incidental things that I'd accumulated over many years. Now that I was an adult bundle of rage knots, my grievances had sort of bonded together and were more pernicious as a group. Over time, recognizing the nature of what aggravated me taught me that I was an extremely petty person.

The memories were of *perceived* slights. Like once my girlfriend accused me of cheating on her (she was right), and I exploded into a rage. I didn't hit her, but what I unleashed on her, both psychological and verbal, was devastating. When we were making up, I told her not to get me mad anymore. I blamed her for setting me off since, as my stupid logic went, she knew that confronting me would make me feel cornered and this would make me ferocious. You've heard it I'm sure, when a guy says, *She pushed my buttons*, as if the guy had no volition, as if his only choice was to get angry, and she must have wanted the drama to call it out of him like that.

My first discovery about my rage was accidental, on that day when I found myself angry while alone in my cell. The second biggest discovery I made about my rage was that it was arbitrary. The first time I remembered that slight by my restaurant manager, I was equally pissed off again. Three days later, when I thought about the same incident again, I wasn't as angry anymore. Two weeks later, and I was less angry. In fact, I was more curious to know why she had behaved that way to me. Something had shifted. The lesson was that the same memory didn't always trigger the same thing. In fact, one day I could be mad about one memory and the next day, if my mood was different, I could have an entirely opposite reaction to the same memory. This was revelatory. All of a sudden I realized that my *reaction* to things, and not the things themselves, was really the cause of my rage. You have to understand that this was a large and fundamental shift in my perspective, a remarkable change. It subverted everything I'd ever known about my anger.

Fast forward again. About two years before I got out of prison, I read the book *Metaphors We Live By*. In it I learned that people automatically believe things about their place in their world that is in fact based on faulty thinking, or thoughtlessness. For example, if you live in a valley, then you will find yourself talking about the surrounding mountains as if they have a front and backside. You will assign a value to them that is in fact inaccurate, since things like mountains and trees and rocks don't have fronts or backs. But we assign fronts and backs to mountains, trees, and rocks because we see them from our point of view. This was a provocative concept to me—that we assign values to phenomena and believe that they are just because we utter the value.

The book goes on to describe how we may look at a hedge in front of our neighbor's home and think him lazy for letting it get overgrown. But the trimmed hedge we have in our imaginations is a false boundary on the hedge. In some cultures, the trimmed hedge that we value as correct may be deemed as unnatural, deforming, or contorting the hedge's natural growth—the way Westerners view the binding of Chinese women's feet. Hedges grow; that's what they do. "Overgrown" is an artificial boundary that we assign to them.

The book says that these objects (mountains and hedges) we treat as discrete entities so that "we can categorize them, group them, and quantify them—and, by this means, reason about them."

At the same time that I was reading this book, I was also trying to figure out ways not to have to confront people who I felt might be disrespecting me. The more I confronted people, the greater the chances that they weren't going to respond well to the confrontation and I would have to take things to the next level. (My ethic had it that I never asked someone to do something that I wasn't prepared to *make* him do if he said no.

Like I'd never ask someone to be quiet unless I was prepared to punch him in the mouth or stab him if he said no.) You can see how my ethic could get me in considerable trouble if I was always going around confronting people. I wanted a way to make myself a smaller target, with less room for volatility in the way I did my time. I needed a way not to care what people were doing around me. That's why I was so prepared for lessons from this book when it started talking about how our concept of boundary is a mutable thing.

What that meant to me was that when I placed a three-foot boundary around my cell door, I quantified it as mine for the purposes of gauging a person's respect for me. Which meant that I could just as easily reverse my thinking and let go of that three-foot boundary and not have to regulate it, and thus lessen the likelihood that I would be confronting people outside of my cell door. Immediately I was able to cut down the possibility of conflict. This was a good thing. So when a guy stood outside my cell door and yelled to his friend on the third tier to throw down some dominoes, I could simply stay on my bunk and not have to feel like I was implicated in his act. When I changed my thinking about space, I took away the violation. This new idea was revolutionary to me. It was very hard not to speak up in the beginning, because I still felt that tug to confront. And I still monitored the boundary at my cell door; if he crossed that, I would have to check him. But he wasn't disrespecting me anymore because I no longer had that arbitrary boundary outside of my cell.

I also let go of my airspace border, relinquishing it as too arbitrary as well. I was looking for ways to live more peacefully, without antagonism and conflict. I was trying to move away from dominion-minded thinking, with its codes of putting boundaries around everything for the purpose of measuring the weak and the strong. I was excited that I had a new linguistic tool to describe things differently to myself.

Most significant about all of this change was my discovering that I got enraged whenever I felt out of control, helpless. This was why I had been so angry all my life, and more so in prison. I was the angriest in solitary because I was super helpless there. I needed to rely on the guard to give me everything, from soap to toilet paper. (This is how prisons infantilize  men.) There I had the least control I'd ever had in my entire life. Feeling that zenith of helplessness killed me. But I learned that I could control *one* thing in my life: my *reaction* to things. This was a big deal for me. All of a sudden I had great control over my life in the most helpless of situations. If a guard acted like an asshole to me, I could look at him and think, *I'm not going to get mad at him. I'm just gonna watch him walk away and wonder at why he is so offensive.* This gave me a power I hadn't ever had. I had volition again. Choice. I was free to choose my reaction to any situation. *choose* So I practiced self-control and tried not to get angry. And I was ever vigilant for the oncoming stomach- or headaches.

I came across Buddhist writings that essentially taught the same point. It wasn't what was done to me that got me angry, it was how I reacted to what was done to me that determined my mood. *(ZEN?)*

▌▌▌▌▌▌▌▌▌

I wrote to Richard about my fears of my upcoming release:

> When I was released from prison last time, I was housebound for a few days. I was excited in the mornings, full of plans to see a movie, eat at a restaurant, go to a real trendy spot for dessert and cappuccinos, but as the day progressed, I began to dread my plans. The thought of the lines, the crowds, the possibility that someone near me would do something that I would respond to with violence, frightened me. I didn't want to go back to prison quickly and I didn't trust myself. Why just that first night someone bumped into me in the line at the supermarket and I swung around reflexively to demand an apology for the blatant act of disrespect. I stopped myself when I saw it was some clueless housewife reaching for a *National Enquirer* on the rack behind me. I could have pummeled her for her slight. Such was my attitude at the time. And my story is not unique. Other men have similar stories about their first

nights out, coming home to hazard. Assimilating is rough. As for the last time, by the end of those first days, I cancelled my big plans and settled instead for a rented video and home-delivered Domino's pizza. Going out of the house scared me and seemed full of peril, in those first few days of freedom. I anticipate the same sort of slow and tentative easing of myself back into the free world. Fortunately there is a pool at my brother's apartment; I don't have a girlfriend; and I have plenty of books to read, articles to catch up on. I will take it slow and easy for the first couple of days. Driving around is about the most I will be able to handle. Looking at places to live. Maybe a ride to the beach. But no restaurants, clubs, theatres. No places of big traffic. I'd consider a museum or a library. Those places don't threaten me. Oh yeah, there is a beautiful Catholic church right off the freeway in Pasadena that I want to go sit in. I will go sit and pray inside, near one of the large pillars. The church is special because when I was a fugitive before, full of intense anxiety, I went inside and sat down on a back pew. I was overcome with a marvelous peace. A sense of awe. I knew about the church because I'd once attended a wedding there. I want to go back.

Thinking a lot lately about going out to face freedom. Going home to find family. Leaving all this prison pollution behind me. Interesting how not all my thoughts are positive. I anticipate antagonisms. I am a livid life incompatible in many ways with the globe's gullible living.

*He was appalled to think that he belonged to a society*
*that existed only on materialism and gave so little*
*thought to its great themes.*

—John Le Carré

My disagreements and antagonisms with the
world are informed by the easy agreements they
have about limitations. Which is why poetry is my
sanctuary. The majority of the world hasn't the
poet's perceptions of space or time.

*Not everyone sees the world in limited ways just because*
*the majority are in agreement about those limitations.*

—Baba

▮▮▮▮▮▮▮▮▮▮

I'll live with my only brother until I can earn
money to rent my own apartment. No more yelling
and arguing with a prison guard to close my cell
door so that I can shit in private. No more having
to submit to spontaneous strip searches. No more
having to intrigue to get an extra pancake or extra
piece of bread in the chow hall. No more washing
my clothes in the shower by hand. No more looking
at myself in a polished stainless-steel mirror that
reflects a dull impression. No more conniving to get
more than one roll of rationed toilet paper a week.

But I'll still have to consider things out here that
will waste my time. A dress code at work. Price
comparisons at local supermarkets. Phone calls
from friends who'll want me to go to see the new
Jackie Chan movie. The crazy choices available in
every restaurant, shoe, or clothing store.
Waitresses pawning off daily specials. The time-
neurosis of ordinary life. Billboards promoting

every hustle and huge busty movie star to come down the pike. Off-ramp this, on-ramp that. No Stopping. No Parking. Keep Off the Grass. Loading Zone Only. School Crossing. Deer Crossing. Ad nauseam.—Price includes 8.5-percent gratuity. 15 percent gratuity added to parties over fifteen. Tax not included. Must be over 18. Must be under 21. Must be over 65. Check-out time is 11:00. Check-in before 6:00 or lose your reservation. Leaded. Unleaded. Super unleaded. Ultra unleaded. Waste of words around the water cooler every morning. Hobson's choice: long slavery or a clean exit.

I don't know how to trust a world conditioned to drudgery and the status quo.

▉▉▉▉▉▉▉▉▉

Prison has been good for me. And bad too. I eat too fast. Both arms on the table. I'm quick to interrupt a conversation I find boring or stupid. Even when I'm happy, I curse like a drunken sailor. I'm a philistine in many ways. I'm also uncomfortable with genuine gestures of kindness. My mind—no matter how hard I try—is still conditioned for a meaner world than the one I will reside in. I am habituated to the grotesque in man.

▉▉▉▉▉▉▉▉▉

I feel anguished for having been robbed of my facility for trust. I was a good-natured boy, so willing to please, to embrace the world. I quite naturally leaned toward the greater themes. I received strong academic training. I knew God, opera music, literature, history. I was deft with the English language. I showed promise. But my

entire life was hijacked by this monstrous rage
that simply would not let me be. It wasn't until I
walked into a horrible silence a few years ago that
I realized my life took a rough detour for 23 years
after the death of my mother.

It was then, in the midst of some great grief
that my anguish and lament assumed the proportion of that self-blinded man bumping into the
temple stones at Colonus. I swear to you that my
new conscience was overwhelmed when I took
stock of my life and the balance came up wanting.
I sympathized with guilt-ridden Oedipus and felt
sometimes what he must have felt the split second
before he dug his fingers into his eye sockets and
blinded himself. I woke from my coma of conscience
and I saw clearly the damage I'd done. My fate was
fulfilled by violence. That's why I was menaced by
a manic grief in my early solitude. I've witnessed
too much and I'm harassed in the end by my keen
vision. It is easy for me to conceive of existential
exile. A deserted future. Suicide.

▦▦▦▦▦▦

Your words:

> The essay has been "finished" for weeks. But of course, I
> have labored and labored over it. I worry whole para-
> graphs until I am no longer certain which version,
> among the many revisions, is best . . . I end up wonder-
> ing which version is truest? A question I cannot always
> answer.

You were talking about your essay writing and
you could have been talking about the shared
human predicament. There are so many versions
of me that I could ask the same question you ask—

*Which version of me is truest?*—and I could too end
up stumped, such is the condition of my identities.

▓▓▓▓▓▓▓▓▓▓

I will be seated at my desk, looking out the window,
at the sky, maybe reminiscing about some fine
moment in my past—like my mother's pride of
me when I was a handsome, well-dressed child—
when apropos of nothing, without warning (or
propriety), a rude image from my dark past will
come barging to the forefront of my mind, abruptly
interrupting my casual, innocent thoughts, brutally
colliding with my recent decency.

An analogy will help. Imagine me and my sweet
wife entertaining her deeply religious parents,
showing them honeymoon slides of she and I in
Cancun. We are all laughing at the tame picture
of her and me by the sea in full snorkeling gear,
goggles, mask, and breathing tubes in our mouths,
*Wham!* then a slide of exquisite color and focus
comes into view, showing Daddy's little girl on her
knees, naked but for a black latex head mask with
three holes, her lips puckered, revealing a twisted
agony through one of the holes, eyes pinched shut
and in pain in the other two holes, her wrists
handcuffed behind her back, metal clamps on her
nipples, and there I am, naked, of course, fucking
her doggy-style, grimacing in mad pleasure,
whipping her ass with a whip in one hand and
yanking her long hair with the other.

That grudge fuck on the hypothetical slide is the
sort of distasteful, demented, stunningly
inappropriate nature of the images in my head.
And I don't mean strictly sexual. Repulsive, more
like it. I mean harsh violence that I'd wish my

mind would forget, cruel uninvited reveries, wickedly out of flow, and always disconcerting. Tormenting images that I lost a fascination for a long time ago.

The truth is a day doesn't go by when I don't entertain some really horrible thoughts. Never! The only consolation today is that those thoughts come and go and find little traction anymore. Although it is nothing for me to entertain a truculent idea now and again, I don't truck in evil visions anymore. Whereas before I surrendered to my demons and would plot revenges and let my rage ferment into despicable visions all day long, now they are lucky if they can get my attention for a total of an hour a day—cumulative. And that may be an hour more than my parole officer, or the FBI, would like me to have; or it may be an intense hour that you or my other friends could not handle; but it is huge improvement for me and I'll take my victories any way I can today.

▮▮▮▮▮▮▮▮▮▮

I told Richard what stabbing my father had done to me:

I look back on that hellish afternoon of attempted patricide and I understand more starkly Shaw's caveat. "There are two tragedies in life. One is not to get your heart's desire. The other is to get it." I stabbed my father and received the deliverance I'd always wept and begged God for. Horribly ignorant, I had no way of knowing how any emancipation from trauma that is underwritten by angry violence is merely a barter for another type of trauma more sublime and menacing than the first.

I lost my faith and became bothered by

optimism. I became an utter nihilist, decadent and
debauched. It is perhaps understandable why I
would eventually blame God for causing so much
grief in my life. My wrath was as naïve as my
relationship with God had been. So I spun my
wheels for years, housing an out of control rage.
I recognized my disillusionment and wrote
this phrase in a journal to describe my callous
condition: *My unbridled audacity would set a
ghost aghast.*

▓▓▓▓▓▓▓▓▓

Six months before I was paroled, I was feeling quite anxious about leaving
prison. I didn't trust that I'd changed enough, and I wasn't yet sure that I
wanted to be the new meek man that I said I was working hard to
become. So, as if to prove myself unworthy of redemption, I got into a fight
with Roc, the largest black man in the prison. I stabbed him in the face because he'd cut in front of me in chow line, but I knew that some fundamental insecurity about my upcoming freedom was really behind the attack.

I was sent back to solitary confinement for two and a half months. In
letters to Richard I fretted that I was like the wolf in that Italian parable.
When he was sick he wanted to be a monk, but when he got well he realized that he was still a wolf. I felt like a fraud, a man who talked about
change but never really changed. Fortunately for me, no charges were
pressed and I was allowed to go home on schedule.

You'll never know how fine it feels to stab a man
for whom you have an animal hate. And you can't
imagine the confusion of hating yourself in the
first place for finding pleasure in such barbarity.
So I stabbed him in the face, aiming for the eye,
hitting the high cheekbone.

And I still want to come home. Leave this prison
and step into society, the larger prison, where at
least I can have conjugal visits, have a burger my

way, or order a wine in a downtown hotel bar, or watch a porno video where the movements have a soundtrack that my imagination lacked for seven years.

I aspire to the higher themes. I want to be at peace with myself. Until Roc's sad day, I hadn't stabbed anyone for two and a half years. I've used well my willpower for inaction. Until last week. I am, of course, saddened that I resorted to violence only six months from my parole date. I need to right the course quickly.

The truth is that after seven years in prison I am afraid of leaving the comfort of what I know. I can't imagine a life out there.

> *A man's life is dyed the color of his imagination.*
> —Marcus Aurelius

I dreamt last night a frenetic vision. I got laid, attended the opera, was visited by dead Creeper's ghost, and I plotted to kill a police officer. One moment I was standing in the corridor of my old high school, then on an airplane over the Atlantic, then at the Pantages Theatre in Los Angeles, then on a prison tier.

The collision of the colors in my imagination produces confusion.

Being a reconfigured man, and having robbed handsome sums, I've been relinquished of a boring desire to get rich. I have no passion to live in gaudy prosperity. As stated before, my needs are minimal. I hope to keep my financial obligations minimal too.

> *Choose the best life and the habit will make it pleasant.*
> —Pythagorean adage

▐▐▐▐▐▐▐▐▐▐

I picked up some books on Buddhism and began imagining my problems differently. In that frame of mind, tracing the origins of my rage, seeking enlightenment, I decided to talk to my father. I shared with him how I wanted to be different when I got out. I wasn't sure how, but upon my release from prison, I planned on being a pacifist.

But sometimes I'd sit on my bed and contemplate walking into the cell next to mine and stabbing the loud bastard who banged on his metal desk at night while he did his rap. Or I'd fantasize about picking up a mop wringer and bludgeoning some knucklehead who cut in the chow line. Still, as powerful as these fantasies felt, I was also utterly disgusted with this part of my petty punitive personality. My disgust for those automatic impulses to harm others did, after all, bode well for my transformation, and was, in fact, the beginning of true change. I only needed this newfound disgust for absurdly violent action to become preemptive, and never to allow me to dwell for even ten seconds on how good injuring another man could feel.

▟▙▟▙▟▙▟▙▟

I felt like I needed to make my father a more complicated character to Richard since all he ever read of my father were only the bad things that he did when I was growing up. So I told him about the most difficult conversation I ever had with my father on a prison phone.

The first thing I wrote in solitary confinement was a story about playing in the bald boy's clubhouse. One story lead to another and another and soon I was organizing my narrative on the page, learning about myself, making connections, giving language to my childhood grievances. Writing about what happened to me as a boy led to my writing about my adult rage, and I saw how my crimes replicated my childhood universe, how I was introducing my victims to the terror I felt as a boy. I saw how I'd patterned my sadistic temper after my father's. My dad's violence in the home was finally making sense to me, because I was making sense to myself. After a couple of years of writing I discovered what I thought was the number one condition that I thought triggered my viciousness, and that was feeling helpless like I had felt at that kitchen sink as a boy when my dad almost drowned my brother. My blood boiled whenever I felt helpless. After I figured that out, every beating that I received as a boy could be explained by a sense of helplessness I identified in my father, one that resembled my own.

Well, not every beating; there was one exception. The time that I was hit for the amnesia of my concussion. I couldn't figure that one out for the life of me, so about a year before I got out of prison, I called Pops and asked him straight-up, *Hey dad, what the hell were you thinking when I came home with amnesia, head trauma, and you started punching me in the head?*

He started his answer by apologizing to me, asking for my forgiveness. He told me that, having matured, he now knew about head traumas and would rush any child of his to the hospital. Then he revealed to me the poignant truth about his vicious reaction.

He explained how my mother was given massive doses of experimental drugs that drove her mad at times. She would wake in the night, panicked because she didn't recognize the stranger sleeping beside her in bed. Occasionally, she tried to jump out of the car on the freeway while my father drove her to the hospital for her dialysis treatments. More bizarrely, several times she believed that she was Elizabeth Taylor and my father was Richard Burton; she'd share glamorous stories with the nurses about Richard and their two boys.

Sometimes, when my father was driving her to the hospital for her weekly dialysis treatment, she would turn to him with a confused expression on her face that quickly turned to panic. Then she'd try to open the door to jump out of the car. My father would grab her blouse and struggle to steer the car to the side of the road, with my mother twisting in his grip.

Her mad amnesia came over her at all times of the day. One night I heard a bottle crash in our bathroom. I woke frightened.

*Leave me alone! Don't touch me!* my mother was screaming.

*Bessie, don't do that! Come here!*

*No! No! No! Not you! Stop!*

*Bessie! Cut it out! Put it down!*

I rolled over and went back to sleep believing that my father was hitting my mother. My father now told me that she had been threatening to hit him.

During that first week of her crisis, nurses and doctors would find her trying to sneak out of the hospital. She was convinced that the staff had inappropriately admitted her, had confused her for a person who was really sick. Not her, she'd argue. She wasn't ill.

But sometimes my mother succeeded in slipping out of her room and into a better role on the telephone. She'd call my grandma Nellie's house. My aunt Rosemary or aunt Margie would answer the phone.

*Hello?*

*Hello, Rosemary. This is Elizabeth Taylor.*

*Bessie?*

*No. This is Elizabeth Taylor calling. I'd like to know if my husband, Richard, has left yet. He's supposed to pick me up so I can visit with our boys, Joey and Paul.*

The doctors blamed her temporary insanity on the high dosage of medication they were giving her to stay alive.

On the phone that day my father explained to me how he'd been able to handle all the pain of my mother's dying. The loss of a sex life. The horrible stress of keeping the news of her dying from Paul and me. Losing sleep and working hard to keep the family going. It was all worth it because he knew that my mother loved him, that she appreciated him. He loved her, and knowing that she was able to recognize his effort was a big deal. But when she began not to know who he was, he lost it. He needed her to know him. This pain was too much for him to bear. So, three years after her death, when I came home and couldn't remember things, my amnesia menaced him. He was immediately and unexpectedly forced to confront his worst nightmare, the grief of those years. And so he responded with violence, which he figured was suitable to squash the torment of his memory. He got mad at himself and punched me in the face.

At the end of my father's telephone explanation, I thought of the book of Ecclesiastes and I pitied us and our violent vanities. I sat on that prison phone listening to my father's tragic explanation and I had a fundamental epiphany about violence. I comprehended how violent anger had been our way of disguising our wounds. It was our first conversation about the senseless brutality in our home. We began swapping stories of remorse, realizing that we were the same, lugging around shared regrets about our lives.

▌▌▌▌▌▌▌▌▌▌

I wrote almost every day for the final three years of my incarceration, struggling to convey my narrative on the page. I wanted to organize my life around honest principles, the higher themes I had so egregiously ridiculed Christians for when I lost my faith. No more hiding from myself behind a mask of bravado.

Generally, my main writing topics were the death of my mother, the beatings I endured in childhood, stabbing my father, and my history of unfaithful relationships. But I also explored my complicated affection for Brenda and the woman who'd raped me as a boy. By the end of my prison term I was somewhat able to parse out on the page the good from the deformed religiosity that had governed my childhood home. To Richard I wrote:

> First, the violent humiliation of my childhood contributed to a hardening in my heart. When the bullies beat and tore my sweater and broke my eyeglasses, my father slapped me for losing the fight, and then he piled my brother and me into the car.
>
> Sitting in that front seat, praying to God that we not find them, taught me the most unglamorous male lesson in my life: The tyranny of the bullied schoolyard extended to the rest of the world. Lose too many fights in school and you become a vassal of the class asshole. Lose too many contests in the larger world and you earn the reputation of a serial sissy. This particular incident stands out in my memory as the one that best exemplifies all my boyhood lessons on maleness.
>
> The ethic of vengeance I learned that day, in the front seat, gestated in me and finally bore itself out

on the afternoon that I stabbed my father. That
event altered me so that as an adult I would
consider every aggression—in sport, in jest,
intellectually—as a challenge to my manhood.
And those challenges always felt like that
catastrophic, split-second decision with my
father when I had to either rapidly (and rabidly)
address the threat or sheepishly accept heaps of
abuse. So I was wound tightly, poised for hostile
action all the time. And one can't underestimate
the force of the vengeance tug that pulled me
toward physical payback. This was one dynamic
turning my boyhood helplessness into active rage.

Stabbing my bully father convinced me that my
road to manhood—like salvation—would require a
periodic sprinkling of blood.

As a boy, I was severely bruised by the multiple
rejections of the pretty daughters of those racist
church-going men. As a young man moving into
the world, I began to fantasize about injuring
those bigoted fathers.

The misogynistic aspect of my rage was a more
elaborate riddle: My desperate need for female
attention deceived me into believing that I cared
deeply for women, when what I really felt was
resentment. The three strongest female relationships of my life until that date—my mother,
Brenda, and Lorelei—had all in the end treated me
and my feelings badly, had proven to be unreliable
trustees of my trust and affection. So I resented the
women who later came into my life, mostly because
their attraction mocked me and reminded me of the
troika of female humiliaters in my imagination.

To cap off a complicated rage, it dawned on me
that if I could beat my father, then who could stop

me? Not God: by bringing my father down, I'd brought his God down too. I stood alone. An odd sense of power swelled in me in the four years after I stabbed my father. I earnestly talked about nothingness and autonomy. This was partially the reason why I had such a fantastic— not "wonderful" fantastic but more like "spacey" fantastic—impression of myself.

Morality became a joke to me, just a tyrant's tool to keep me in check. I started to hate society for its moral imposition, its timid conventions, and I took it as my honorable mission to act with complete contempt for its rules and moralities. I never suspected that I was simply one of those morally lazy people who abhor restrictions or hard work so much that they find intellectual reasons to reject morals or a work ethic ad hoc.

In that time of brooding, all these tugs on my mind, violent fantasies of payback, humiliations accrued in childhood, resentment of women, and a real crisis of faith, nurtured a burgeoning rage.

▥▥▥▥▥▥▥▥▥

Later, many years later, I realized in prison that stabbing my father wasn't the only call that afternoon, as it seemed to me at the time. Many men in prison were beat by their fathers. Sure, some fought back. Shoved their drunken fathers to the ground when they got big or old enough. Or jumped in and told their father that he wasn't going to take a swing at mom anymore. But most of them swallowed their humiliation and waited till they grew up and it was their turn to have easy captive victims, like wives, children, or pets who they could pummel their rage into.

> Or they took it out on themselves. Unable to face
> the sorrowful shame and humiliation of their lives,
> many of those brutalized boys turned into criminal
> men who became addicted to every drug available
> to them.

▐▌▐▌▐▌▐▌▐▌

Most men fantasize about getting laid or getting high when they get out of prison. But as my release day neared, I fantasized about getting a facial. This from the man who once bit off a piece of a guy's ear because he had sold my *Playboy* magazine.

I never wore a mask as a criminal—that is, until I got to prison. Just take a look at my mug shot. People say I look like a corpse, with my dead stare and slack facial muscles.

While I was in prison I wanted to be like a Gambino family crime boss, John Gotti, *capo di tutti capi*, who on the morning of a court appearance, prison lore tells, scrubbed his face with a hard-bristle brush to make it look tough for the cameras and jury. I fed into the macho prison ethic that bad-asses weren't supposed to look pretty. In fact, the first time I met Steven, a lifer who as a teenager was likened by courtroom journalists to James Dean, I couldn't believe that he was actually incarcerated like me. Such was my expectation that beauty was a currency that could keep people out of prison.

I had never been mistaken for one of those pretty boys. During my seven years in prison, my skin broke out badly because of severe stress and cheap soap. I picked at the unruly pimples on my face, and they finally scabbed so badly that the blemishes turned brown and eventually became permanent craters on my face. My nose was dotted with grimy blackheads. But I wore the scars and acne and dark circles under my eyes (from insomnia) as a badge of honor—evidence to other men that I survived in those mean corridors because I had overcome the outside world's preoccupation with looking attractive.

Sometimes when I was a boy my father slugged my face so hard that he forced me to stay home from school to hide the bruises. So I could only imagine my facial features as permanently contorted, after years of seeing my face swollen and bruised in the mirror.

But now I wanted a facial. I'd paid for girlfriends to get facials. Bought them gift certificates for birthdays or Christmas. If it hadn't been for Oprah, I'd never have thought about getting one myself.

Almost every inmate in the last prison where I did my time owned a thirteen-inch TV. They mostly watched cartoons in the morning, Ricky Lake, Montel, or Jerry Springer. In the afternoon, the Colombians and Dominicans bettered their English with cartoons. Ricky Lake often featured young, half-dressed, heavy-cleavaged, slutty girls, strutting on stage, defending their dangerous promiscuity. Incarcerated guys loved watching all that wild fleshiness. I considered daytime talk shows beneath me. They reminded me of wrestling: phony and vaudevillian.

But one day, when the entire prison was on lockdown because an Irish kid had stabbed a black guy, I was alone in the cell watching TV, and, while channel surfing, I stumbled across an *Oprah* makeover show. Oprah's guests were five women from domestic abuse shelters. Some of them were strikingly pretty, which threw me for a minute. Why did *they* need makeovers? Then the confessions came out, one interview after the next: after years of relentless domestic abuse they all saw themselves as ugly. After only seven months of intense daily therapy, they finally felt like they deserved to become attractive.

Normally, I'd be embarrassed to watch or be caught watching all that touchy-feely TV, but the seven months of daily therapy for the women put me in mind of my seven years in prison. I thought, "Could I, dare I, risk becoming attractive to society again?"

I couldn't think about getting a facial without thinking about my fear of being touched by strangers. When the occasion called for it, I'd hugged friends in prison, when they left to go home or were transferred to another prison. Bear hugs. But I hadn't been touched sensually for seven years. A simple touch from a woman sounded scary. I was afraid of feeling something, anything, but especially of remembering my father's punches.

When I was a kid, I associated every blow and explosion of feeling in my head with eroticism. And why not? Nerves are densely bundled in that small oval space. It's an intimate, sensual zone. When the head gets slapped or punched hard enough—or pounded with a metal teapot like my father once did to my head—it's easy to suffer major head concussions. Movement slows, things turn blurry, and the body goes numb. Like a stunning orgasm after exhausting lovemaking. That's why I'd always been terrified of loitering too long in a woman's bed after sex. I both desired and feared erotic human touch.

I didn't presume that I'd be made handsome by the facial. In fact, I was sort of put off by the whole Palm Springs treatment I'd seen in magazines—red mud caked on the face and cucumbers worn on the eyes like matching monocles. I just wanted to wipe clean the grime that had become caked on my face in those dungeons. And it would be a real challenge to see if I could allow myself to be touched without flinching. I wanted to prove, right out of the joint, that I could accept a softer version of myself.

My father never really recovered from his life's plunge in the late 1970s. For twenty years he skipped from one manufacturing job to another, never saving enough money, always staying in debt. He had a heart attack the first week I went into prison, when he was forty-four.

During the last few months before I got out of prison, my brother and father and I began a conversation about how to be a closer family. Being the two people who knew me best, they more than anyone recognized that I was indeed different, willing now to talk freely about my fears and resentments and the various anxieties I had about my freedom. I told them that I'd wasted my early adult years, not caring about life, but that now I wanted to make amends, to develop new patterns of thinking and behaving.

I told my father that I'd adopted all his faults and expanded upon them, therefore I could no longer presume to judge him. I understood his past and present fear, deceit, and desperation.

*I've changed, so I believe anyone can change. Let's be honest here. You and I have done many bad things and hurt each other in horrible ways. We share the same grief and regrets for past mistakes. I suggest that we let my wrongs cancel out your wrongs.*

He and my brother agreed to try my revised approach to life, to be more truthful, mindful, less aggressive. I'd modeled my rage after my father's anger. He agreed to model his reform after mine.

▮▮▮▮▮▮▮▮▮

*Do you blame your father's violence for your growing up to rob banks?*

My answer is always the same: No. I don't blame my father's violence for the bank robberies. A lot of people get beaten up by their parents and they don't grow up and pick up a gun to rob banks. In fact, I'd venture to say that most abused kids grow up and pick up lunch pails and become functioning citizens in society. So we can't blame my pop for my criminal behavior. I take responsibility for my choice to commit those crimes.

However, we can blame my father's fist in my mouth for altering my imagination, my idea of what was possible when I felt my world was out of control. He gave me occasion to contemplate committing violence on others whenever I felt they were stopping me from achieving some satisfaction in my crummy life. We can blame his banging my body with a metal teapot for giving me a stark example of terror and overkill.

My father has always appreciated one thing about me. Even when I was behaving like an asshole to him or to my friends, or robbing banks and going off to prison, he was grateful that I never blamed him for my criminal activities.

*Believe me dad,* I've replied, *I give you all the credit that you deserve for other truly stupid decisions in my life, but on this one score—the bank jobs and me ending up in prison—I'll never shirk my responsibility. I did it and I'll always be here to represent it.*

▮▮▮▮▮▮▮▮▮

In one of my last letters to Richard I wrote:

> There's a song by Peter Gabriel—"Don't Give Up"—
> that always takes me to my bunk when it plays on
> my radio. In the song the seductive voice of Kate

Bush acts like a reassuring conscience to Peter Gabriel's muscular suicidal despair. The duet resembles the kind of angry discourse that occurs in my head at the precise moment when total anguish and complete optimism have equal sway on my imagination. The sorrow of existence is acute in the throes of my interior turmoil. Kate Bush implores Peter Gabriel to choose life.

> *Don't give up*
> *'Cause somewhere there's a place,*
> *There's a place where we belong*

A place where I belong: a splendid hope for the alienated person who has repented of a vicious antisocial bent. Exploring ways to again belong in society emancipated my thinking and took me away from the drudgery that is confinement.

I want to make it clear that I never connived at liberation. If this were all a charade, it would be much easier. Less conviction would require less stamina. But you know that I have struggled for my blessing. Wrestled with those familiar demons at the foot of my bed. This last year has found me both wanting to belong to society and me wanting to again rip myself from this body of polluted humanity. The medical procedure of grafting flesh onto a different part of the body is a procedure that doesn't always take. A risk. A baboon heart can only survive for a brief time in a human bosom. And isn't that the better metaphor? I am a beast attempting to be tamed by a human heartbeat.

I have yet to see if I'll belong in that place outside of these walls.

# De Profundis

*Only where there are tombs are there resurrections.*

—Friedrich Nietzsche

Lazarus's tomb was a cave in the hills above the village of Bethany. "Take away the stone!" Jesus commanded. Martha, sister to the corpse, was always the first one to fret. "Master, by this time there is a bad odor for he has been there four days." But unsanitary things never dissuaded Jesus. "Lazarus come out!" Silence for several moments. One desperate gasp. A cough. Barklike wheezing. Lazarus shuffled from the dark hole in the hill, his hands lifted to shade the slits in the cloth that covered his face. Martha and Mary wept as their brother unraveled the strips of linen they'd wrapped around his hands and feet. But being miracle minded, they were insulted when Lazarus dusted himself off with malice and hastily departed. They couldn't know why he was angry to be brought back to life.

The electric gate shut slowly behind me—and there I stood, two seconds into my freedom, my back to the prison, a Lazarus moment.

For years I'd bragged to other prisoners that once outside the prison gate I'd turn around and hold up my middle finger to the prison that had mistakenly released me. I intended to come out and start where I left off—robbing banks. My "fuck you" gesture was to be my boast to the

Federal Bureau of Prisons that I, Joe Loya, could be knocked down but never counted out.

But I opted not to sully the moment with such a vulgarity. A different man than the one who walked into prison seven years earlier stood at that gate.

An hour earlier I had been seated near my cell window, staring out into the parking lot of the prison. Three fences, all topped with barbed wire, surrounded our confined compound. A space of thirty feet separated each fence. The inmates referred to the empty patch of dirt between the fences as No Man's Land.

In the cell, I'd sat gazing past No Man's Land, trying to guess which of the cars driving into the parking lot was the one coming to take me away. Over the last seven years the car designs had all begun to blur and resemble one another when I saw them in commercials during televised sports events. I couldn't tell the difference between a Chevy Cutlass and a Honda Accord. Richard said that he would not visit me. But he sent a friend of his, Mark Serna, abbot of the Portsmouth Abbey in Rhode Island. He visited me for the final six months of my sentence.

I never saw Mark arrive. I only know that I could barely contain myself at that window. I was trying to be cool, stoic. I didn't want to flaunt my freedom in front of men who might never have a chance to get out. Some of the friends I'd made at that last prison were lifers, and I felt bad for them. There was a certain melancholy to the goodbyes and good lucks I received from other inmates in the early hours before my release that morning. Friends would come and shake my hand, reach to hug me, peer deeply into my eyes.

I was also uncomfortable with the notion that my release from prison could lead to discouragement in my friends. It is a strange paradox. The first to celebrate another inmate's parole and good fortune are also the ones who turn what should be an occasion for celebration into an opportunity to succumb to envy and despair. There is a dejection that can settle on inmates when one of their own either dies in prison or gets released.

For my part, when my name was called by the guard (*Loya, pack it up!*) I was nervous. (I wouldn't feel the loss of the place for a few weeks.) I was escorted to the front offices and taken to a room where I was handed a check for a hundred fifty bucks and a plane ticket from Logan Airport to LAX. It was ten o'clock in the morning.

I knew that my brother had sent Mark a backpack for me with a new pair of Reebok sneakers in it. (A twenty dollar bill would be in one of the shoes.) Knowing this, I gave my used pair of sneakers to a friend. Nothing is worthless in prison. I knew that the sneakers, although second-hand, would eventually be used by an inmate who'd show up to the prison without a decent pair of shoes. Or they would be washed and sold. The shoes were no longer of any concern to me. All I cared about was leaving, even if it meant that I walked out of the prison wearing a pair of dollar shower shoes, the kind of cheap flip-flop sandals you find in any drugstore.

After I was handed the check and plane ticket I was escorted to the front gate. The last bars I would ever have to stand behind separated me from the lobby, where I could see Mark standing. The guard verified that I was in fact Joe Loya and not some impostor cunningly attempting to break out.

Mark was kind when first we met outside the gate. We hugged, and he handed me the backpack. I sat on the bench where he'd been waiting for me and put on the gift Reeboks. Plain bright white. No colorful design.

Mark and I lifted two boxes of books—all the property I owned—and walked to his black Lincoln Continental in the parking lot. There was a brief moment while Mark fiddled with a lever in the car for popping open the trunk when I turned back to steal a last glimpse of my prison. I felt peculiar, like I was betraying my friends with my freedom.

A brisk breeze slapped my face and made my eyes water. I raised my chin, closed my eyes for a moment, then opened them and scanned the overcast sky. I lowered my head and trained my eyes on the wall of deep green trees circumscribing the parking lot. The cars parked there were clean and shiny from the morning mist.

*You got it?* Mark shouted from inside the car when the trunk popped open.

*Yeah, no problem.*

I placed the heavy boxes inside and slammed the trunk shut.

There were reasons to be anxious. There was the near legendary story of Paddy's foiled parole, told to me by Paddy himself when we were drunk in my cell. Paroled from Lompoc Penitentiary, Paddy stopped at a liquor store to buy a bottle of whiskey before he boarded a Greyhound bus headed for San Diego. A male passenger didn't apologize when his luggage accidentally knocked Paddy into a seat. For a while Paddy drank his booze and stewed in the back of the bus, his prison ego bruised. At the next long stop, Paddy got off the bus to buy a drugstore knife. An hour later he brandished the knife on the bus. He didn't stab the man, but he used the knife to scare him before he slugged him unconscious, only to pass out himself in the toilet compartment at the back of the bus. The bus driver telephoned ahead and notified the authorities. When the bus pulled into the San Diego Greyhound Station the police arrested Paddy: He'd been out of prison—free in only the most technical sense—for exactly eight hours.

After Mark and I left the prison, we immediately drove to the local bank from which the prison check was drawn. I stepped out of the Lincoln and froze in my tracks.

It is said that one's life flashes before them right before they die. I was experiencing the reverse; my dying flashed before my eyes, as I was being reborn.

*Are you all right, Joe?* Mark asked.

I told him a story.

I flashbacked to 1988. I was halfway between Los Angeles and San Diego in my car, on the way to rob a bank, when my knees began to tremble. My hands jerked violently, almost jumping off the steering wheel. My stomach was queasy, and sharp pains stabbed my lower abdomen, forcing me to bend over. My eyes burned. My temples throbbed. A wave of intense fatigue finally splashed over me. I could barely keep my eyelids open. If I'd pulled to the side of the road, I could have capitulated to my body's revolt and fallen instantly asleep.

My panicky reaction was like a train crossing with bells ringing and red lights flashing: *STOP! DO NOT PROCEED! DANGER AHEAD!*

But I ignored the warning.

Instead, I played in my head a scene of me in the sixth grade on my knees, trying hard not to cry, my sweater pulled over my head, and the neighborhood bullies—Jerry, Mikey, and José—standing over me, laughing because I was scrambling for the pieces of my broken eyeglasses.

I called up the memory of defeat and humiliation and allowed the anger to rise and swell. Then I corralled and marshaled my special rage to crush my body's attempt to abort my mission.

Then *BLAM!* It happened. I detached from my body's fear and walked into a silence—like a special effect on TV that has a boat at sea being tossed about by treacherous hurricane waves one moment, only to place it in the tranquil eye of the storm the next. I'd achieved that moment of clean exhilaration past the edge of fear, that brief and seldom occurring clarity of purpose when we don't play life safe.

I exited the freeway in La Jolla, a city north of San Diego, and parked my car behind a row of financial buildings—three of them banks. I tucked a .357 magnum in my khaki pants, under my blue blazer, got out of the car, and walked to rob the bank farthest from where I'd parked.

A woman—blond, early thirties, freckles—was the only person in the bank. She was on the telephone. We exchanged smiles.

*Okay, I've got to go now. A customer just came in. Yeah. All right. Bye.*

She hung up the phone and walked to her teller station, fumbling with the keys as she unlocked her cash drawer.

*How can I help you today, sir?*

My voice was low spoken, but fiercely matter of fact.

*This is a bank robbery. We have a bomb. I have a gun. Give me the money now or I'll blow your fuckin' head off.*

My words slugged her.

There was a metallic taste in my mouth, a crisp electrical charge between us, the antiseptic smell of ammonia in my nostrils, something whistling clean about the truth of that furious moment. Ferocious as nature, my vehemence did not lie.

I told Mark that I loved the expression of sheer lucidity on my victim's shocked faces, suddenly in the grip of more pernicious instincts than they'd ever imagined possible. Like a vampire, I thirsted to suck from them all their red terror. I never pulled out a gun during a bank robbery.

I didn't need to. Tellers handed over the money without seeing a weapon. In their statements to the FBI, tellers said that my dead stare was convincing enough. And I stood there satiated from lapping up the fear on their faces, the twitch at the corner of the mouth, soft tears on the cheeks, the supplication in their eyes, the trembling hand emptying the money drawer, the low murmur and pleading, *Please don't hurt me, Mister. I'll do what you say.* My violence intersected with their calm, and they were introduced to the universe I'd occupied since age seven, where everything about my life spun into mad flux, nothing was as it seemed, and one could survive in that thin air only by snatching breaths of pure humility.

She was slow in handing over the loot. I threatened to pull out my weapon or jump over the counter if she didn't hurry. Time sped up. I shoved the cash in a large fanny pack around my waist.

Outside, walking to my car, I unzipped the fanny pack and became enraged when I counted less than two thousand dollars. I felt cheated. *That bitch!*

As I zipped my fanny pack shut, I looked up and noticed that I was in front of another bank. I knew that the cops were coming, but in that fluid moment of criminal contingency I felt like I was the top of the food chain. So I walked into the second bank and robbed it. Five minutes later I was driving on Interstate 5, blasting Pink Floyd's "Comfortably Numb" (soundtrack to all my getaways) on my recently installed ten-disc CD player.

Mark hadn't heard that story, but confessions weren't new to him.

As Mark and I approached the front doors of the bank, I placed both my hands firmly on the handles. I'd leave evidence everywhere. On glass. On the pen attached to the lobby desk. I'd looked every employee in the eye. All seven cameras mounted behind the teller stations photographed me dumbly staring at them like a heavily medicated mental patient. I wanted to be seen, known, to withstand daylight scrutiny—in that way, I thought, I'd also become less suspicious to myself.

I walked to the window of a young, pretty black female teller.

*How are you today, sir?*

I smiled broadly, loose in the neck, eyebrows slightly raised, both hands in front of me, trying to show her that I posed no threat.

*Fine, thanks. I just need to cash this check, but I just got out of prison so I don't have a driver's license.*

I slid the check to her and then placed my open palms flat on the counter. I followed her eyes, measured her reaction, waited for the shifting eyes or flinch of panic. She simply picked up the check, turned it over, and then slid it back to me.

*No problem, sir. Just sign the back again. Do you have your prison ID with you?*

*Yeah. I got it right here.*

The ID was the typical mug shot; one picture of me in profile, the other facing the camera. My hair was shaved low to the scalp, my eyes were a menacing dare, my facial muscles flat, corpse-like. The teller compared the photo in her hand to the more animated face in front of her.

*Please don't take this wrong, Mr. Loya, but you look much better now.* She smiled.

I chuckled, *Yeah, I know. I wasn't trying to make myself look pretty in there.*

▮▮▮▮▮▮▮▮▮▮

I called my brother from a telephone down the road from the prison.

*Hello?*

*The Eagle has landed.*

We laughed and chatted for only a few minutes. Then I phoned Richard Rodriguez. We'd never spoken to each other; he'd never visited me. We talked on that phone for fifteen minutes. I'll never forget the heartiness of our laughter. Exchanging private thoughts of relief. It was something fantastic to be out of prison at the side of the road on a long-distance call—jovial, ripe with emotion, thrilled and charged with possibility, tripping over my words to explain my feelings. We said goodbye, and he promised to come down from the Bay area to see me in L.A. in a few weeks.

After the calls Mark and I went to eat breakfast. Light rain started to fall. Mark offered me his umbrella. I smiled and told him that in prison it was a point of pride to protect oneself from the elements as little as possible. I declined his offer and joked that he should leave his umbrella in the car since he and I weren't made of paper. He opened the umbrella, hunched under it, and told me his mother had spoiled him. She had told him never to go outside in the rain without an umbrella. I playfully called him a momma's boy.

The sign outside the diner advertised the best breakfast on earth. Something about how you'd have to be in heaven to get a better breakfast. It seemed appropriate to be eating with a monk, a holy man.

The menu overwhelmed me. Choices I hadn't been afforded in years. In prison, I'd grown accustomed to being served children's portions. Hungry most of the time. No choice in the matter. The restaurant menu folded open three or four times. The best breakfast on earth seemed to mean the most selections. I glanced at the menu and put it down just as fast. I was intimidated by the options. Not a good augury. Little things like menus would overwhelm me all day long.

*You all right?*

*Yeah, Mark. I already know what I want. I've dreamt about this breakfast for more years than I can remember.*

I ordered bacon and three eggs over easy, with wheat toast and hash browns. I also ordered a coffee and a *large* orange juice. I believe I ate some of Mark's pancakes too.

Halfway through the meal the waitress placed the bill at the edge of the table. Then it hit me. I had money. I hadn't had money in my pocket for over seven years. I hadn't even seen dollar bills. (Visitors to the prison can bring only change into the visiting rooms. And the guards aren't supposed to bring bills into the prison.) Cash. Scratch. Greenbacks. Legal tender. Call it what you want. I had it on me. And the immensity of that realization struck me hard.

I reached for the bill.

*Let me pay for the meal, Mark.*

*No Joe, I can't let you do that.*

*Please, Mark. This is big. I need to pay for this because I've felt impotent for so long, having to rely on everybody who visited me to buy sodas and snacks at those cheesy vending machines in the visiting rooms.*

He thought for a moment. *Okay. But let me get the tip.*

*You got it.*

I walked up to the cashier like a sixteen-year-old boy paying a restaurant bill on his first date, proud to be flexing his monetary muscle in front of adults.

▬▬▬▬▬▬▬▬

Mark drove me into Boston and parked the car near Harvard Square. I was bowled over by the traffic and the bustling crowds of people walking and jogging and riding bicycles. Even though I wasn't literally bumped into by many people, the space I was accustomed to keeping between me and other people was repeatedly violated on those Boston sidewalks.

I walked with my head loose, looking down at the ground a few paces ahead of me. I didn't look into people's eyes as they passed me. I kept my head lowered to hear and sense movements around me, like on a prison tier. I watched shadows pass me. I heard the clip-clop of student clogs approaching and passing. Lovely tanned flesh in tight, baby-blue shorts. No threat. Charcoal gray worsted wool pants with burgundy wingtips walked fast and indifferently past me. Very good. Birkenstocks under a long flowing flowery dress strolled lazily in front of me, then turned and stopped to look in shop windows. No threat again. Van sneakers with graffiti on them with a skateboard dangling from a hand above them. Could be trouble. The young are notoriously unaware of who is around them. I never walked in town that day without deciphering the intentions of the bodies in my space. I was a free man, but I couldn't shake my prison habit of gauging the level of threats around me. I found it difficult to adjust my sense of perception, which had served me so well in prison. Mine was a prisoner's paranoia.

We entered a store organized in the standard 7-Eleven mini-mart design. I selected a bottle of Tylenol; a pen and pad of paper; a pack of gum; and postcards, mostly of the famous Charles River in Boston, shot from various angles in the air.

The cashier was a pointy-shouldered scarecrow, a gangly rail of a boy in a bright red convenience-store apron. He hunched slightly over the counter, his left face and ear awkwardly inclined to the voices of shorter customers, as if he were hard of hearing. He had short, disheveled hair and an almost painful-looking jutting Adam's apple. Wild red pimples covered his face; craters displayed his losing battle with adolescent acne.

He was a conscientious worker, moving each item out of the way after a computer beep logged the purchase. A bottle of Gatorade brushed over a computerized price scanner. Then Chap Stick. The boy's eyebrows twitched when he saw the price of each item. His concentration was like the entranced arcade adolescent whose facial muscles contort and grimace at a video game screen every time a battleship gets cremated in space.

*Is that gonna be all for you, sir? OK, then that'll be twelve dollars and seventy-four cents. All right, twelve dollars and seventy-four cents from twenty gives you back seven dollars and twenty-six cents. Here you go. Thank you, sir. Have a nice day, and come again.*

The man in front of me picked up his purchases and left the store.

I placed my items on the counter.

*Hello, sir. Will that be all?*

*Yeah.*

I handed him a twenty-dollar bill before he could tell me the cost of my items. He gave me my change. On the way to the bag—*whoosh!*—the postcards fell to the floor.

*Oops!* He apologized as he knelt to retrieve them.

*No problem*, I muttered.

Then the pen rolled off the counter. The receipt got into the act and drifted by the cashier's ear.

*I'm really sorry, sir.*

All afternoon I'd absorbed every pulsation in an acute and intimate way. So I heard echoes in the boy's formal courtesy that sounded like my early, gullible boy's voice before the world taught me to distrust. His voice agitated me, reminded me how wholly removed I was, at age thirty-five, from my irreproachable beginning.

In that instant at the counter, the cashier's transparency jolted me. There, crouched on the floor and reaching under the counter for my stray pen, was innocence personified, an embodiment of virtue, flustered and apologizing profusely. He was not me, not a slacker Generation Xer either. He didn't remotely resemble anyone I'd recently known in prison.

Instinctively, I feared that the sludge of my life would besmirch this boy. (Like all the self-despising men I knew in prison, I willingly chose to play the unclean leper to his spotless vulnerability.) I wanted to spare him my dirtiness, run and hide from him, from myself, my own shame—like the instant when Adam and Eve recognized their nakedness and ran for cover behind large avocado leaves. I feared that he would see right through me. That the lens of his guileless soul would glimpse a clear picture of the tar in my heart, the obscene images that burned in my imagination. I didn't want him to see me lying like a beaten dog on the floor, whimpering, telling my father that I loved him in hopes that my teary voice would induce him to quit kicking my head and chest. I didn't want him to see me as the twelve-year-old boy lying in bed naked with a twenty-two-year-old married neighbor who suggested that I recruit my younger brother to our secret bed. I didn't want him to see me at my mother's funeral, curious and scared when I touched her cold, stiff hand in the coffin. I didn't want him to know the cum smell of a prison cell; to know about the men murdered while they slept in their cells because they'd been ignorant of the drug-buy double-cross. I didn't want him to know how I'd once plotted with friends to extort money from a legless man in prison.

I never wanted the boy to glimpse the depth of depravity that we humans can stoop to when we've given up on ourselves. I was afraid that he might see me locked in solitary confinement, squatting in front of the toilet, stirring my shit so I could scoop some of it into a cup and toss it on an obnoxious prison guard when he delivered my food—wet retaliation for telling me that I'd have to wait two days for toilet paper. I felt as if the din and racket of my life—the gratuitous lies, the rabid insecurities, the fantasies of suicide, the nightmare of men begging me to quit injuring them—were all welling up in me, and risked spilling on that boy.

The boy cashier knew nothing of the intensity of my discomfort in front of his counter. He was too preoccupied with his own clumsy predicament. I grabbed my purchase and walked fast out of the store. I stood paralyzed on the curb, my thoughts racing, scaring me, trying to figure out why it felt as if my anger had been ignited. Mark was halfway in the car when I asked him if we could stand out in the cool air for a moment. I breathed deeply. Panting almost.

*Did you see him, Mark? The boy, did you see him?*

Mark nodded slowly, not understanding where my inquiry was leading.

*Did you see how innocent he looked? Did you notice how selfless he seemed?*

I was glad to be away from the store. But it distressed me to think that I might continually panic when I encountered the boy's brand of innocence in another clerk, far away in some other store. A melancholy descended on me as my imagination lurched back toward prison.

It was a cinch to live among the despised wrongdoers. Sometimes the shadowy criminal mind can become permanently unsuited to the overt life of John Q. Citizen. For weeks before my release I'd stayed up late at night pondering if that would be my new condition—whether George Herbert's axiom that "a wolf must die in its own skin" applied to me. That's why standing in front of that cashier I felt alien, silent as a spy, like a ghost inhabiting a citizen's space.

Only then did I appreciate how I'd earned a lonely, lesser freedom than the one I anticipated after my release from prison. Even though I faithfully dreamt of a good reform during my last three years in prison, I often doubted that I'd really arrested my criminal appetite. There seemed to be some romantic disappointment designed into my hope. Of course, every criminal wants to become a monk when they've hit rock bottom. St. Dismas, the good thief hanging on the cross next to Jesus, was promised Paradise at the end because he'd hit the skids and finally reached out for divine deliverance. But I knew that I would be released from prison, that my punishment, my confinement, was finite, so my need for redemption was not as compelling as the dying thief's. I considered that maybe I was telling myself I could change as a way to cope with the banalities of my prison existence. Which, if true, meant that I would leave prison and go right back to doing what I did to get myself in there in the first place, not fearing eternal repercussions. Needless to say, this dog-returning-to-his-own-vomit scenario frightened me.

I'd cried out for redemption, of course—during the darkest moments of my confinement—but I worried that I'd disqualified myself from the company of good people by living too long on the other side of taboo. Had I seen and done so much hard wrong that I would forever sound an inferior voice in the conversation that occurred among virtue, innocence, integrity, and beauty? More than any other, this question had harassed me for the final six months of my incarceration.

So, on that first day, when I had access to the most possible hope, I was only meagerly surprised when I found that my thoughts had turned negative and that, like Lazarus at the entrance to his cave, I could only hypothesize a fierce hopelessness ahead of me. Lazarus's sisters, Mary and Martha, too readily equated their brother's resurrection with twice being alive. Meanwhile, Lazarus, with some wisdom from the other side, quickly discerned that resurrection literally meant twice having to die.

▮▮▮▮▮▮▮▮▮▮

At the airport, Mark and I embraced, then he reached into his bag and handed me a gift: a wooden plaque of a medieval impression with the Madonna laminated on the surface. I turned it around and saw Mark's small scribble on the back:

> *"God, who is rich in mercy, out of the great love with which he loved us, even when we were dead through our trespasses, made us alive together with Christ . . ." (Ephesians 2: 4–5) With respect and love, Mark.*

▮▮▮▮▮▮▮▮▮▮

Fidgety and unable to doze comfortably, she finally placed the pillow beneath her seat and asked the stewardess for coffee.

*An airplane is the worst place to be when you're sleepy,* I remarked.

*You're right. It's impossible to relax comfortably.* She reached into her purse for some gum. *And yet you'd think that as exhausted as I am right now, sleep would come easier.*

Her accent was Australian. I'd seen enough *Mad Max* and *Crocodile Dundee* movies to spot the outback accent.

She offered me a stick of gum. *Do you live in Los Angeles?* she asked.

*Not really. But I was raised in L.A. so this is a kind of coming home.*

*Nice. To visit? Or to stay?*

*To stay.*

*I'm going home too.*

*Is that right?*

*Yes. I've been away for a month and I've got to get home to my husband and children.*

*I'm sure they understand that whatever it was you did here in Boston was important enough for you to leave them for a whole month.*

I didn't want my prying to sound too obvious, like asking outright, "So tell me. Why were you here in Boston?" I didn't know if she had been in Boston for some secret government assignment or whether she might think my question inappropriate, seeing as we'd just started our conversation. Of course, her remark about being away for a month was encouraging and sounded to me like she wouldn't mind if I pried just a tiny bit. But like in prison, where you never ask a man what crime he was found guilty of to land him in there, I wanted to play safe and gingerly approach the topic of her stay.

All my worrying was for naught. She bravely opened up and told me that Sidney Hospital had sent her to Harvard Medical Center for training, something about how to counsel patients through the various mental phases they go through after surviving life-threatening surgery. Apparently, big macho men fall into grave depressions after a period of initial elation for surviving heart surgery. The slow process of rehabilitation, and the drastic loss of control over everything from their diet to their calendar, is a total diminishment that they find debilitating. She'd learned enough about this psychological phenomenon to return home and train therapists in Australia.

*So what type of work do you do?*

In my cell the night before my release, I'd rehearsed the answer to this question. I decided I would respond in a guarded way, assessing first the questioner's temperament. I thought that quiet people would be more pensive, be more inclined to mull over my answer before saying anything rude in return. Chatterers unnerved me. They always want to fill silences with words. So they ended up speaking without putting too much thought into the words that dropped out of their mouths. Chatty Cathies were the ones who typically said regrettable things, more out of ignorance than design. I hadn't been one to tolerate offensive comments spoken to me in the past, so my strategy for answering the question about what type of work I did was to proceed with caution and try to avoid engaging in personal conversation with babblers.

But the woman's open friendliness was more than I anticipated. She was warm, and perhaps because I had been so guarded for so long, and also knowing about her work with depressed men who struggled with alienation, I found myself feeling expansive toward her question. I smiled, looked down at my hands on my lap, and said, *Well, I was released from prison less than eight hours ago, so I don't have a job. Not yet anyway.*

*How long were you in prison?*

*Seven years.*

*Oh my. Seven years? Straight?*

*Yep.*

My stomach bothered me. Nerves. I hid them well in prison, but she'd looked at me in such a way that I knew she was sizing me up, like a good therapist would. Then I became even more uneasy, thinking that even though I thought my façade was calm, I suspected that there were tells that I didn't know about. It was easy work to disguise my level of fear from dumb prisoners, but I imagined that this therapist next to me had sophisticated ways to read what was really going on inside of me.

*If you don't mind my asking, what were you in there for?*

*I don't mind. I don't mind at all.* This is where I felt bold. I looked her in the eyes. *I used to rob banks.*

She didn't flinch. Nice. A real pro. I pulled out my prison ID, emboldened by the favorable impression it had earlier made on the teller.

*Here's the proof.*

She pulled eyeglasses out of her purse and reached for the ID.

*Oh my. You look so different now. So much better.*

She handed the ID back to me, and we smiled to each other as I pocketed it.

*Thanks. Yeah, I intend to keep it as a reminder of my survival and the way I dreamed so hard of never going back.*

*Who will you live with? Do you have a job waiting for you? Some meaningful work?*

*My brother lined up a job for me at the health-food store where he works. I just have to speak to his boss, and the job's pretty much all mine.*

*What else will you do?*

*I plan to write an autobiography. And I'll live with my brother until I can earn money to rent my own apartment.*

Then she asked me in her therapist's soft voice, *What does freedom feel like?*

I think I mumbled something about being joyous, relieved, something along those lines. But I couldn't tell her the other, equal truth: Seven years away from improvisational living and spontaneous conversation meant that freedom was menacing me all day, and that I was already weary as we sat and talked on that plane.

She said that as excited as I was, as relieved as I felt for being free, sometime, not too long in the future, I'd wake up and feel depressed and dread the day ahead of me. I was liberated, true, she said, but on that fateful morning I'd only be able to associate my freedom with a kind of bondage. She talked like a poet. Paul Valéry, she told me, remarked how for him illumination was always associated with sorrow. I thought of my experience with the boy cashier in Harvard Square. And I also thought of my dread when I was first paroled from prison nine years earlier.

I thanked her for the advice. She shook my hand and congratulated me. We talked for the next few hours, Chatty Cathies both of us. She told me about her husband's work, her children's schooling, her decision to go back to school and pursue the field of study she was presently working in. I told her I'd robbed more than thirty banks. I told her how I'd had an epiphany in prison while locked in solitary confinement for almost two years, how I'd decided to become a writer by writing about my childhood and education. We discussed politics, religion, poetry.

My new Australian friend and I walked off the airplane together. She wanted to meet my father and younger brother who were waiting for me at the arrival gate. The ramp from the airplane to the terminal door was crowded. Up ahead I glimpsed my brother's head bobbing beyond the heads of the people in front of me. Once I was in the clear, Paul and my father walked up to me. Several aunts and uncles stood nearby. I stopped and turned to the Australian woman, then made introductions. She shook Paul and my father's hands and remarked that it was an honor to meet them. My father gave her a gracious half-bow as he held her hand in both of his. Then she reached for my hand and wished me luck. She was crying. We said goodbye.

I turned and was immediately encircled by other family members, being kissed and hugged. The woman was walking away but had looked back to witness the tearful reunion. Our eyes momentarily met again as I hugged an aunt. We both smiled and nodded, then she turned a corner and left my family to our private joy as the airport loudspeaker called out another flight number departing on time to somewhere else across the sky, over the Pacific Ocean.

## Author's Note

Much of what I write about in this book occurred long ago, and involved people with whom I no longer have any contact. To avoid embarrassing childhood friends and enemies, classmates, co-workers, partners in crime, and former girlfriends, I have changed their names and in some cases changed other identifying details. I have also changed the names of men who were in prison with me, and our jailers.